PROMETHEA BOOK 2

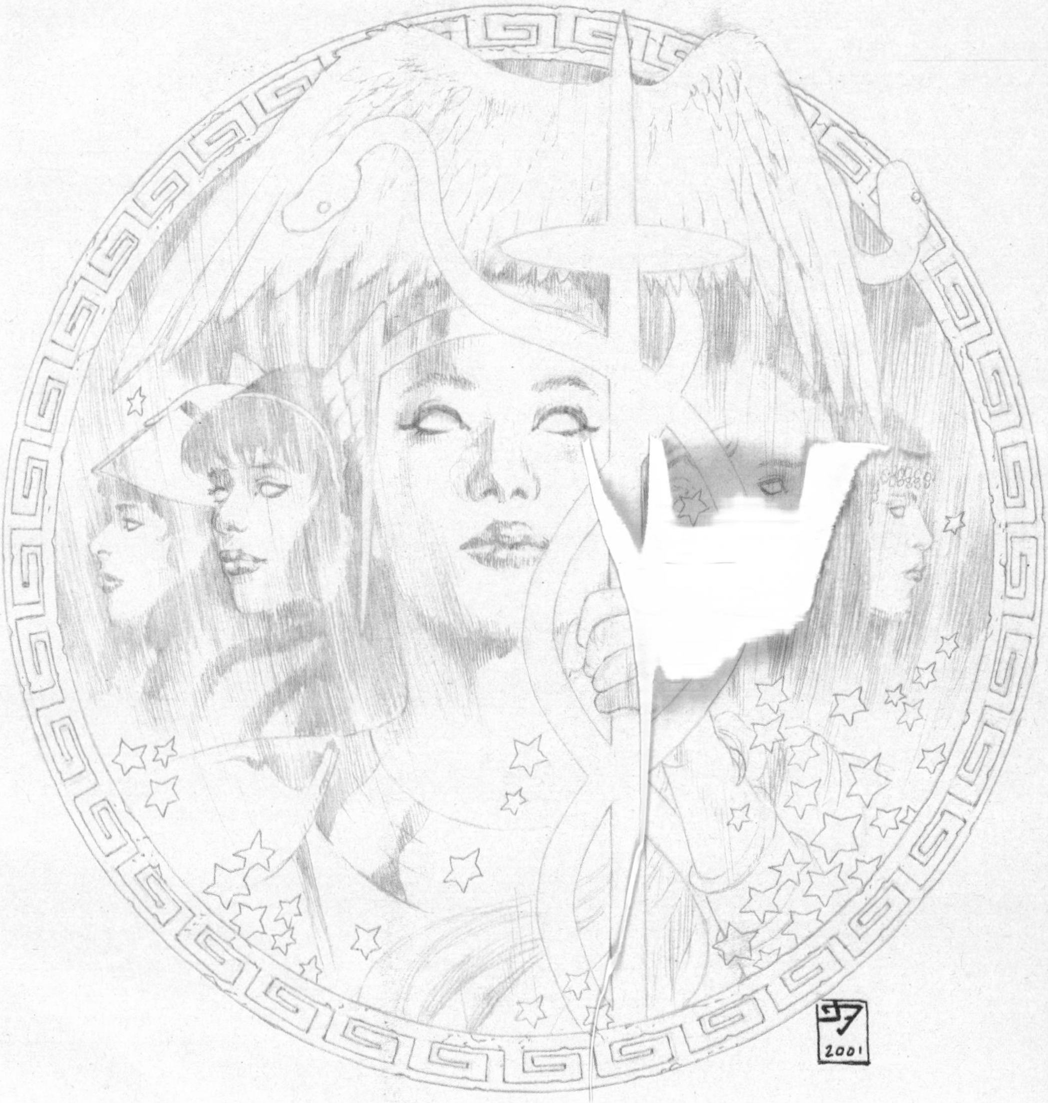

PROMETHEA

COLLECTED EDITION BOOK 2

ALAN MOORE
writer

J.H. WILLIAMS III
penciller

MICK GRAY
inker

JEROMY COX
coloring

JOSE VILLARRUBIA
digital art, painted color

TODD KLEIN
lettering, logos & design

Promethea created by
Alan Moore and
J.H. Williams III

CAST AND CREDITS - DIGITAL SEQUENCE
Promethea and The Universe:
Audrey Causilla
Sophie Bangs: Jeannie Lobato
Bill Woolcott: Douglas Bayne
Dirk Dangerfield/Dennis Drucker:
Tom Burke
Prometheus, Taurus and Colossal Figures:
Pawel Pagan-Piskorski
Aquarius: Alan Fluharty
Marv: Everett Boyd

Crowd: Carlos, Lisa, Elena and Sarah Taylor,
Nacho Muñoz-Sanjuán and
Aleksey Zolotaryov
Digital Snake and Promethea Moths:
Aleksey Zolotaryov
Hair and Makeup: Gregory Malone
Wigs courtesy of Matthew and Ingrid
Hair Replacement
Promethea's Costume: Todd Douglass
Straitjacket and Padded Cell: David Page
Background Research: Fehl Cannon

JIM LEE
Editorial Director

JOHN NEE
VP and General Manager

AMERICA'S
BEST COMICS

SCOTT DUNBIER
Group & Promethea Editor

JEFF MARIOTTE
Assistant Editor

PROMETHEA Book Two, published by WildStorm Productions, an imprint of DC Comics,
editorial offices: 888 Prospect St, Suite 240, La Jolla, CA 92037. Cover, design pages, and
compilation Copyright © 2001 DC Comics. America's Best Comics, Promethea and all
related characters and elements are trademarks of DC Comics. All Rights Reserved.

Originally published in single magazine form as PROMETHEA #7-12, © 2000, 2001 DC
Comics. Any similarities to persons living or dead is purely coincidental. Printed in Canada.
This book is manufactured at a facility holding chain-of-custody certification. This paper is
made with sustainably managed North American fiber. Third Printing.
ISBN: 978-1-56389-957-7

CHAPTER ONE

A girl dreams – romantic pictures and earthly themes.

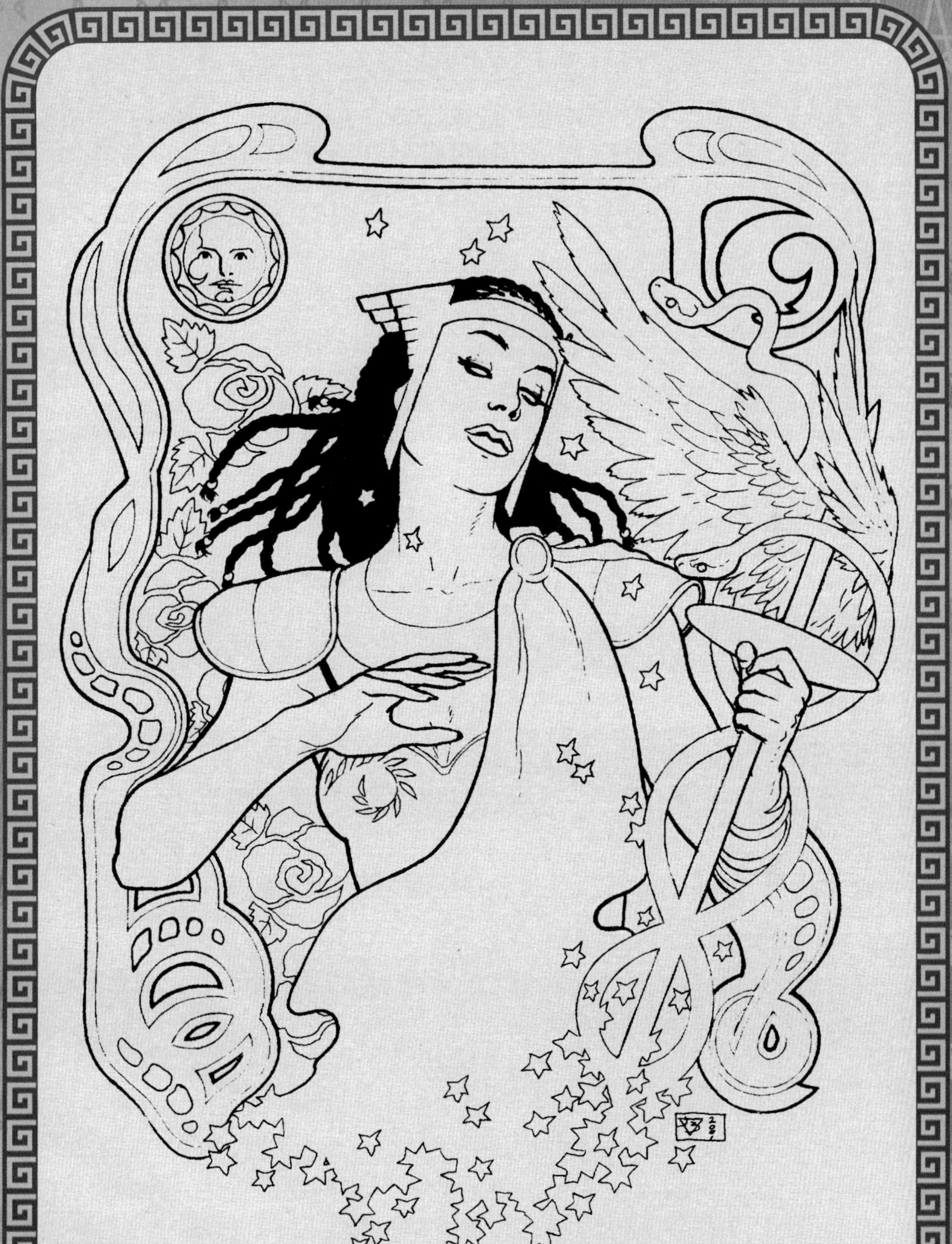

Cover art: J.H. Williams III, Mick Gray & WildStorm FX

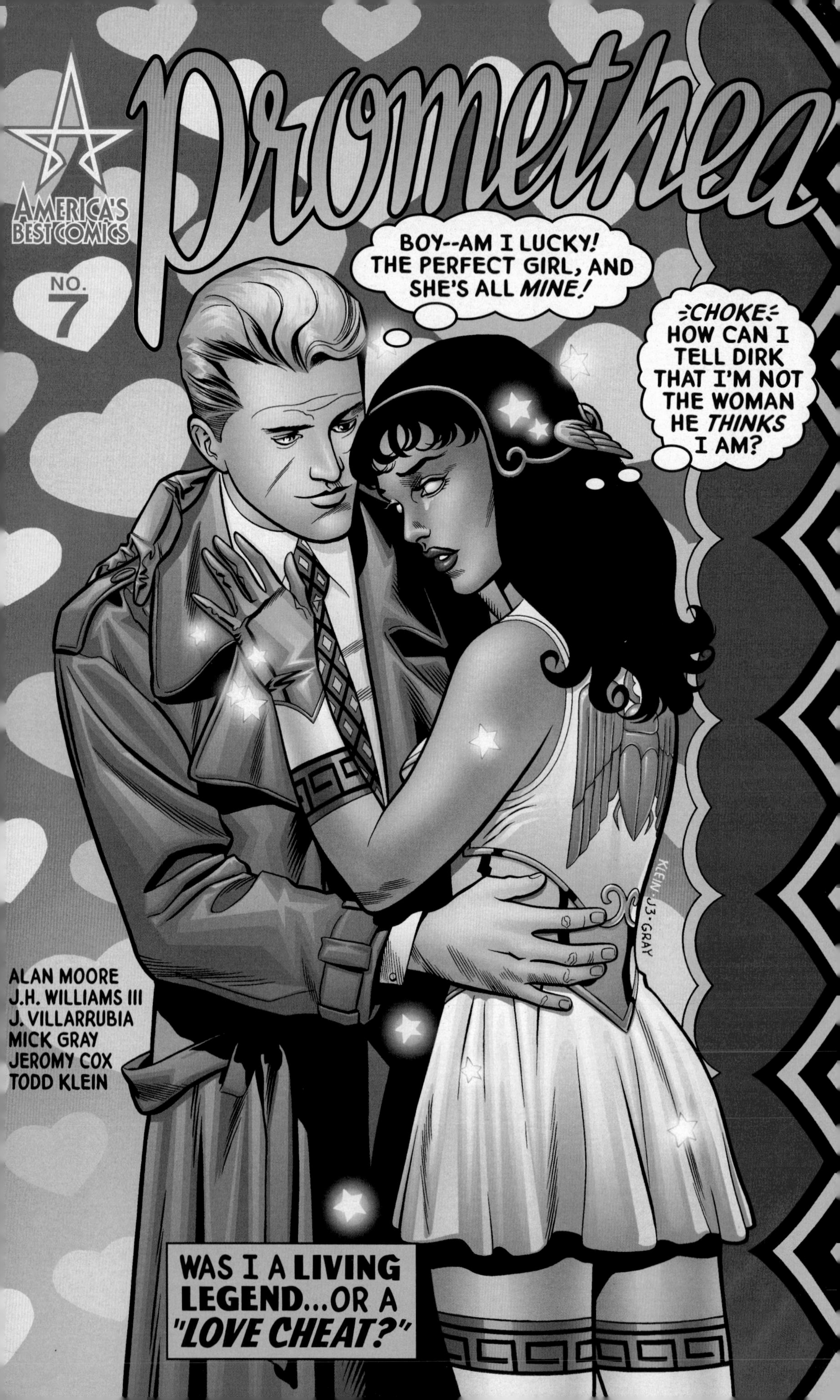

AMERICA'S BEST COMICS
Promethea
NO. 7
BOY--AM I LUCKY! THE PERFECT GIRL, AND SHE'S ALL MINE!
CHOKE HOW CAN I TELL DIRK THAT I'M NOT THE WOMAN HE THINKS I AM?
KLEIN · J3 · GRAY
ALAN MOORE
J.H. WILLIAMS III
J. VILLARRUBIA
MICK GRAY
JEROMY COX
TODD KLEIN
WAS I A LIVING LEGEND...OR A "LOVE CHEAT?"

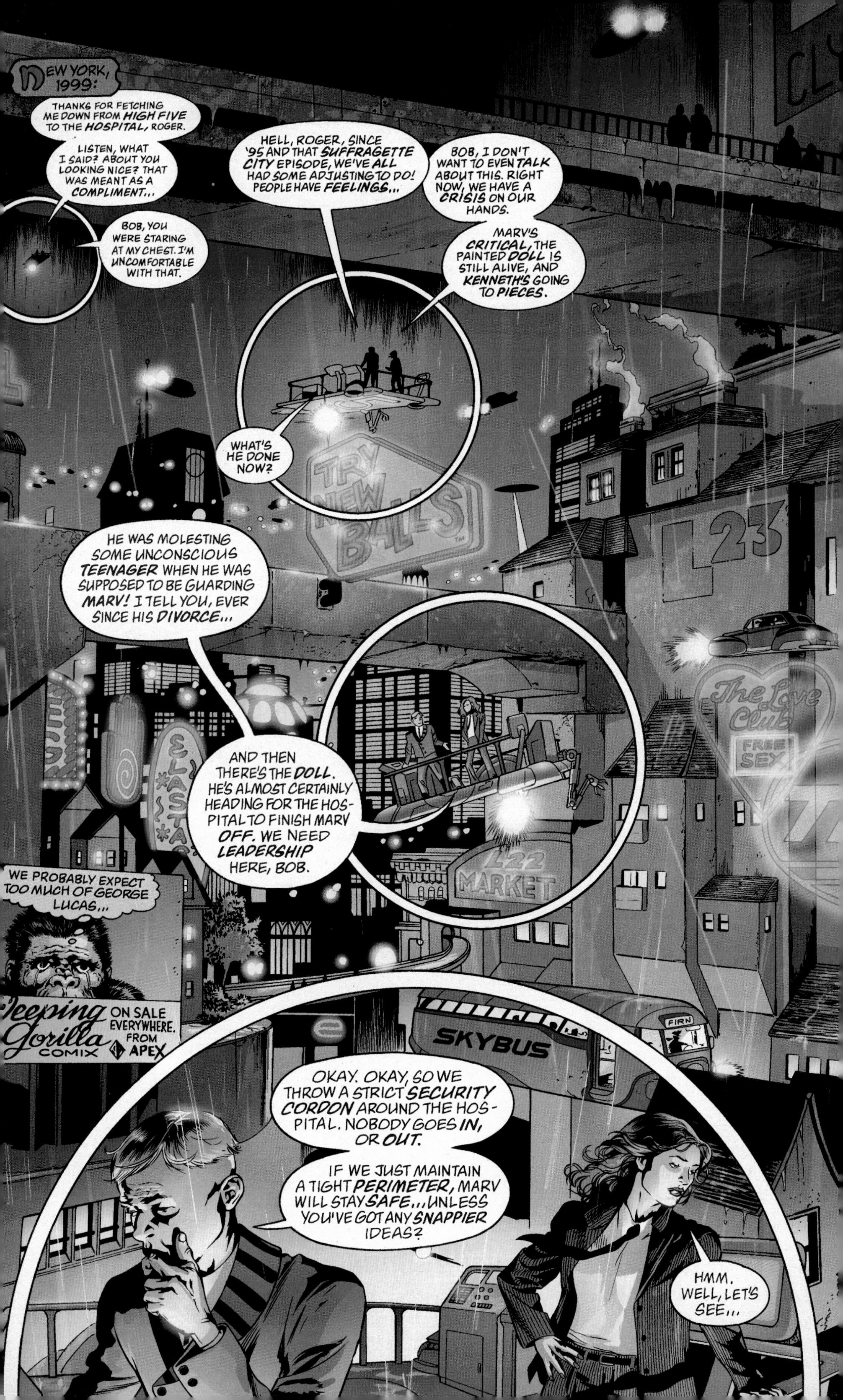
NEW YORK, 1999:
THANKS FOR FETCHING ME DOWN FROM HIGH FIVE TO THE HOSPITAL, ROGER.
LISTEN, WHAT I SAID? ABOUT YOU LOOKING NICE? THAT WAS MEANT AS A COMPLIMENT...
BOB, YOU WERE STARING AT MY CHEST. I'M UNCOMFORTABLE WITH THAT.
HELL, ROGER, SINCE '95 AND THAT SUFFRAGETTE CITY EPISODE, WE'VE ALL HAD SOME ADJUSTING TO DO! PEOPLE HAVE FEELINGS...
BOB, I DON'T WANT TO EVEN TALK ABOUT THIS. RIGHT NOW, WE HAVE A CRISIS ON OUR HANDS.
MARV'S CRITICAL, THE PAINTED DOLL IS STILL ALIVE, AND KENNETH'S GOING TO PIECES.
WHAT'S HE DONE NOW?
TRY NEW BALLS
L23
HE WAS MOLESTING SOME UNCONSCIOUS TEENAGER WHEN HE WAS SUPPOSED TO BE GUARDING MARV! I TELL YOU, EVER SINCE HIS DIVORCE...
The Love Club
FREE SEX
AND THEN THERE'S THE DOLL. HE'S ALMOST CERTAINLY HEADING FOR THE HOSPITAL TO FINISH MARV OFF. WE NEED LEADERSHIP HERE, BOB.
L22 MARKET
WE PROBABLY EXPECT TOO MUCH OF GEORGE LUCAS...
Weeping Gorilla COMIX
ON SALE EVERYWHERE. FROM APEX
SKYBUS
FIRN
OKAY. OKAY, SO WE THROW A STRICT SECURITY CORDON AROUND THE HOSPITAL. NOBODY GOES IN, OR OUT.
IF WE JUST MAINTAIN A TIGHT PERIMETER, MARV WILL STAY SAFE... UNLESS YOU'VE GOT ANY SNAPPIER IDEAS?
HMM. WELL, LET'S SEE...

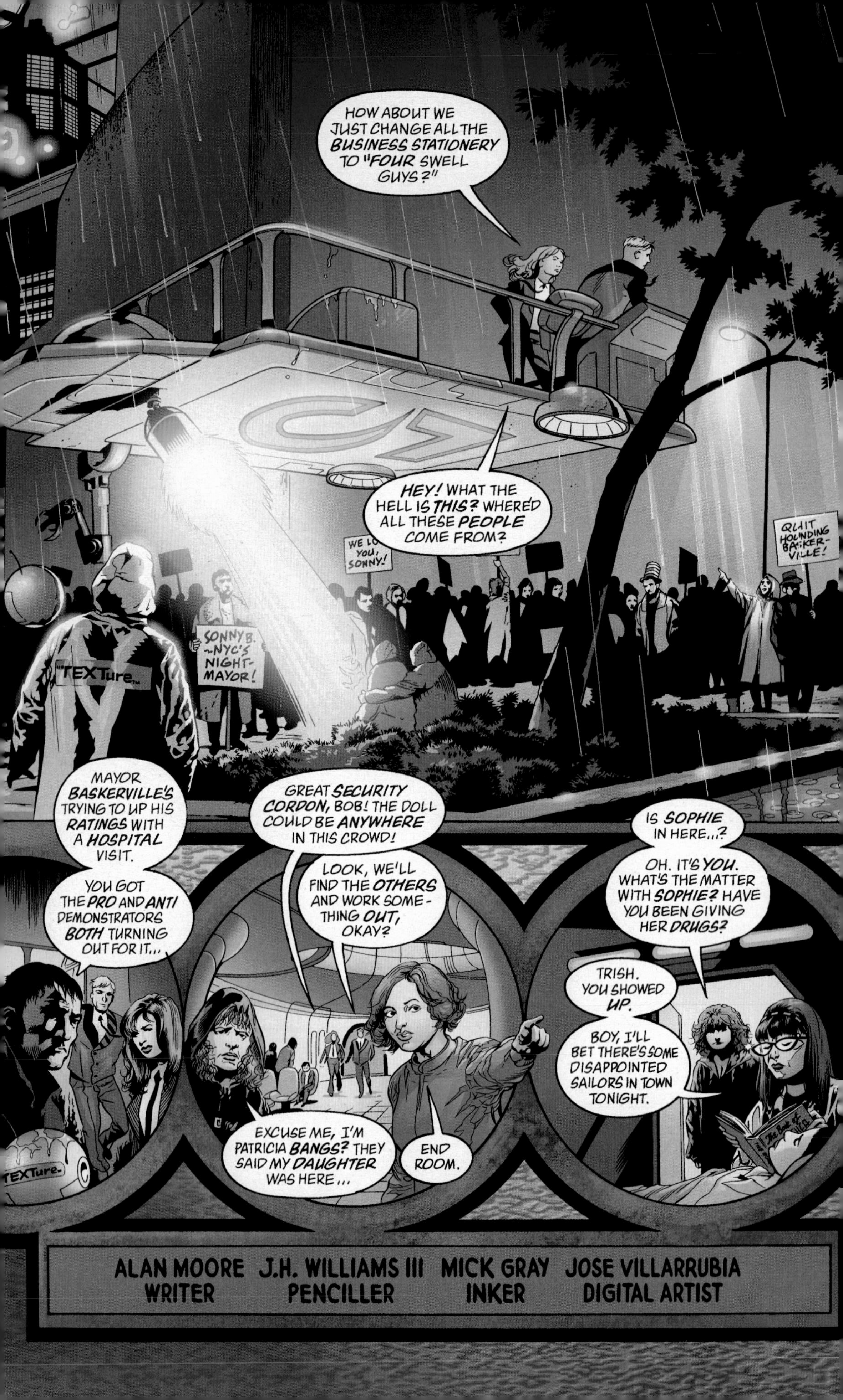
HOW ABOUT WE JUST CHANGE ALL THE BUSINESS STATIONERY TO "FOUR SWELL GUYS?"
HEY! WHAT THE HELL IS THIS? WHERE'D ALL THESE PEOPLE COME FROM?
QUIT HOUNDING BASKER-VILLE!
YOU, SONNY!
SONNY B. ~NYC'S NIGHT-MAYOR!
TEXTure
MAYOR BASKERVILLE'S TRYING TO UP HIS RATINGS WITH A HOSPITAL VISIT.
YOU GOT THE PRO AND ANTI DEMONSTRATORS BOTH TURNING OUT FOR IT...
TEXTure
GREAT SECURITY CORDON, BOB! THE DOLL COULD BE ANYWHERE IN THIS CROWD!
LOOK, WE'LL FIND THE OTHERS AND WORK SOME-THING OUT, OKAY?
EXCUSE ME, I'M PATRICIA BANGS? THEY SAID MY DAUGHTER WAS HERE...
END ROOM.
IS SOPHIE IN HERE...?
OH. IT'S YOU. WHAT'S THE MATTER WITH SOPHIE? HAVE YOU BEEN GIVING HER DRUGS?
TRISH. YOU SHOWED UP.
BOY, I'LL BET THERE'S SOME DISAPPOINTED SAILORS IN TOWN TONIGHT.

ALAN MOORE WRITER | J.H. WILLIAMS III PENCILLER | MICK GRAY INKER | JOSE VILLARRUBIA DIGITAL ARTIST

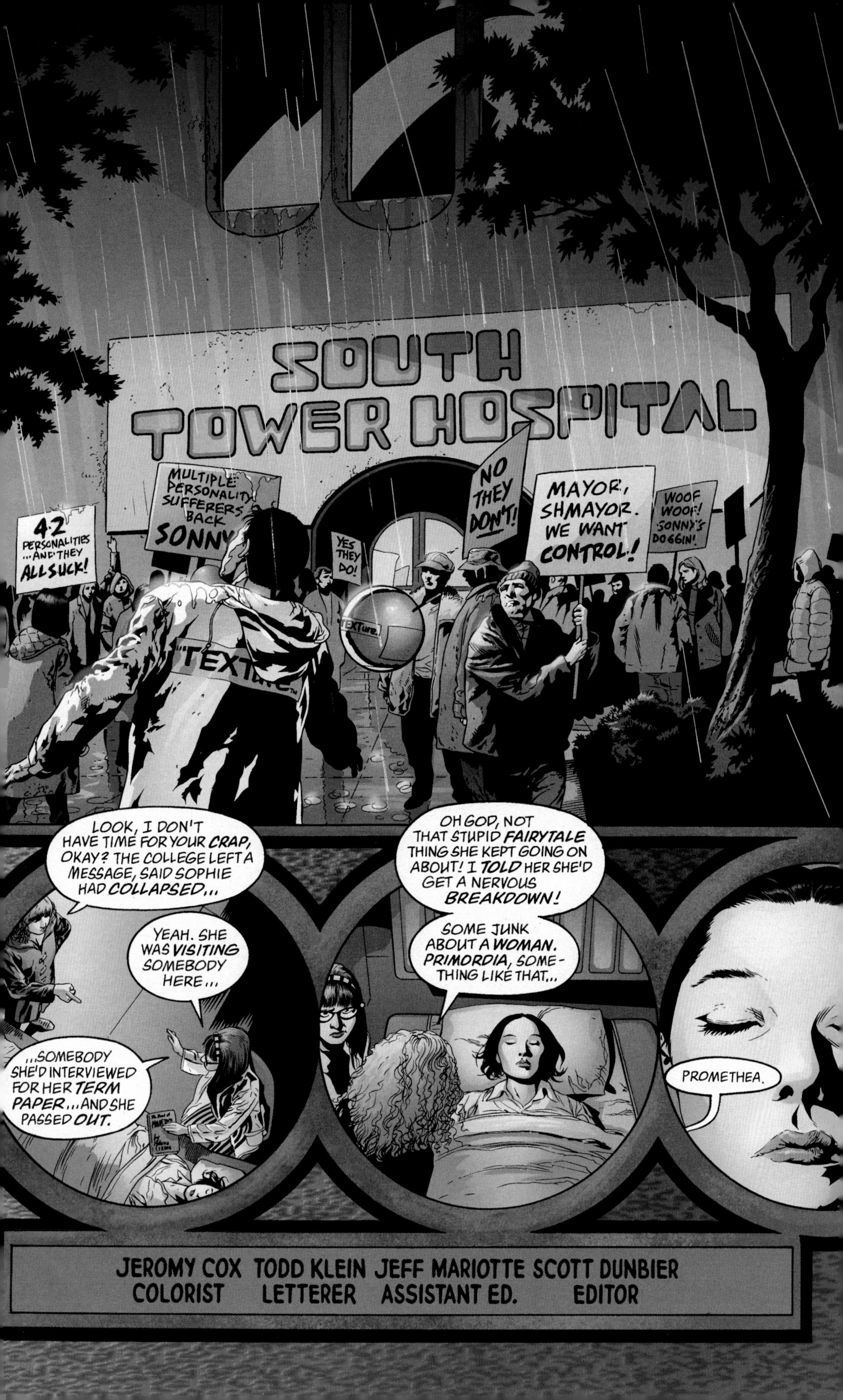
SOUTH TOWER HOSPITAL
4-2 PERSONALITIES ...AND THEY ALL SUCK!
MULTIPLE PERSONALITY SUFFERERS BACK SONNY
YES THEY DO!
NO THEY DON'T!
MAYOR, SHMAYOR. WE WANT CONTROL!
WOOF WOOF! SONNY'S DOGGIN'!
TEXTure
LOOK, I DON'T HAVE TIME FOR YOUR CRAP, OKAY? THE COLLEGE LEFT A MESSAGE, SAID SOPHIE HAD COLLAPSED...
YEAH. SHE WAS VISITING SOMEBODY HERE...
...SOMEBODY SHE'D INTERVIEWED FOR HER TERM PAPER...AND SHE PASSED OUT.
OH GOD, NOT THAT STUPID FAIRYTALE THING SHE KEPT GOING ON ABOUT! I TOLD HER SHE'D GET A NERVOUS BREAKDOWN!
SOME JUNK ABOUT A WOMAN. PRIMORDIA, SOME-THING LIKE THAT...
PROMETHEA.
JEROMY COX COLORIST
TODD KLEIN LETTERER
JEFF MARIOTTE ASSISTANT ED.
SCOTT DUNBIER EDITOR

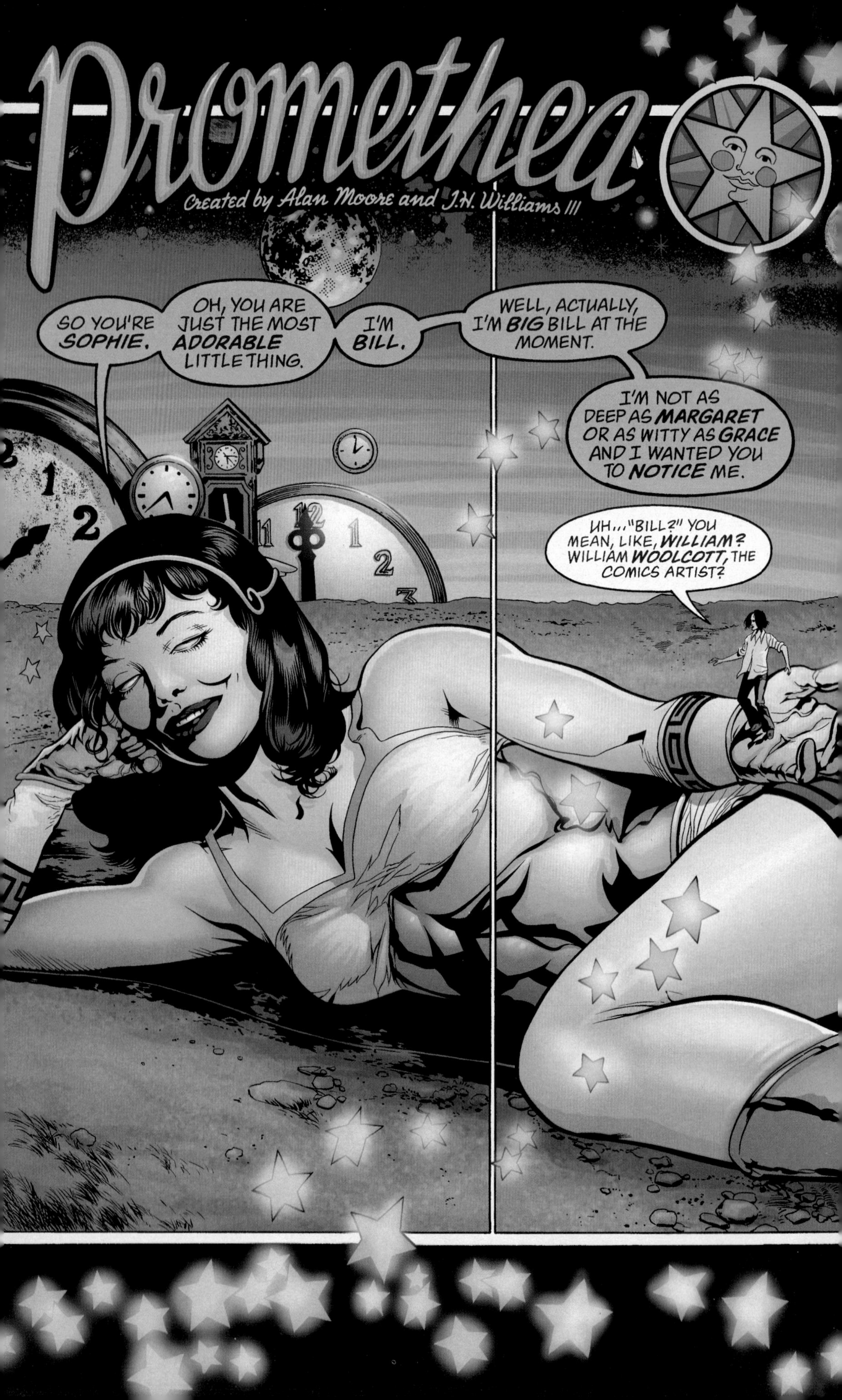
Promethea
Created by Alan Moore and J.H. Williams III
SO YOU'RE SOPHIE.
OH, YOU ARE JUST THE MOST ADORABLE LITTLE THING.
I'M BILL.
WELL, ACTUALLY, I'M BIG BILL AT THE MOMENT.
I'M NOT AS DEEP AS MARGARET OR AS WITTY AS GRACE AND I WANTED YOU TO NOTICE ME.
UH..."BILL?" YOU MEAN, LIKE, WILLIAM? WILLIAM WOOLCOTT, THE COMICS ARTIST?

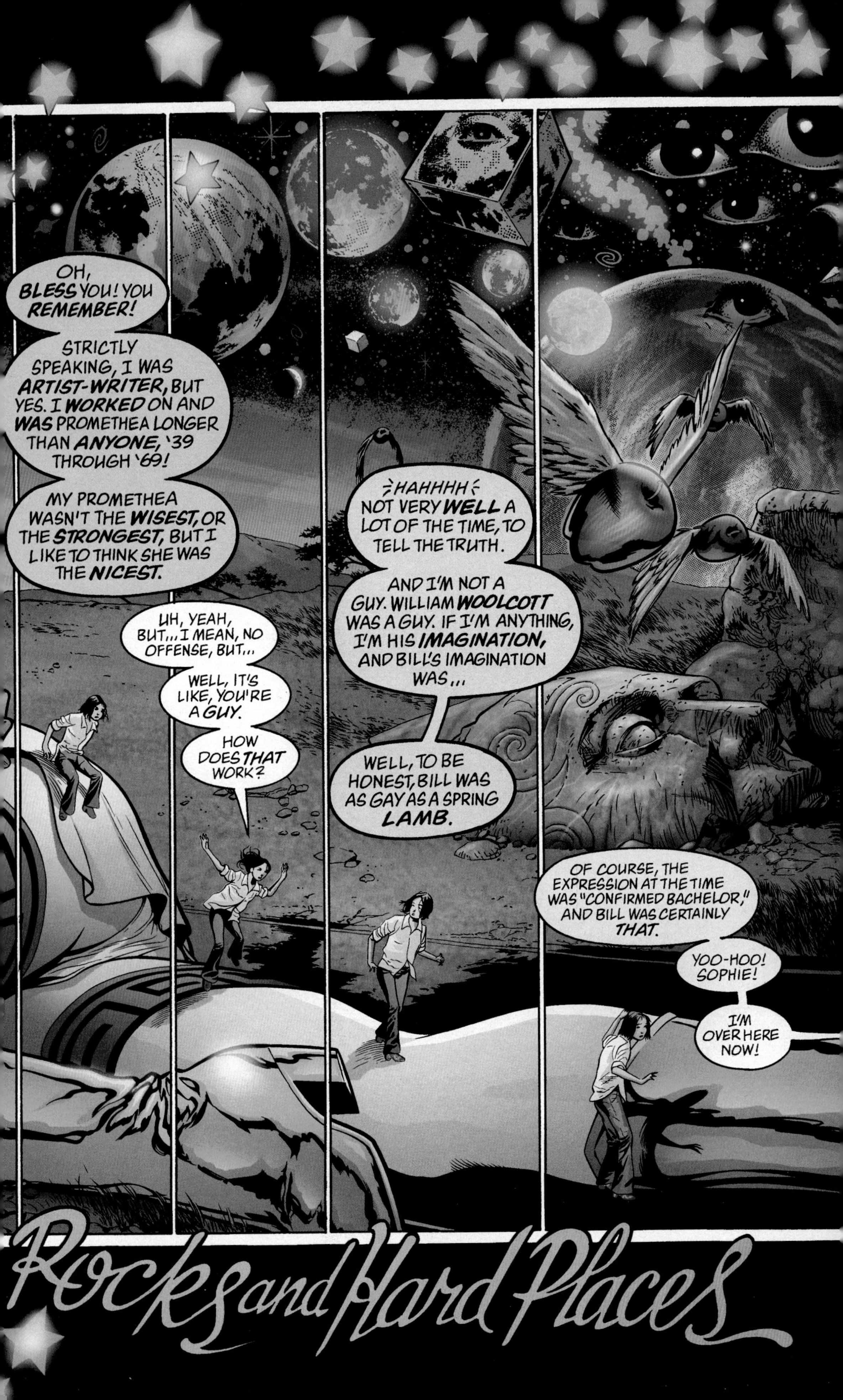
OH, BLESS YOU! YOU REMEMBER!
STRICTLY SPEAKING, I WAS ARTIST-WRITER, BUT YES. I WORKED ON AND WAS PROMETHEA LONGER THAN ANYONE, '39 THROUGH '69!
MY PROMETHEA WASN'T THE WISEST, OR THE STRONGEST, BUT I LIKE TO THINK SHE WAS THE NICEST.
UH, YEAH, BUT... I MEAN, NO OFFENSE, BUT...
WELL, IT'S LIKE, YOU'RE A GUY.
HOW DOES THAT WORK?
HAHHHH NOT VERY WELL A LOT OF THE TIME, TO TELL THE TRUTH.
AND I'M NOT A GUY. WILLIAM WOOLCOTT WAS A GUY. IF I'M ANYTHING, I'M HIS IMAGINATION, AND BILL'S IMAGINATION WAS...
WELL, TO BE HONEST, BILL WAS AS GAY AS A SPRING LAMB.
OF COURSE, THE EXPRESSION AT THE TIME WAS "CONFIRMED BACHELOR," AND BILL WAS CERTAINLY THAT.
YOO-HOO! SOPHIE!
I'M OVER HERE NOW!
Rocks and Hard Places

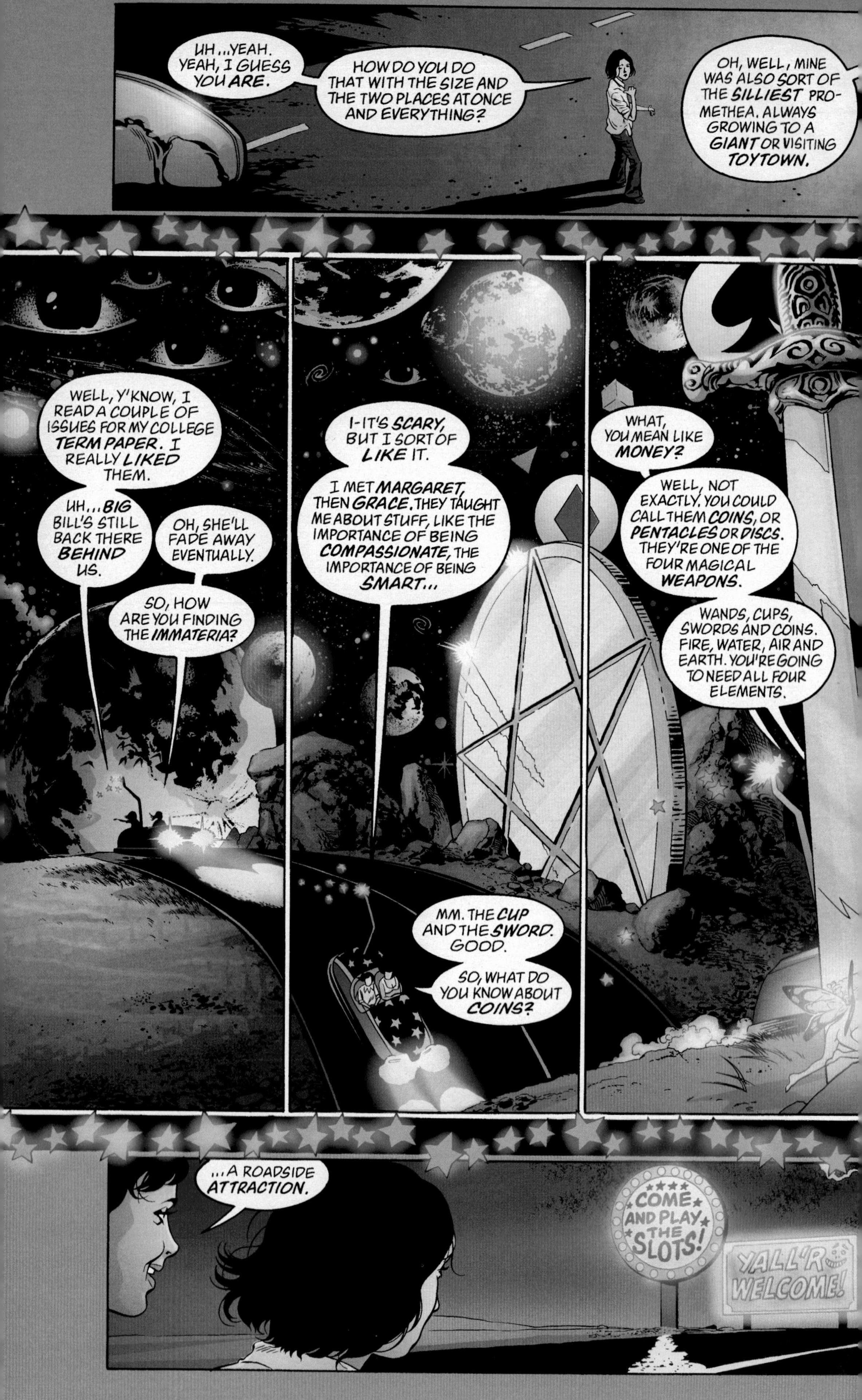
UH...YEAH. YEAH, I GUESS YOU ARE.
HOW DO YOU DO THAT WITH THE SIZE AND THE TWO PLACES AT ONCE AND EVERYTHING?
OH, WELL, MINE WAS ALSO SORT OF THE SILLIEST PROMETHEA. ALWAYS GROWING TO A GIANT OR VISITING TOYTOWN.
WELL, Y'KNOW, I READ A COUPLE OF ISSUES FOR MY COLLEGE TERM PAPER. I REALLY LIKED THEM.
UH...BIG BILL'S STILL BACK THERE BEHIND US.
OH, SHE'LL FADE AWAY EVENTUALLY.
SO, HOW ARE YOU FINDING THE IMMATERIA?
I-IT'S SCARY, BUT I SORT OF LIKE IT.
I MET MARGARET, THEN GRACE. THEY TAUGHT ME ABOUT STUFF, LIKE THE IMPORTANCE OF BEING COMPASSIONATE, THE IMPORTANCE OF BEING SMART...
MM. THE CUP AND THE SWORD. GOOD.
SO, WHAT DO YOU KNOW ABOUT COINS?
WHAT, YOU MEAN LIKE MONEY?
WELL, NOT EXACTLY. YOU COULD CALL THEM COINS, OR PENTACLES OR DISCS. THEY'RE ONE OF THE FOUR MAGICAL WEAPONS.
WANDS, CUPS, SWORDS AND COINS. FIRE, WATER, AIR AND EARTH. YOU'RE GOING TO NEED ALL FOUR ELEMENTS.
...A ROADSIDE ATTRACTION.
COME AND PLAY THE SLOTS!
YALL'R WELCOME!

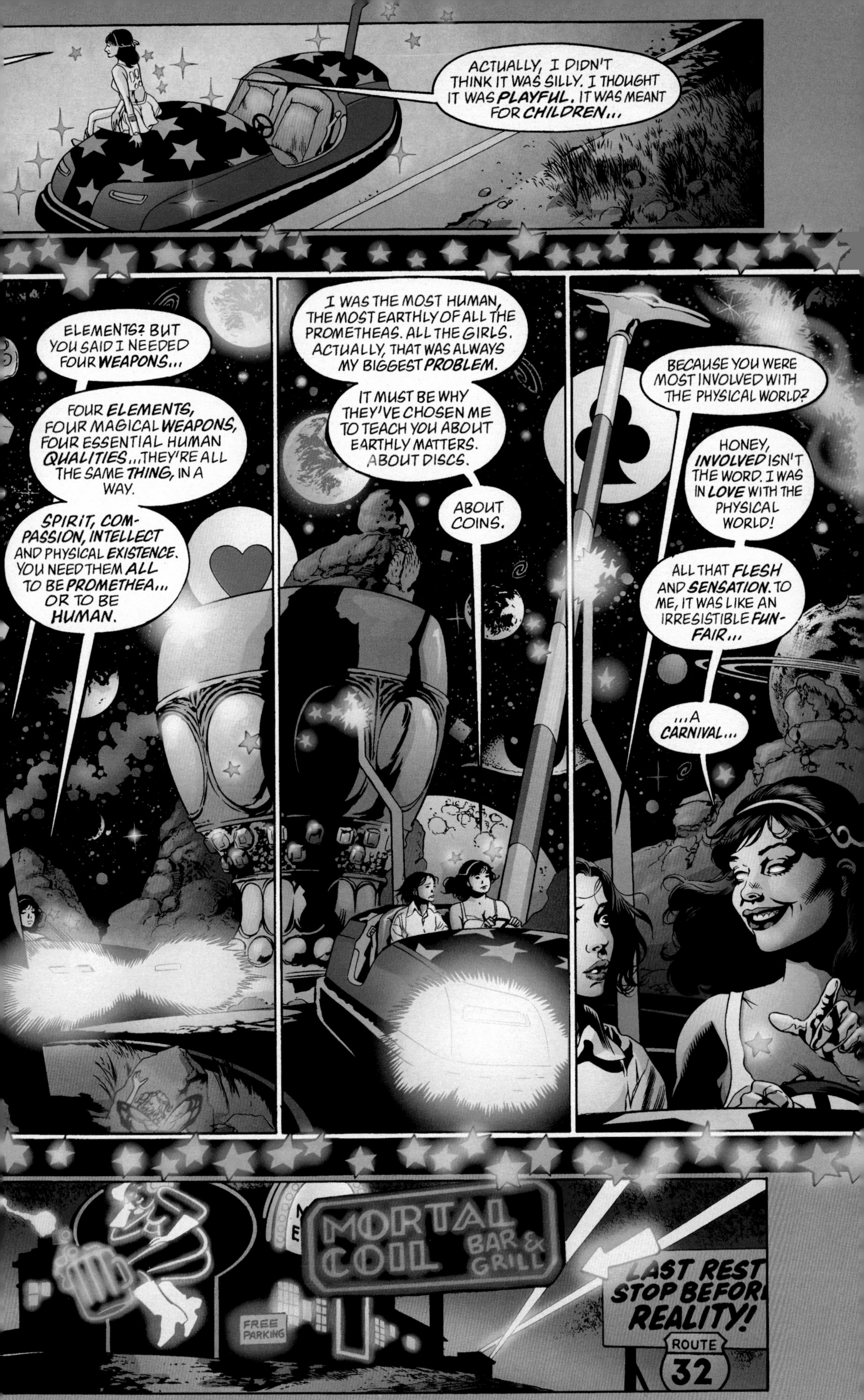
ACTUALLY, I DIDN'T THINK IT WAS SILLY. I THOUGHT IT WAS PLAYFUL. IT WAS MEANT FOR CHILDREN...
ELEMENTS? BUT YOU SAID I NEEDED FOUR WEAPONS...
FOUR ELEMENTS, FOUR MAGICAL WEAPONS, FOUR ESSENTIAL HUMAN QUALITIES... THEY'RE ALL THE SAME THING, IN A WAY.
SPIRIT, COMPASSION, INTELLECT AND PHYSICAL EXISTENCE. YOU NEED THEM ALL TO BE PROMETHEA... OR TO BE HUMAN.
I WAS THE MOST HUMAN, THE MOST EARTHLY OF ALL THE PROMETHEAS. ALL THE GIRLS. ACTUALLY, THAT WAS ALWAYS MY BIGGEST PROBLEM.
IT MUST BE WHY THEY'VE CHOSEN ME TO TEACH YOU ABOUT EARTHLY MATTERS. ABOUT DISCS.
ABOUT COINS.
BECAUSE YOU WERE MOST INVOLVED WITH THE PHYSICAL WORLD?
HONEY, INVOLVED ISN'T THE WORD. I WAS IN LOVE WITH THE PHYSICAL WORLD!
ALL THAT FLESH AND SENSATION. TO ME, IT WAS LIKE AN IRRESISTIBLE FUN-FAIR...
...A CARNIVAL...
MORTAL COIL BAR & GRILL
FREE PARKING
LAST REST STOP BEFORE REALITY!
ROUTE 32

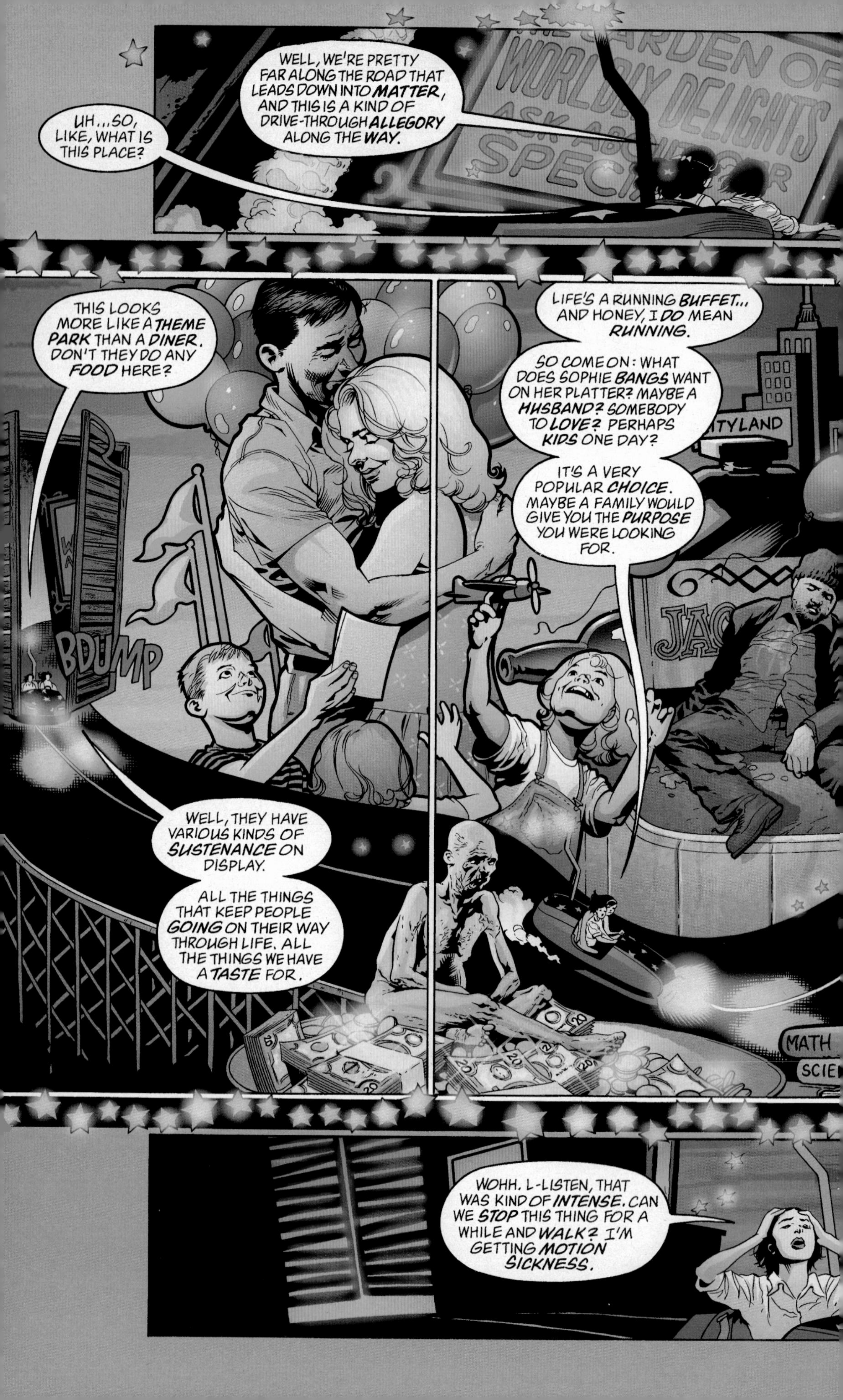
THE GARDEN OF WORLDLY DELIGHTS
UH...SO, LIKE, WHAT IS THIS PLACE?
WELL, WE'RE PRETTY FAR ALONG THE ROAD THAT LEADS DOWN INTO MATTER, AND THIS IS A KIND OF DRIVE-THROUGH ALLEGORY ALONG THE WAY.
THIS LOOKS MORE LIKE A THEME PARK THAN A DINER. DON'T THEY DO ANY FOOD HERE?
BDUMP
WELL, THEY HAVE VARIOUS KINDS OF SUSTENANCE ON DISPLAY.
ALL THE THINGS THAT KEEP PEOPLE GOING ON THEIR WAY THROUGH LIFE. ALL THE THINGS WE HAVE A TASTE FOR.
LIFE'S A RUNNING BUFFET... AND HONEY, I DO MEAN RUNNING.
SO COME ON: WHAT DOES SOPHIE BANGS WANT ON HER PLATTER? MAYBE A HUSBAND? SOMEBODY TO LOVE? PERHAPS KIDS ONE DAY?
IT'S A VERY POPULAR CHOICE. MAYBE A FAMILY WOULD GIVE YOU THE PURPOSE YOU WERE LOOKING FOR.
MATH
WOHH. L-LISTEN, THAT WAS KIND OF INTENSE. CAN WE STOP THIS THING FOR A WHILE AND WALK? I'M GETTING MOTION SICKNESS.

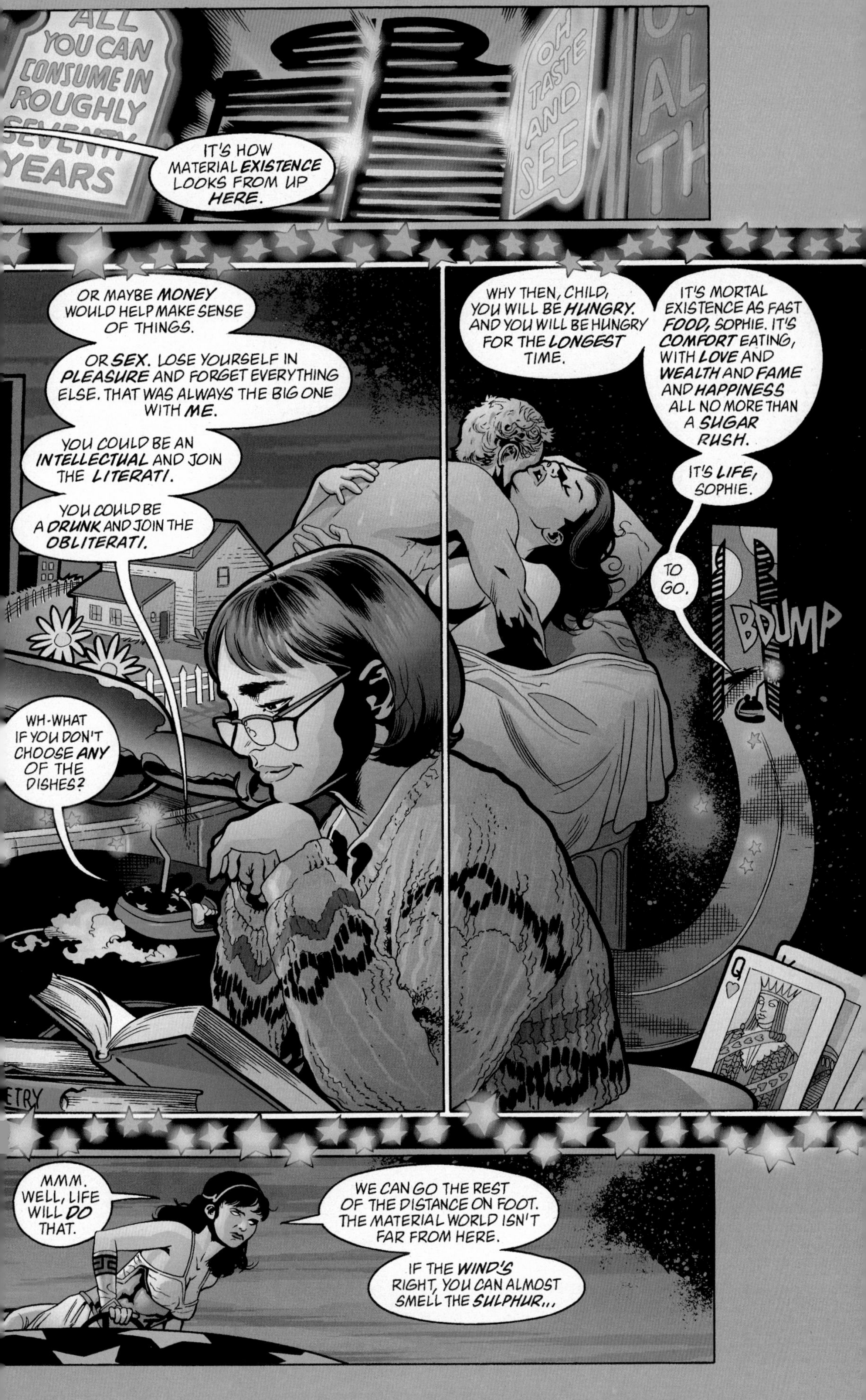
ALL YOU CAN CONSUME IN ROUGHLY SEVENTY YEARS
OH TASTE AND SEE
IT'S HOW MATERIAL EXISTENCE LOOKS FROM UP HERE.
OR MAYBE MONEY WOULD HELP MAKE SENSE OF THINGS.
OR SEX. LOSE YOURSELF IN PLEASURE AND FORGET EVERYTHING ELSE. THAT WAS ALWAYS THE BIG ONE WITH ME.
YOU COULD BE AN INTELLECTUAL AND JOIN THE LITERATI.
YOU COULD BE A DRUNK AND JOIN THE OBLITERATI.
WH-WHAT IF YOU DON'T CHOOSE ANY OF THE DISHES?
WHY THEN, CHILD, YOU WILL BE HUNGRY. AND YOU WILL BE HUNGRY FOR THE LONGEST TIME.
IT'S MORTAL EXISTENCE AS FAST FOOD, SOPHIE. IT'S COMFORT EATING, WITH LOVE AND WEALTH AND FAME AND HAPPINESS ALL NO MORE THAN A SUGAR RUSH.
IT'S LIFE, SOPHIE.
TO GO.
BDUMP
ETRY
MMM. WELL, LIFE WILL DO THAT.
WE CAN GO THE REST OF THE DISTANCE ON FOOT. THE MATERIAL WORLD ISN'T FAR FROM HERE.
IF THE WIND'S RIGHT, YOU CAN ALMOST SMELL THE SULPHUR...

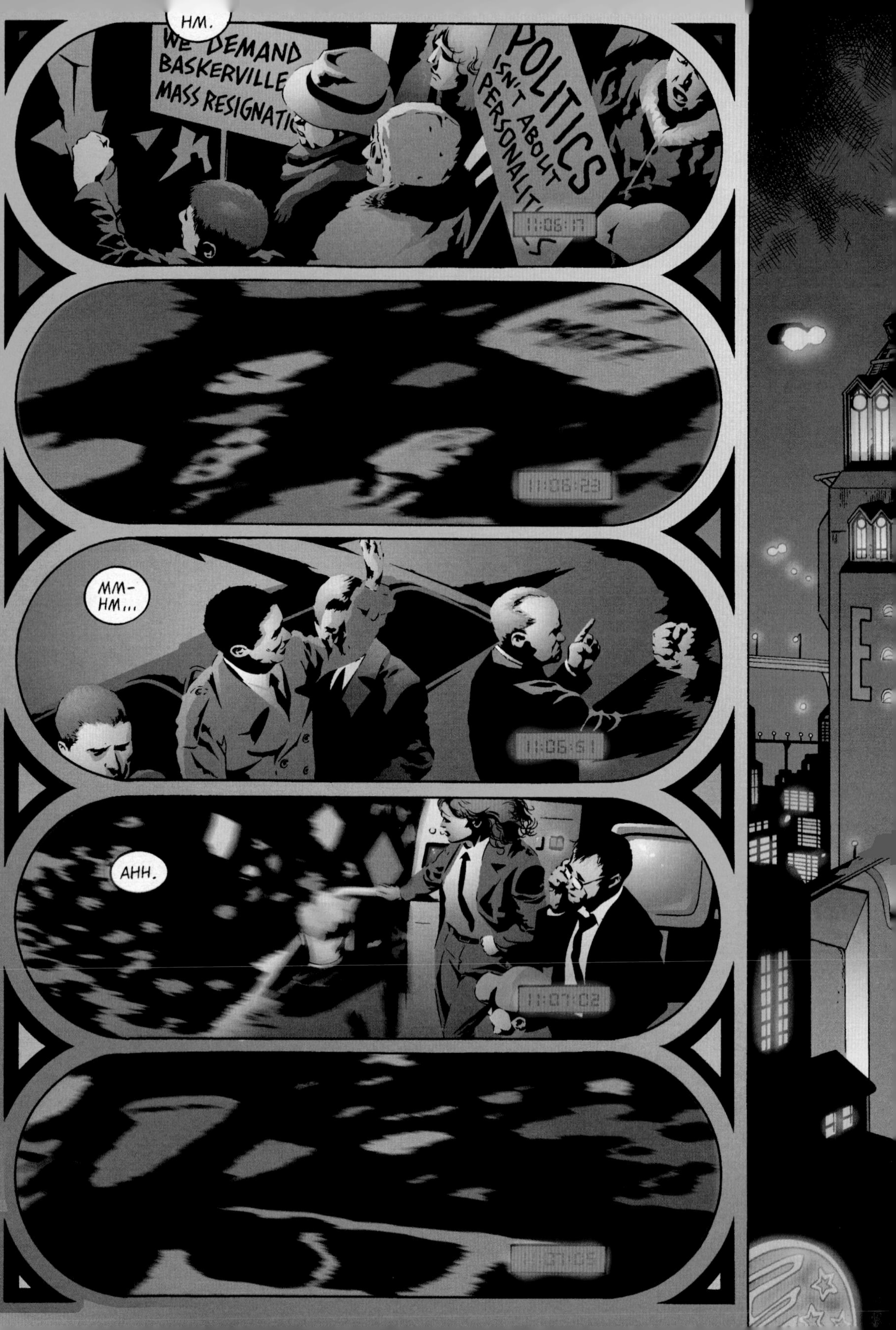
HM.
WE DEMAND BASKERVILLE MASS RESIGNATI
POLITICS ISN'T ABOUT PERSONALITI
11:06:17
11:06:23
MM-HM...
11:06:51
AHH.
11:07:02

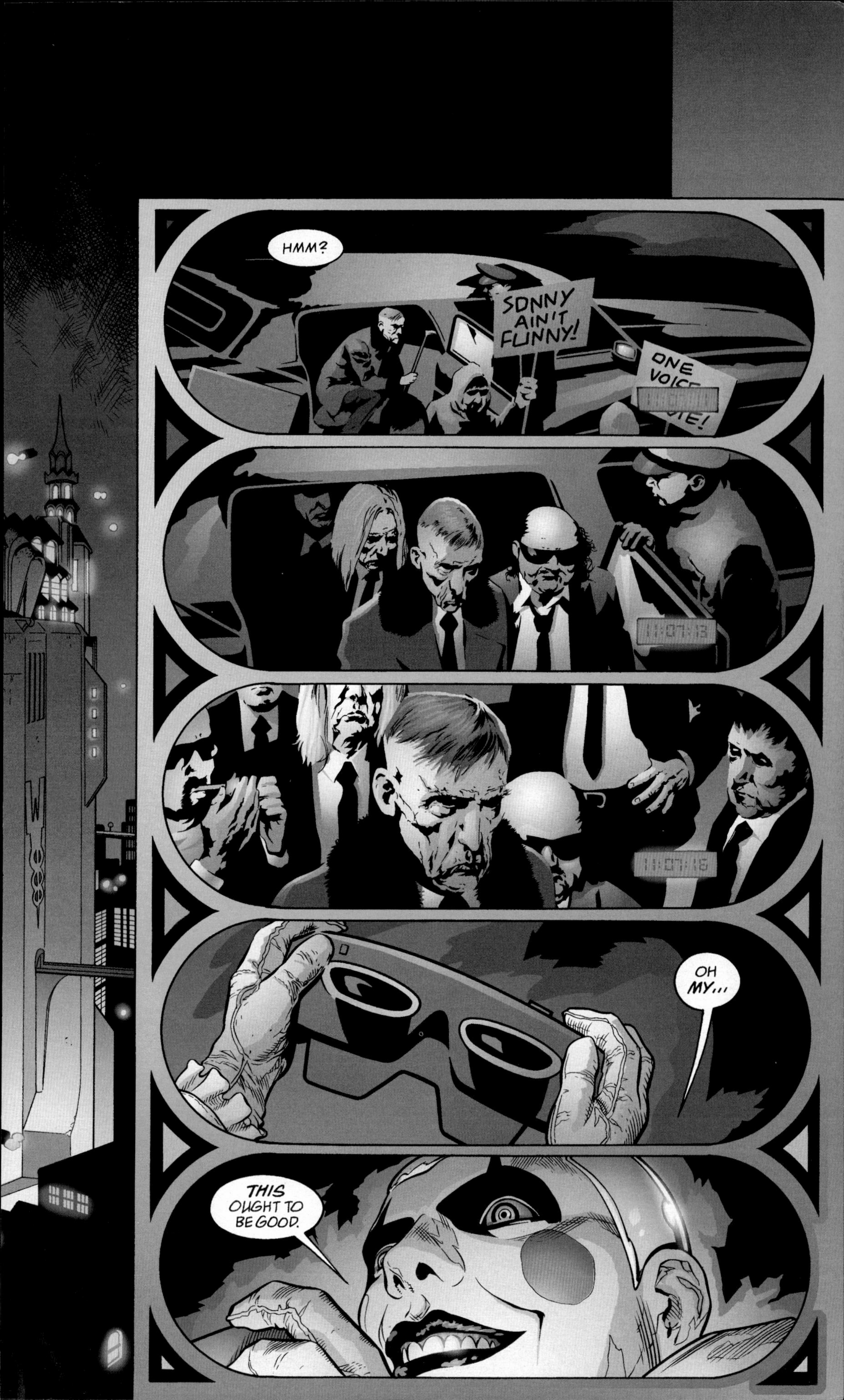
HMM?
SONNY AIN'T FUNNY!
ONE VOICE
11:07:13
11:07:16
OH MY...
THIS OUGHT TO BE GOOD.

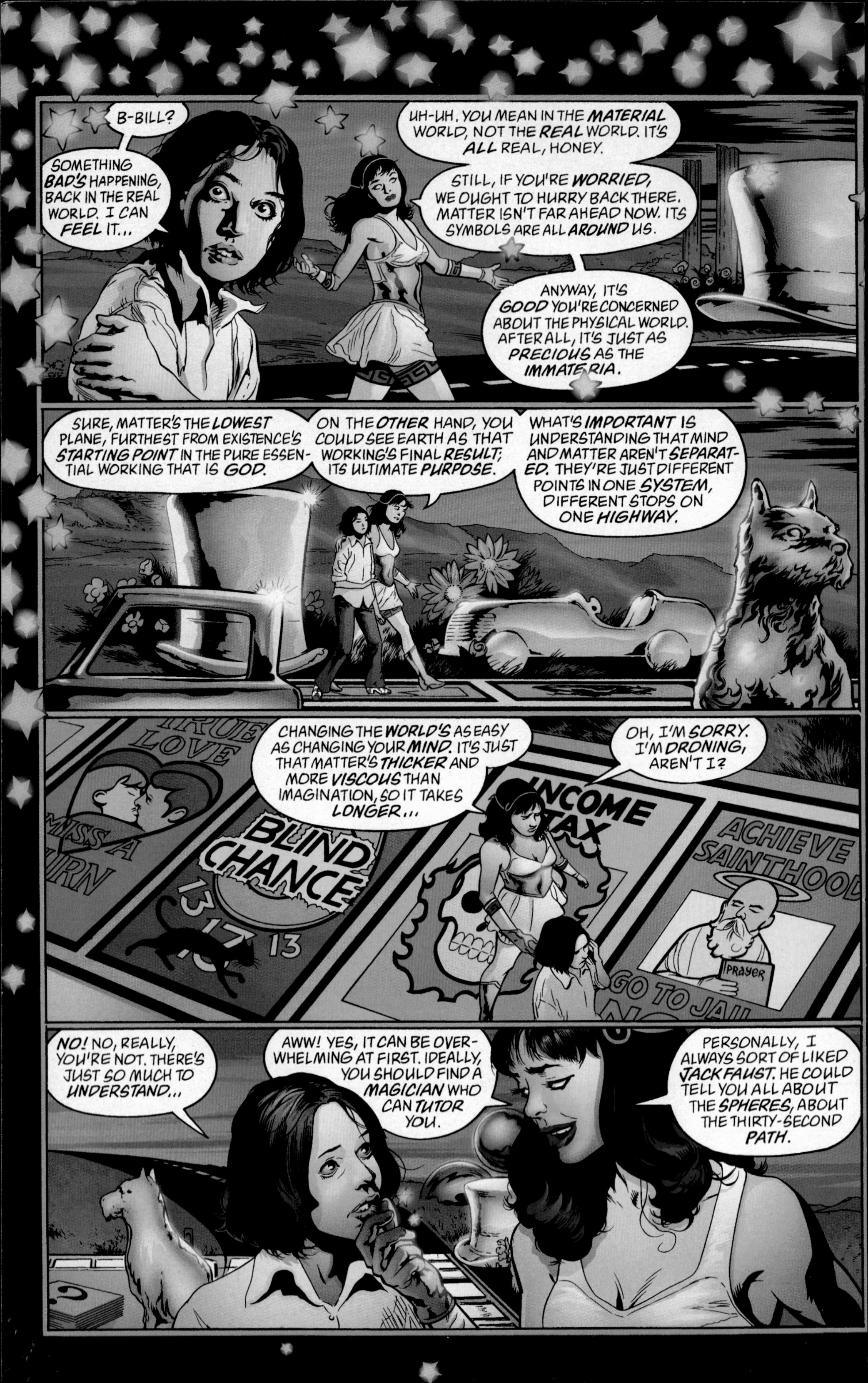
B-BILL?
SOMETHING BAD'S HAPPENING, BACK IN THE REAL WORLD. I CAN FEEL IT...
UH-UH. YOU MEAN IN THE MATERIAL WORLD, NOT THE REAL WORLD. IT'S ALL REAL, HONEY.
STILL, IF YOU'RE WORRIED, WE OUGHT TO HURRY BACK THERE. MATTER ISN'T FAR AHEAD NOW. ITS SYMBOLS ARE ALL AROUND US.
ANYWAY, IT'S GOOD YOU'RE CONCERNED ABOUT THE PHYSICAL WORLD. AFTER ALL, IT'S JUST AS PRECIOUS AS THE IMMATERIA.
SURE, MATTER'S THE LOWEST PLANE, FURTHEST FROM EXISTENCE'S STARTING POINT IN THE PURE ESSENTIAL WORKING THAT IS GOD.
ON THE OTHER HAND, YOU COULD SEE EARTH AS THAT WORKING'S FINAL RESULT; ITS ULTIMATE PURPOSE.
WHAT'S IMPORTANT IS UNDERSTANDING THAT MIND AND MATTER AREN'T SEPARATED. THEY'RE JUST DIFFERENT POINTS IN ONE SYSTEM, DIFFERENT STOPS ON ONE HIGHWAY.
TRUE LOVE
MISS A TURN
BLIND CHANCE
13
17
13
CHANGING THE WORLD'S AS EASY AS CHANGING YOUR MIND. IT'S JUST THAT MATTER'S THICKER AND MORE VISCOUS THAN IMAGINATION, SO IT TAKES LONGER...
INCOME TAX
OH, I'M SORRY. I'M DRONING, AREN'T I?
ACHIEVE SAINTHOOD
PRAYER
GO TO JAIL
NO! NO, REALLY, YOU'RE NOT. THERE'S JUST SO MUCH TO UNDERSTAND...
AWW! YES, IT CAN BE OVERWHELMING AT FIRST. IDEALLY, YOU SHOULD FIND A MAGICIAN WHO CAN TUTOR YOU.
PERSONALLY, I ALWAYS SORT OF LIKED JACK FAUST. HE COULD TELL YOU ALL ABOUT THE SPHERES, ABOUT THE THIRTY-SECOND PATH.

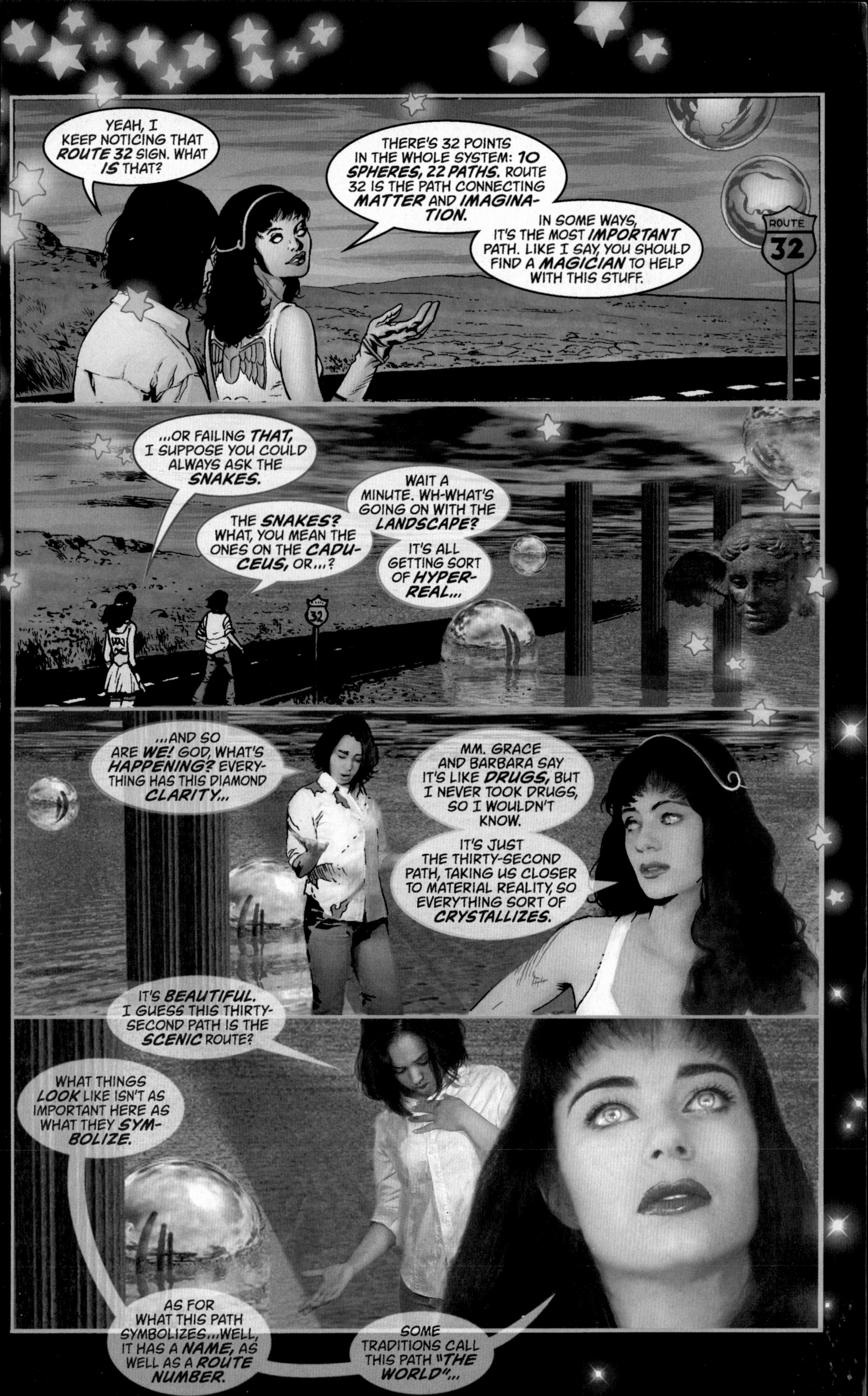

YEAH, I KEEP NOTICING THAT ROUTE 32 SIGN. WHAT IS THAT?
THERE'S 32 POINTS IN THE WHOLE SYSTEM: 10 SPHERES, 22 PATHS. ROUTE 32 IS THE PATH CONNECTING MATTER AND IMAGINATION.
IN SOME WAYS, IT'S THE MOST IMPORTANT PATH. LIKE I SAY, YOU SHOULD FIND A MAGICIAN TO HELP WITH THIS STUFF.
ROUTE 32
...OR FAILING THAT, I SUPPOSE YOU COULD ALWAYS ASK THE SNAKES.
THE SNAKES? WHAT, YOU MEAN THE ONES ON THE CADUCEUS, OR...?
WAIT A MINUTE. WH-WHAT'S GOING ON WITH THE LANDSCAPE?
IT'S ALL GETTING SORT OF HYPER-REAL...
...AND SO ARE WE! GOD, WHAT'S HAPPENING? EVERYTHING HAS THIS DIAMOND CLARITY...
MM. GRACE AND BARBARA SAY IT'S LIKE DRUGS, BUT I NEVER TOOK DRUGS, SO I WOULDN'T KNOW.
IT'S JUST THE THIRTY-SECOND PATH, TAKING US CLOSER TO MATERIAL REALITY, SO EVERYTHING SORT OF CRYSTALLIZES.
IT'S BEAUTIFUL. I GUESS THIS THIRTY-SECOND PATH IS THE SCENIC ROUTE?
WHAT THINGS LOOK LIKE ISN'T AS IMPORTANT HERE AS WHAT THEY SYMBOLIZE.
AS FOR WHAT THIS PATH SYMBOLIZES...WELL, IT HAS A NAME, AS WELL AS A ROUTE NUMBER.
SOME TRADITIONS CALL THIS PATH "THE WORLD"...

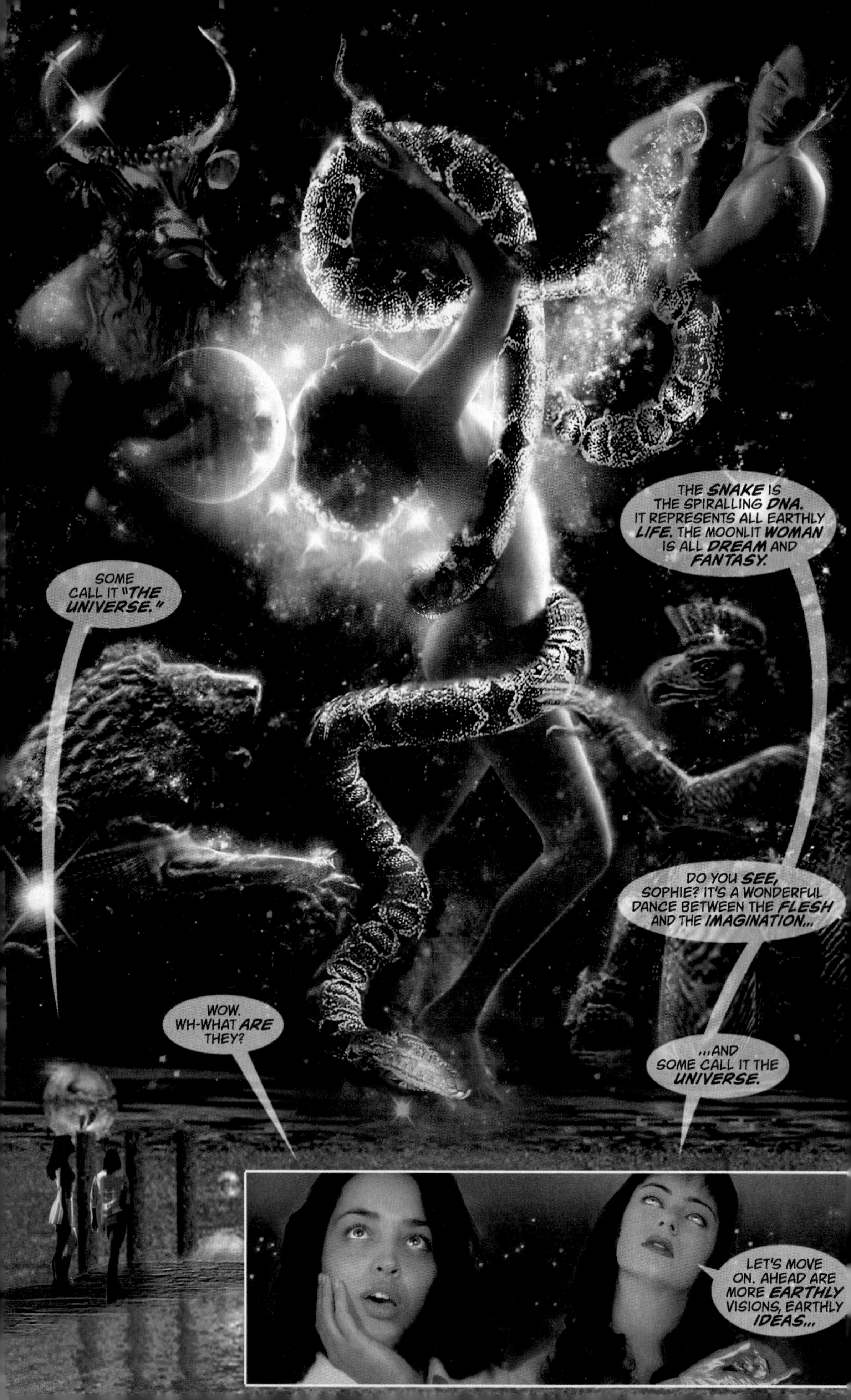
THE SNAKE IS THE SPIRALLING DNA. IT REPRESENTS ALL EARTHLY LIFE. THE MOONLIT WOMAN IS ALL DREAM AND FANTASY.
DO YOU SEE, SOPHIE? IT'S A WONDERFUL DANCE BETWEEN THE FLESH AND THE IMAGINATION...
...AND SOME CALL IT THE UNIVERSE.
SOME CALL IT "THE UNIVERSE."
WOW. WH-WHAT ARE THEY?
LET'S MOVE ON. AHEAD ARE MORE EARTHLY VISIONS, EARTHLY IDEAS...

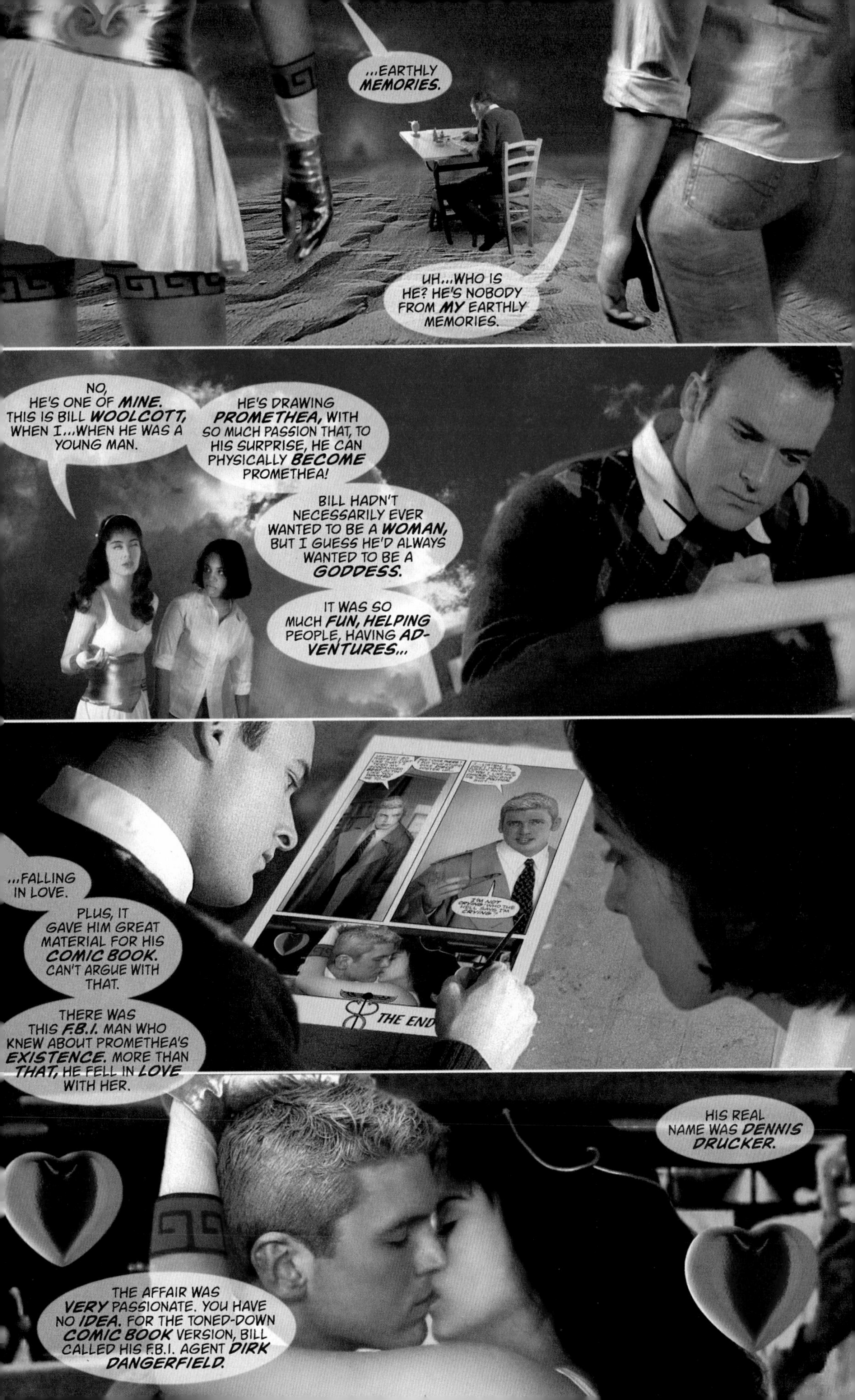
...EARTHLY MEMORIES.
UH...WHO IS HE? HE'S NOBODY FROM MY EARTHLY MEMORIES.
NO, HE'S ONE OF MINE. THIS IS BILL WOOLCOTT, WHEN I...WHEN HE WAS A YOUNG MAN.
HE'S DRAWING PROMETHEA, WITH SO MUCH PASSION THAT, TO HIS SURPRISE, HE CAN PHYSICALLY BECOME PROMETHEA!
BILL HADN'T NECESSARILY EVER WANTED TO BE A WOMAN, BUT I GUESS HE'D ALWAYS WANTED TO BE A GODDESS.
IT WAS SO MUCH FUN, HELPING PEOPLE, HAVING ADVENTURES...
...FALLING IN LOVE.
PLUS, IT GAVE HIM GREAT MATERIAL FOR HIS COMIC BOOK. CAN'T ARGUE WITH THAT.
THE END
THERE WAS THIS F.B.I. MAN WHO KNEW ABOUT PROMETHEA'S EXISTENCE. MORE THAN THAT, HE FELL IN LOVE WITH HER.
HIS REAL NAME WAS DENNIS DRUCKER.
THE AFFAIR WAS VERY PASSIONATE. YOU HAVE NO IDEA. FOR THE TONED-DOWN COMIC BOOK VERSION, BILL CALLED HIS F.B.I. AGENT DIRK DANGERFIELD.

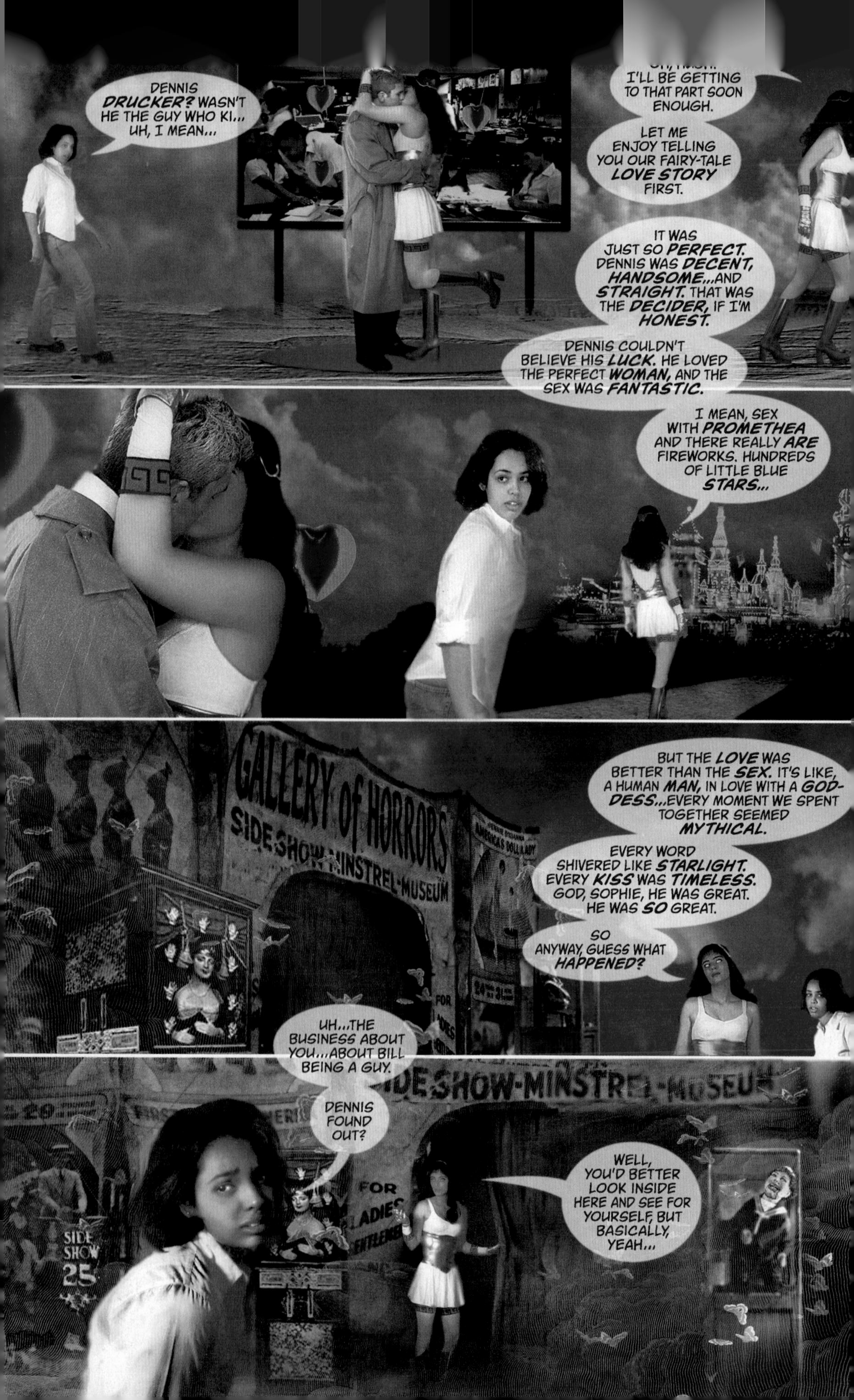
DENNIS DRUCKER? WASN'T HE THE GUY WHO KI... UH, I MEAN...
I'LL BE GETTING TO THAT PART SOON ENOUGH.
LET ME ENJOY TELLING YOU OUR FAIRY-TALE LOVE STORY FIRST.
IT WAS JUST SO PERFECT. DENNIS WAS DECENT, HANDSOME...AND STRAIGHT. THAT WAS THE DECIDER, IF I'M HONEST.
DENNIS COULDN'T BELIEVE HIS LUCK. HE LOVED THE PERFECT WOMAN, AND THE SEX WAS FANTASTIC.
I MEAN, SEX WITH PROMETHEA AND THERE REALLY ARE FIREWORKS. HUNDREDS OF LITTLE BLUE STARS...
GALLERY of HORRORS
SIDE-SHOW-MINSTREL-MUSEUM
BUT THE LOVE WAS BETTER THAN THE SEX. IT'S LIKE, A HUMAN MAN, IN LOVE WITH A GOD-DESS...EVERY MOMENT WE SPENT TOGETHER SEEMED MYTHICAL.
EVERY WORD SHIVERED LIKE STARLIGHT. EVERY KISS WAS TIMELESS. GOD, SOPHIE, HE WAS GREAT. HE WAS SO GREAT.
SO ANYWAY, GUESS WHAT HAPPENED?
UH...THE BUSINESS ABOUT YOU...ABOUT BILL BEING A GUY.
DENNIS FOUND OUT?
SIDE SHOW 25
FOR LADIES
WELL, YOU'D BETTER LOOK INSIDE HERE AND SEE FOR YOURSELF, BUT BASICALLY, YEAH...

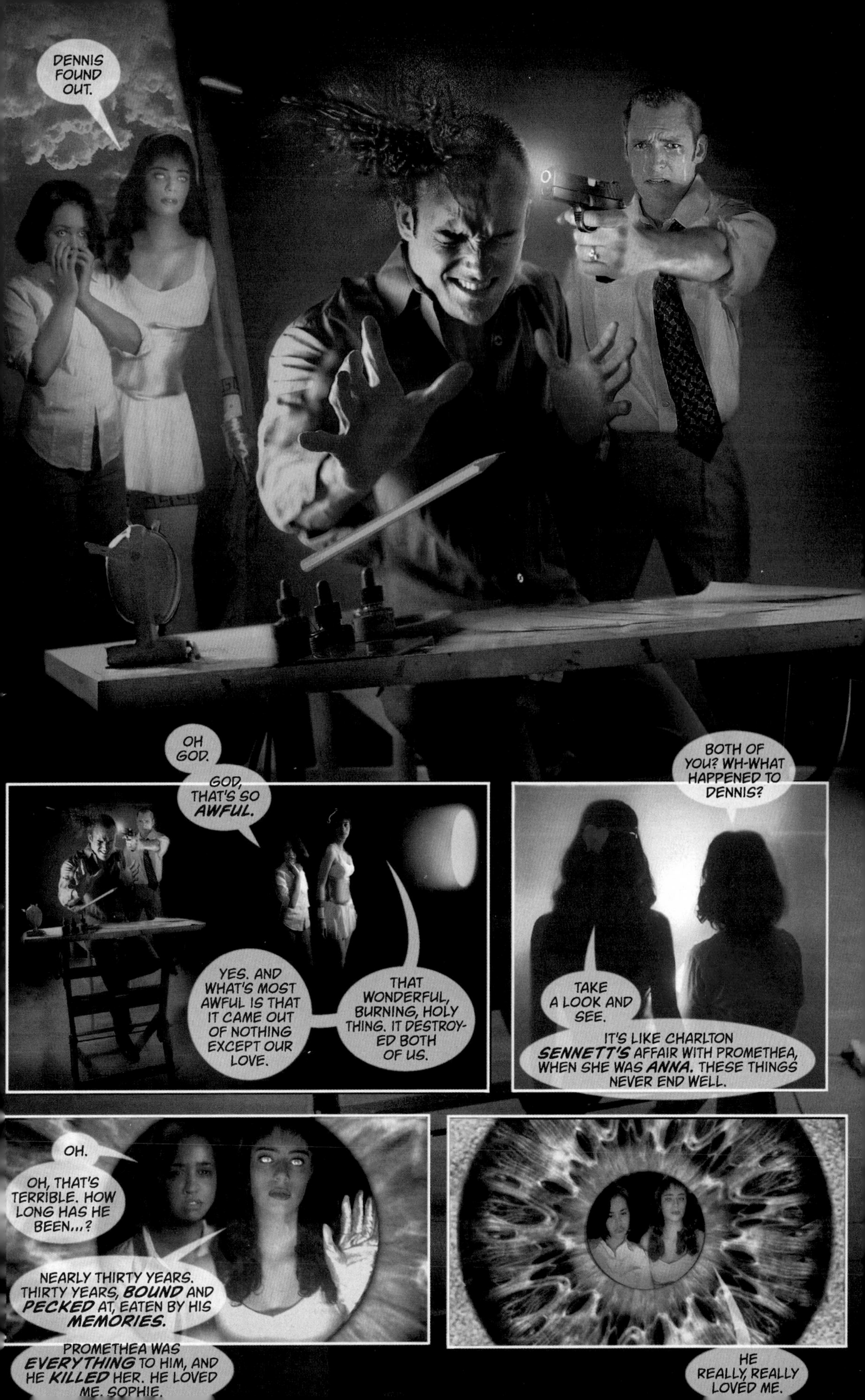
DENNIS FOUND OUT.
OH GOD.
GOD, THAT'S SO AWFUL.
YES. AND WHAT'S MOST AWFUL IS THAT IT CAME OUT OF NOTHING EXCEPT OUR LOVE.
THAT WONDERFUL, BURNING, HOLY THING. IT DESTROY-ED BOTH OF US.
BOTH OF YOU? WH-WHAT HAPPENED TO DENNIS?
TAKE A LOOK AND SEE.
IT'S LIKE CHARLTON SENNETT'S AFFAIR WITH PROMETHEA, WHEN SHE WAS ANNA. THESE THINGS NEVER END WELL.
OH.
OH, THAT'S TERRIBLE. HOW LONG HAS HE BEEN...?
NEARLY THIRTY YEARS. THIRTY YEARS, BOUND AND PECKED AT, EATEN BY HIS MEMORIES.
PROMETHEA WAS EVERYTHING TO HIM, AND HE KILLED HER. HE LOVED ME. SOPHIE.
HE REALLY, REALLY LOVED ME.

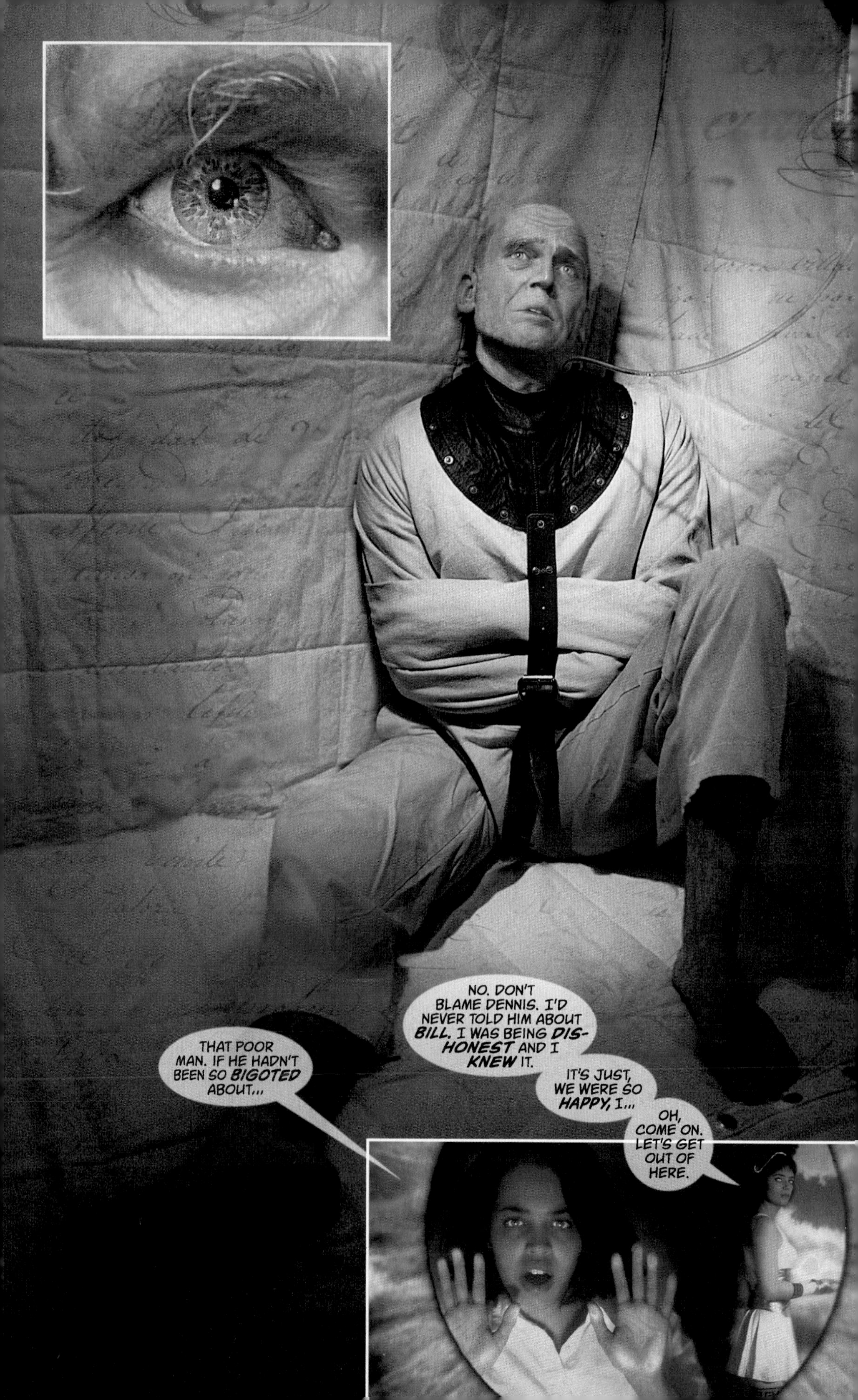
THAT POOR MAN. IF HE HADN'T BEEN SO BIGOTED ABOUT...
NO. DON'T BLAME DENNIS. I'D NEVER TOLD HIM ABOUT BILL. I WAS BEING DIS-HONEST AND I KNEW IT.
IT'S JUST, WE WERE SO HAPPY, I...
OH, COME ON. LET'S GET OUT OF HERE.

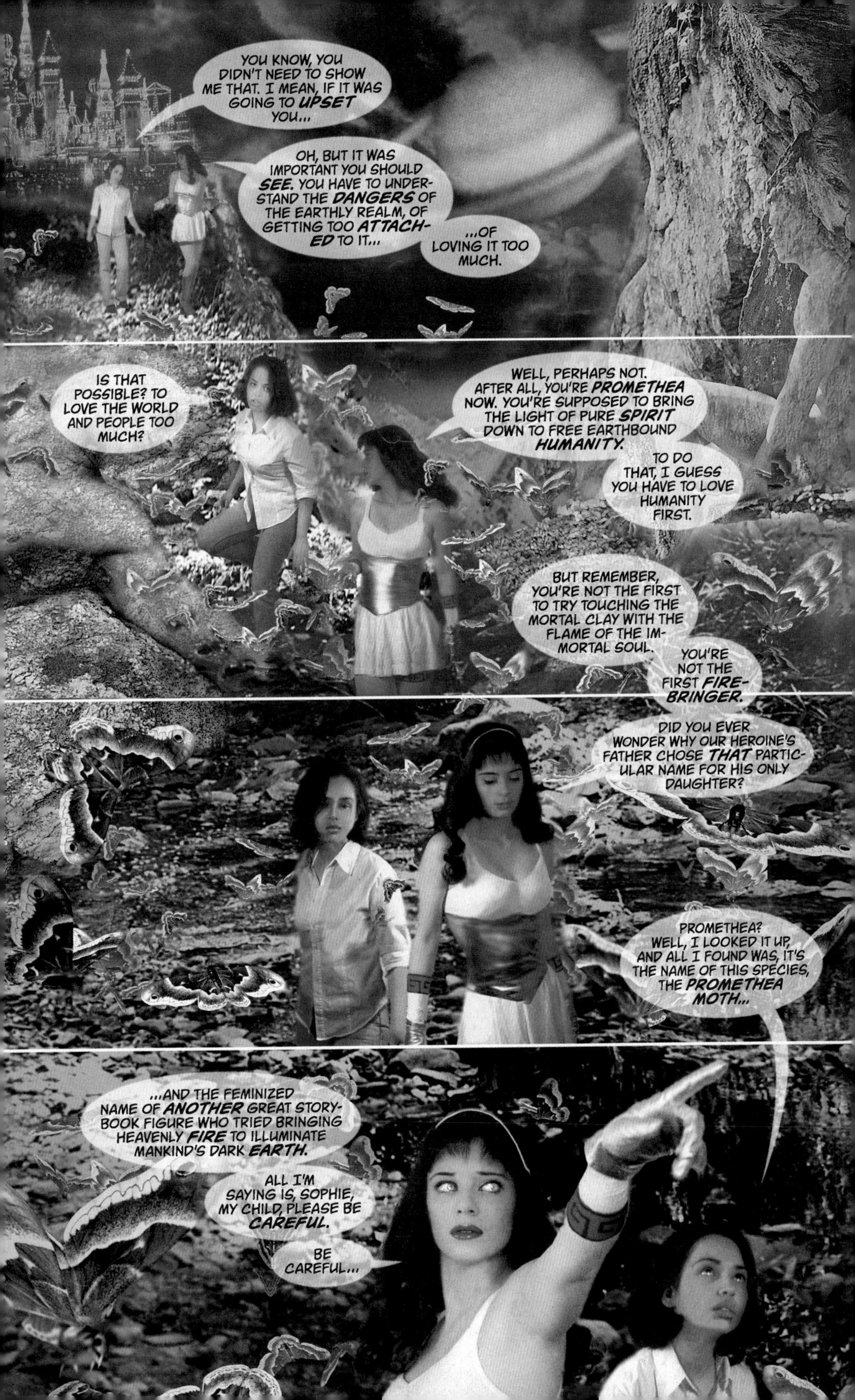
YOU KNOW, YOU DIDN'T NEED TO SHOW ME THAT. I MEAN, IF IT WAS GOING TO UPSET YOU...
OH, BUT IT WAS IMPORTANT YOU SHOULD SEE. YOU HAVE TO UNDER-STAND THE DANGERS OF THE EARTHLY REALM, OF GETTING TOO ATTACH-ED TO IT...
...OF LOVING IT TOO MUCH.
IS THAT POSSIBLE? TO LOVE THE WORLD AND PEOPLE TOO MUCH?
WELL, PERHAPS NOT. AFTER ALL, YOU'RE PROMETHEA NOW. YOU'RE SUPPOSED TO BRING THE LIGHT OF PURE SPIRIT DOWN TO FREE EARTHBOUND HUMANITY.
TO DO THAT, I GUESS YOU HAVE TO LOVE HUMANITY FIRST.
BUT REMEMBER, YOU'RE NOT THE FIRST TO TRY TOUCHING THE MORTAL CLAY WITH THE FLAME OF THE IM-MORTAL SOUL.
YOU'RE NOT THE FIRST FIRE-BRINGER.
DID YOU EVER WONDER WHY OUR HEROINE'S FATHER CHOSE THAT PARTIC-ULAR NAME FOR HIS ONLY DAUGHTER?
PROMETHEA? WELL, I LOOKED IT UP, AND ALL I FOUND WAS, IT'S THE NAME OF THIS SPECIES, THE PROMETHEA MOTH...
...AND THE FEMINIZED NAME OF ANOTHER GREAT STORY-BOOK FIGURE WHO TRIED BRINGING HEAVENLY FIRE TO ILLUMINATE MANKIND'S DARK EARTH.
ALL I'M SAYING IS, SOPHIE, MY CHILD, PLEASE BE CAREFUL.
BE CAREFUL...

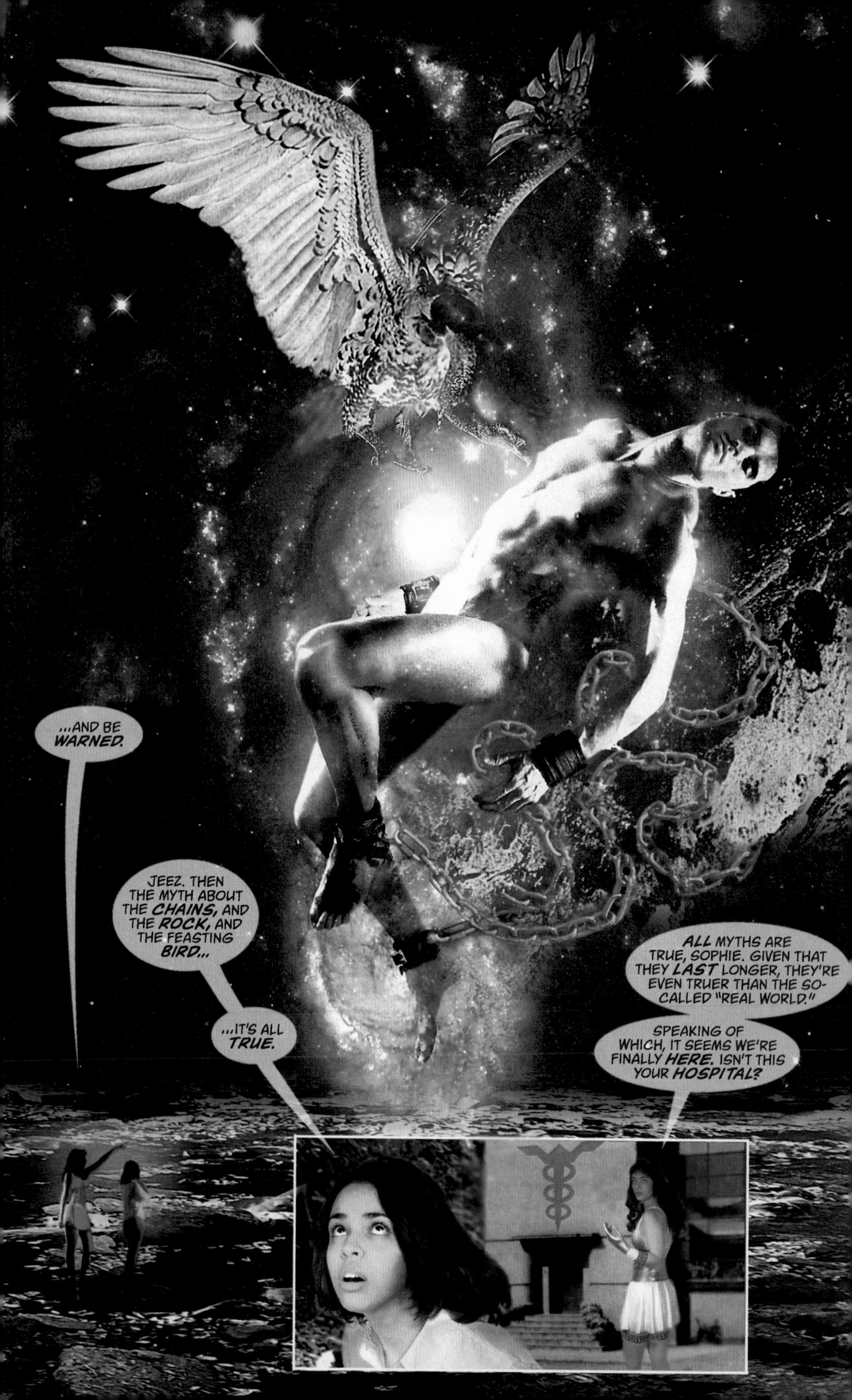
...AND BE WARNED.
JEEZ. THEN THE MYTH ABOUT THE CHAINS, AND THE ROCK, AND THE FEASTING BIRD...
...IT'S ALL TRUE.
ALL MYTHS ARE TRUE, SOPHIE. GIVEN THAT THEY LAST LONGER, THEY'RE EVEN TRUER THAN THE SO-CALLED "REAL WORLD."
SPEAKING OF WHICH, IT SEEMS WE'RE FINALLY HERE. ISN'T THIS YOUR HOSPITAL?

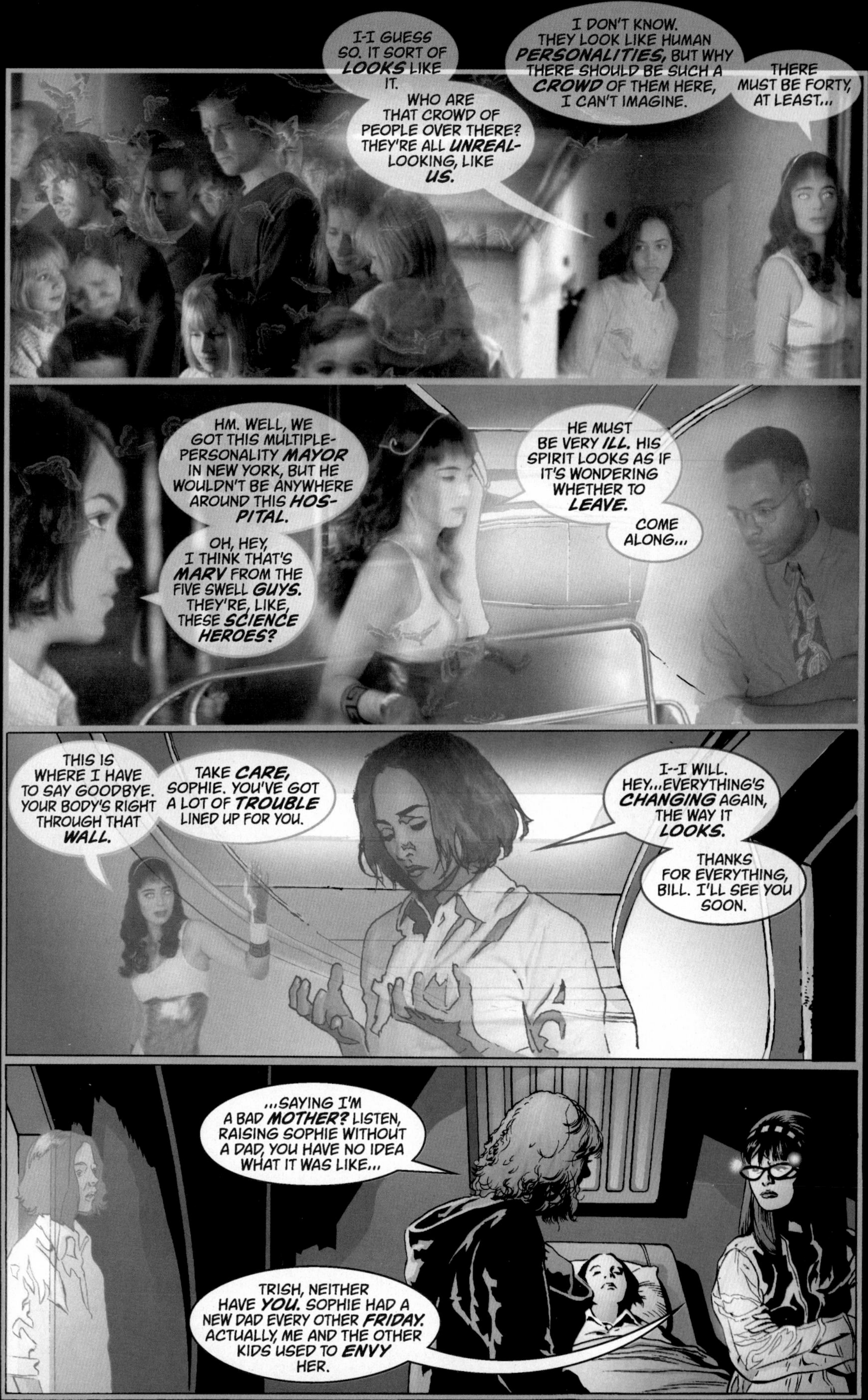
I-I GUESS SO. IT SORT OF LOOKS LIKE IT.
WHO ARE THAT CROWD OF PEOPLE OVER THERE? THEY'RE ALL UNREAL-LOOKING, LIKE US.
I DON'T KNOW. THEY LOOK LIKE HUMAN PERSONALITIES, BUT WHY THERE SHOULD BE SUCH A CROWD OF THEM HERE, I CAN'T IMAGINE.
THERE MUST BE FORTY, AT LEAST...
HM. WELL, WE GOT THIS MULTIPLE-PERSONALITY MAYOR IN NEW YORK, BUT HE WOULDN'T BE ANYWHERE AROUND THIS HOS-PITAL.
OH, HEY, I THINK THAT'S MARV FROM THE FIVE SWELL GUYS. THEY'RE, LIKE, THESE SCIENCE HEROES?
HE MUST BE VERY ILL. HIS SPIRIT LOOKS AS IF IT'S WONDERING WHETHER TO LEAVE.
COME ALONG...
THIS IS WHERE I HAVE TO SAY GOODBYE. YOUR BODY'S RIGHT THROUGH THAT WALL.
TAKE CARE, SOPHIE. YOU'VE GOT A LOT OF TROUBLE LINED UP FOR YOU.
I--I WILL. HEY...EVERYTHING'S CHANGING AGAIN, THE WAY IT LOOKS.
THANKS FOR EVERYTHING, BILL. I'LL SEE YOU SOON.
...SAYING I'M A BAD MOTHER? LISTEN, RAISING SOPHIE WITHOUT A DAD, YOU HAVE NO IDEA WHAT IT WAS LIKE...
TRISH, NEITHER HAVE YOU. SOPHIE HAD A NEW DAD EVERY OTHER FRIDAY. ACTUALLY, ME AND THE OTHER KIDS USED TO ENVY HER.

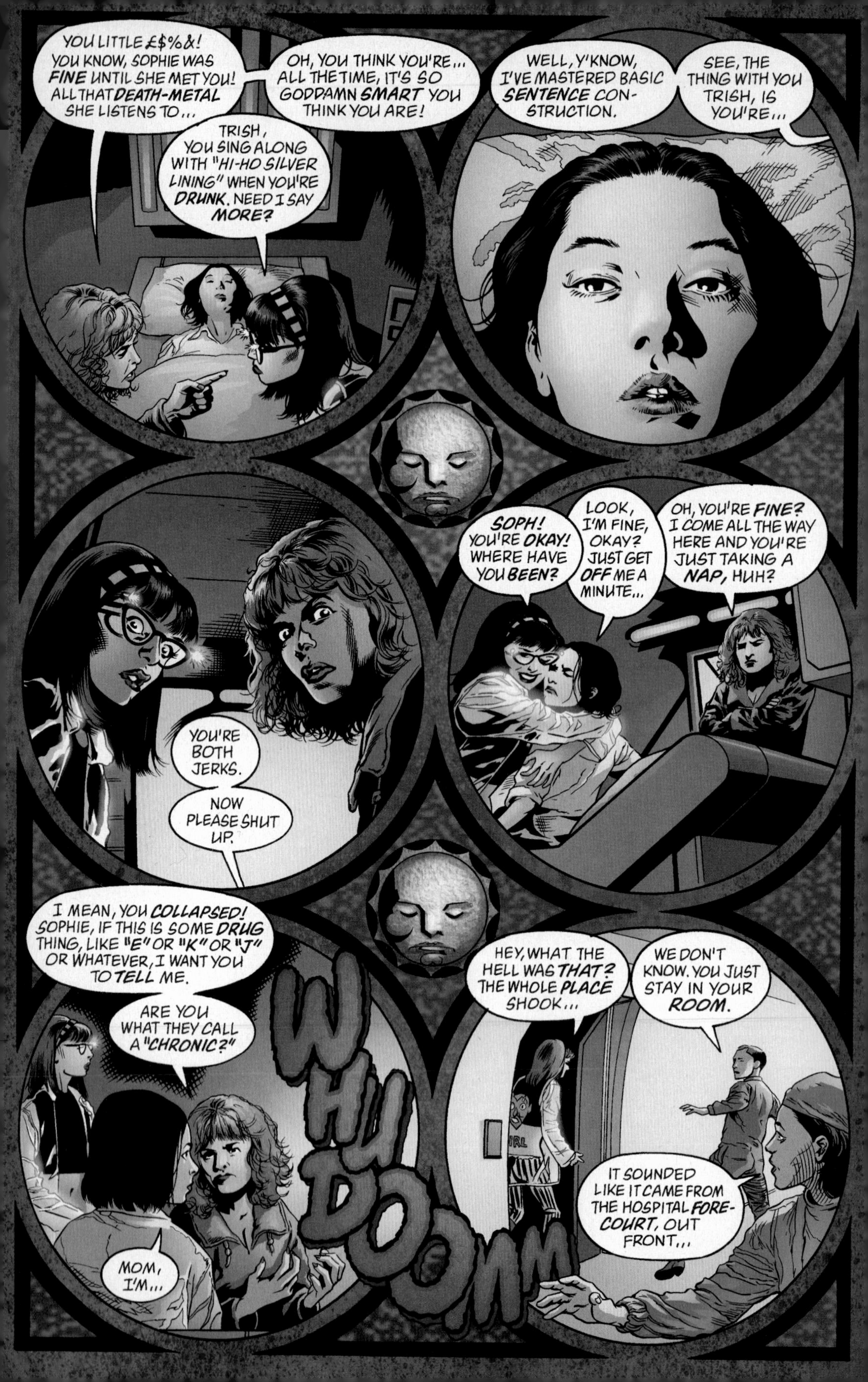
YOU LITTLE £$%&! YOU KNOW, SOPHIE WAS FINE UNTIL SHE MET YOU! ALL THAT DEATH-METAL SHE LISTENS TO...
OH, YOU THINK YOU'RE... ALL THE TIME, IT'S SO GODDAMN SMART YOU THINK YOU ARE!
TRISH, YOU SING ALONG WITH "HI-HO SILVER LINING" WHEN YOU'RE DRUNK. NEED I SAY MORE?
WELL, Y'KNOW, I'VE MASTERED BASIC SENTENCE CONSTRUCTION.
SEE, THE THING WITH YOU TRISH, IS YOU'RE...
YOU'RE BOTH JERKS.
NOW PLEASE SHUT UP.
SOPH! YOU'RE OKAY! WHERE HAVE YOU BEEN?
LOOK, I'M FINE, OKAY? JUST GET OFF ME A MINUTE...
OH, YOU'RE FINE? I COME ALL THE WAY HERE AND YOU'RE JUST TAKING A NAP, HUH?
I MEAN, YOU COLLAPSED! SOPHIE, IF THIS IS SOME DRUG THING, LIKE "E" OR "K" OR "J" OR WHATEVER, I WANT YOU TO TELL ME.
ARE YOU WHAT THEY CALL A "CHRONIC?"
MOM, I'M...
WHUDOOM
HEY, WHAT THE HELL WAS THAT? THE WHOLE PLACE SHOOK...
WE DON'T KNOW. YOU JUST STAY IN YOUR ROOM.
IT SOUNDED LIKE IT CAME FROM THE HOSPITAL FORECOURT, OUT FRONT...

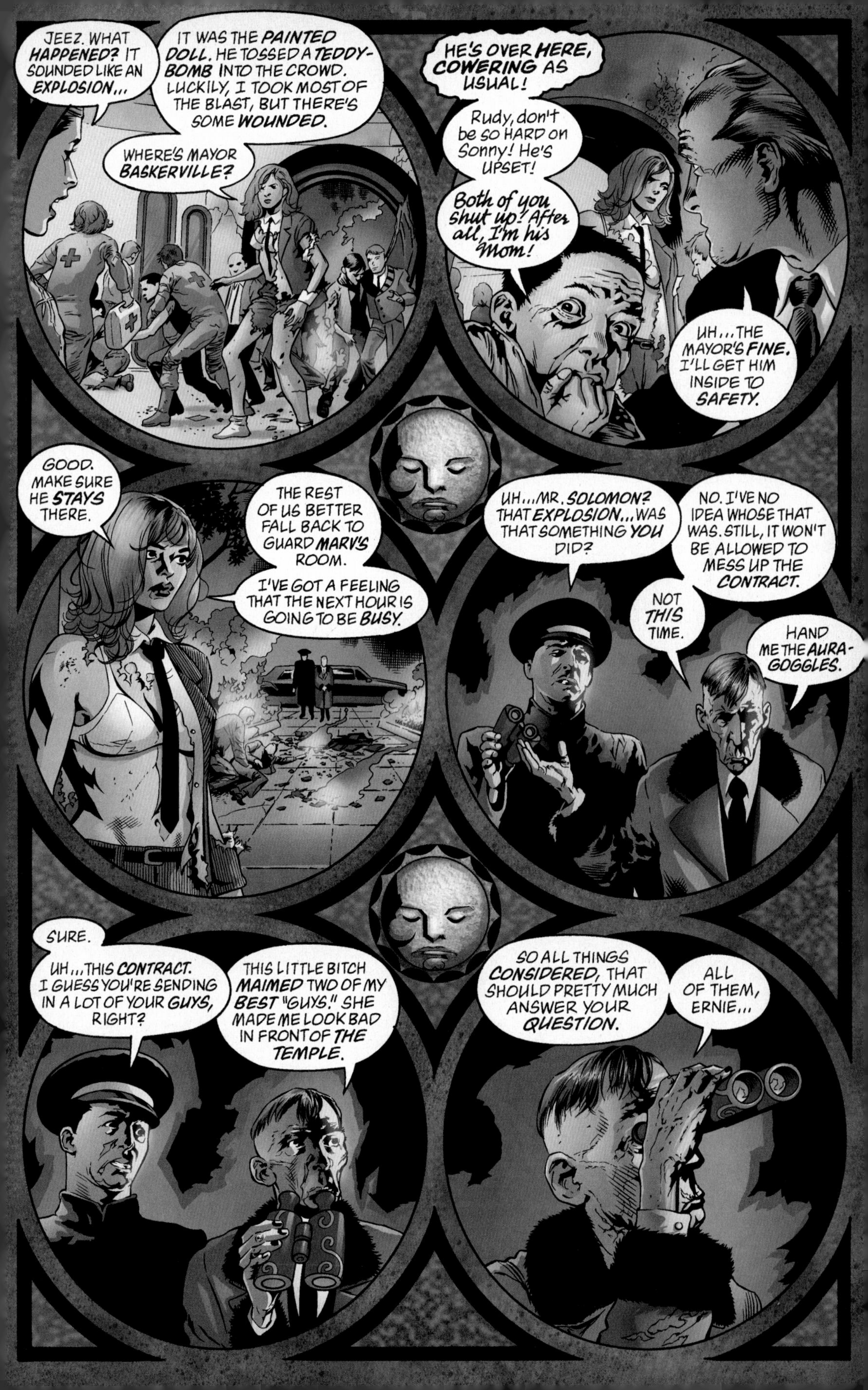
JEEZ. WHAT HAPPENED? IT SOUNDED LIKE AN EXPLOSION...
IT WAS THE PAINTED DOLL. HE TOSSED A TEDDY-BOMB INTO THE CROWD. LUCKILY, I TOOK MOST OF THE BLAST, BUT THERE'S SOME WOUNDED.
WHERE'S MAYOR BASKERVILLE?
HE'S OVER HERE, COWERING AS USUAL!
Rudy, don't be so HARD on Sonny! He's UPSET!
Both of you shut up! After all, I'm his Mom!
UH... THE MAYOR'S FINE. I'LL GET HIM INSIDE TO SAFETY.
GOOD. MAKE SURE HE STAYS THERE.
THE REST OF US BETTER FALL BACK TO GUARD MARV'S ROOM.
I'VE GOT A FEELING THAT THE NEXT HOUR IS GOING TO BE BUSY.
UH... MR. SOLOMON? THAT EXPLOSION... WAS THAT SOMETHING YOU DID?
NO. I'VE NO IDEA WHOSE THAT WAS. STILL, IT WON'T BE ALLOWED TO MESS UP THE CONTRACT.
NOT THIS TIME.
HAND ME THE AURA-GOGGLES.
SURE.
UH... THIS CONTRACT. I GUESS YOU'RE SENDING IN A LOT OF YOUR GUYS, RIGHT?
THIS LITTLE BITCH MAIMED TWO OF MY BEST "GUYS." SHE MADE ME LOOK BAD IN FRONT OF THE TEMPLE.
SO ALL THINGS CONSIDERED, THAT SHOULD PRETTY MUCH ANSWER YOUR QUESTION.
ALL OF THEM, ERNIE...

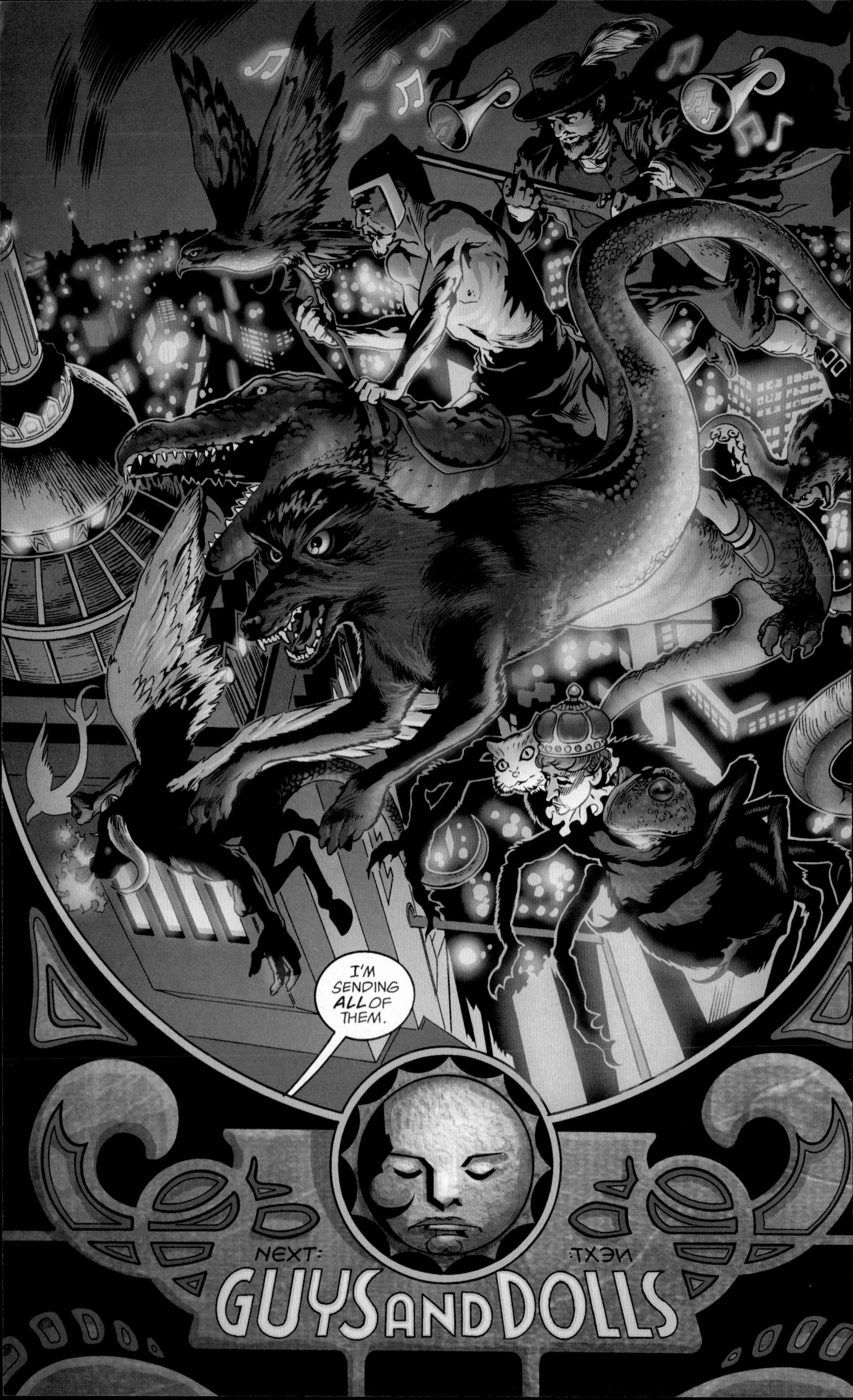
I'M SENDING ALL OF THEM.
NEXT:
:TXƎN
GUYS AND DOLLS

CHAPTER TWO

A sleeper wakes, empowering friends as battle breaks.

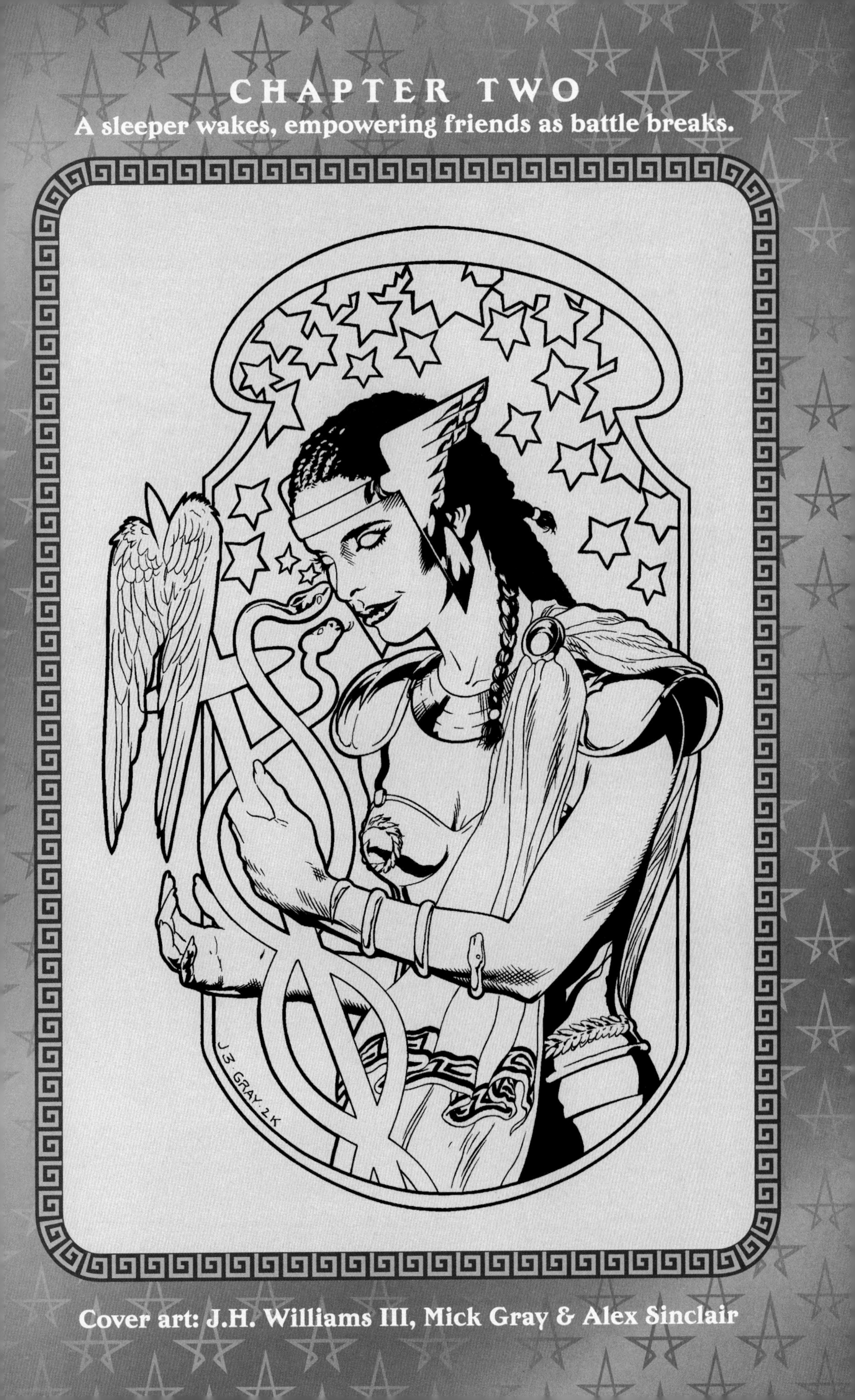
J.H. GRAY. 2K

Cover art: J.H. Williams III, Mick Gray & Alex Sinclair

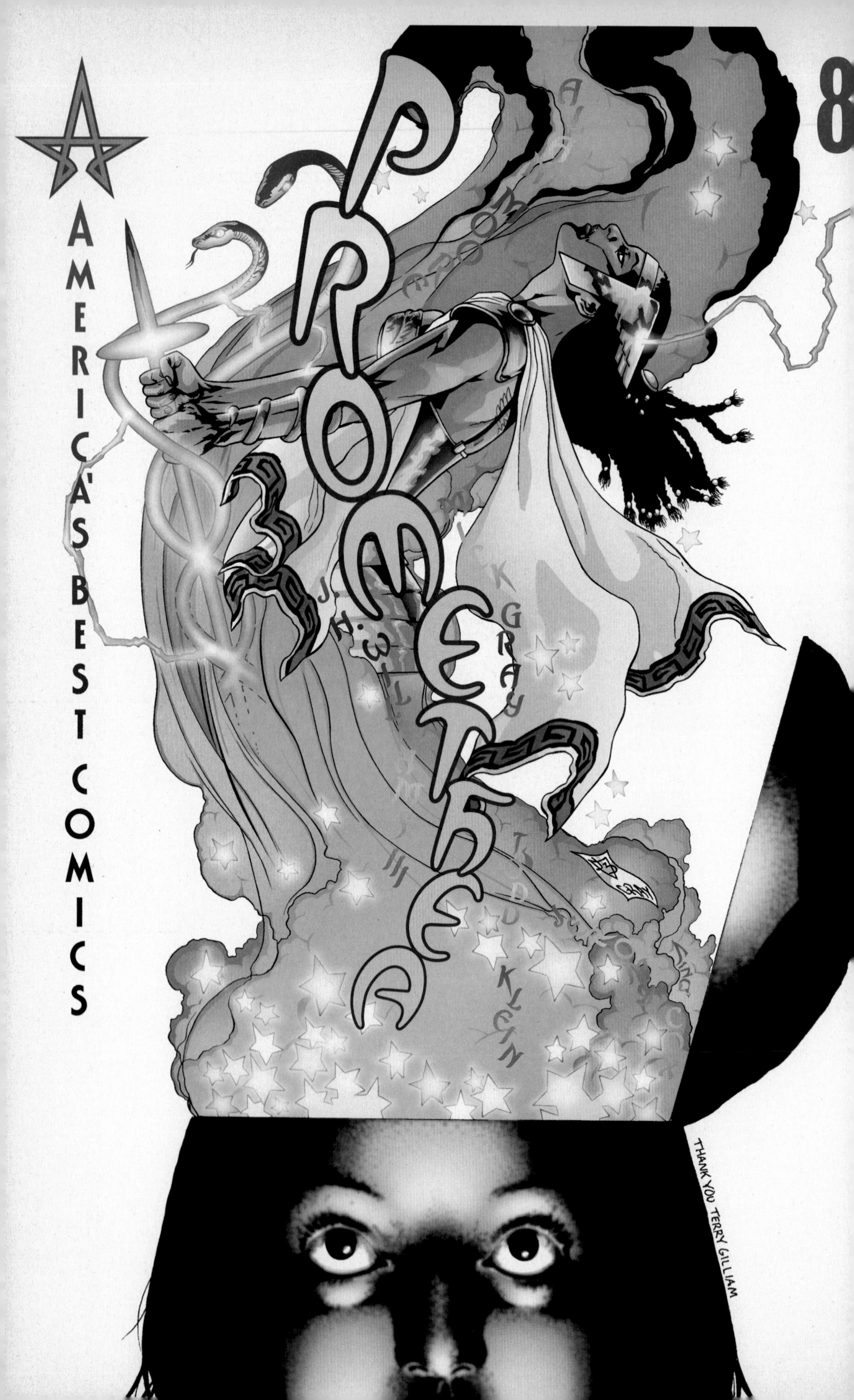
AMERICA'S BEST COMICS
PROMETHEA
8
THANK YOU TERRY GILLIAM

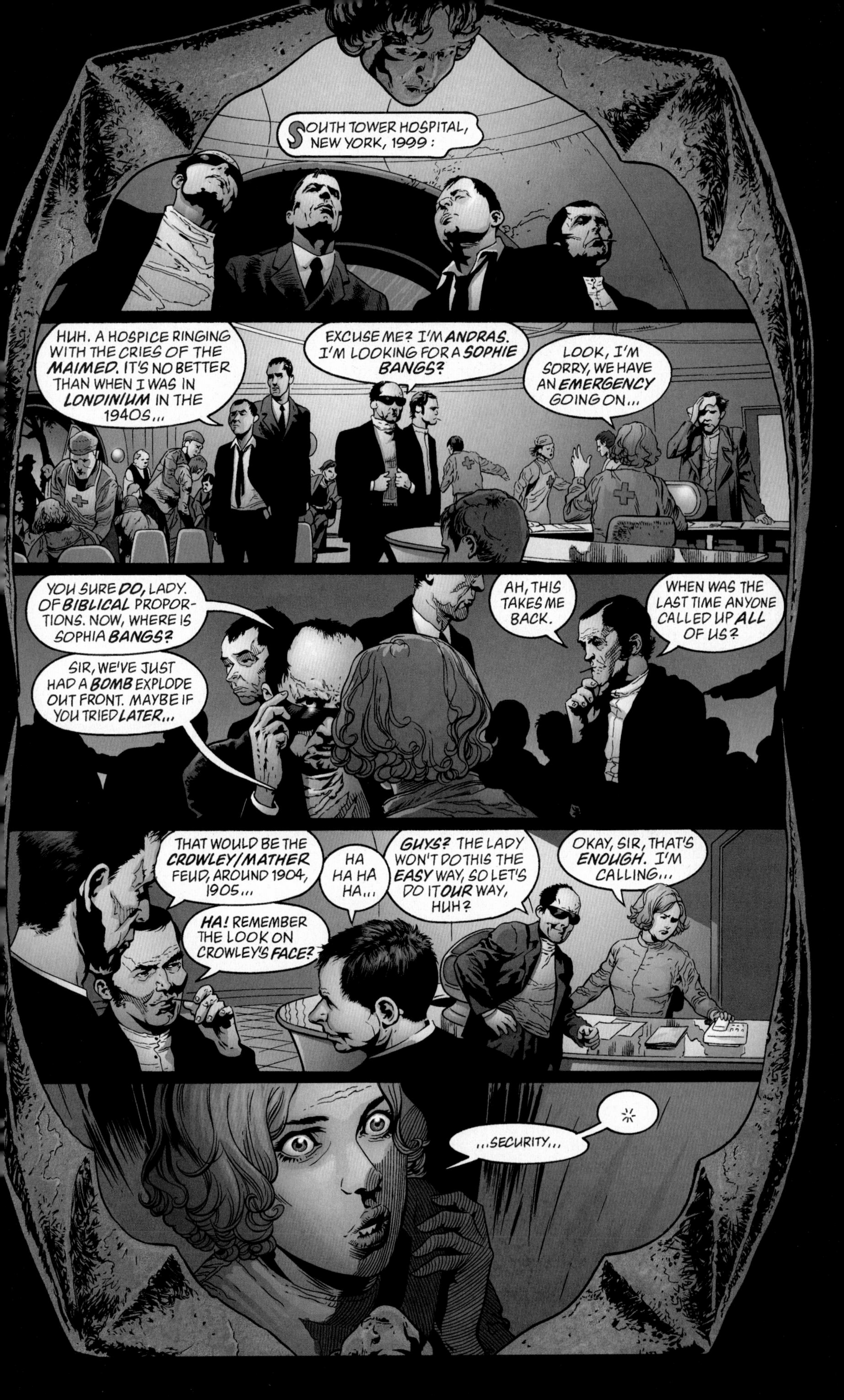
SOUTH TOWER HOSPITAL, NEW YORK, 1999:
HUH. A HOSPICE RINGING WITH THE CRIES OF THE MAIMED. IT'S NO BETTER THAN WHEN I WAS IN LONDINIUM IN THE 1940S...
EXCUSE ME? I'M ANDRAS. I'M LOOKING FOR A SOPHIE BANGS?
LOOK, I'M SORRY, WE HAVE AN EMERGENCY GOING ON...
YOU SURE DO, LADY. OF BIBLICAL PROPORTIONS. NOW, WHERE IS SOPHIA BANGS?
SIR, WE'VE JUST HAD A BOMB EXPLODE OUT FRONT. MAYBE IF YOU TRIED LATER...
AH, THIS TAKES ME BACK.
WHEN WAS THE LAST TIME ANYONE CALLED UP ALL OF US?
THAT WOULD BE THE CROWLEY/MATHER FEUD, AROUND 1904, 1905...
HA! REMEMBER THE LOOK ON CROWLEY'S FACE?
HA HA HA HA...
GUYS? THE LADY WON'T DO THIS THE EASY WAY, SO LET'S DO IT OUR WAY, HUH?
OKAY, SIR, THAT'S ENOUGH. I'M CALLING...
...SECURITY...

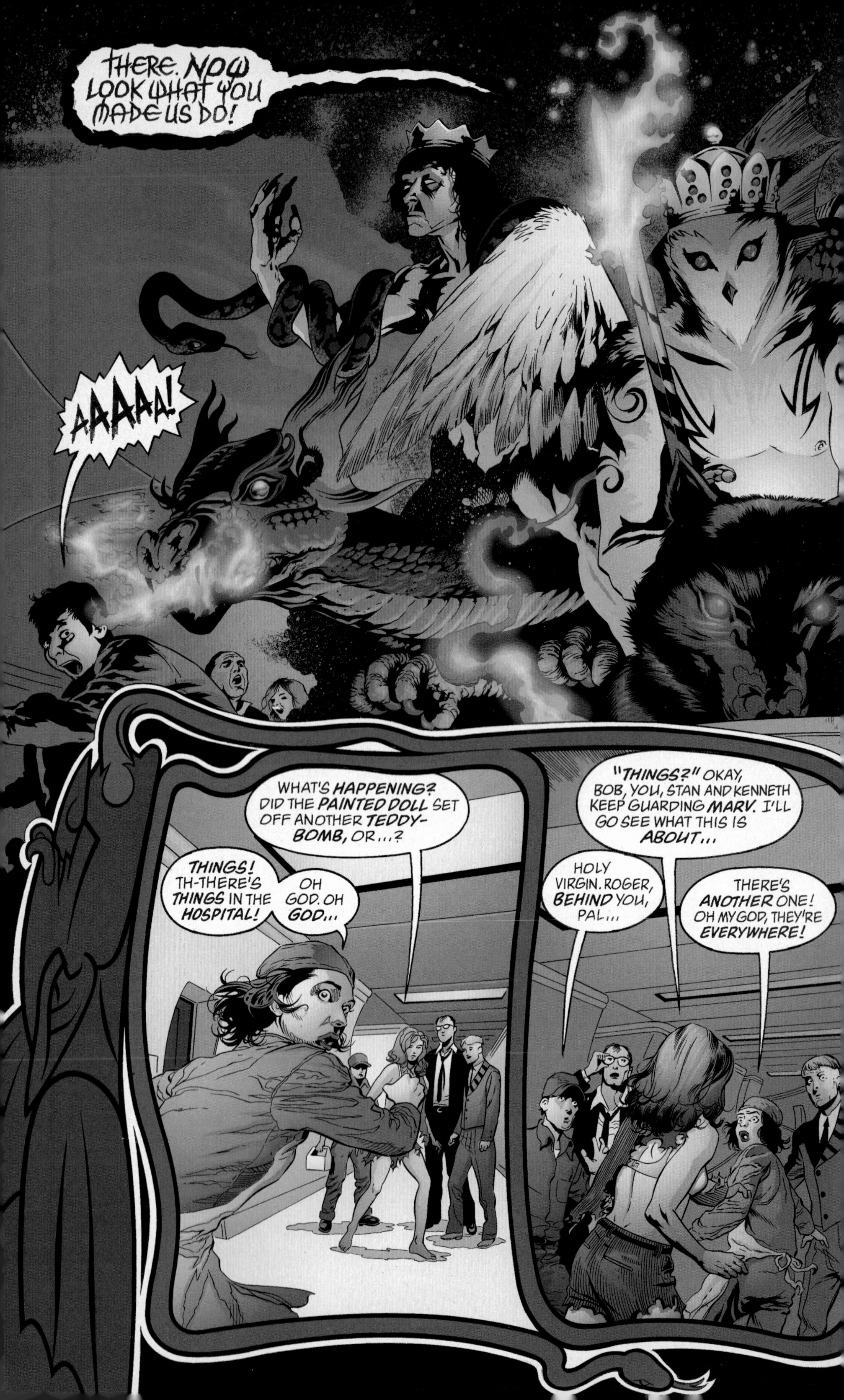
THERE. NOW LOOK WHAT YOU MADE US DO!
AAAAA!
WHAT'S HAPPENING? DID THE PAINTED DOLL SET OFF ANOTHER TEDDY-BOMB, OR...?
THINGS! TH-THERE'S THINGS IN THE HOSPITAL!
OH GOD. OH GOD...
"THINGS?" OKAY, BOB, YOU, STAN AND KENNETH KEEP GUARDING MARV. I'LL GO SEE WHAT THIS IS ABOUT...
HOLY VIRGIN. ROGER, BEHIND YOU, PAL...
THERE'S ANOTHER ONE! OH MY GOD, THEY'RE EVERYWHERE!

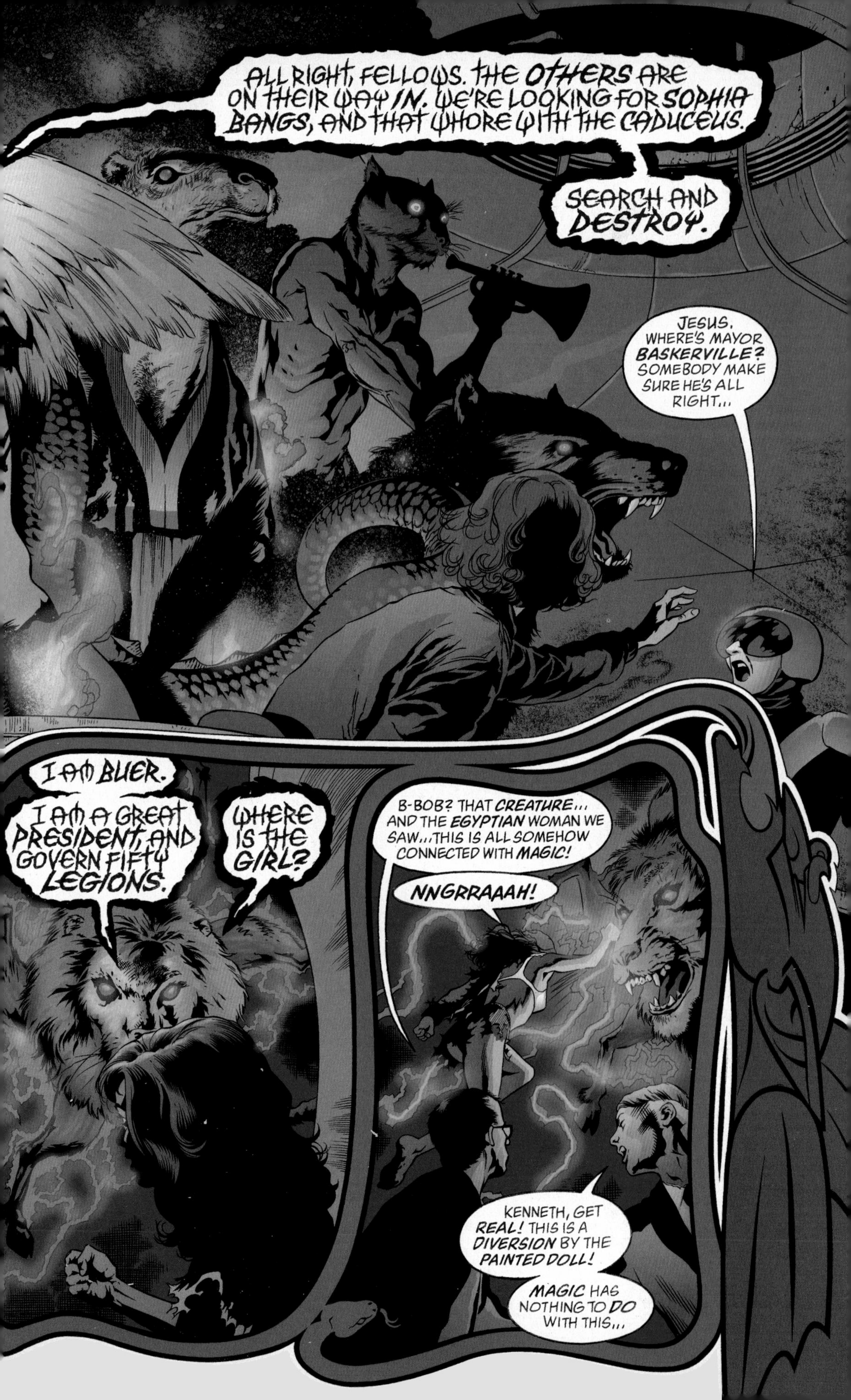
ALL RIGHT, FELLOWS. THE OTHERS ARE ON THEIR WAY IN. WE'RE LOOKING FOR SOPHIA BANGS, AND THAT WHORE WITH THE CADUCEUS.
SEARCH AND DESTROY.
JESUS. WHERE'S MAYOR BASKERVILLE? SOMEBODY MAKE SURE HE'S ALL RIGHT...
I AM BUER.
I AM A GREAT PRESIDENT, AND GOVERN FIFTY LEGIONS.
WHERE IS THE GIRL?
B-BOB? THAT CREATURE... AND THE EGYPTIAN WOMAN WE SAW... THIS IS ALL SOMEHOW CONNECTED WITH MAGIC!
NNGRRAAAH!
KENNETH, GET REAL! THIS IS A DIVERSION BY THE PAINTED DOLL!
MAGIC HAS NOTHING TO DO WITH THIS...

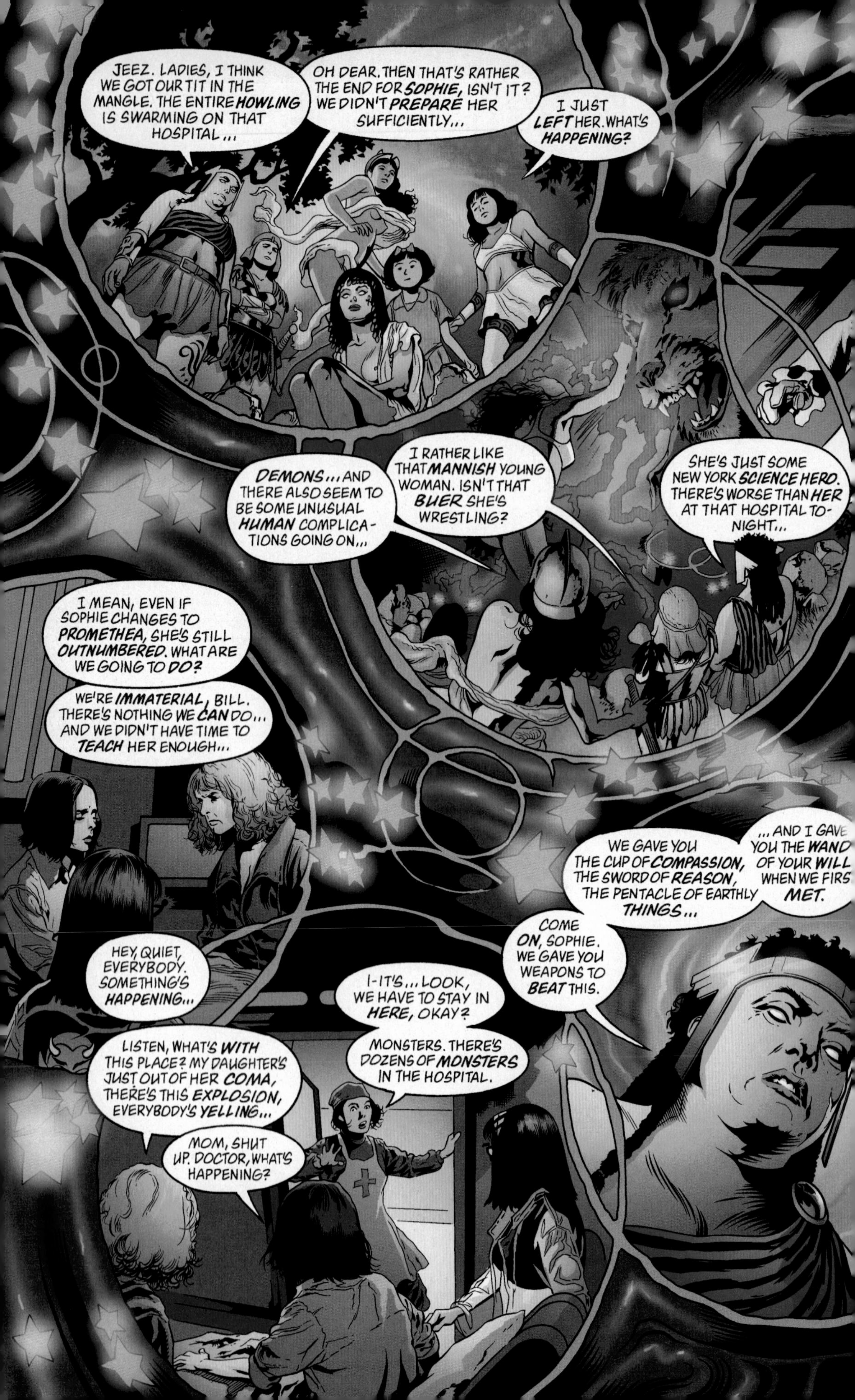
JEEZ. LADIES, I THINK WE GOT OUR TIT IN THE MANGLE. THE ENTIRE HOWLING IS SWARMING ON THAT HOSPITAL...
OH DEAR. THEN THAT'S RATHER THE END FOR SOPHIE, ISN'T IT? WE DIDN'T PREPARE HER SUFFICIENTLY...
I JUST LEFT HER. WHAT'S HAPPENING?
DEMONS... AND THERE ALSO SEEM TO BE SOME UNUSUAL HUMAN COMPLICATIONS GOING ON...
I RATHER LIKE THAT MANNISH YOUNG WOMAN. ISN'T THAT BUER SHE'S WRESTLING?
SHE'S JUST SOME NEW YORK SCIENCE HERO. THERE'S WORSE THAN HER AT THAT HOSPITAL TO-NIGHT...
I MEAN, EVEN IF SOPHIE CHANGES TO PROMETHEA, SHE'S STILL OUTNUMBERED. WHAT ARE WE GOING TO DO?
WE'RE IMMATERIAL, BILL. THERE'S NOTHING WE CAN DO... AND WE DIDN'T HAVE TIME TO TEACH HER ENOUGH...
WE GAVE YOU THE CUP OF COMPASSION, THE SWORD OF REASON, THE PENTACLE OF EARTHLY THINGS...
...AND I GAVE YOU THE WAND OF YOUR WILL WHEN WE FIRS MET.
COME ON, SOPHIE. WE GAVE YOU WEAPONS TO BEAT THIS.
HEY, QUIET, EVERYBODY. SOMETHING'S HAPPENING...
I-IT'S... LOOK, WE HAVE TO STAY IN HERE, OKAY?
MONSTERS. THERE'S DOZENS OF MONSTERS IN THE HOSPITAL.
LISTEN, WHAT'S WITH THIS PLACE? MY DAUGHTER'S JUST OUT OF HER COMA, THERE'S THIS EXPLOSION, EVERYBODY'S YELLING...
MOM, SHUT UP. DOCTOR, WHAT'S HAPPENING?

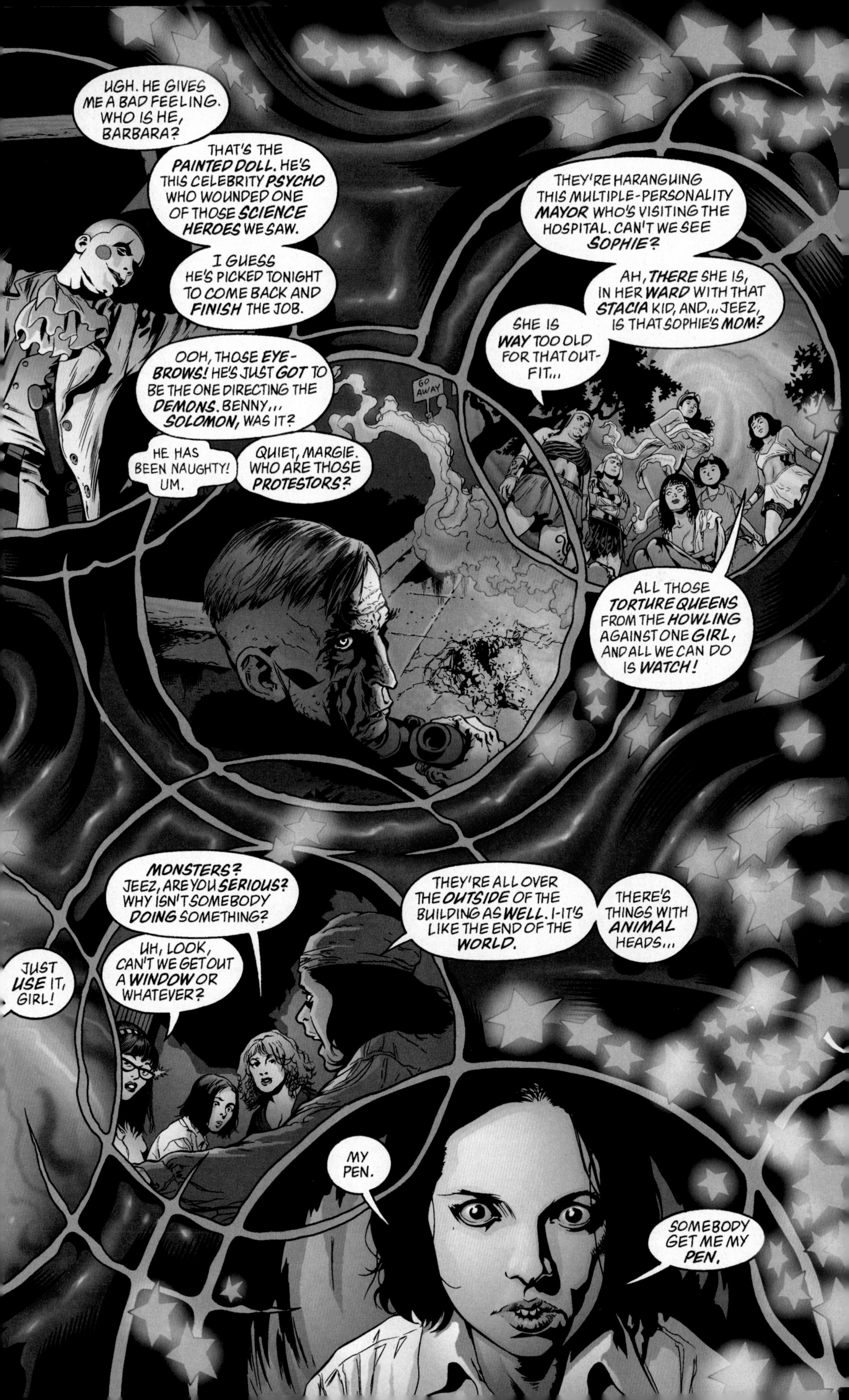
UGH. HE GIVES ME A BAD FEELING. WHO IS HE, BARBARA?
THAT'S THE PAINTED DOLL. HE'S THIS CELEBRITY PSYCHO WHO WOUNDED ONE OF THOSE SCIENCE HEROES WE SAW.
I GUESS HE'S PICKED TONIGHT TO COME BACK AND FINISH THE JOB.
THEY'RE HARANGUING THIS MULTIPLE-PERSONALITY MAYOR WHO'S VISITING THE HOSPITAL. CAN'T WE SEE SOPHIE?
AH, THERE SHE IS, IN HER WARD WITH THAT STACIA KID, AND... JEEZ, IS THAT SOPHIE'S MOM?
SHE IS WAY TOO OLD FOR THAT OUT-FIT...
OOH, THOSE EYE-BROWS! HE'S JUST GOT TO BE THE ONE DIRECTING THE DEMONS. BENNY... SOLOMON, WAS IT?
HE HAS BEEN NAUGHTY! UM.
QUIET, MARGIE. WHO ARE THOSE PROTESTORS?
GO AWAY
ALL THOSE TORTURE QUEENS FROM THE HOWLING AGAINST ONE GIRL, AND ALL WE CAN DO IS WATCH!
MONSTERS? JEEZ, ARE YOU SERIOUS? WHY ISN'T SOMEBODY DOING SOMETHING?
THEY'RE ALL OVER THE OUTSIDE OF THE BUILDING AS WELL. I-IT'S LIKE THE END OF THE WORLD.
THERE'S THINGS WITH ANIMAL HEADS...
JUST USE IT, GIRL!
UH, LOOK, CAN'T WE GET OUT A WINDOW OR WHATEVER?
MY PEN.
SOMEBODY GET ME MY PEN.

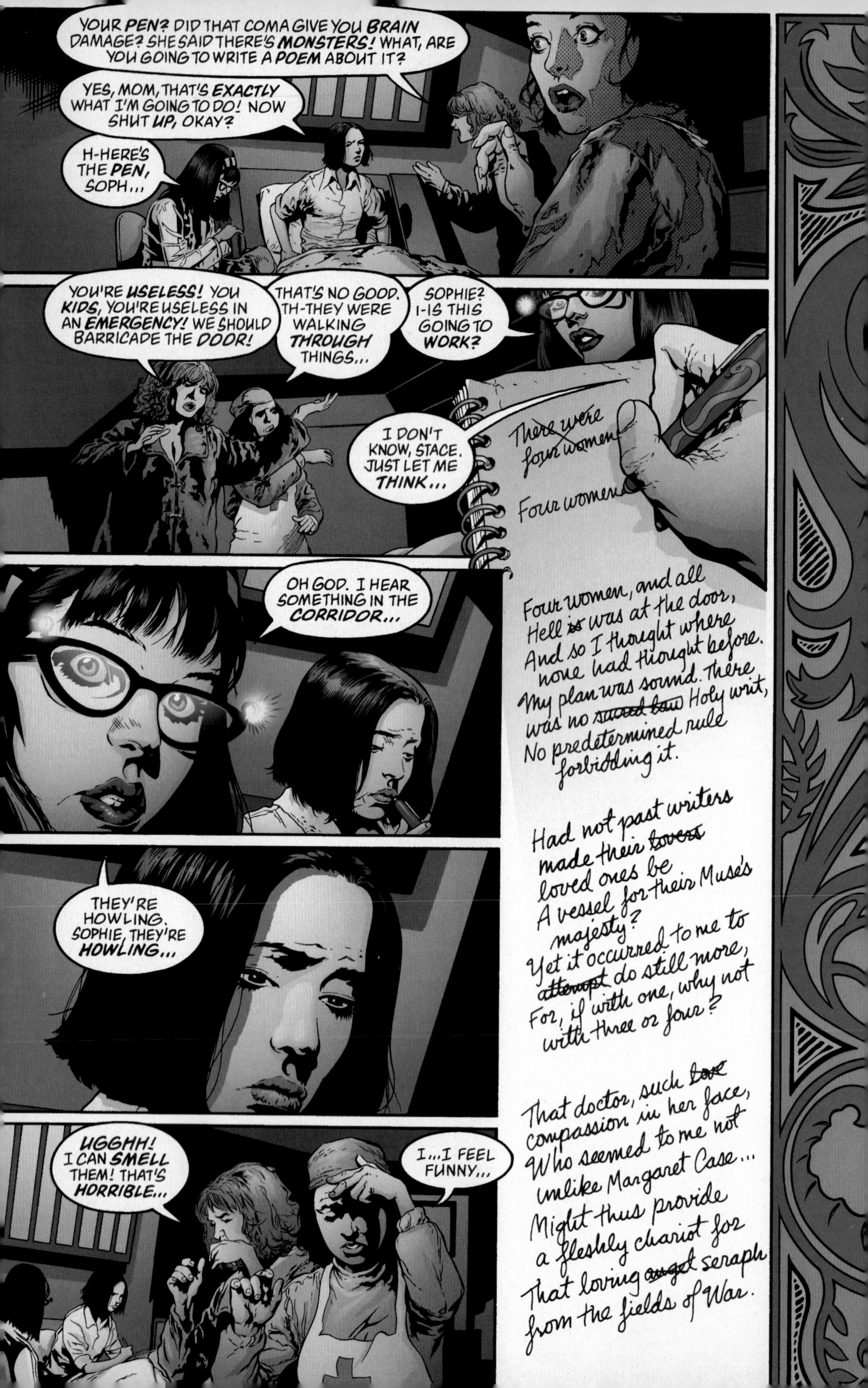
YOUR PEN? DID THAT COMA GIVE YOU BRAIN DAMAGE? SHE SAID THERE'S MONSTERS! WHAT, ARE YOU GOING TO WRITE A POEM ABOUT IT?
YES, MOM, THAT'S EXACTLY WHAT I'M GOING TO DO! NOW SHUT UP, OKAY?
H-HERE'S THE PEN, SOPH...
YOU'RE USELESS! YOU KIDS, YOU'RE USELESS IN AN EMERGENCY! WE SHOULD BARRICADE THE DOOR!
THAT'S NO GOOD. TH-THEY WERE WALKING THROUGH THINGS...
SOPHIE? I-IS THIS GOING TO WORK?
I DON'T KNOW, STACE. JUST LET ME THINK...
~~There were four women~~
Four women
OH GOD. I HEAR SOMETHING IN THE CORRIDOR...
Four women, and all
Hell ~~so~~ was at the door,
And so I thought where
none had thought before.
My plan was sound. There
was no ~~sacred law~~ Holy writ,
No predetermined rule
forbidding it.
THEY'RE HOWLING. SOPHIE, THEY'RE HOWLING...
Had not past writers
made their ~~lovers~~
loved ones be
A vessel for their Muse's
majesty?
Yet it occurred to me to
~~attempt~~ do still more,
For, if with one, why not
with three or four?
UGGHH! I CAN SMELL THEM! THAT'S HORRIBLE...
I...I FEEL FUNNY...
That doctor, such ~~love~~
compassion in her face,
Who seemed to me not
unlike Margaret Case...
Might thus provide
a fleshly chariot for
That loving ~~angel~~ seraph
from the fields of War.

Or might my Mother's
life contain less ~~strife~~
harm
If she possessed Bill
Woolcott's female charm?

Would my companion
Stacia's caustic wit
Together with Grace
Brannagh's make a fit?

That fortunate ~~event~~
eventuality
Would leave nobody
untransformed save me.

~~As for~~ Myself, I'll conjure
with a single line
The fiction of a ~~woman~~
mortal made divine.

Eyes dark with kohl,
her breath like ocean
breeze,
There in her hand the
wand of swift Hermes.

Winged god of ~~writers~~
scribes, who writes
the fates of men
With the Caduceus as
his wand, his pen.

By his art, let Her
blazing form descend
On me, alike with
Mother, stranger,
friend.

And in each soul
let burn a single
star

Whose light is all
Mankind's:

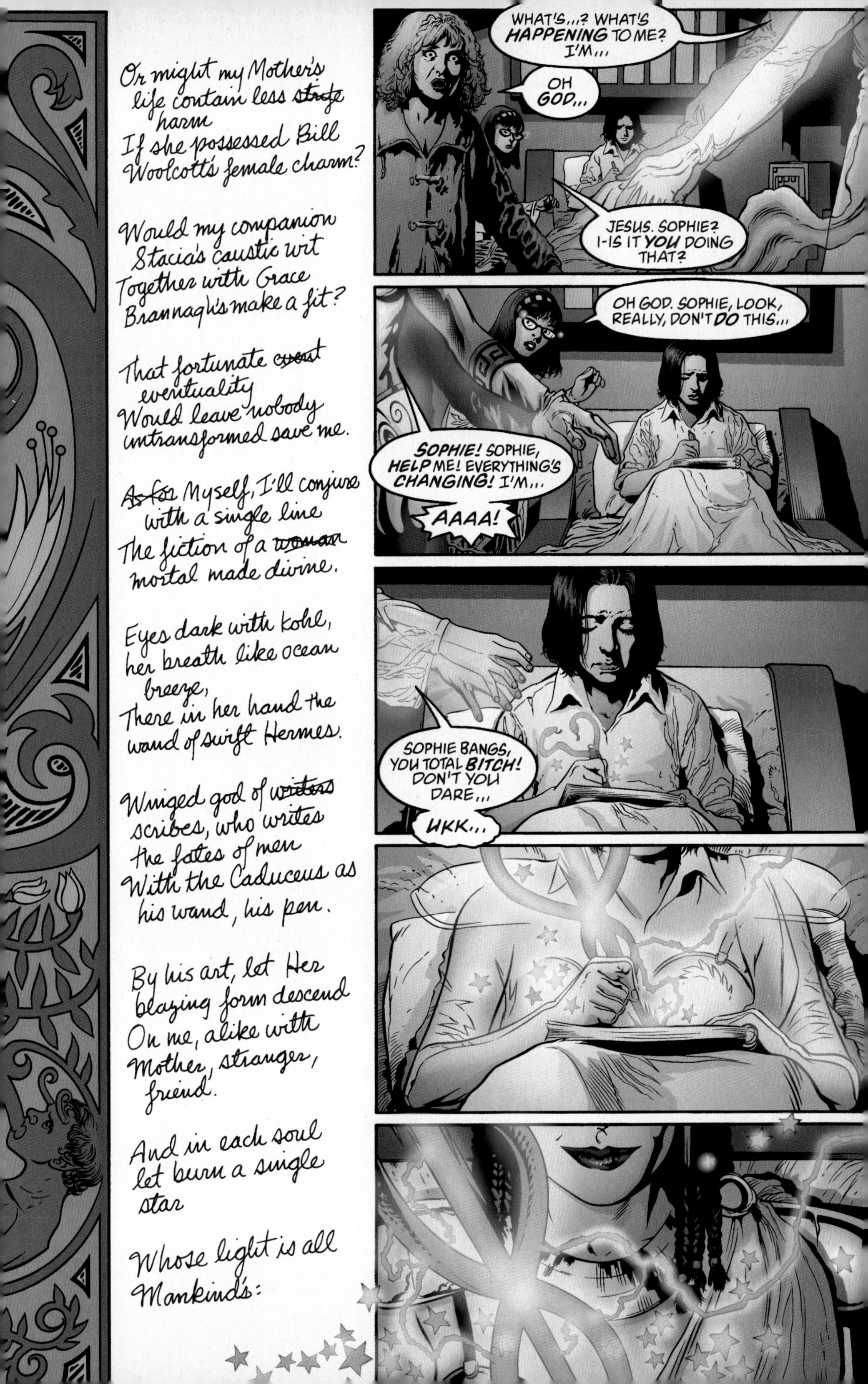
WHAT'S...? WHAT'S HAPPENING TO ME? I'M...
OH GOD...
JESUS. SOPHIE? I-IS IT YOU DOING THAT?
OH GOD. SOPHIE, LOOK, REALLY, DON'T DO THIS...
SOPHIE! SOPHIE, HELP ME! EVERYTHING'S CHANGING! I'M...
AAAA!
SOPHIE BANGS, YOU TOTAL BITCH! DON'T YOU DARE...
UKK...

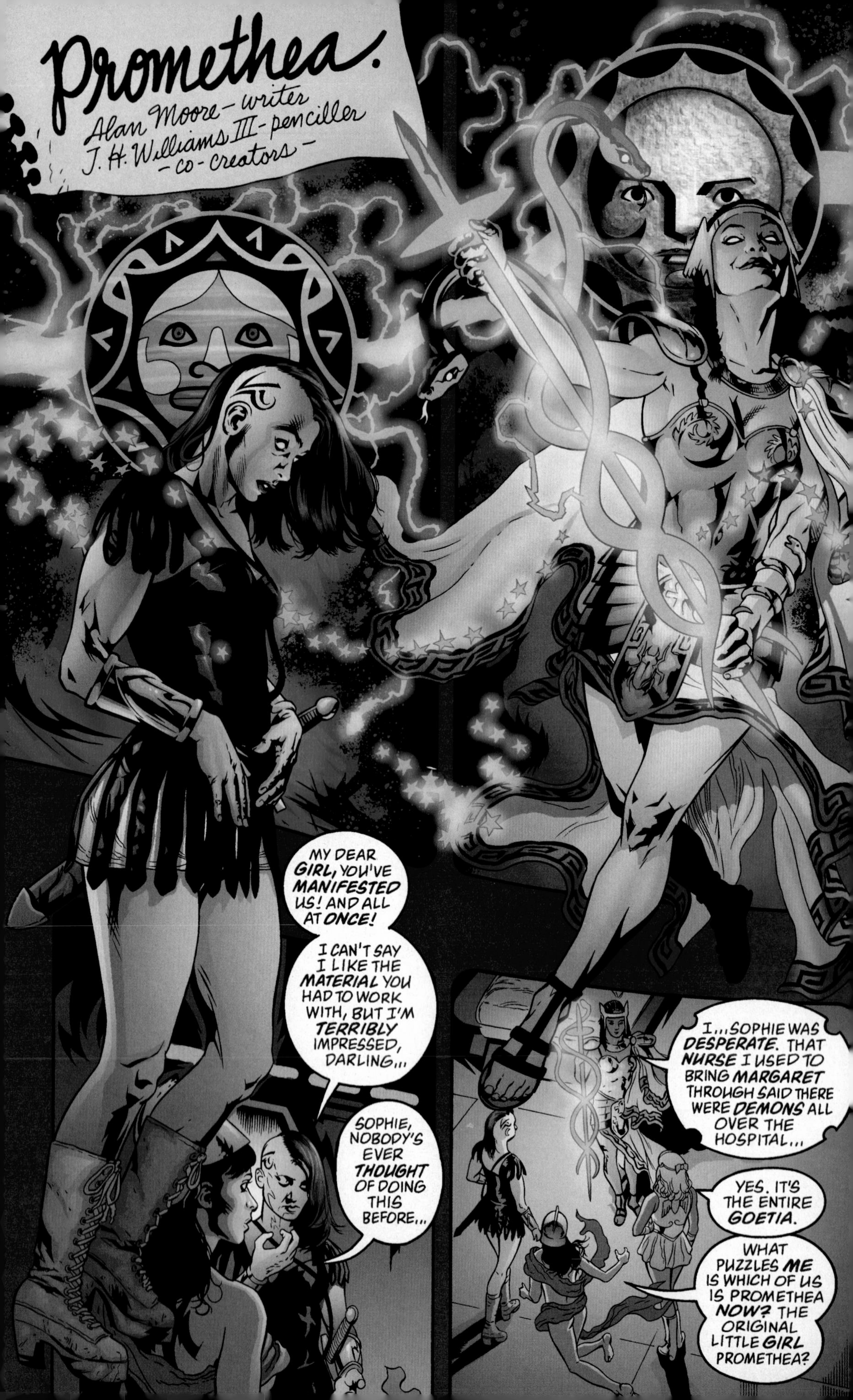
Promethea.
Alan Moore-writer
J. H. Williams III-penciller
-co-creators-
MY DEAR GIRL, YOU'VE MANIFESTED US! AND ALL AT ONCE!
I CAN'T SAY I LIKE THE MATERIAL YOU HAD TO WORK WITH, BUT I'M TERRIBLY IMPRESSED, DARLING...
SOPHIE, NOBODY'S EVER THOUGHT OF DOING THIS BEFORE...
I... SOPHIE WAS DESPERATE. THAT NURSE I USED TO BRING MARGARET THROUGH SAID THERE WERE DEMONS ALL OVER THE HOSPITAL...
YES. IT'S THE ENTIRE GOETIA.
WHAT PUZZLES ME IS WHICH OF US IS PROMETHEA NOW? THE ORIGINAL LITTLE GIRL PROMETHEA?

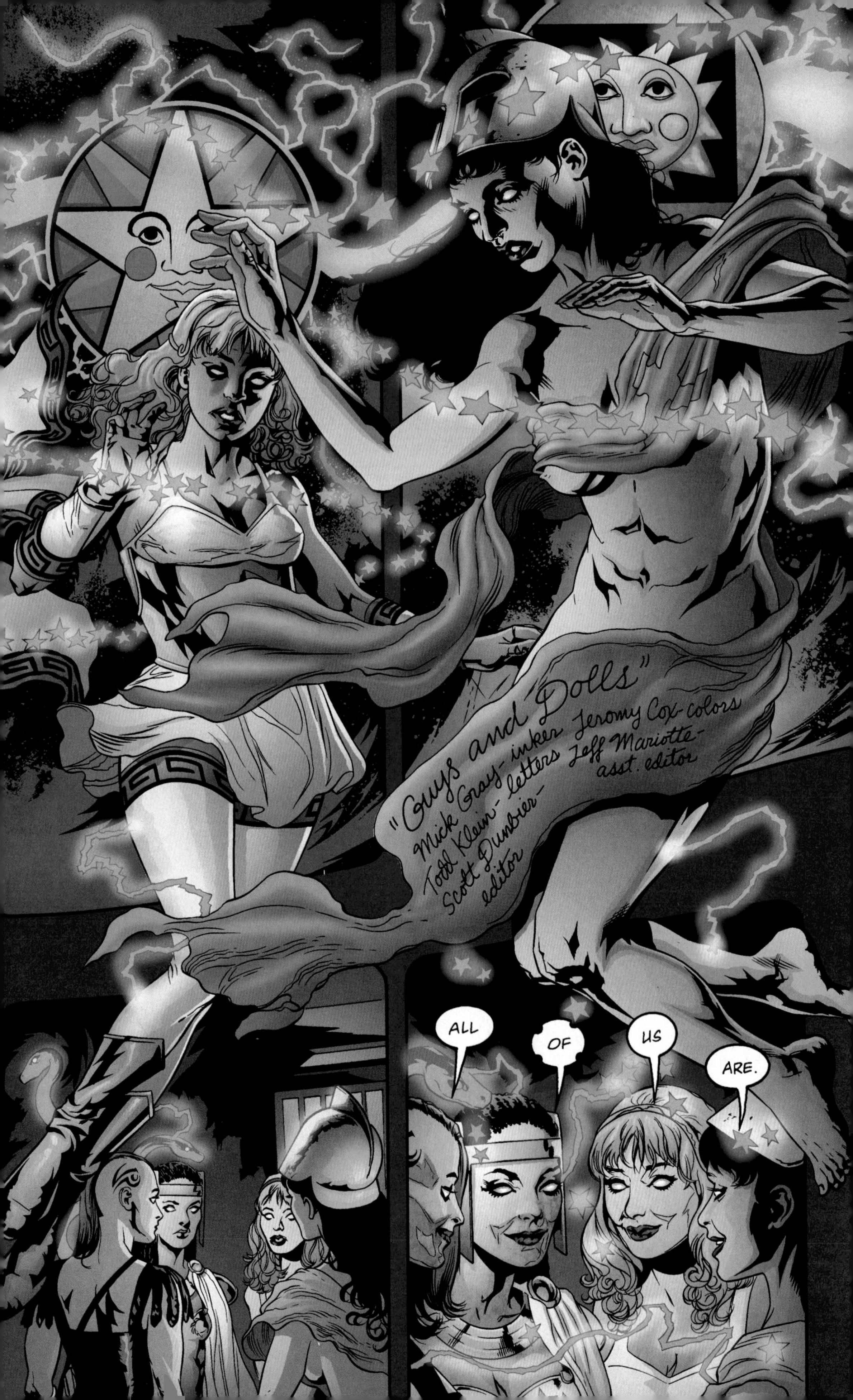
"Guys and Dolls"
Mick Gray- inker Jeromy Cox-colors
Todd Klein- letters Jeff Mariotte-
asst. editor
Scott Dunbier-
editor
ALL
OF
US
ARE.

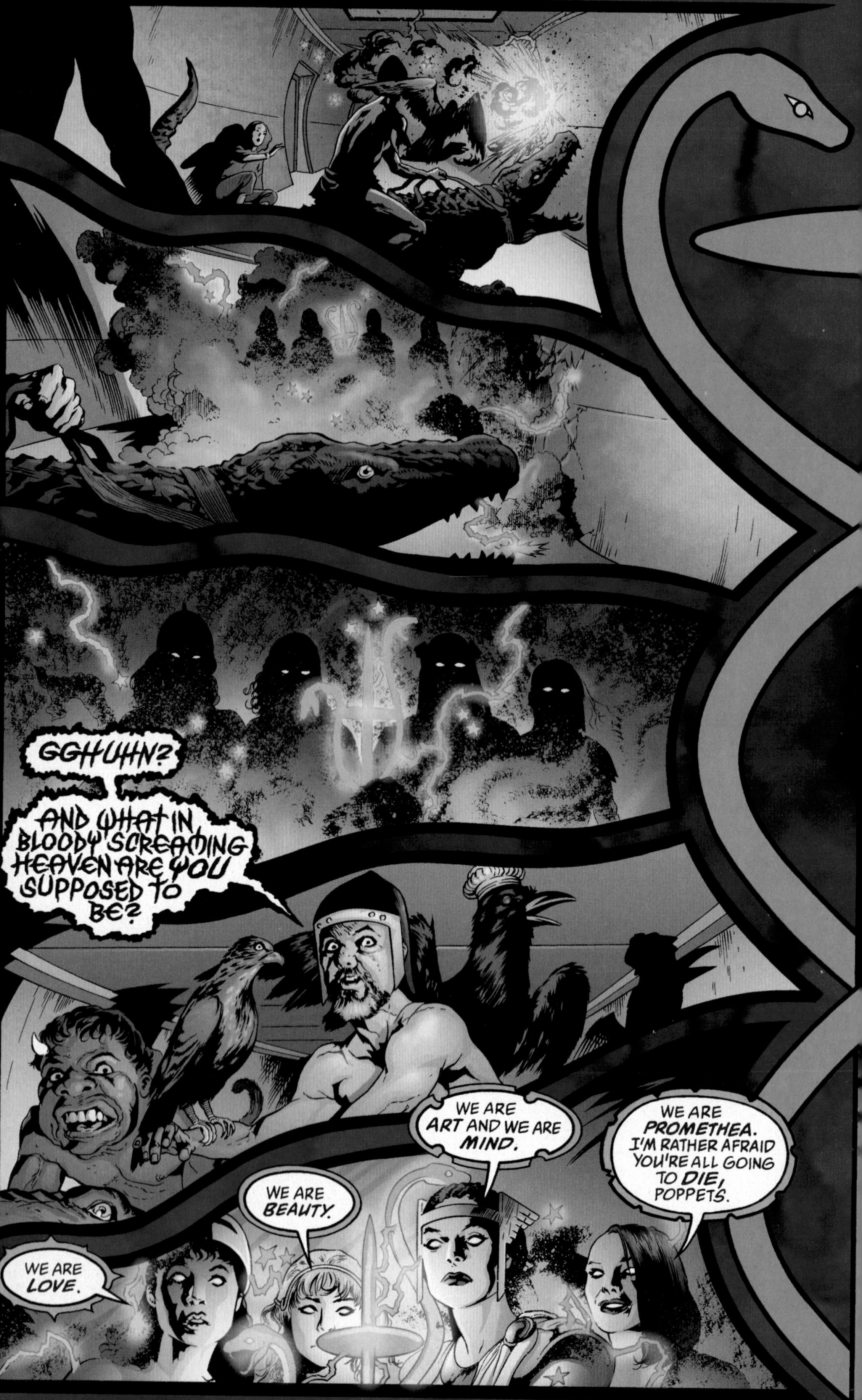
GGHUHN?
AND WHAT IN BLOODY SCREAMING HEAVEN ARE YOU SUPPOSED TO BE?
WE ARE ART AND WE ARE MIND.
WE ARE PROMETHEA. I'M RATHER AFRAID YOU'RE ALL GOING TO DIE, POPPETS.
WE ARE BEAUTY.
WE ARE LOVE.

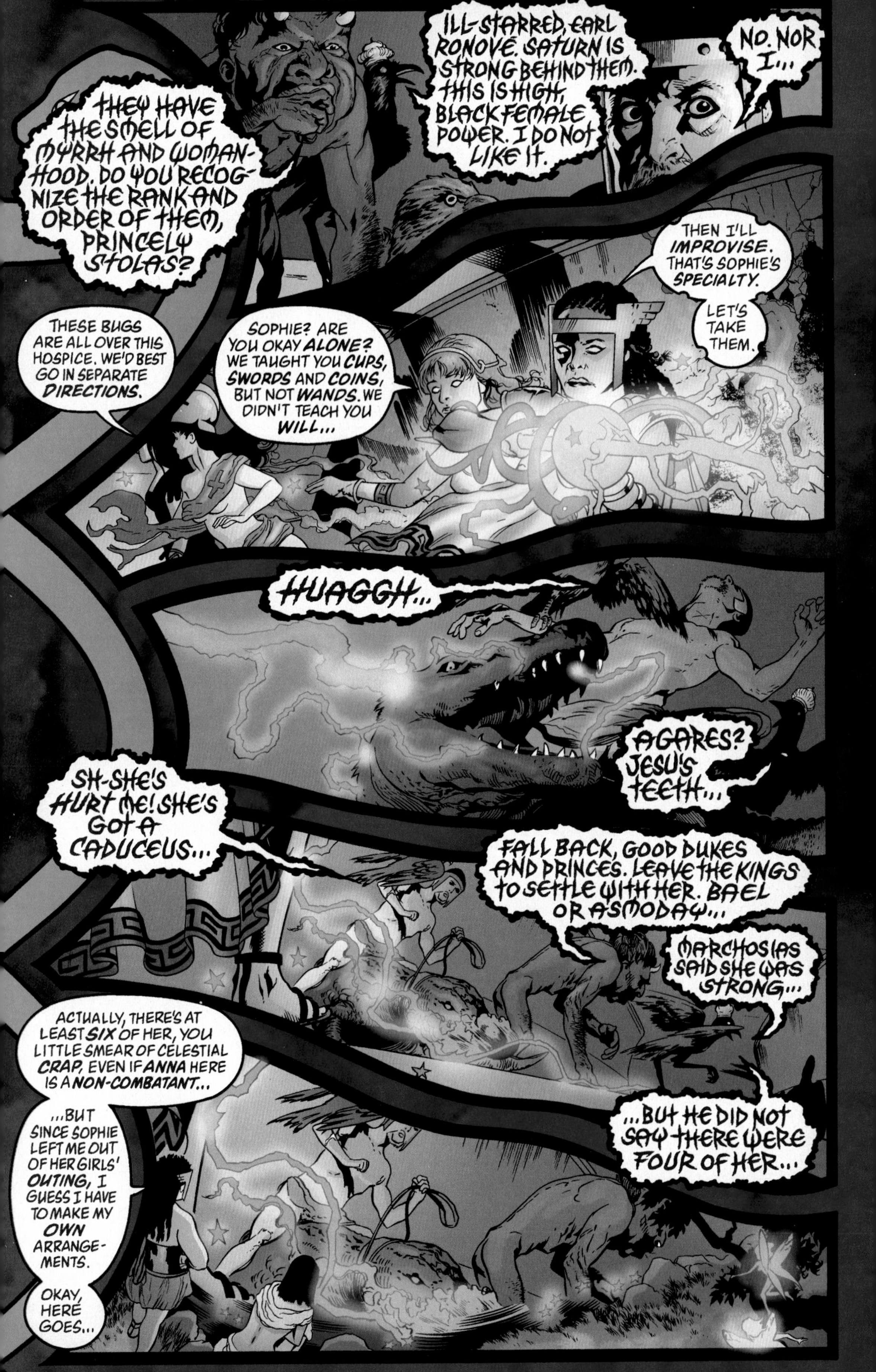
THEY HAVE THE SMELL OF MYRRH AND WOMANHOOD. DO YOU RECOGNIZE THE RANK AND ORDER OF THEM, PRINCELY STOLAS?
ILL-STARRED, EARL RONOVE. SATURN IS STRONG BEHIND THEM. THIS IS HIGH, BLACK FEMALE POWER. I DO NOT LIKE IT.
NO. NOR I...
THESE BUGS ARE ALL OVER THIS HOSPICE. WE'D BEST GO IN SEPARATE DIRECTIONS.
SOPHIE? ARE YOU OKAY ALONE? WE TAUGHT YOU CUPS, SWORDS AND COINS, BUT NOT WANDS. WE DIDN'T TEACH YOU WILL...
THEN I'LL IMPROVISE. THAT'S SOPHIE'S SPECIALTY.
LET'S TAKE THEM.
HUAGGH...
AGARES? JESU'S TEETH...
SH-SHE'S HURT ME! SHE'S GOT A CADUCEUS...
FALL BACK, GOOD DUKES AND PRINCES. LEAVE THE KINGS TO SETTLE WITH HER. BAEL OR ASMODAY...
MARCHOSIAS SAID SHE WAS STRONG...
...BUT HE DID NOT SAY THERE WERE FOUR OF HER...
ACTUALLY, THERE'S AT LEAST SIX OF HER, YOU LITTLE SMEAR OF CELESTIAL CRAP, EVEN IF ANNA HERE IS A NON-COMBATANT...
...BUT SINCE SOPHIE LEFT ME OUT OF HER GIRLS' OUTING, I GUESS I HAVE TO MAKE MY OWN ARRANGEMENTS.
OKAY, HERE GOES...

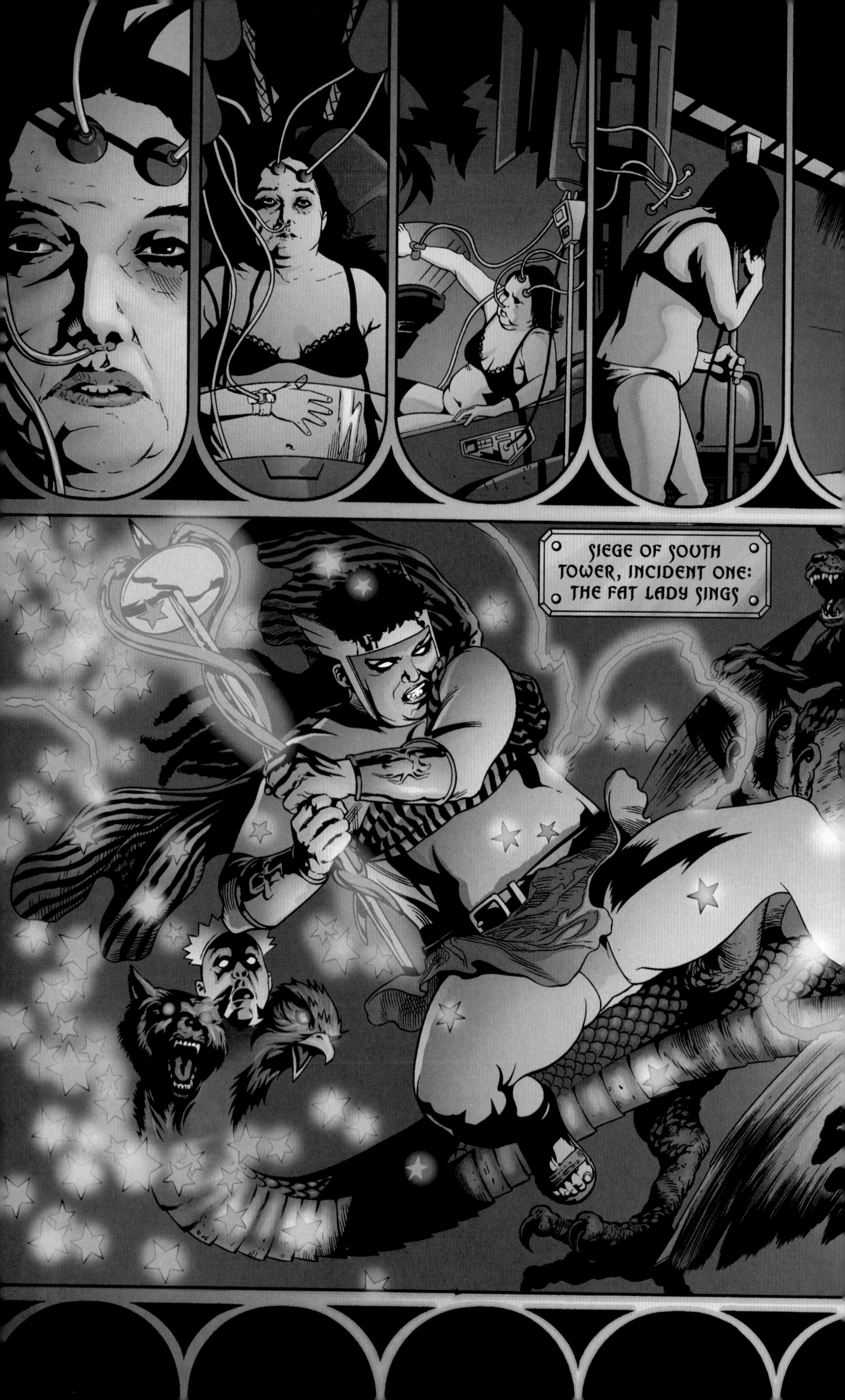
SIEGE OF SOUTH TOWER, INCIDENT ONE: THE FAT LADY SINGS

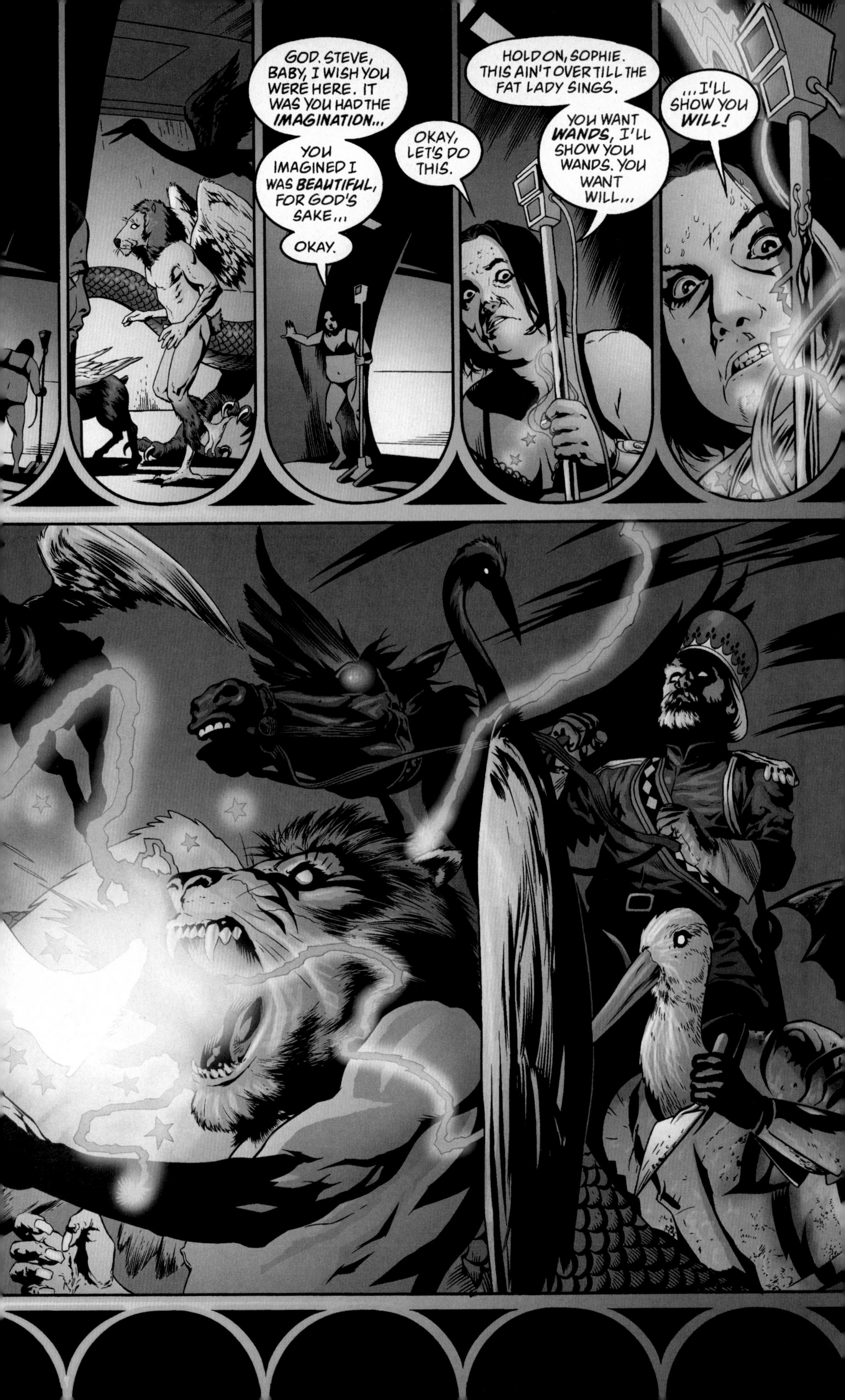
GOD. STEVE, BABY, I WISH YOU WERE HERE. IT WAS YOU HAD THE IMAGINATION...
YOU IMAGINED I WAS BEAUTIFUL, FOR GOD'S SAKE...
OKAY.
OKAY, LET'S DO THIS.
HOLD ON, SOPHIE. THIS AIN'T OVER TILL THE FAT LADY SINGS.
YOU WANT WANDS, I'LL SHOW YOU WANDS. YOU WANT WILL...
...I'LL SHOW YOU WILL!

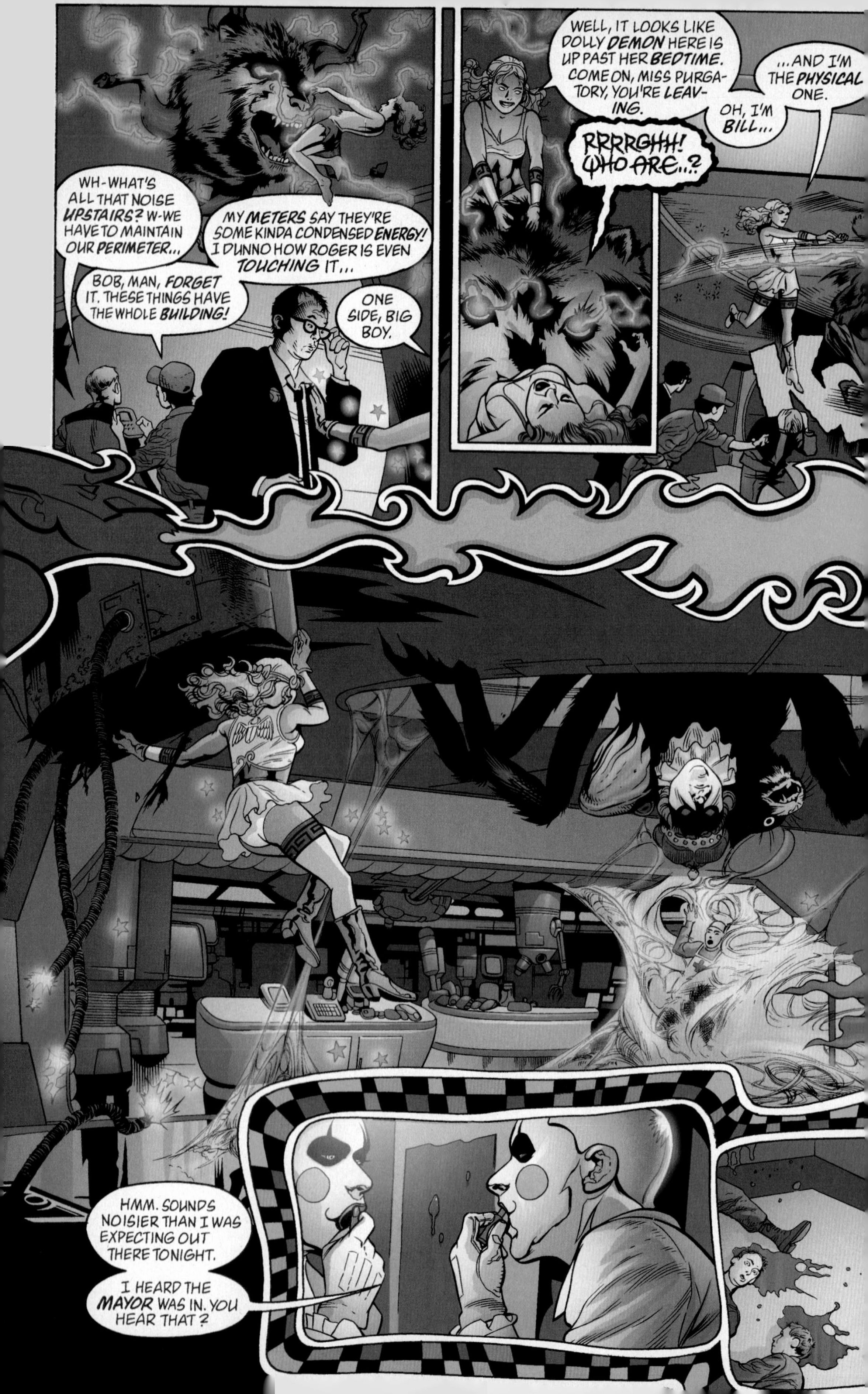
WH-WHAT'S ALL THAT NOISE UPSTAIRS? W-WE HAVE TO MAINTAIN OUR PERIMETER...
MY METERS SAY THEY'RE SOME KINDA CONDENSED ENERGY! I DUNNO HOW ROGER IS EVEN TOUCHING IT...
BOB, MAN, FORGET IT. THESE THINGS HAVE THE WHOLE BUILDING!
ONE SIDE, BIG BOY.
WELL, IT LOOKS LIKE DOLLY DEMON HERE IS UP PAST HER BEDTIME. COME ON, MISS PURGATORY, YOU'RE LEAVING.
RRRRGHH! WHO ARE...?
OH, I'M BILL...
...AND I'M THE PHYSICAL ONE.
HMM. SOUNDS NOISIER THAN I WAS EXPECTING OUT THERE TONIGHT.
I HEARD THE MAYOR WAS IN. YOU HEAR THAT?

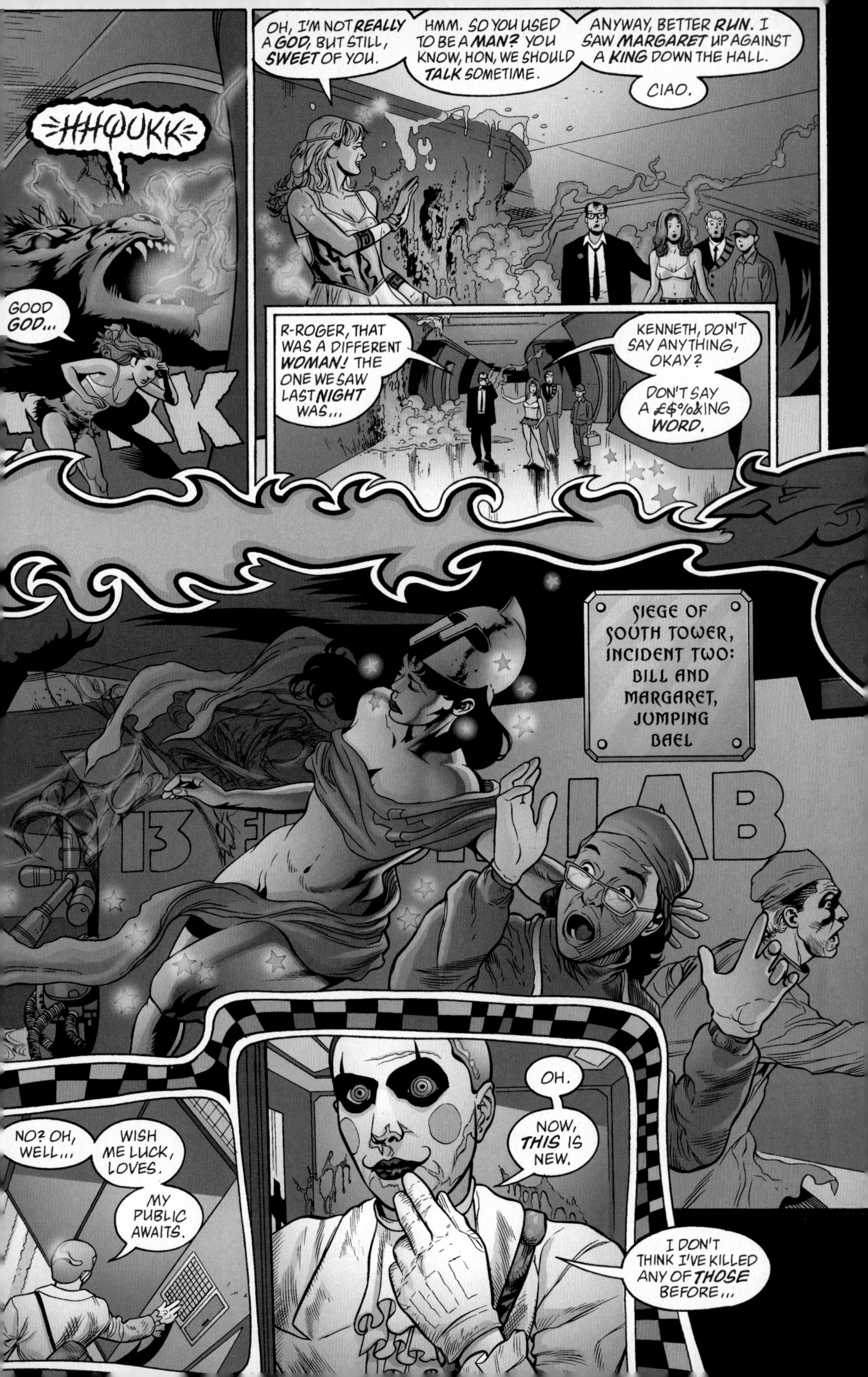
HHΦUKK
GOOD GOD...
OH, I'M NOT REALLY A GOD, BUT STILL, SWEET OF YOU.
HMM. SO YOU USED TO BE A MAN? YOU KNOW, HON, WE SHOULD TALK SOMETIME.
ANYWAY, BETTER RUN. I SAW MARGARET UP AGAINST A KING DOWN THE HALL.
CIAO.
R-ROGER, THAT WAS A DIFFERENT WOMAN! THE ONE WE SAW LAST NIGHT WAS...
KENNETH, DON'T SAY ANYTHING, OKAY?
DON'T SAY A £$%&ING WORD.
SIEGE OF SOUTH TOWER, INCIDENT TWO: BILL AND MARGARET, JUMPING BAEL
13
LAB
NO? OH, WELL...
WISH ME LUCK, LOVES.
MY PUBLIC AWAITS.
OH.
NOW, THIS IS NEW.
I DON'T THINK I'VE KILLED ANY OF THOSE BEFORE...

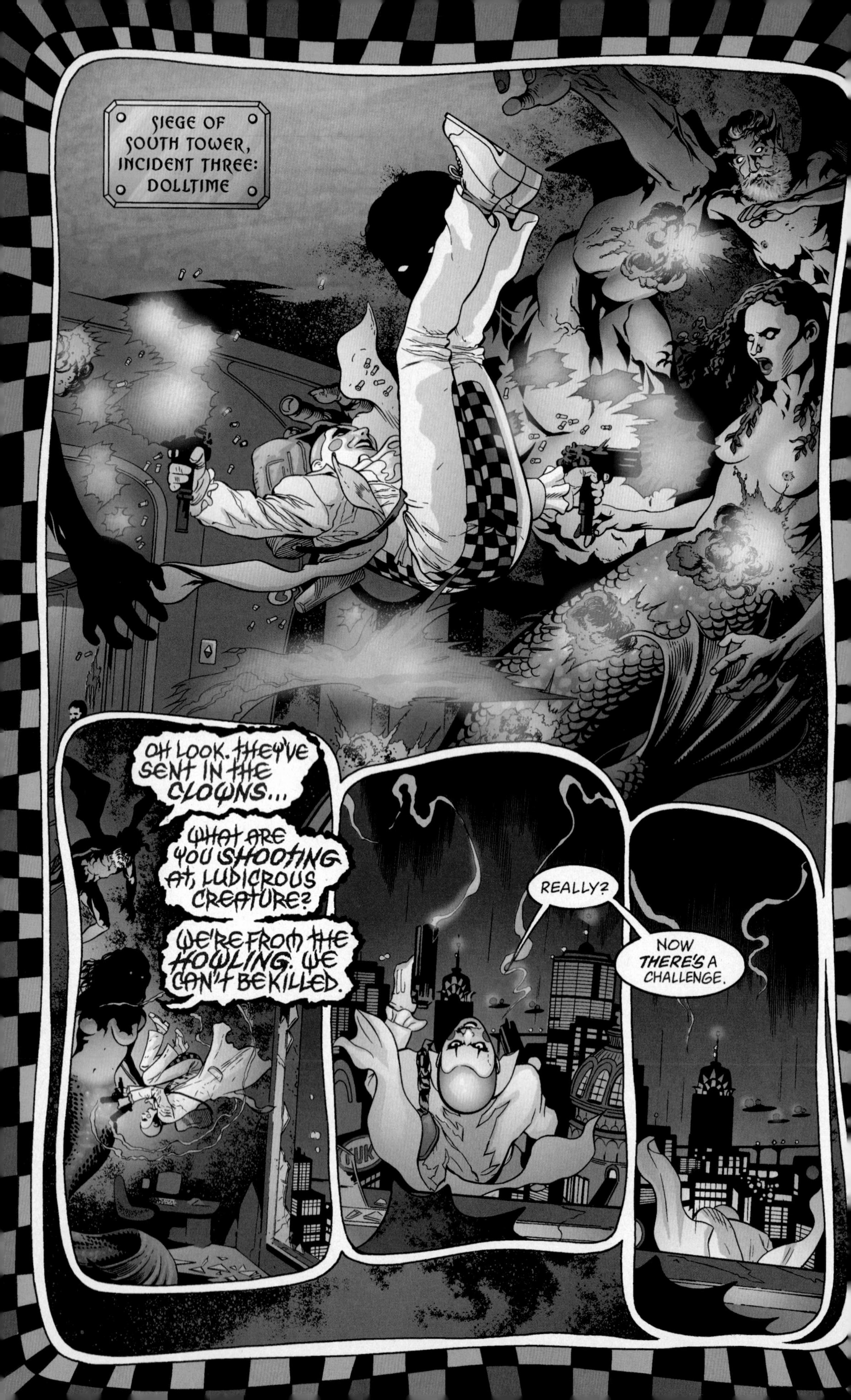
SIEGE OF SOUTH TOWER, INCIDENT THREE: DOLLTIME
OH LOOK. THEY'VE SENT IN THE CLOWNS...
WHAT ARE YOU SHOOTING AT, LUDICROUS CREATURE?
WE'RE FROM THE HOWLING. WE CAN'T BE KILLED.
REALLY?
NOW THERE'S A CHALLENGE.

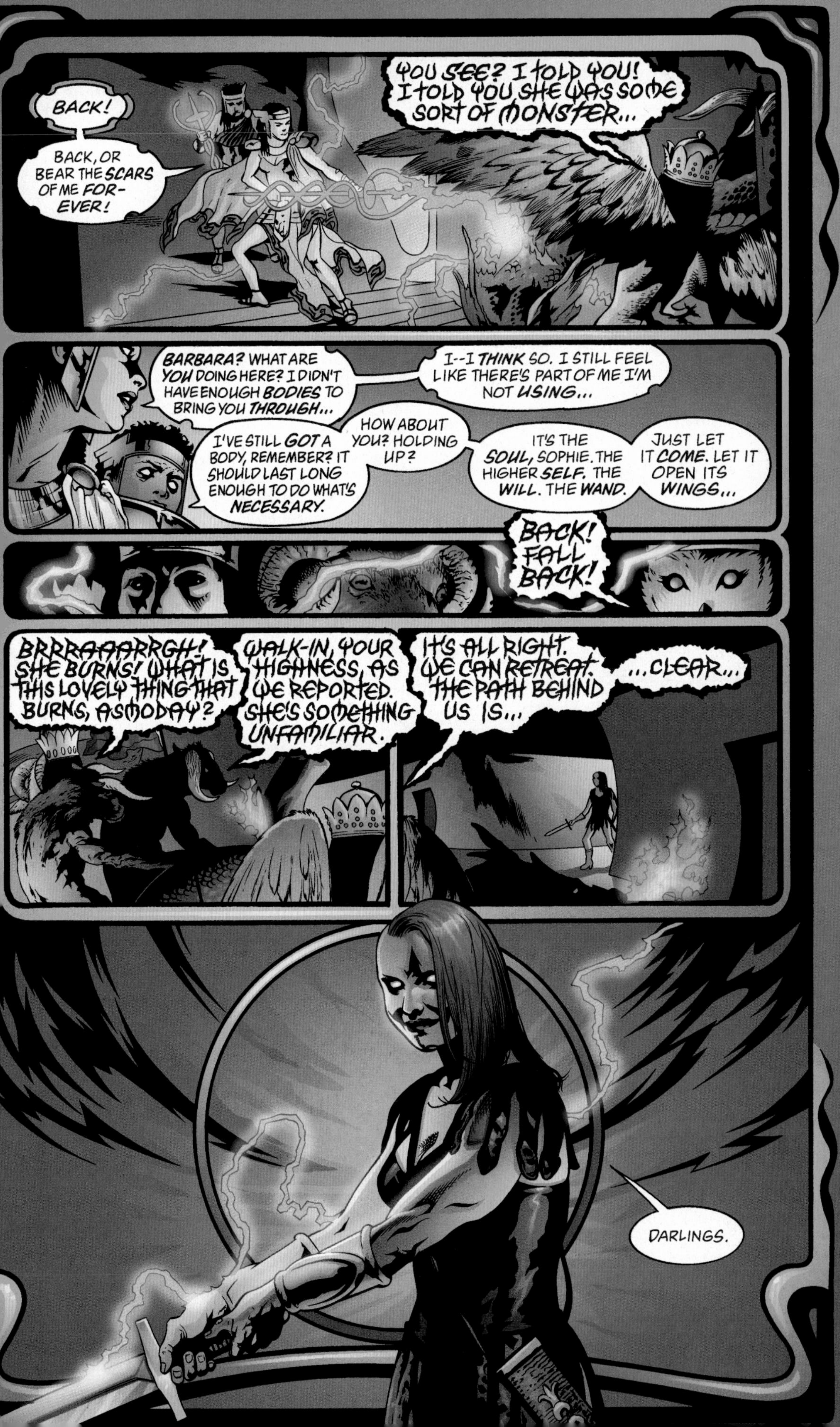
BACK!
BACK, OR BEAR THE SCARS OF ME FOR-EVER!
YOU SEE? I TOLD YOU! I TOLD YOU SHE WAS SOME SORT OF MONSTER...
BARBARA? WHAT ARE YOU DOING HERE? I DIDN'T HAVE ENOUGH BODIES TO BRING YOU THROUGH...
I'VE STILL GOT A BODY, REMEMBER? IT SHOULD LAST LONG ENOUGH TO DO WHAT'S NECESSARY.
HOW ABOUT YOU? HOLDING UP?
I--I THINK SO. I STILL FEEL LIKE THERE'S PART OF ME I'M NOT USING...
IT'S THE SOUL, SOPHIE. THE HIGHER SELF. THE WILL. THE WAND.
JUST LET IT COME. LET IT OPEN ITS WINGS...
BACK! FALL BACK!
BRRRAAAARRGH! SHE BURNS! WHAT IS THIS LOVELY THING THAT BURNS, ASMODAY?
WALK-IN, YOUR HIGHNESS, AS WE REPORTED. SHE'S SOMETHING UNFAMILIAR.
IT'S ALL RIGHT. WE CAN RETREAT. THE PATH BEHIND US IS...
...CLEAR...
DARLINGS.

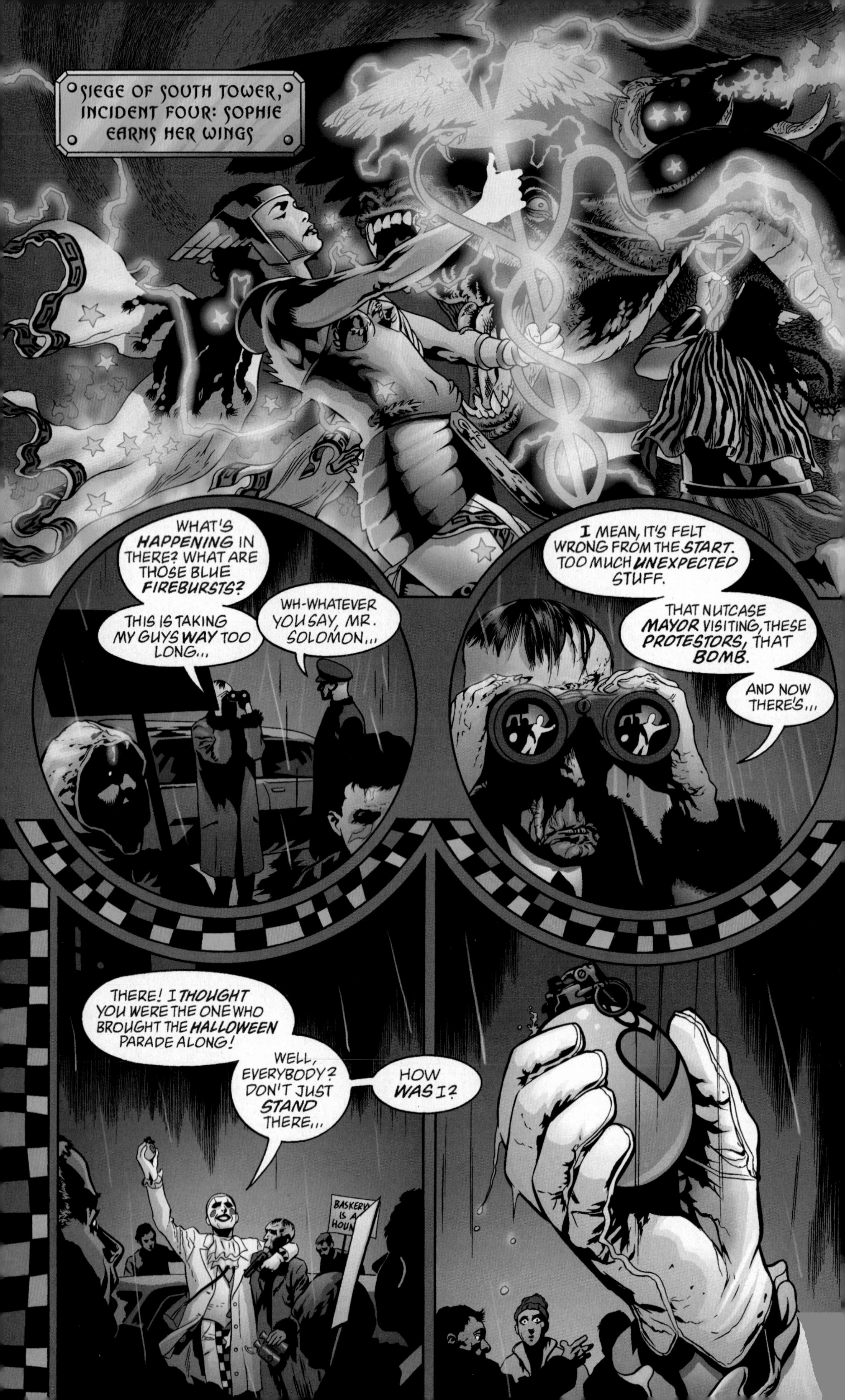
SIEGE OF SOUTH TOWER, INCIDENT FOUR: SOPHIE EARNS HER WINGS
WHAT'S HAPPENING IN THERE? WHAT ARE THOSE BLUE FIREBURSTS?
THIS IS TAKING MY GUYS WAY TOO LONG...
WH-WHATEVER YOU SAY, MR. SOLOMON...
I MEAN, IT'S FELT WRONG FROM THE START. TOO MUCH UNEXPECTED STUFF.
THAT NUTCASE MAYOR VISITING, THESE PROTESTORS, THAT BOMB.
AND NOW THERE'S...
THERE! I THOUGHT YOU WERE THE ONE WHO BROUGHT THE HALLOWEEN PARADE ALONG!
WELL, EVERYBODY? DON'T JUST STAND THERE...
HOW WAS I?

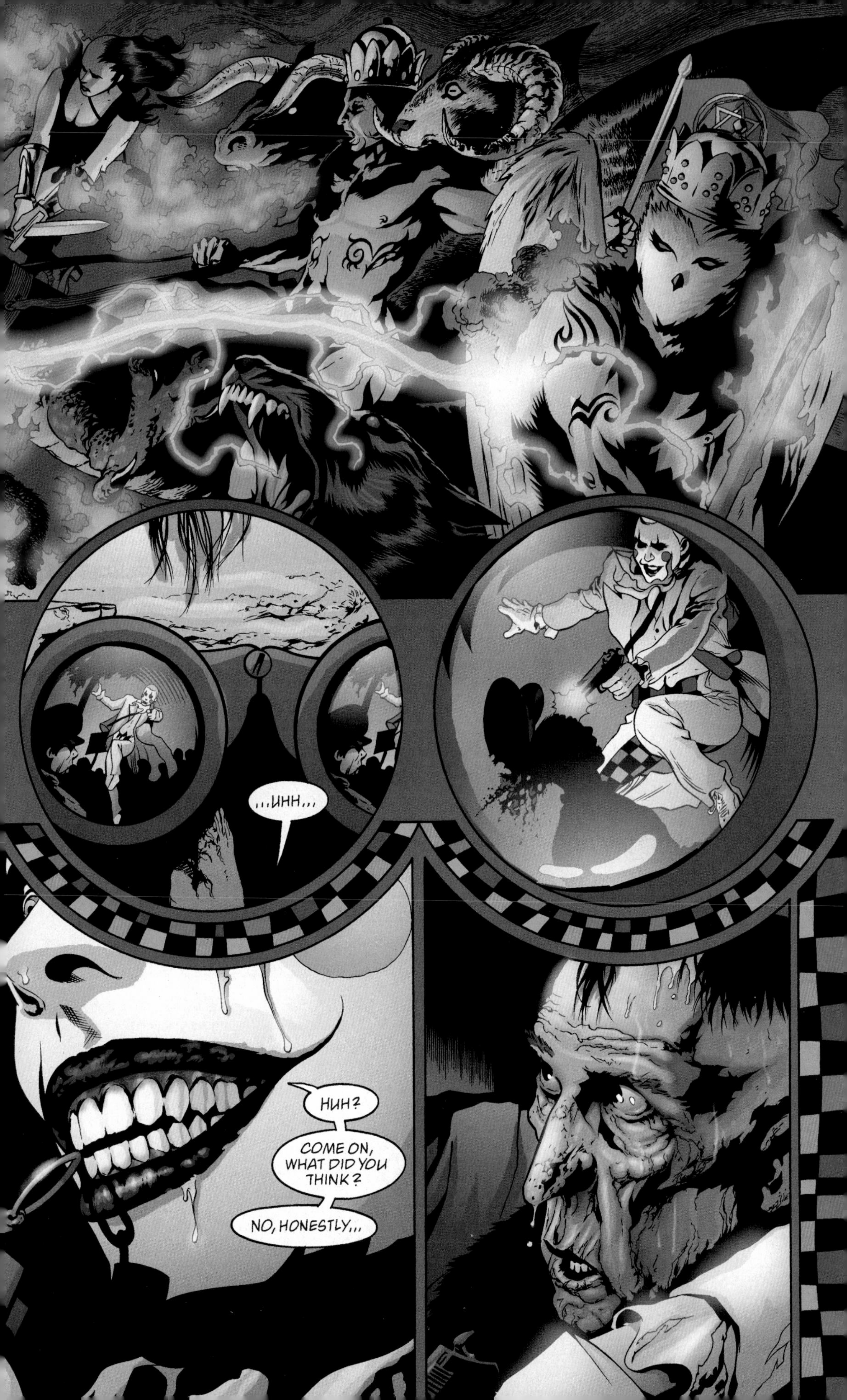
...UHH...
HUH?
COME ON, WHAT DID YOU THINK?
NO, HONESTLY...

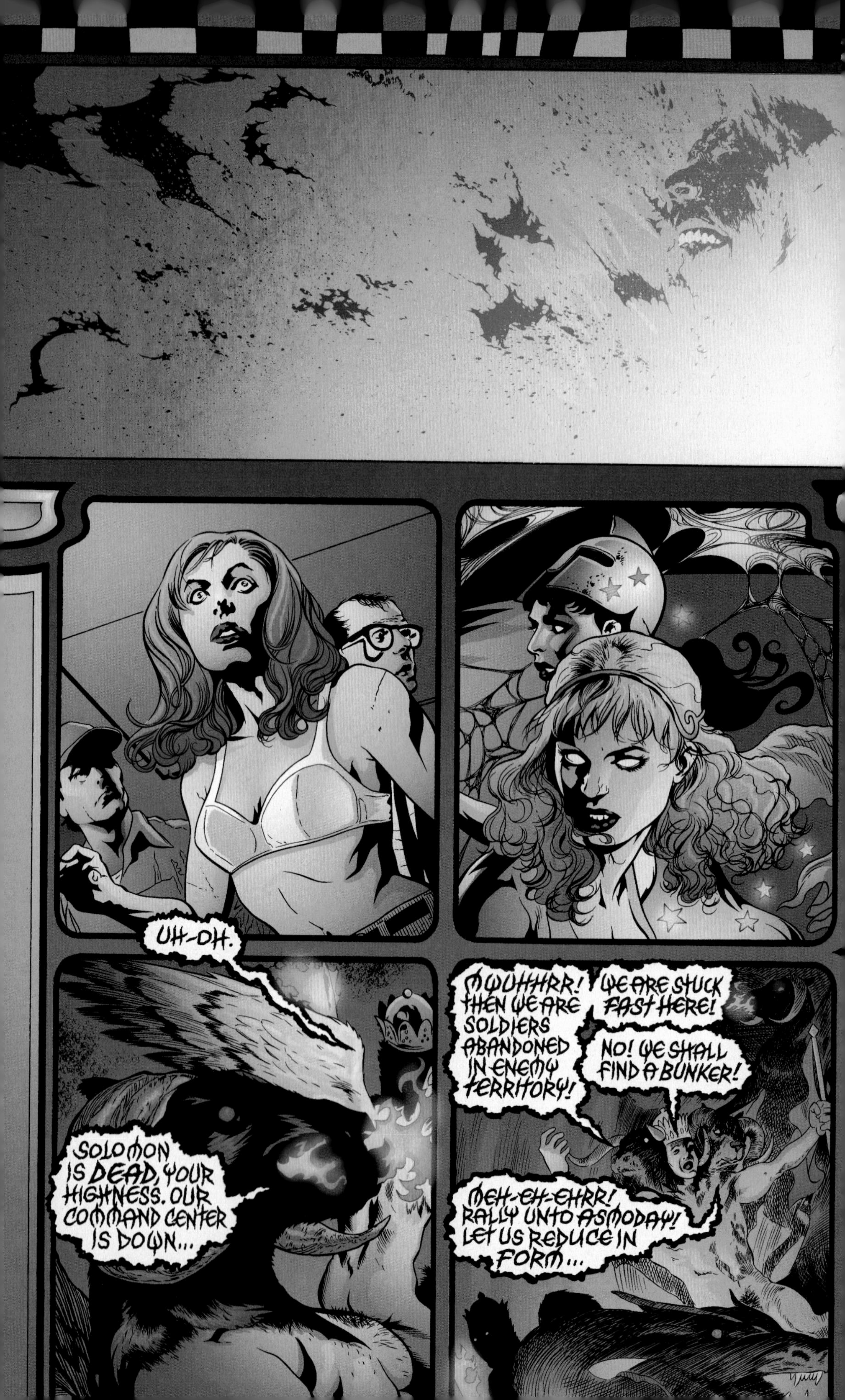
UH-OH.
SOLOMON IS DEAD, YOUR HIGHNESS. OUR COMMAND CENTER IS DOWN...
MWUHHRR! THEN WE ARE SOLDIERS ABANDONED IN ENEMY TERRITORY!
WE ARE STUCK FAST HERE!
NO! WE SHALL FIND A BUNKER!
MEH-EH-EHRR! RALLY UNTO ASMODAY! LET US REDUCE IN FORM...

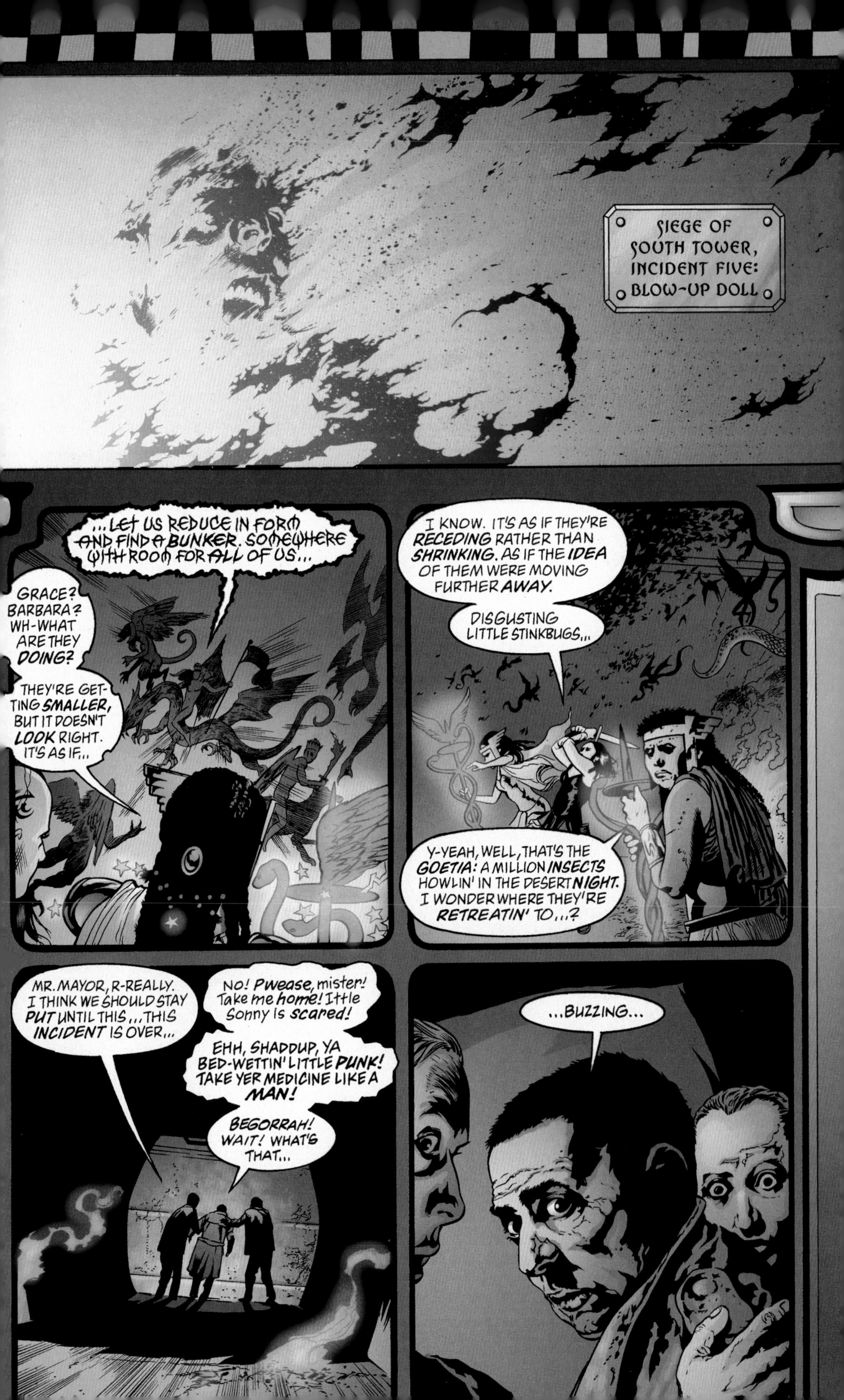
SIEGE OF SOUTH TOWER, INCIDENT FIVE: BLOW-UP DOLL
...LET US REDUCE IN FORM AND FIND A BUNKER. SOMEWHERE WITH ROOM FOR ALL OF US...
GRACE? BARBARA? WH-WHAT ARE THEY DOING?
THEY'RE GETTING SMALLER, BUT IT DOESN'T LOOK RIGHT. IT'S AS IF...
I KNOW. IT'S AS IF THEY'RE RECEDING RATHER THAN SHRINKING. AS IF THE IDEA OF THEM WERE MOVING FURTHER AWAY.
DISGUSTING LITTLE STINKBUGS...
Y-YEAH, WELL, THAT'S THE GOETIA: A MILLION INSECTS HOWLIN' IN THE DESERT NIGHT. I WONDER WHERE THEY'RE RETREATIN' TO...?
MR. MAYOR, R-REALLY. I THINK WE SHOULD STAY PUT UNTIL THIS... THIS INCIDENT IS OVER...
NO! Pwease, mister! Take me home! Ittle Sonny is scared!
EHH, SHADDUP, YA BED-WETTIN' LITTLE PUNK! TAKE YER MEDICINE LIKE A MAN!
BEGORRAH! WAIT! WHAT'S THAT...
...BUZZING...

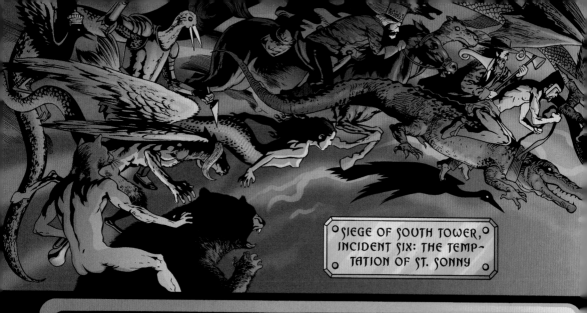

SIEGE OF SOUTH TOWER, INCIDENT SIX: THE TEMP- TATION OF ST. SONNY

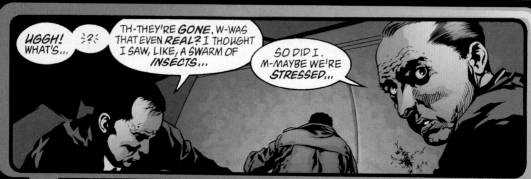

UGGH! WHAT'S...

?!?

TH-THEY'RE *GONE*. W-WAS THAT EVEN *REAL?* I THOUGHT I SAW, LIKE, A SWARM OF *INSECTS*...

SO DID I. M-MAYBE WE'RE *STRESSED*...

BUT...THAT WAS SO *WEIRD!* IT WASN'T EVEN, LIKE, ALL ONE *KIND* OF BUG. THEY ALL LOOKED *DIFFERENT*...

UH...MR. MAYOR? ARE YOU *OKAY?*

WE'RE FINE.

NOW, IF YOU'LL *ESCORT* US TO OUR *TRANSPORT*...

...WE HAVE *WORK* TO DO.

AHHH...

THANK GOODNESS FOR THAT. THAT INFERNAL *CHITTERING* IN MY HEAD HAS STOPPED. THEY'RE *GONE*.

WE'D PROBABLY BEST BE GONE *OUR- SELVES*, BEFORE THIS ERA'S *POLICEMEN* ARRIVE...

MARGARET HAS A *POINT*, GIRLS.

DON'T FORGET TO WIPE OUR VESSEL'S *MEMORIES* CLEAN ON OUR WAY *OUT*. SOPHIE HAS ENOUGH EXPLAINING TO DO *ALREADY*.

WELL, *NATURALLY*. I ALWAYS LIKE TO LEAVE A MIND AS I *FOUND* IT...

G-GOODBYE, SOPHIE. S-SEE YOU SOONNNHHHH...

W-WE'LL *ALL* SEE YOU SOON, BABY. Y-YOU TAKE CARE NOWUHHHHH...

SOPHIE, TAKE A *WARRIOR'S* ADVICE: PRESS YOUR *ADVANTAGE*. DON'T LET THE *TEMPLE* GET AWAY WITH DOING THIS TO YOU AND BARBARA...

BARBARA? BUT...OH *JEEZ!* BARBARA, ARE YOU *OKAY*?

FINE, JUST WINDED.

NONSENSE. SHE'S *DYING*. IT'S JUST SHE'S A VERY, VERY BRAVE LITTLE LATINA GIRL, AREN'T YOU DARLING?

L-LOOK AFTER HER. S-SEE THAT SH-SHE'S C-COMFORTABUHHHHH...

£$%& YOU, GRACE. I'M OKAY.

LISTEN, KID, WORRY ABOUT *YOURSELF*. Y-YOU WANNA BE *SOPHIE* WHEN THE *COPS* ARRIVE...

I CAN DO THAT. I KNOW HOW TO LET

OH, DON'T WORRY ABOUT *ME*. I CAN LET GO OF BEING PROMETHEA JUST *FINE*.

HEH HEH

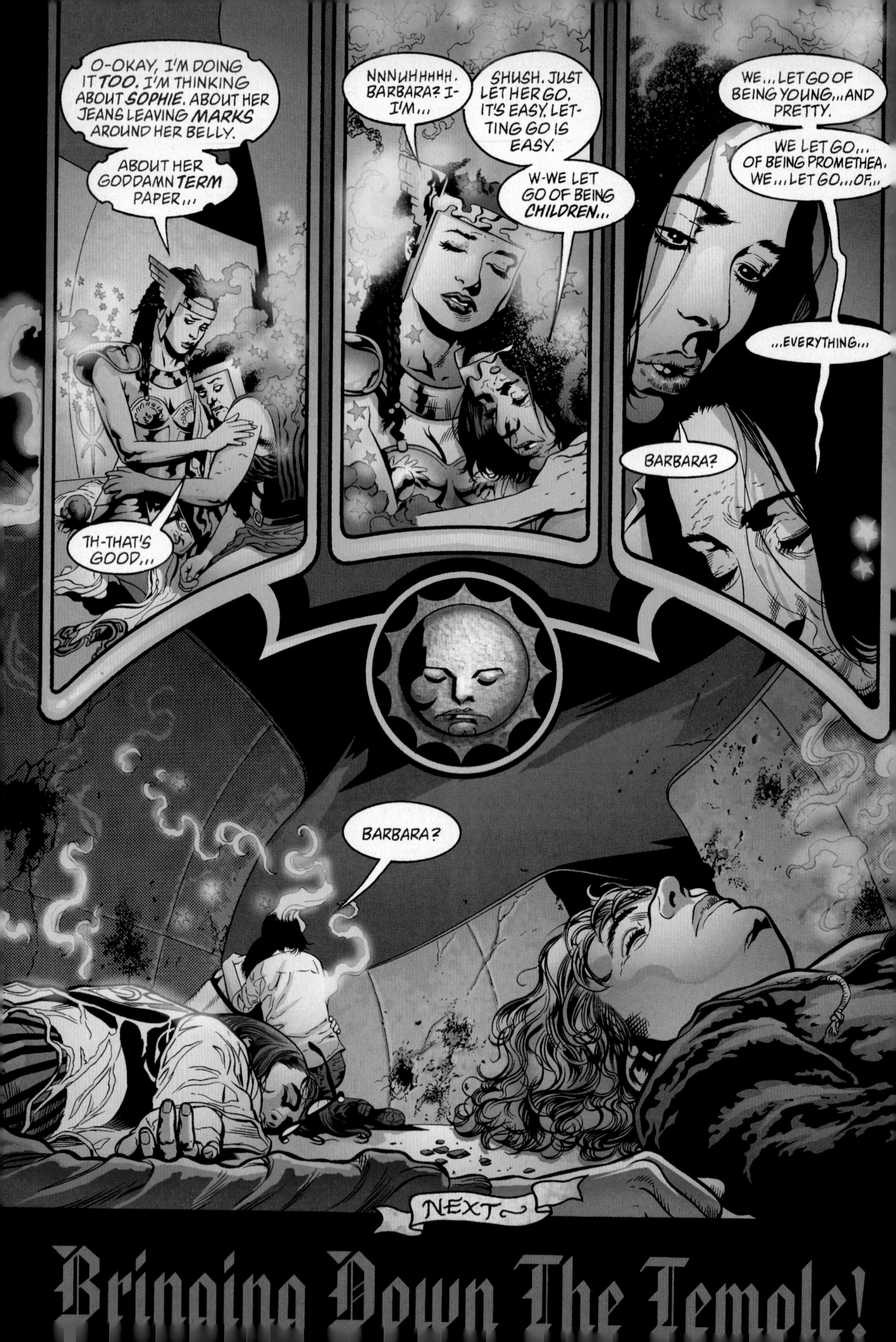
O-OKAY, I'M DOING IT TOO. I'M THINKING ABOUT SOPHIE. ABOUT HER JEANS LEAVING MARKS AROUND HER BELLY.
ABOUT HER GODDAMN TERM PAPER...
TH-THAT'S GOOD...
NNNUHHHHH. BARBARA? I-I'M...
SHUSH. JUST LET HER GO. IT'S EASY. LETTING GO IS EASY.
W-WE LET GO OF BEING CHILDREN...
WE... LET GO OF BEING YOUNG... AND PRETTY.
WE LET GO... OF BEING PROMETHEA. WE... LET GO... OF...
...EVERYTHING...
BARBARA?
BARBARA?
NEXT
Bringing Down The Temple!

CHAPTER THREE

A plot fails, before her anger the Temple quails.

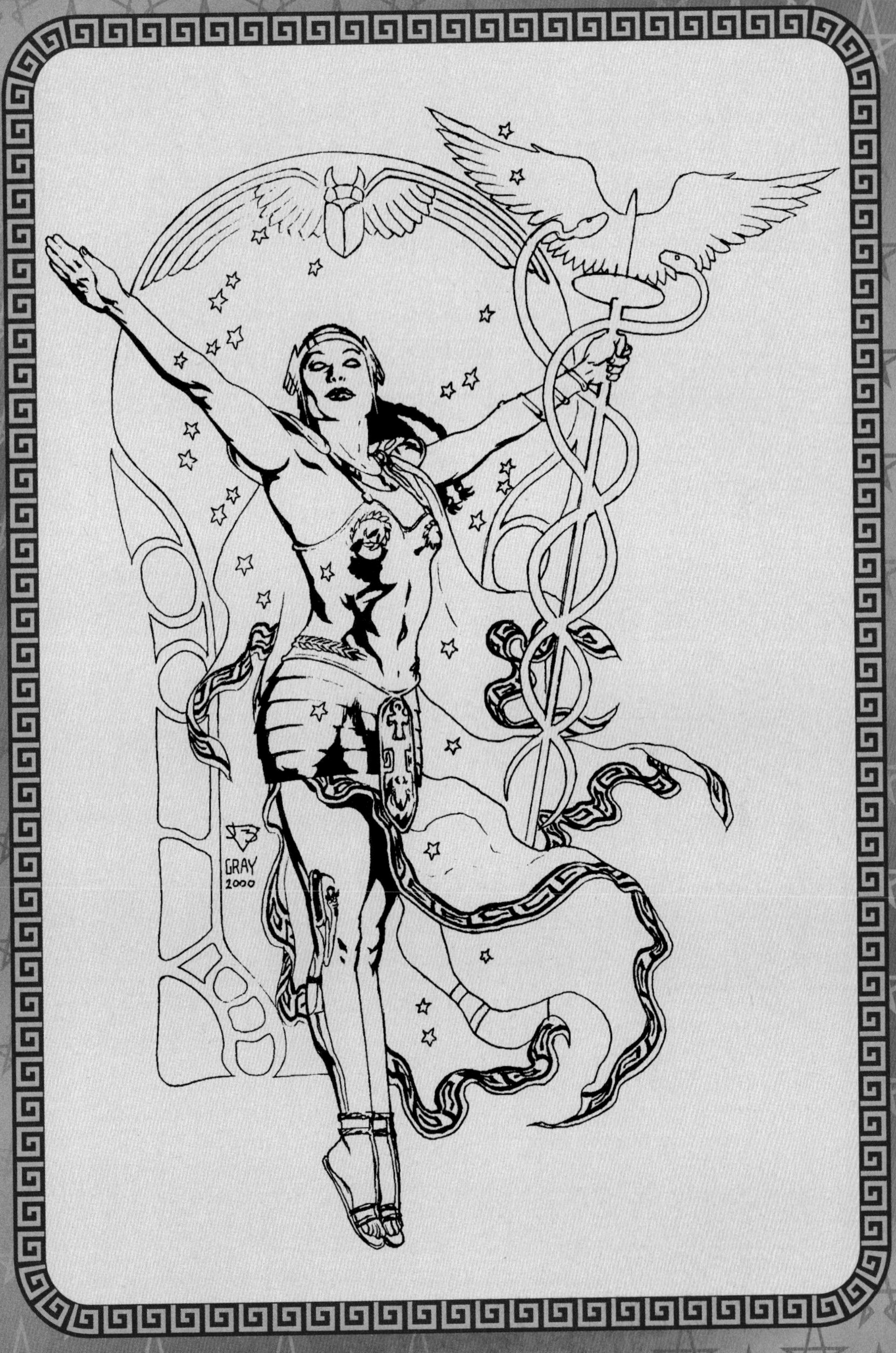
GRAY
2000

Cover art: J.H. Williams III, Mick Gray & Alex Sinclair

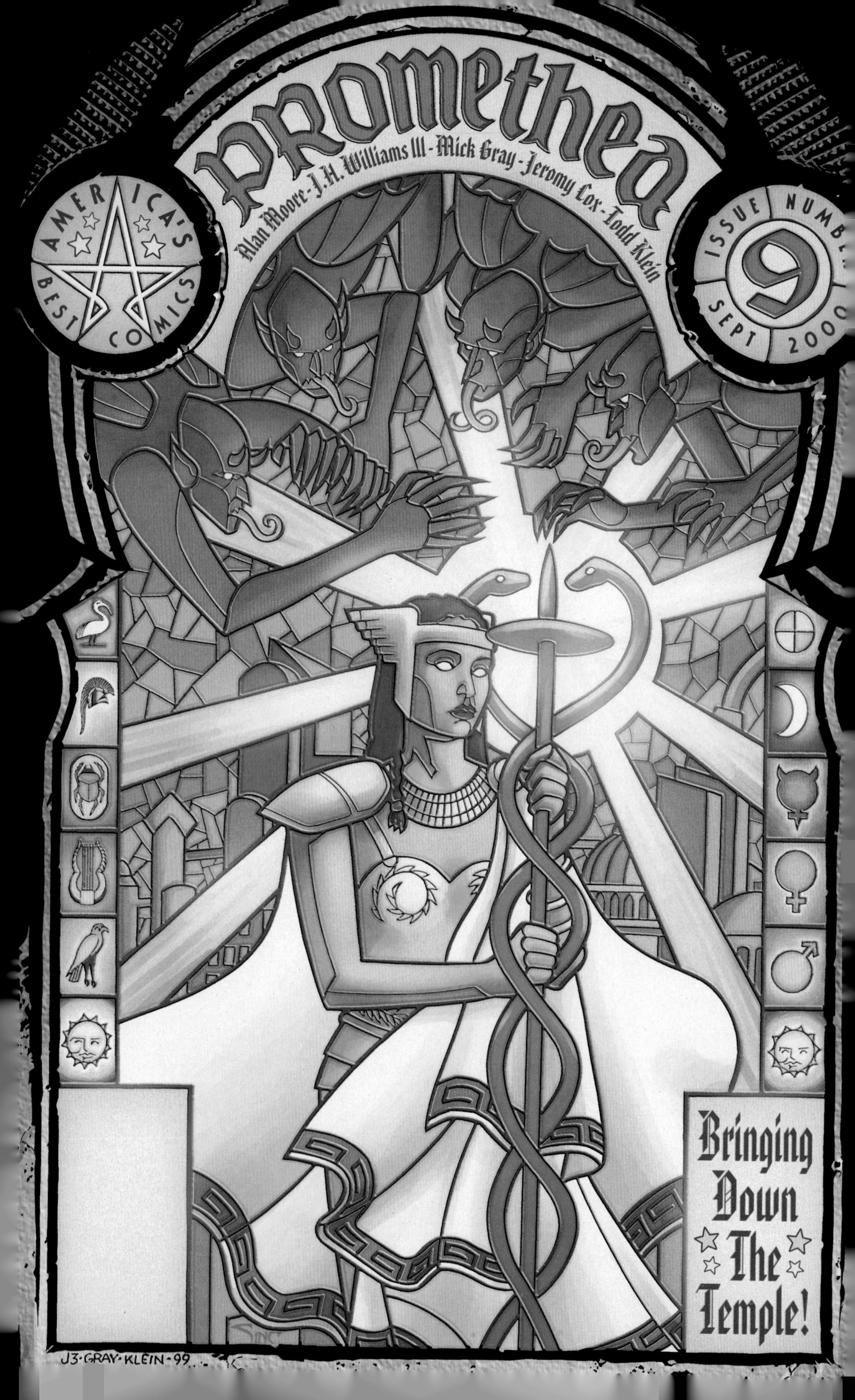

PROMETHEA
Alan Moore - J.H. Williams III - Mick Gray - Jeromy Cox - Todd Klein
AMERICA'S BEST COMICS
ISSUE NUMBER 9
SEPT 2000
Bringing Down The Temple!
J3·GRAY·KLEIN·99

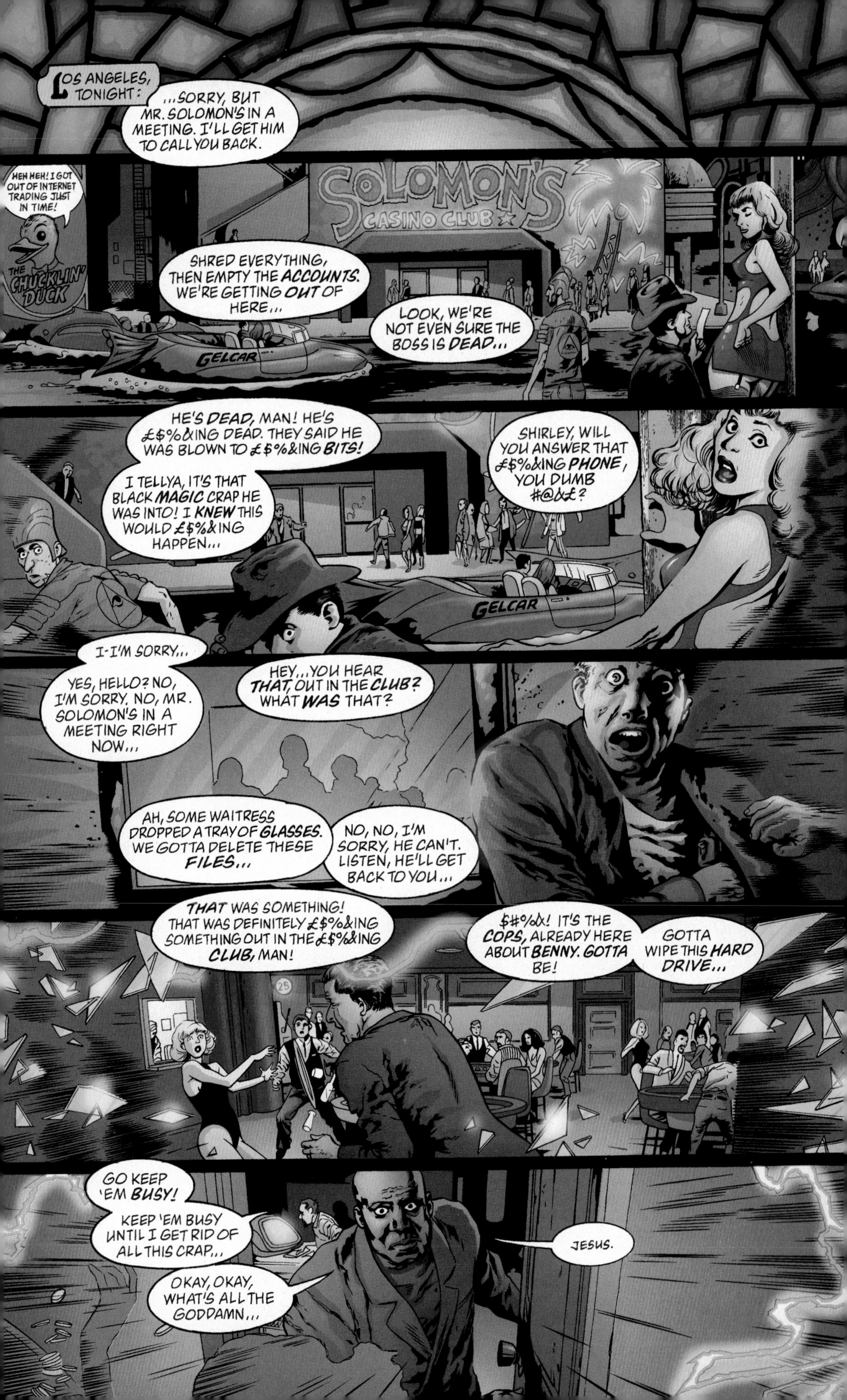
LOS ANGELES, TONIGHT:
...SORRY, BUT MR. SOLOMON'S IN A MEETING. I'LL GET HIM TO CALL YOU BACK.
HEH HEH! I GOT OUT OF INTERNET TRADING JUST IN TIME!
THE CHUCKLIN' DUCK
SOLOMON'S CASINO CLUB
SHRED EVERYTHING, THEN EMPTY THE ACCOUNTS. WE'RE GETTING OUT OF HERE...
LOOK, WE'RE NOT EVEN SURE THE BOSS IS DEAD...
GELCAR
HE'S DEAD, MAN! HE'S £$%&ING DEAD. THEY SAID HE WAS BLOWN TO £$%&ING BITS!
I TELLYA, IT'S THAT BLACK MAGIC CRAP HE WAS INTO! I KNEW THIS WOULD £$%&ING HAPPEN...
SHIRLEY, WILL YOU ANSWER THAT £$%&ING PHONE, YOU DUMB #@&£?
GELCAR
I-I'M SORRY...
YES, HELLO? NO, I'M SORRY. NO, MR. SOLOMON'S IN A MEETING RIGHT NOW...
HEY... YOU HEAR THAT, OUT IN THE CLUB? WHAT WAS THAT?
AH, SOME WAITRESS DROPPED A TRAY OF GLASSES. WE GOTTA DELETE THESE FILES...
NO, NO, I'M SORRY, HE CAN'T. LISTEN, HE'LL GET BACK TO YOU...
THAT WAS SOMETHING! THAT WAS DEFINITELY £$%&ING SOMETHING OUT IN THE £$%&ING CLUB, MAN!
$#%&! IT'S THE COPS, ALREADY HERE ABOUT BENNY. GOTTA BE!
GOTTA WIPE THIS HARD DRIVE...
25
GO KEEP 'EM BUSY!
KEEP 'EM BUSY UNTIL I GET RID OF ALL THIS CRAP...
OKAY, OKAY, WHAT'S ALL THE GODDAMN...
JESUS.

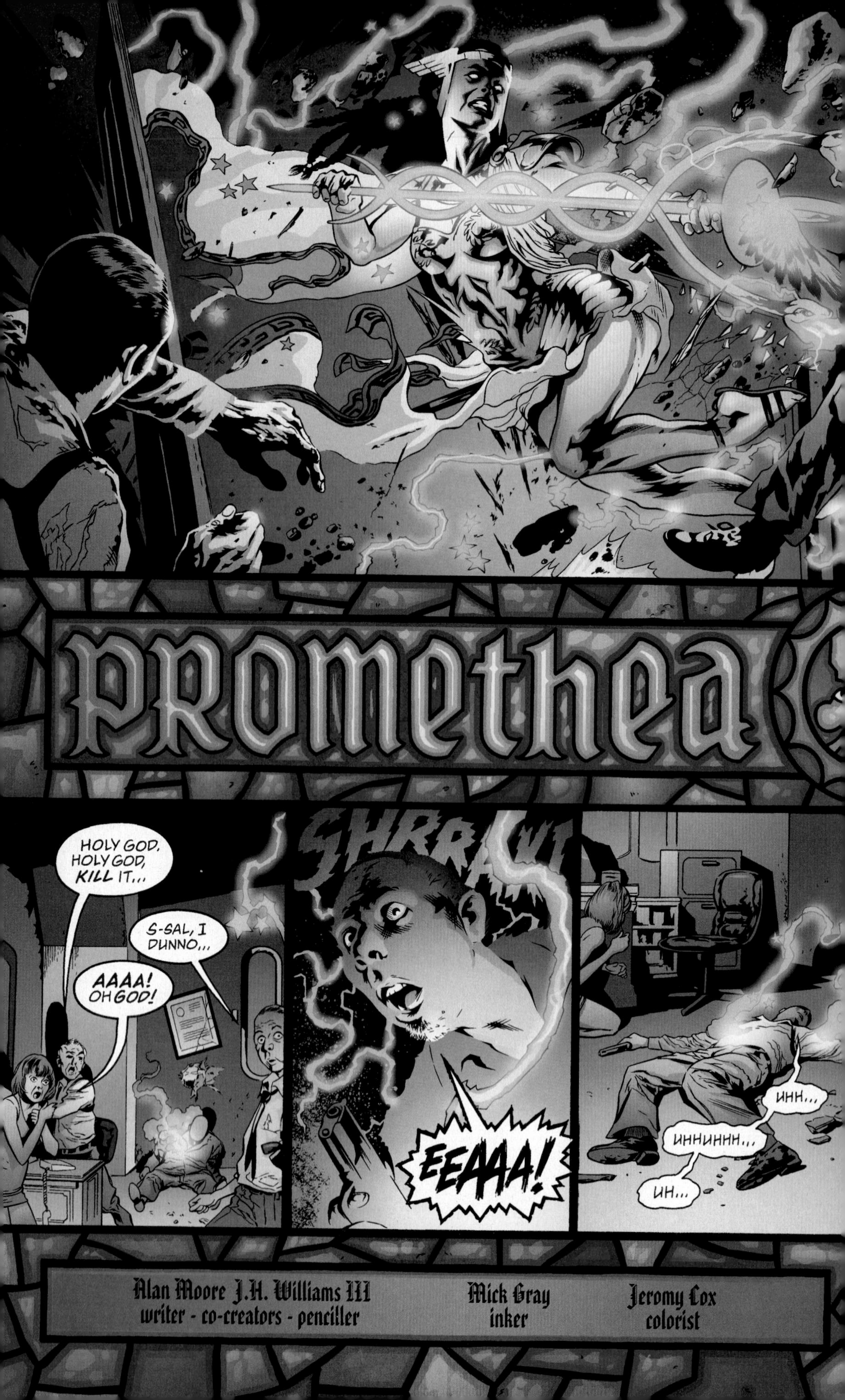
PROMETHEA
HOLY GOD, HOLY GOD, KILL IT...
S-SAL, I DUNNO...
AAAA! OH GOD!
EEAAA!
UHH...
UHHUHHH...
UH...
Alan Moore J.H. Williams III
writer - co-creators - penciller
Mick Gray
inker
Jeromy Cox
colorist

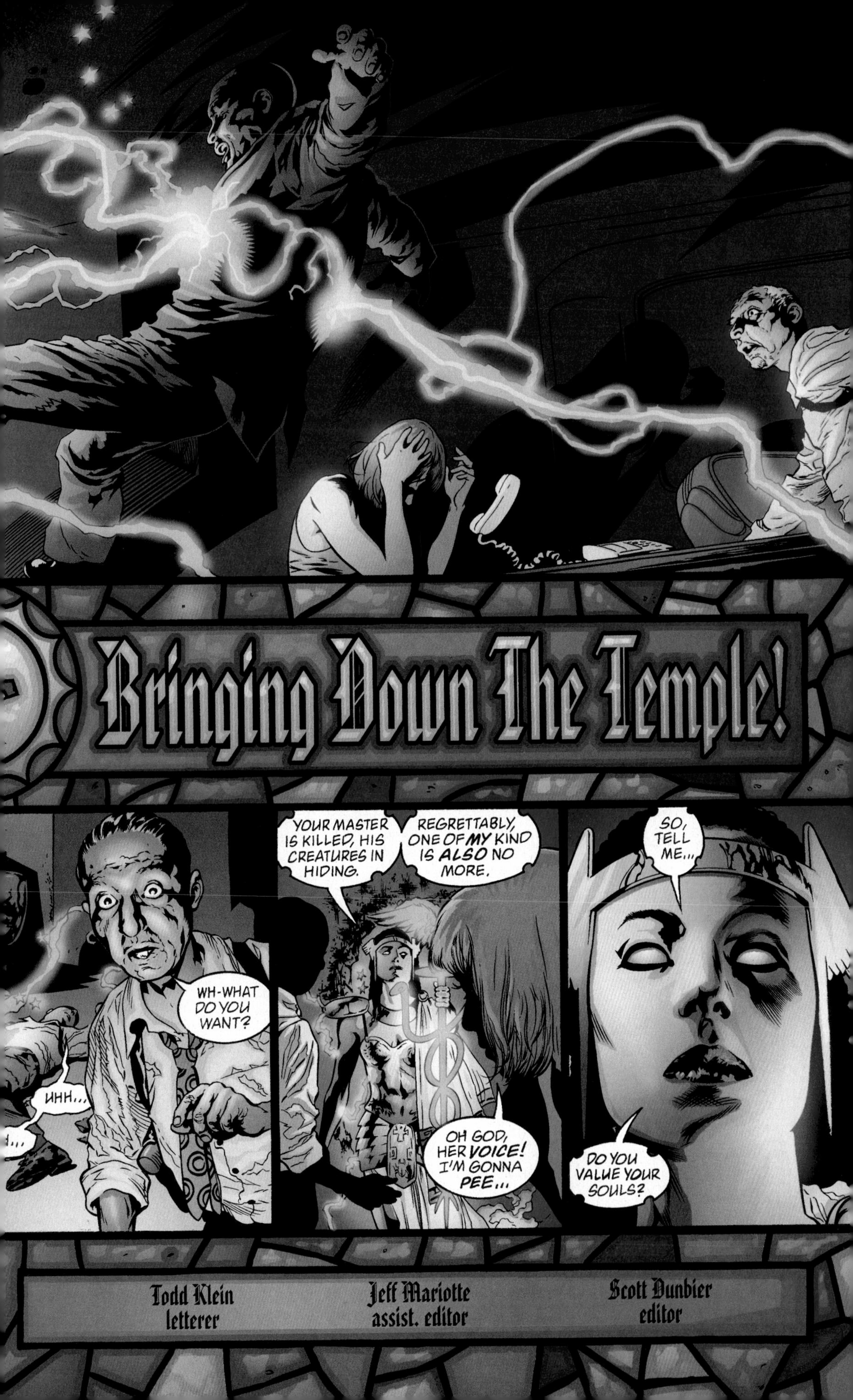
Bringing Down The Temple!
WH-WHAT DO YOU WANT?
UHH...
YOUR MASTER IS KILLED, HIS CREATURES IN HIDING.
REGRETTABLY, ONE OF MY KIND IS ALSO NO MORE.
OH GOD, HER VOICE! I'M GONNA PEE...
SO, TELL ME...
DO YOU VALUE YOUR SOULS?
Todd Klein letterer
Jeff Mariotte assist. editor
Scott Dunbier editor

NEW YORK, MONDAY:

I'M REALLY SORRY.

WOULD YOU LIKE TO SEE HER?

UH...YEAH, YEAH, I--I THINK I WOULD.

OH GOD, WHEN DID...WHEN DID SHE, Y'KNOW...?

SHE HUNG ON A DAY OR SO AFTER WE FOUND HER OUT OF BED DURING THAT...THAT STUFF THAT HAPPENED AT THE HOSPITAL.

THEY PRONOUNCED HER DEAD EARLY THIS MORNING...

LOOK, YOU PROBABLY WANT A FEW MINUTES ALONE WITH HER. I'LL BE RIGHT OUTSIDE.

SOPH? YOU WANT ME TO STAY HERE, OR...?

THIS IS SCREWED. STACE, THIS IS SO SCREWED. I MEAN, LOOK AT HER...

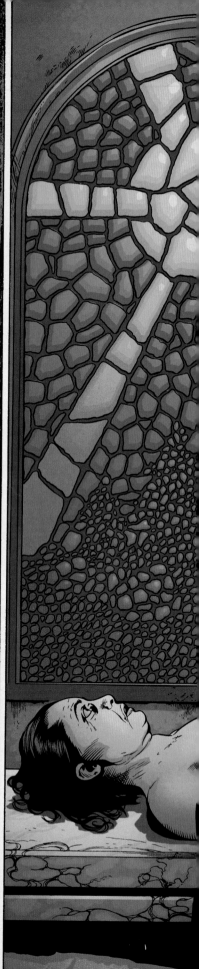

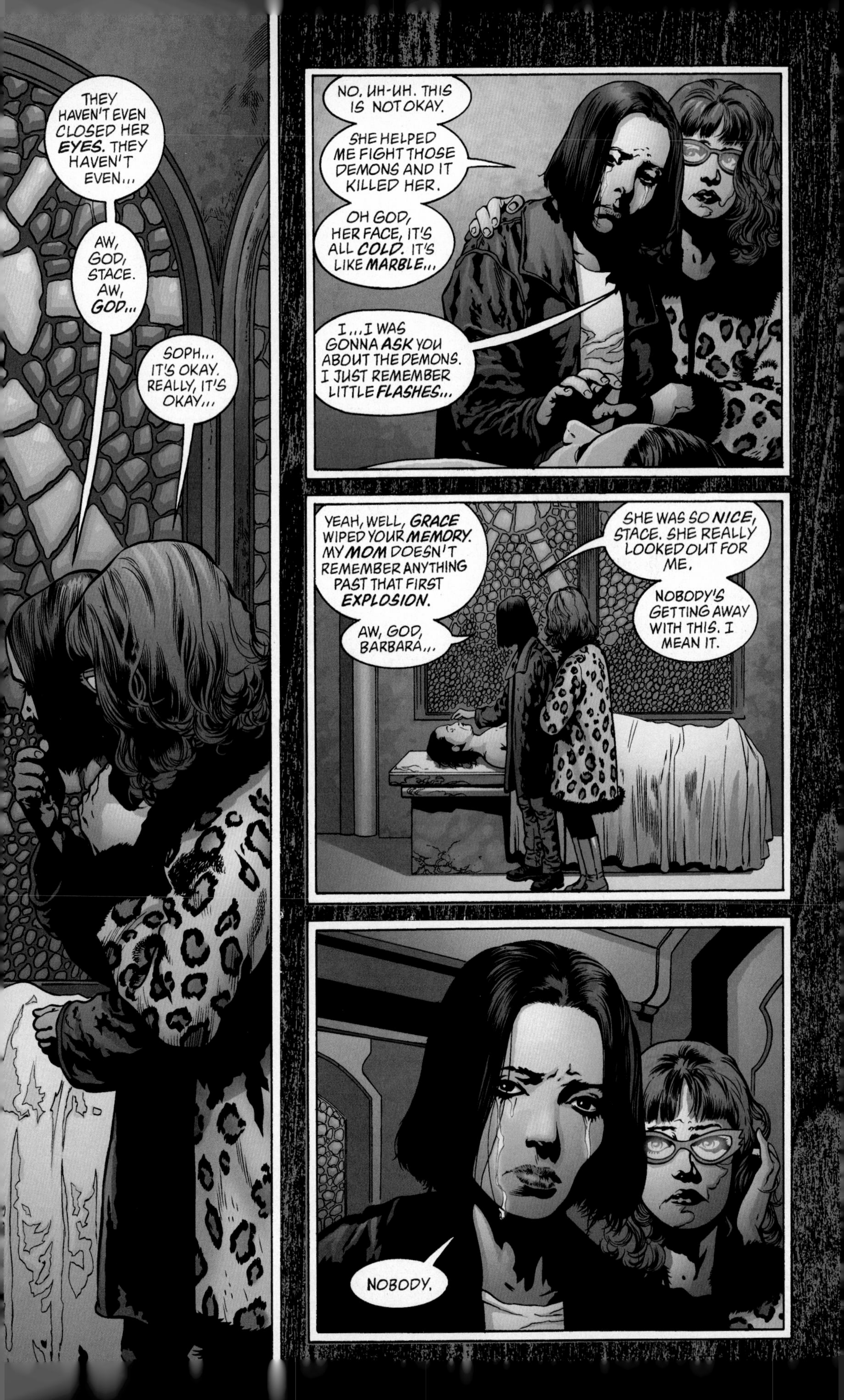
THEY HAVEN'T EVEN CLOSED HER EYES. THEY HAVEN'T EVEN...
AW, GOD, STACE. AW, GOD...
SOPH... IT'S OKAY. REALLY, IT'S OKAY...
NO, UH-UH. THIS IS NOT OKAY.
SHE HELPED ME FIGHT THOSE DEMONS AND IT KILLED HER.
OH GOD, HER FACE, IT'S ALL COLD. IT'S LIKE MARBLE...
I... I WAS GONNA ASK YOU ABOUT THE DEMONS. I JUST REMEMBER LITTLE FLASHES...
YEAH, WELL, GRACE WIPED YOUR MEMORY. MY MOM DOESN'T REMEMBER ANYTHING PAST THAT FIRST EXPLOSION.
AW, GOD, BARBARA...
SHE WAS SO NICE, STACE. SHE REALLY LOOKED OUT FOR ME.
NOBODY'S GETTING AWAY WITH THIS. I MEAN IT.
NOBODY.

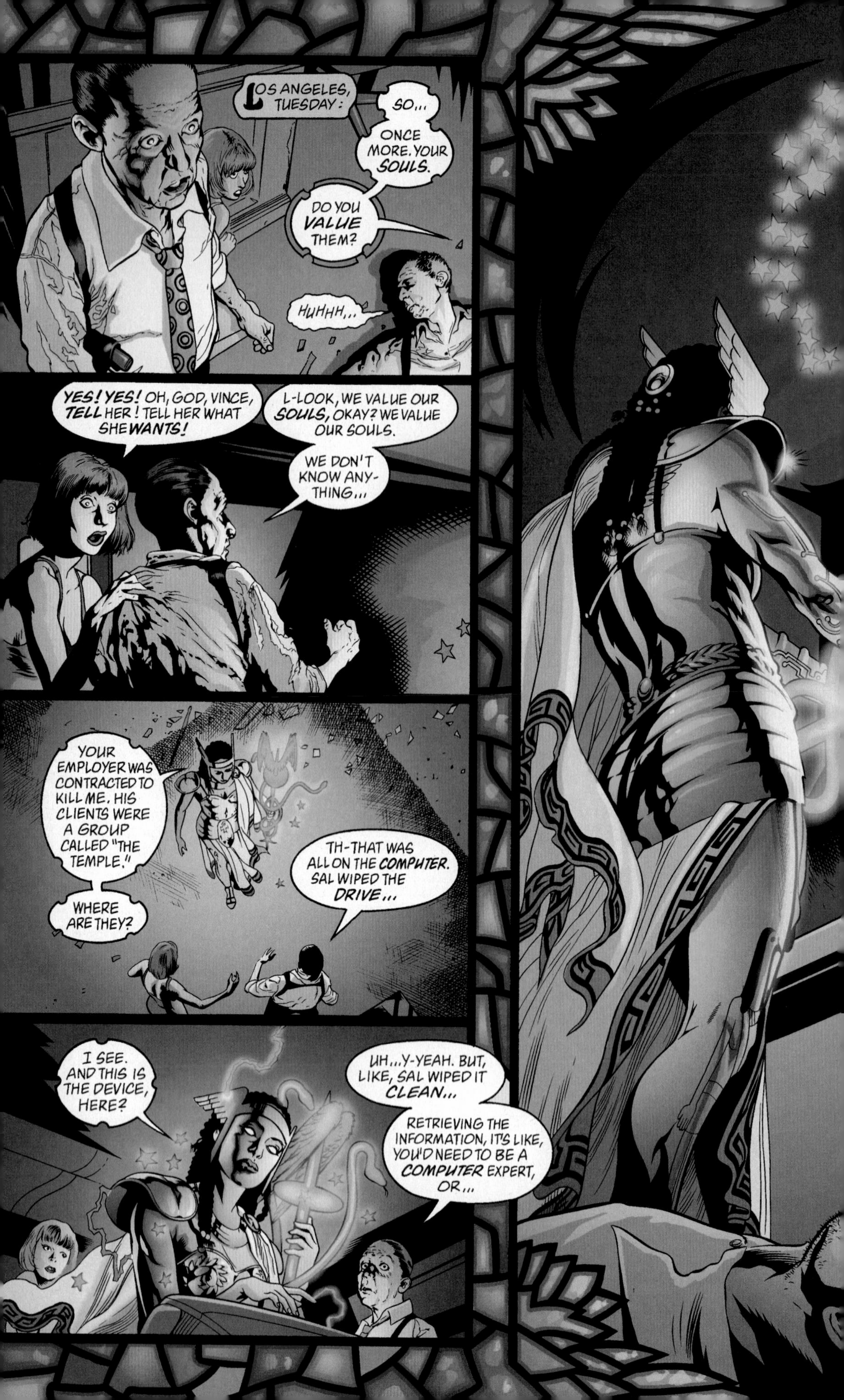
LOS ANGELES, TUESDAY:
SO...
ONCE MORE. YOUR SOULS.
DO YOU VALUE THEM?
HUHHH...
YES! YES! OH, GOD, VINCE, TELL HER! TELL HER WHAT SHE WANTS!
L-LOOK, WE VALUE OUR SOULS, OKAY? WE VALUE OUR SOULS.
WE DON'T KNOW ANYTHING...
YOUR EMPLOYER WAS CONTRACTED TO KILL ME. HIS CLIENTS WERE A GROUP CALLED "THE TEMPLE."
WHERE ARE THEY?
TH-THAT WAS ALL ON THE COMPUTER. SAL WIPED THE DRIVE...
I SEE. AND THIS IS THE DEVICE, HERE?
UH...Y-YEAH. BUT, LIKE, SAL WIPED IT CLEAN...
RETRIEVING THE INFORMATION, IT'S LIKE, YOU'D NEED TO BE A COMPUTER EXPERT, OR...

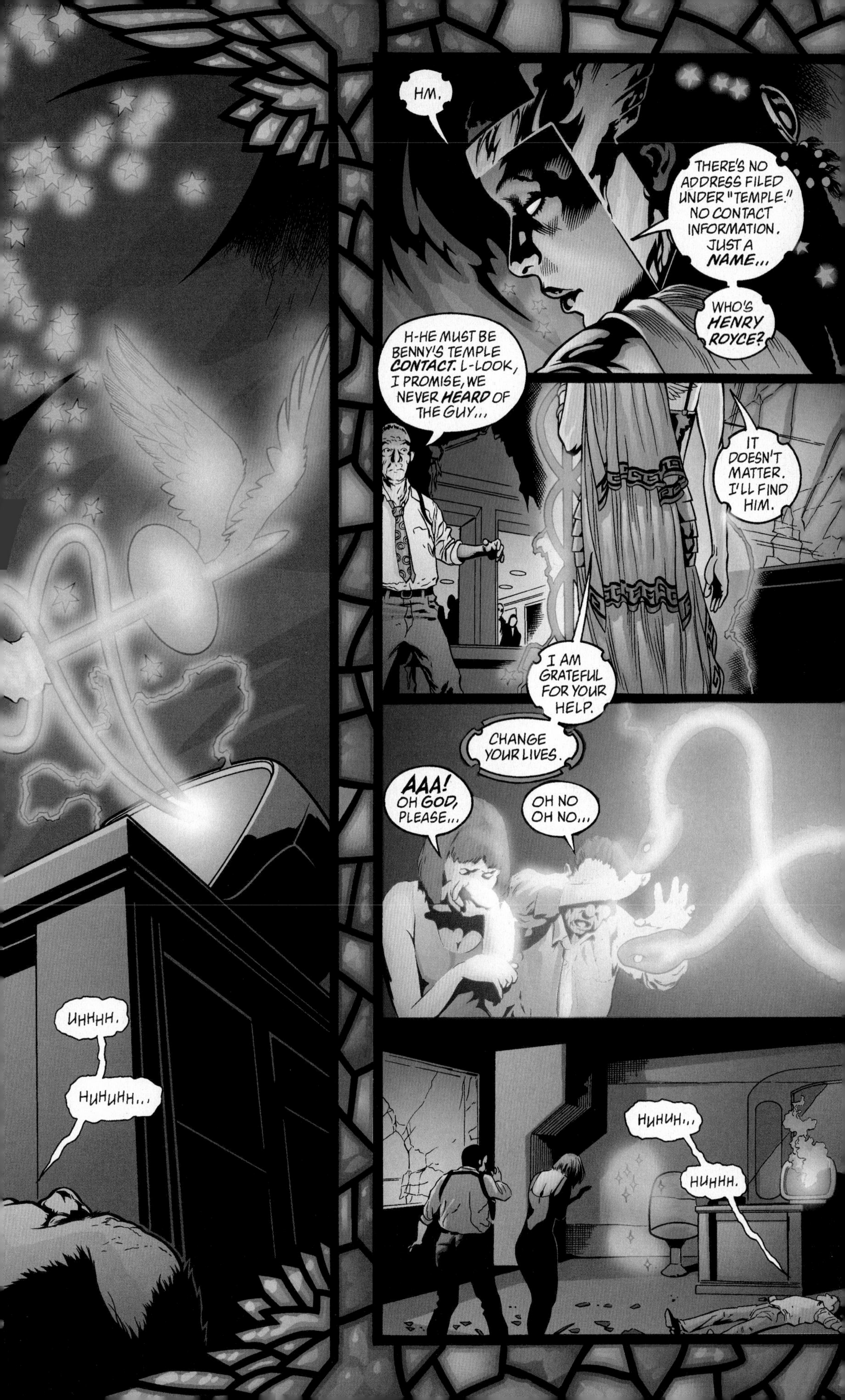
HM.
THERE'S NO ADDRESS FILED UNDER "TEMPLE." NO CONTACT INFORMATION. JUST A NAME...
WHO'S HENRY ROYCE?
H-HE MUST BE BENNY'S TEMPLE CONTACT. L-LOOK, I PROMISE, WE NEVER HEARD OF THE GUY...
IT DOESN'T MATTER. I'LL FIND HIM.
I AM GRATEFUL FOR YOUR HELP.
CHANGE YOUR LIVES.
AAA! OH GOD, PLEASE...
OH NO OH NO...
UHHHH.
HUHUHH...
HUHUH...
HUHHH.

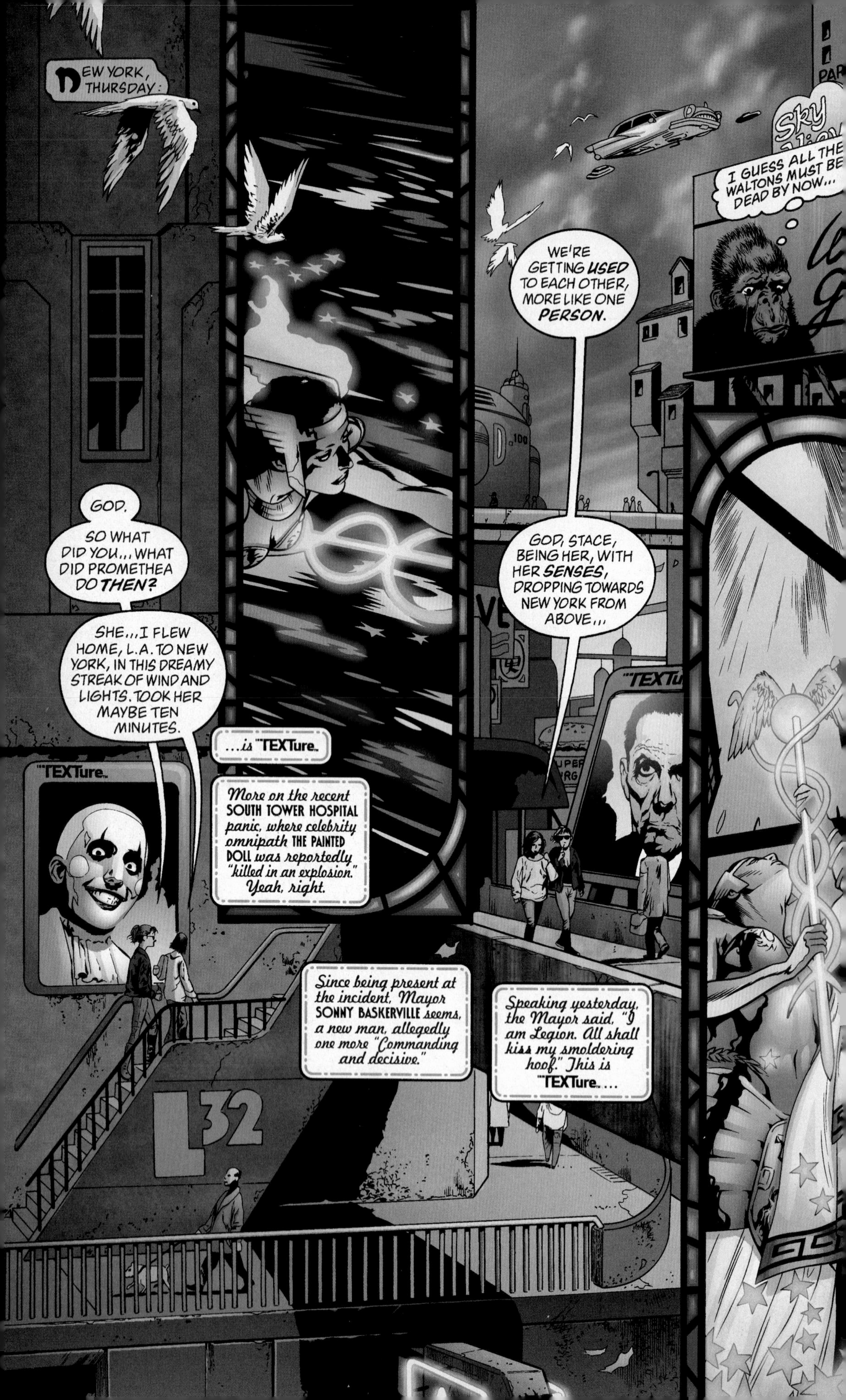
NEW YORK, THURSDAY:
GOD.
SO WHAT DID YOU... WHAT DID PROMETHEA DO THEN?
SHE... I FLEW HOME, L.A. TO NEW YORK, IN THIS DREAMY STREAK OF WIND AND LIGHTS. TOOK HER MAYBE TEN MINUTES.
WE'RE GETTING USED TO EACH OTHER, MORE LIKE ONE PERSON.
GOD, STACE, BEING HER, WITH HER SENSES, DROPPING TOWARDS NEW YORK FROM ABOVE...
I GUESS ALL THE WALTONS MUST BE DEAD BY NOW...
"TEXTure
...is "TEXTure
More on the recent SOUTH TOWER HOSPITAL panic, where celebrity omnipath THE PAINTED DOLL was reportedly "killed in an explosion." Yeah, right.
Since being present at the incident, Mayor SONNY BASKERVILLE seems, a new man, allegedly one more "Commanding and decisive."
Speaking yesterday, the Mayor said, "I am Legion. All shall kiss my smoldering hoof." This is "TEXTure...
L32

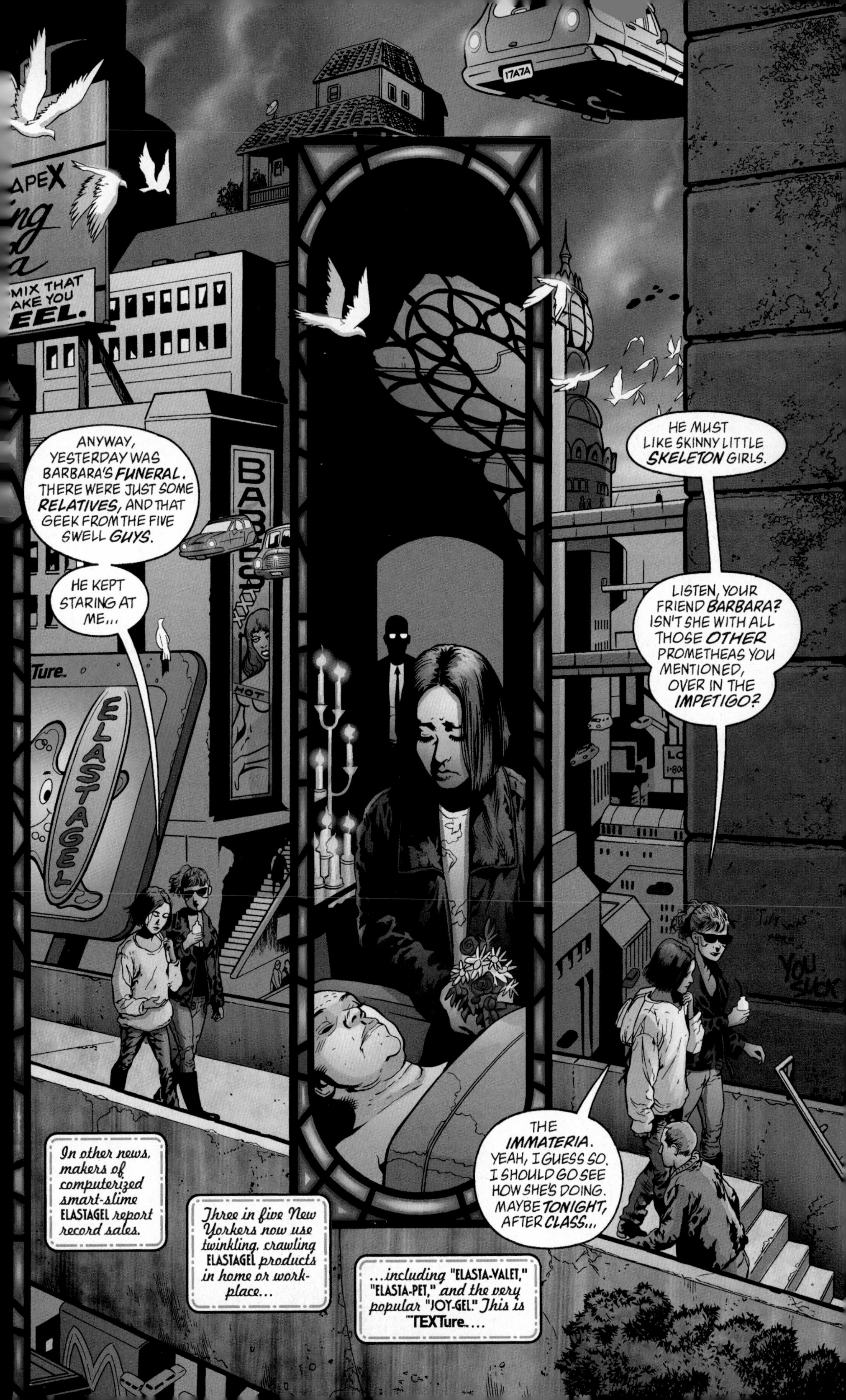
ANYWAY, YESTERDAY WAS BARBARA'S FUNERAL. THERE WERE JUST SOME RELATIVES, AND THAT GEEK FROM THE FIVE SWELL GUYS.
HE KEPT STARING AT ME...
HE MUST LIKE SKINNY LITTLE SKELETON GIRLS.
LISTEN, YOUR FRIEND BARBARA? ISN'T SHE WITH ALL THOSE OTHER PROMETHEAS YOU MENTIONED, OVER IN THE IMPETIGO?
THE IMMATERIA. YEAH, I GUESS SO. I SHOULD GO SEE HOW SHE'S DOING. MAYBE TONIGHT, AFTER CLASS...
In other news, makers of computerized smart-slime ELASTAGEL report record sales.
Three in five New Yorkers now use twinkling, crawling ELASTAGEL products in home or work-place...
...including "ELASTA-VALET," "ELASTA-PET," and the very popular "JOY-GEL." This is "TEXTure....
ELASTAGEL
MIX THAT AKE YOU EEL.
17A7A
TIM was here
YOU SUCK

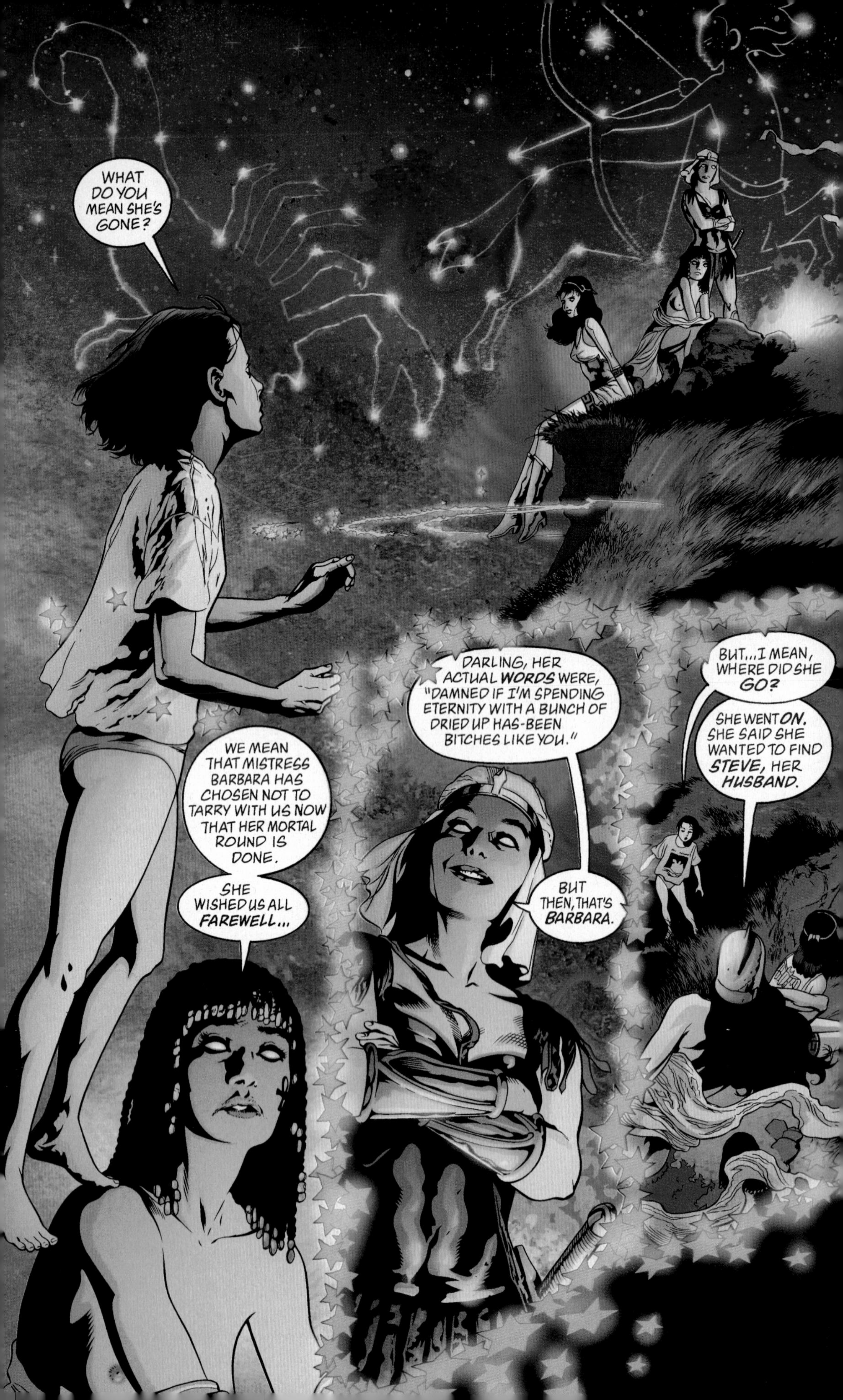
WHAT DO YOU MEAN SHE'S GONE?
WE MEAN THAT MISTRESS BARBARA HAS CHOSEN NOT TO TARRY WITH US NOW THAT HER MORTAL ROUND IS DONE.
SHE WISHED US ALL FAREWELL...
DARLING, HER ACTUAL WORDS WERE, "DAMNED IF I'M SPENDING ETERNITY WITH A BUNCH OF DRIED UP HAS-BEEN BITCHES LIKE YOU."
BUT THEN, THAT'S BARBARA.
BUT... I MEAN, WHERE DID SHE GO?
SHE WENT ON. SHE SAID SHE WANTED TO FIND STEVE, HER HUSBAND.

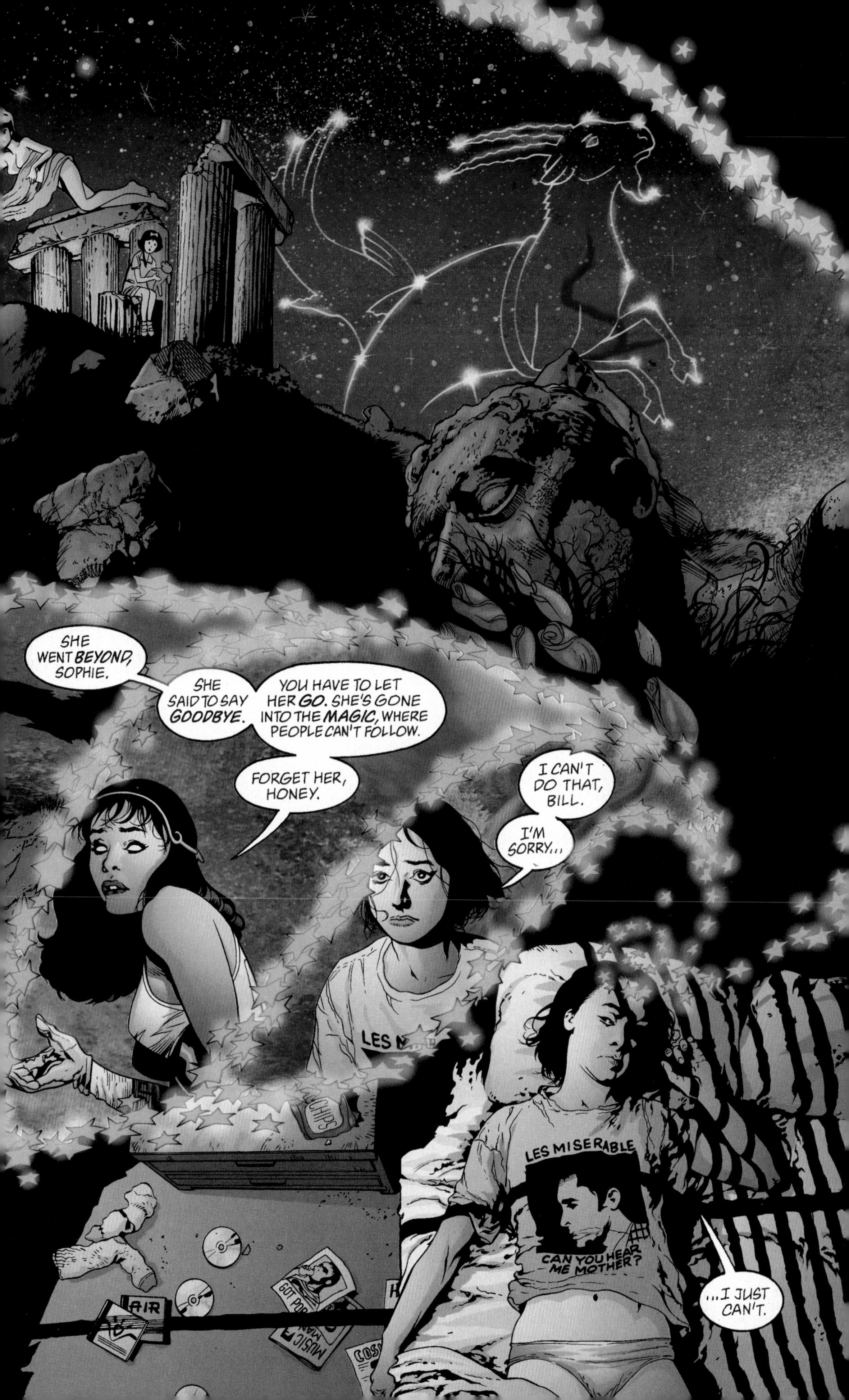
SHE WENT BEYOND, SOPHIE.
SHE SAID TO SAY GOODBYE.
YOU HAVE TO LET HER GO. SHE'S GONE INTO THE MAGIC, WHERE PEOPLE CAN'T FOLLOW.
FORGET HER, HONEY.
I CAN'T DO THAT, BILL.
I'M SORRY...
LES MISERABLE
CAN YOU HEAR ME MOTHER?
...I JUST CAN'T.

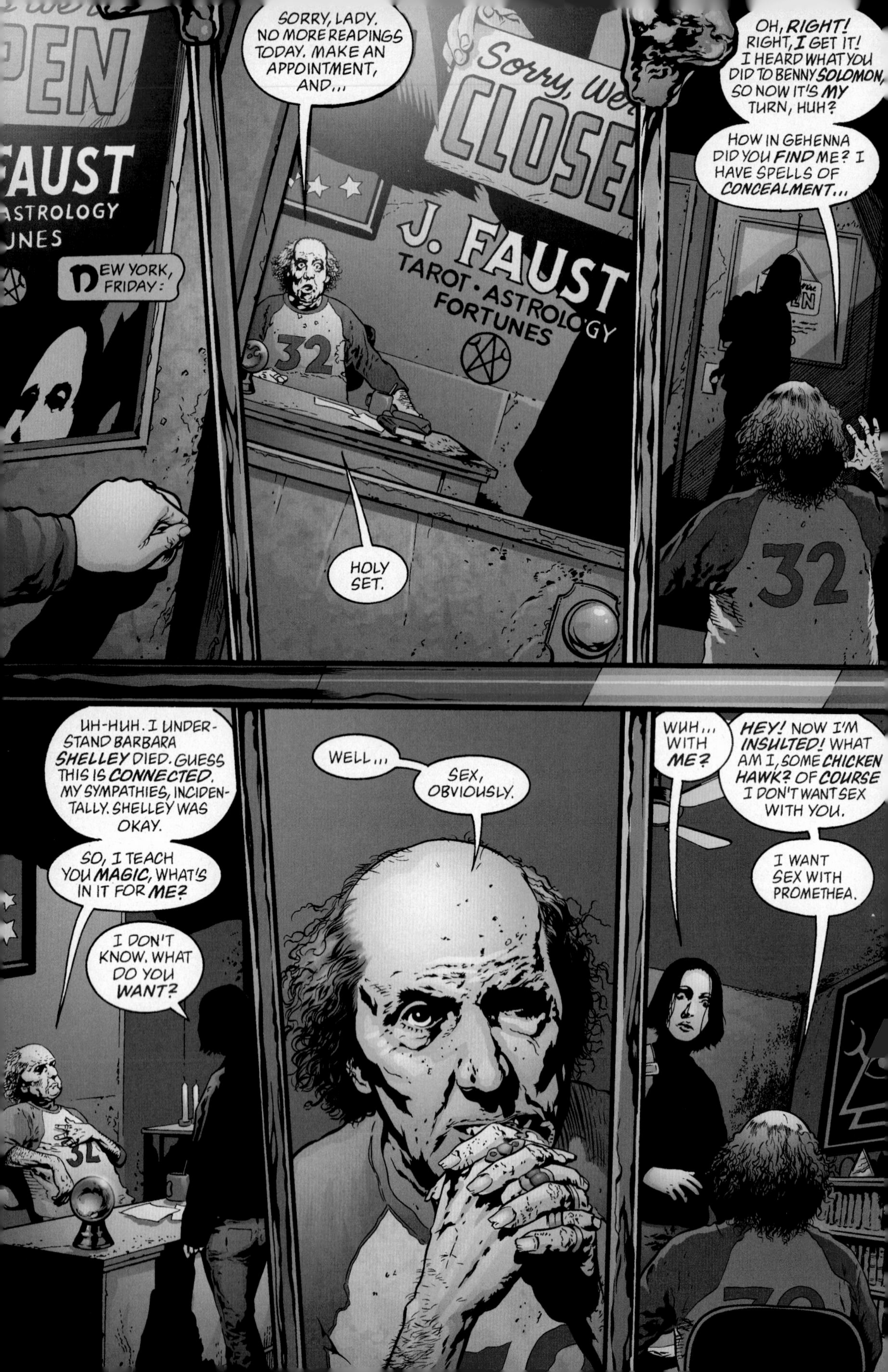
NEW YORK, FRIDAY:
SORRY, LADY. NO MORE READINGS TODAY. MAKE AN APPOINTMENT, AND...
Sorry, We're CLOSED
J. FAUST TAROT · ASTROLOGY FORTUNES
HOLY SET.
OH, RIGHT! RIGHT, I GET IT! I HEARD WHAT YOU DID TO BENNY SOLOMON, SO NOW IT'S MY TURN, HUH?
HOW IN GEHENNA DID YOU FIND ME? I HAVE SPELLS OF CONCEALMENT...
UH-HUH. I UNDERSTAND BARBARA SHELLEY DIED. GUESS THIS IS CONNECTED. MY SYMPATHIES, INCIDENTALLY. SHELLEY WAS OKAY.
SO, I TEACH YOU MAGIC, WHAT'S IN IT FOR ME?
I DON'T KNOW. WHAT DO YOU WANT?
WELL...
SEX, OBVIOUSLY.
WUH... WITH ME?
HEY! NOW I'M INSULTED! WHAT AM I, SOME CHICKEN HAWK? OF COURSE I DON'T WANT SEX WITH YOU.
I WANT SEX WITH PROMETHEA.

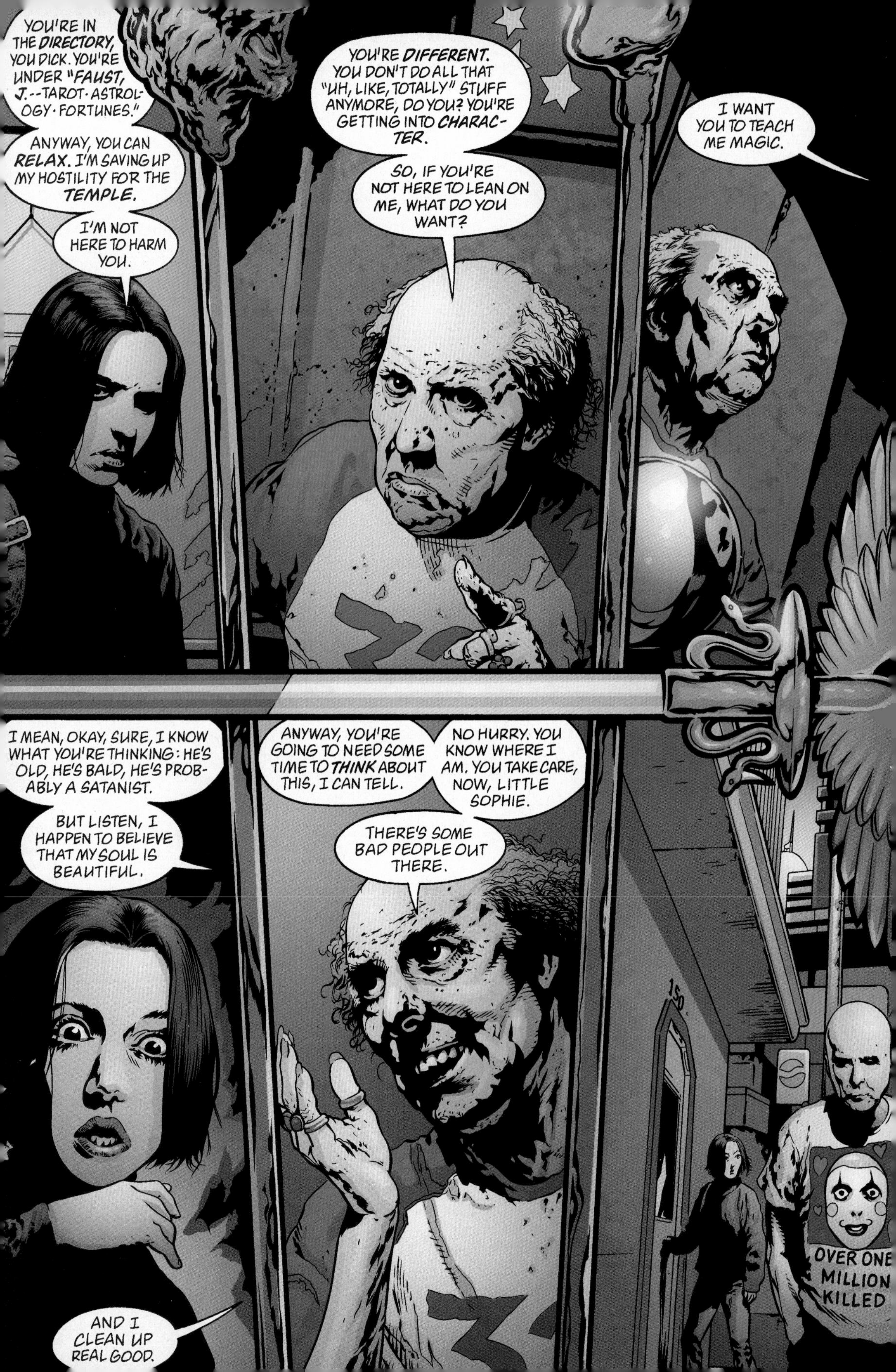
YOU'RE IN THE DIRECTORY, YOU DICK. YOU'RE UNDER "FAUST, J.--TAROT·ASTROLOGY·FORTUNES."
ANYWAY, YOU CAN RELAX. I'M SAVING UP MY HOSTILITY FOR THE TEMPLE.
I'M NOT HERE TO HARM YOU.
YOU'RE DIFFERENT. YOU DON'T DO ALL THAT "UH, LIKE, TOTALLY" STUFF ANYMORE, DO YOU? YOU'RE GETTING INTO CHARACTER.
SO, IF YOU'RE NOT HERE TO LEAN ON ME, WHAT DO YOU WANT?
I WANT YOU TO TEACH ME MAGIC.
I MEAN, OKAY, SURE, I KNOW WHAT YOU'RE THINKING: HE'S OLD, HE'S BALD, HE'S PROBABLY A SATANIST.
BUT LISTEN, I HAPPEN TO BELIEVE THAT MY SOUL IS BEAUTIFUL.
AND I CLEAN UP REAL GOOD.
ANYWAY, YOU'RE GOING TO NEED SOME TIME TO THINK ABOUT THIS, I CAN TELL.
NO HURRY. YOU KNOW WHERE I AM. YOU TAKE CARE, NOW, LITTLE SOPHIE.
THERE'S SOME BAD PEOPLE OUT THERE.
150
OVER ONE MILLION KILLED

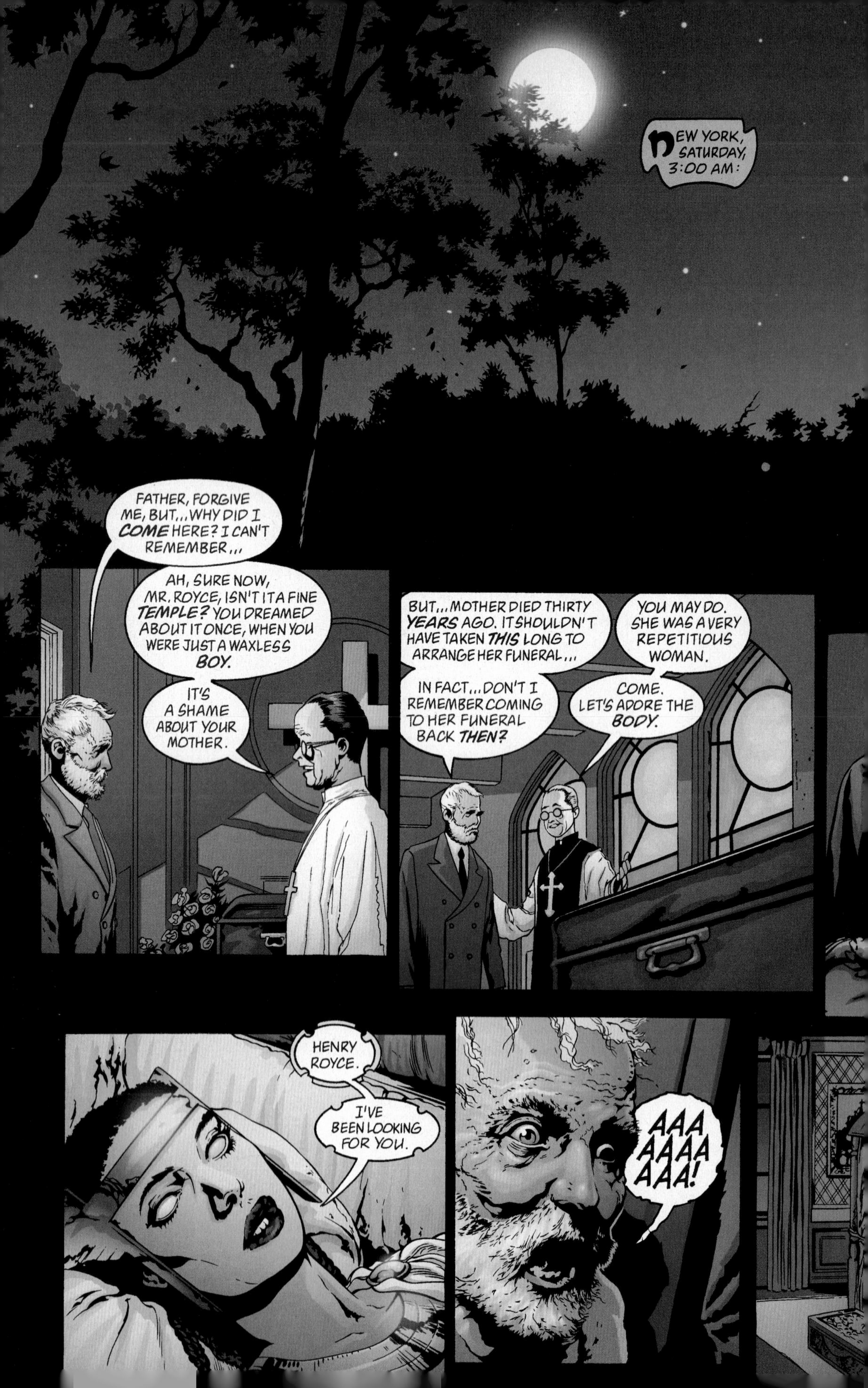
NEW YORK, SATURDAY, 3:00 AM:
FATHER, FORGIVE ME, BUT... WHY DID I COME HERE? I CAN'T REMEMBER...
AH, SURE NOW, MR. ROYCE, ISN'T IT A FINE TEMPLE? YOU DREAMED ABOUT IT ONCE, WHEN YOU WERE JUST A WAXLESS BOY.
IT'S A SHAME ABOUT YOUR MOTHER.
BUT... MOTHER DIED THIRTY YEARS AGO. IT SHOULDN'T HAVE TAKEN THIS LONG TO ARRANGE HER FUNERAL...
IN FACT... DON'T I REMEMBER COMING TO HER FUNERAL BACK THEN?
YOU MAY DO. SHE WAS A VERY REPETITIOUS WOMAN.
COME. LET'S ADORE THE BODY.
HENRY ROYCE.
I'VE BEEN LOOKING FOR YOU.
AAAAAAAAAA!

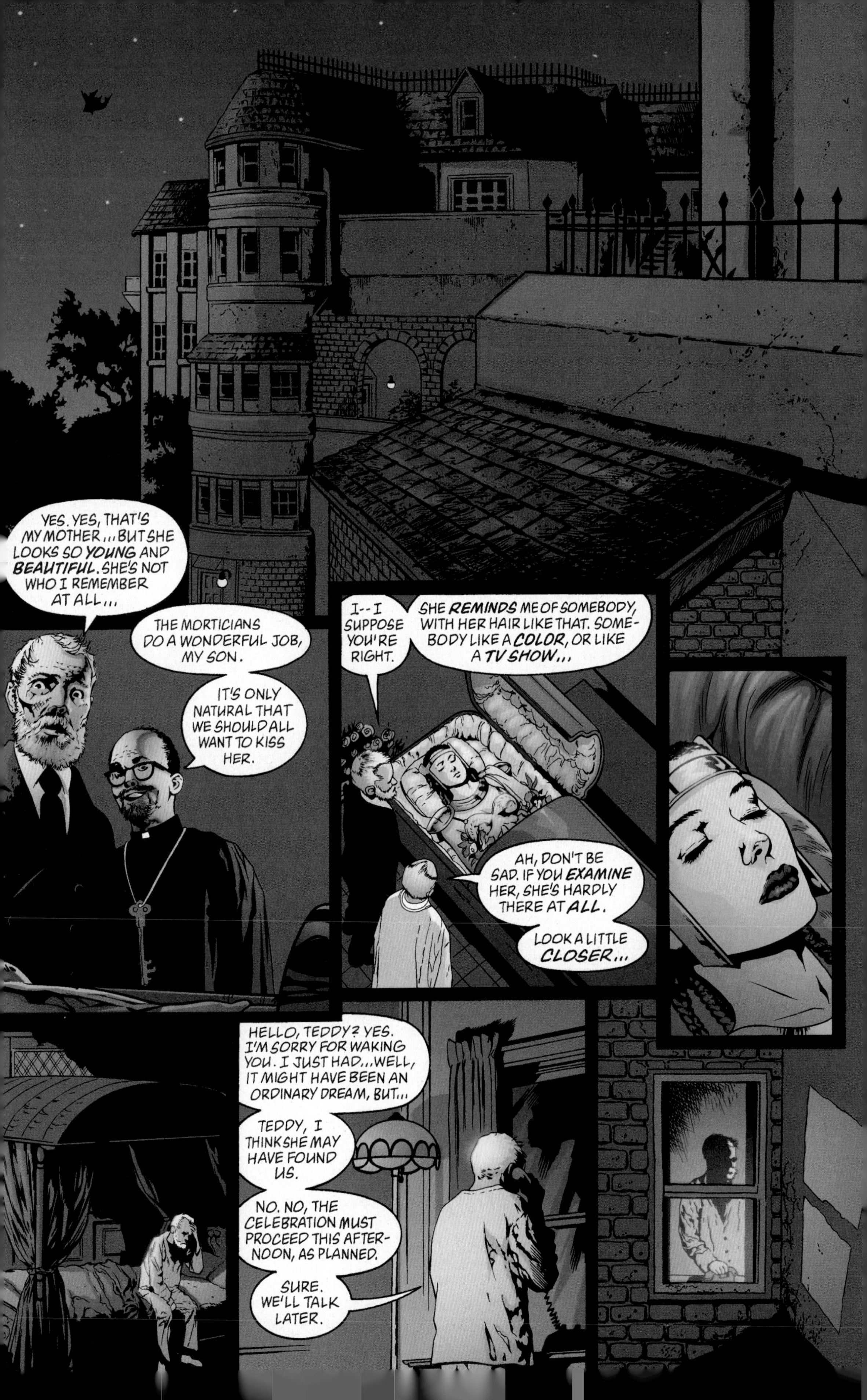
YES. YES, THAT'S MY MOTHER... BUT SHE LOOKS SO YOUNG AND BEAUTIFUL. SHE'S NOT WHO I REMEMBER AT ALL...
THE MORTICIANS DO A WONDERFUL JOB, MY SON.
IT'S ONLY NATURAL THAT WE SHOULD ALL WANT TO KISS HER.
I--I SUPPOSE YOU'RE RIGHT.
SHE REMINDS ME OF SOMEBODY, WITH HER HAIR LIKE THAT. SOMEBODY LIKE A COLOR, OR LIKE A TV SHOW...
AH, DON'T BE SAD. IF YOU EXAMINE HER, SHE'S HARDLY THERE AT ALL.
LOOK A LITTLE CLOSER...
HELLO, TEDDY? YES. I'M SORRY FOR WAKING YOU. I JUST HAD... WELL, IT MIGHT HAVE BEEN AN ORDINARY DREAM, BUT...
TEDDY, I THINK SHE MAY HAVE FOUND US.
NO. NO, THE CELEBRATION MUST PROCEED THIS AFTERNOON, AS PLANNED.
SURE. WE'LL TALK LATER.

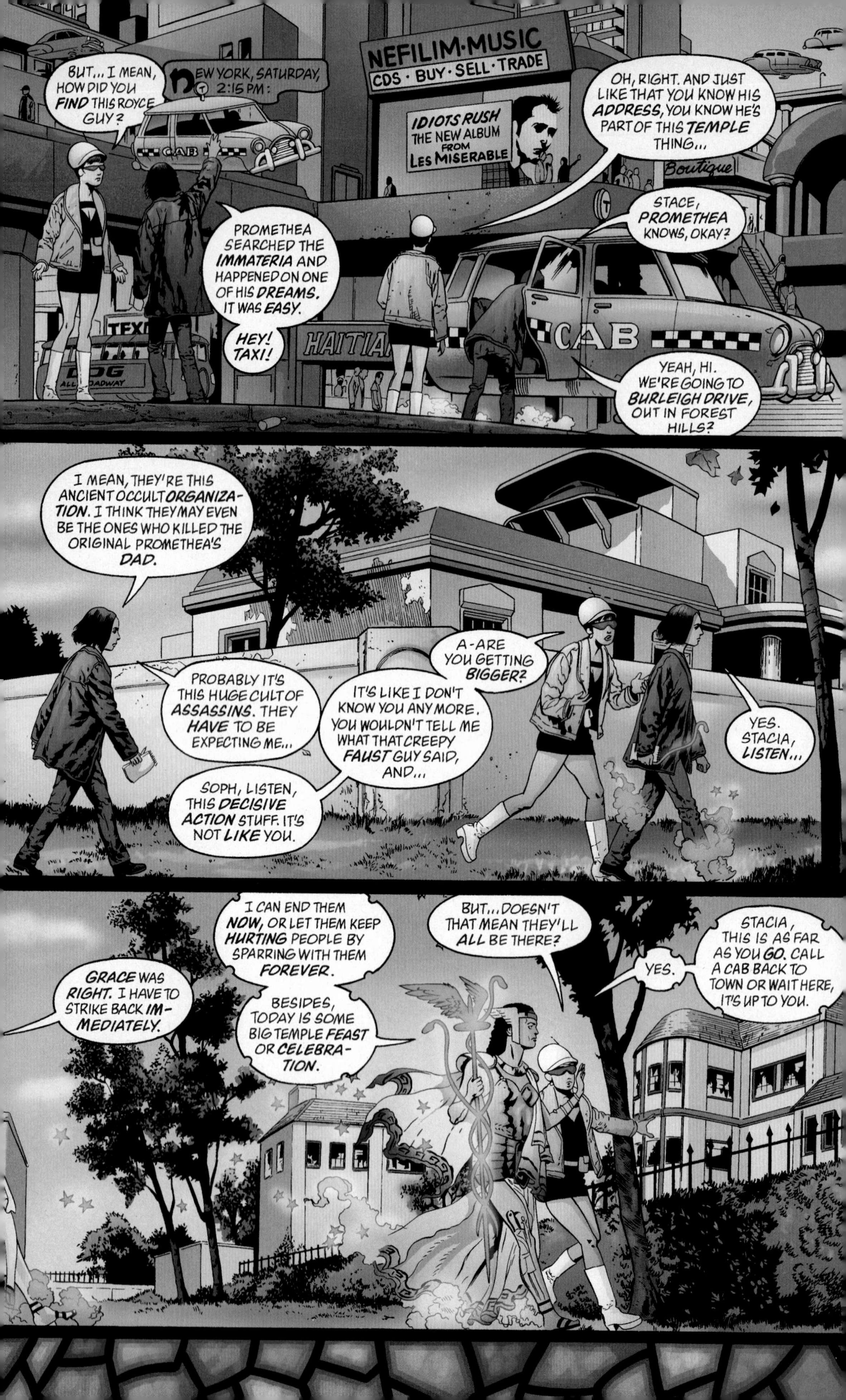
BUT... I MEAN, HOW DID YOU FIND THIS ROYCE GUY?
NEW YORK, SATURDAY, 2:15 PM:
NEFILIM·MUSIC
CDS · BUY · SELL · TRADE
IDIOTS RUSH THE NEW ALBUM FROM LES MISERABLE
OH, RIGHT. AND JUST LIKE THAT YOU KNOW HIS ADDRESS, YOU KNOW HE'S PART OF THIS TEMPLE THING...
PROMETHEA SEARCHED THE IMMATERIA AND HAPPENED ON ONE OF HIS DREAMS. IT WAS EASY.
HEY! TAXI!
Boutique
STACE, PROMETHEA KNOWS, OKAY?
CAB
YEAH, HI. WE'RE GOING TO BURLEIGH DRIVE, OUT IN FOREST HILLS?
I MEAN, THEY'RE THIS ANCIENT OCCULT ORGANIZATION. I THINK THEY MAY EVEN BE THE ONES WHO KILLED THE ORIGINAL PROMETHEA'S DAD.
PROBABLY IT'S THIS HUGE CULT OF ASSASSINS. THEY HAVE TO BE EXPECTING ME...
A-ARE YOU GETTING BIGGER?
IT'S LIKE I DON'T KNOW YOU ANY MORE. YOU WOULDN'T TELL ME WHAT THAT CREEPY FAUST GUY SAID, AND...
SOPH, LISTEN, THIS DECISIVE ACTION STUFF. IT'S NOT LIKE YOU.
YES. STACIA, LISTEN...
GRACE WAS RIGHT. I HAVE TO STRIKE BACK IMMEDIATELY.
I CAN END THEM NOW, OR LET THEM KEEP HURTING PEOPLE BY SPARRING WITH THEM FOREVER.
BESIDES, TODAY IS SOME BIG TEMPLE FEAST OR CELEBRATION.
BUT... DOESN'T THAT MEAN THEY'LL ALL BE THERE?
YES.
STACIA, THIS IS AS FAR AS YOU GO. CALL A CAB BACK TO TOWN OR WAIT HERE, IT'S UP TO YOU.

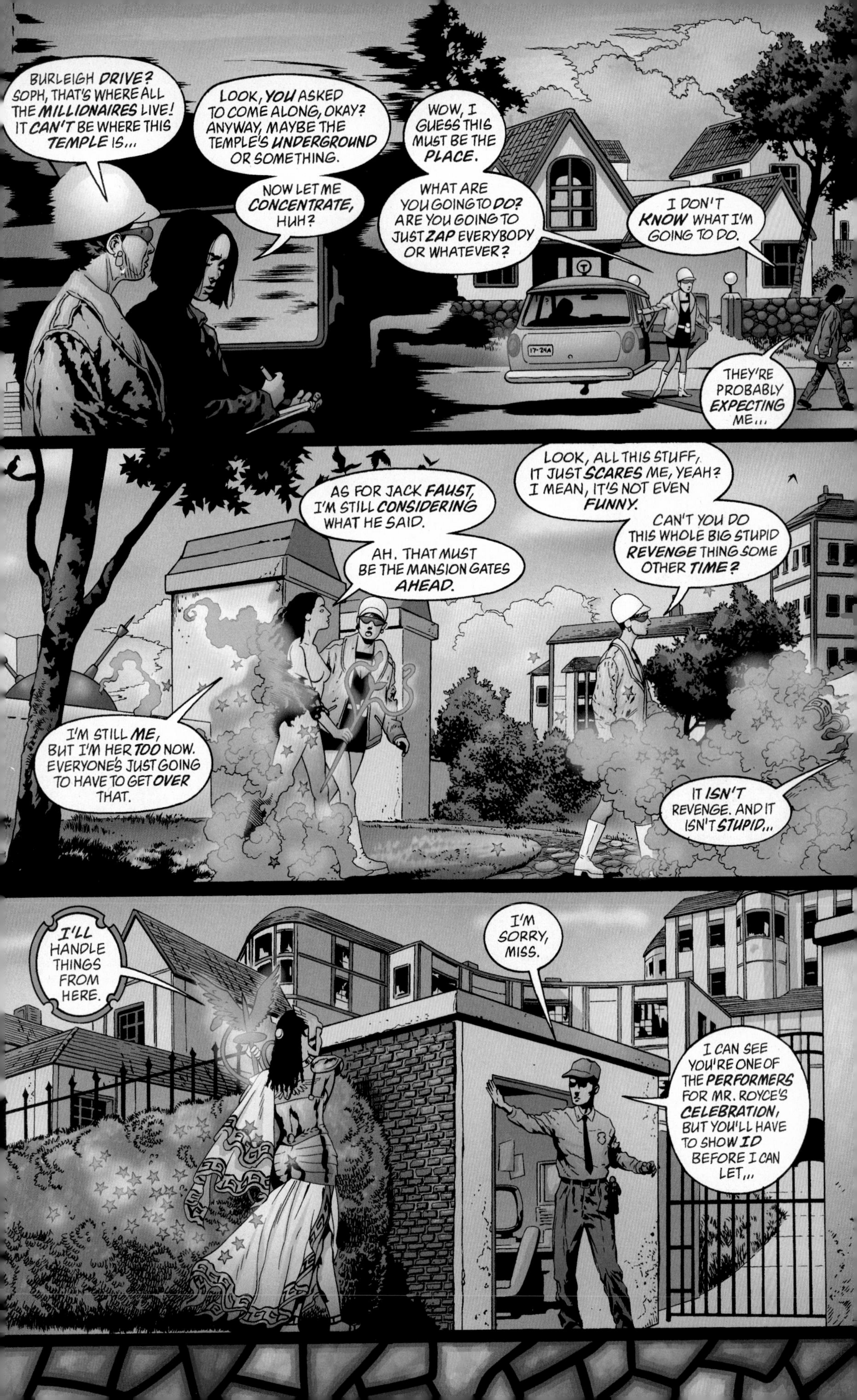
BURLEIGH DRIVE? SOPH, THAT'S WHERE ALL THE MILLIONAIRES LIVE! IT CAN'T BE WHERE THIS TEMPLE IS...
LOOK, YOU ASKED TO COME ALONG, OKAY? ANYWAY, MAYBE THE TEMPLE'S UNDERGROUND OR SOMETHING.
NOW LET ME CONCENTRATE, HUH?
WOW, I GUESS THIS MUST BE THE PLACE.
WHAT ARE YOU GOING TO DO? ARE YOU GOING TO JUST ZAP EVERYBODY OR WHATEVER?
I DON'T KNOW WHAT I'M GOING TO DO.
THEY'RE PROBABLY EXPECTING ME...
AS FOR JACK FAUST, I'M STILL CONSIDERING WHAT HE SAID.
AH. THAT MUST BE THE MANSION GATES AHEAD.
I'M STILL ME, BUT I'M HER TOO NOW. EVERYONE'S JUST GOING TO HAVE TO GET OVER THAT.
LOOK, ALL THIS STUFF, IT JUST SCARES ME, YEAH? I MEAN, IT'S NOT EVEN FUNNY.
CAN'T YOU DO THIS WHOLE BIG STUPID REVENGE THING SOME OTHER TIME?
IT ISN'T REVENGE. AND IT ISN'T STUPID...
I'LL HANDLE THINGS FROM HERE.
I'M SORRY, MISS.
I CAN SEE YOU'RE ONE OF THE PERFORMERS FOR MR. ROYCE'S CELEBRATION, BUT YOU'LL HAVE TO SHOW ID BEFORE I CAN LET...

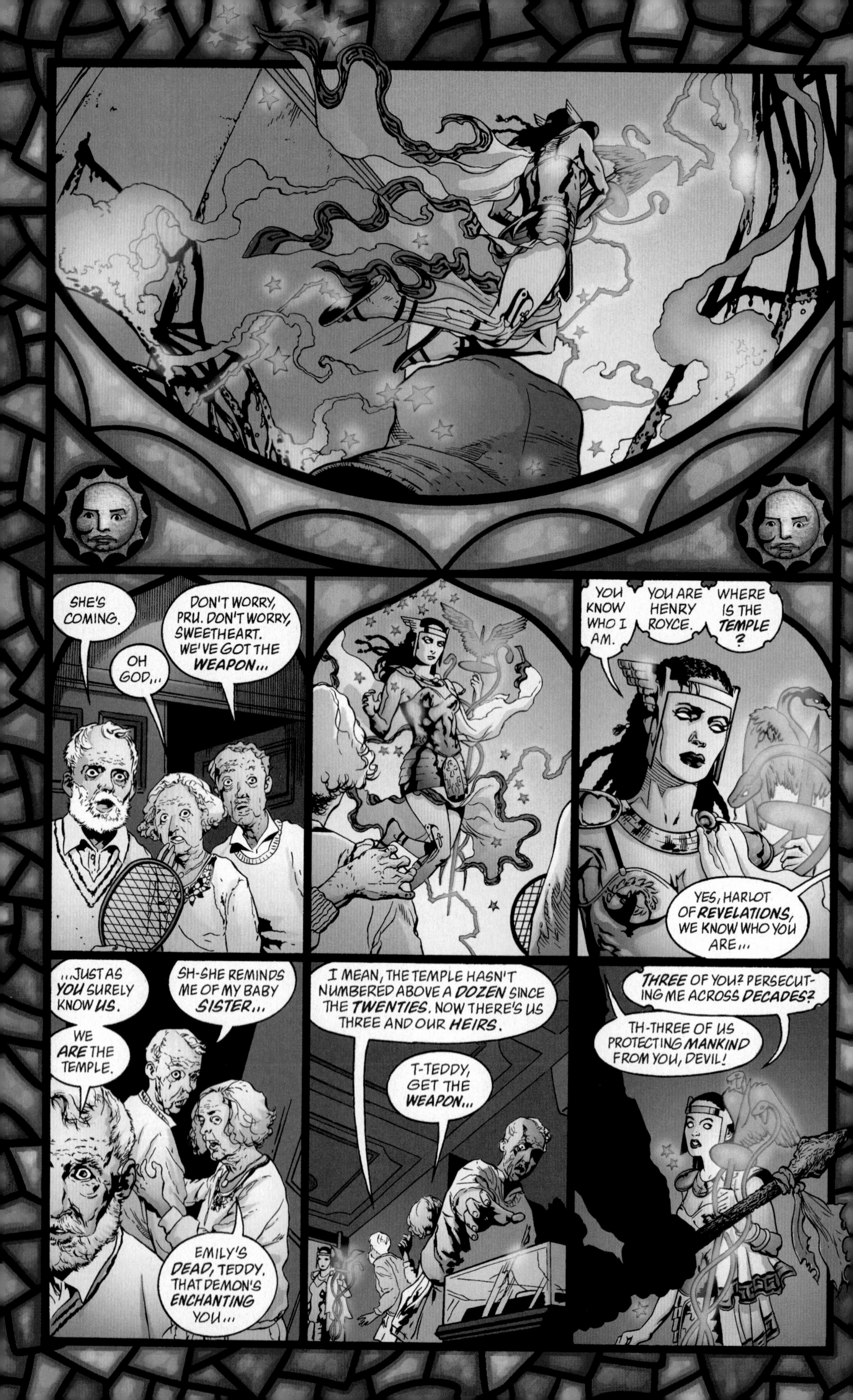
SHE'S COMING.
OH GOD,...
DON'T WORRY, PRU. DON'T WORRY, SWEETHEART. WE'VE GOT THE WEAPON...
YOU KNOW WHO I AM.
YOU ARE HENRY ROYCE.
WHERE IS THE TEMPLE?
YES, HARLOT OF REVELATIONS, WE KNOW WHO YOU ARE...
...JUST AS YOU SURELY KNOW US.
WE ARE THE TEMPLE.
SH-SHE REMINDS ME OF MY BABY SISTER...
EMILY'S DEAD, TEDDY. THAT DEMON'S ENCHANTING YOU...
I MEAN, THE TEMPLE HASN'T NUMBERED ABOVE A DOZEN SINCE THE TWENTIES. NOW THERE'S US THREE AND OUR HEIRS.
T-TEDDY, GET THE WEAPON...
THREE OF YOU? PERSECUTING ME ACROSS DECADES?
TH-THREE OF US PROTECTING MANKIND FROM YOU, DEVIL!

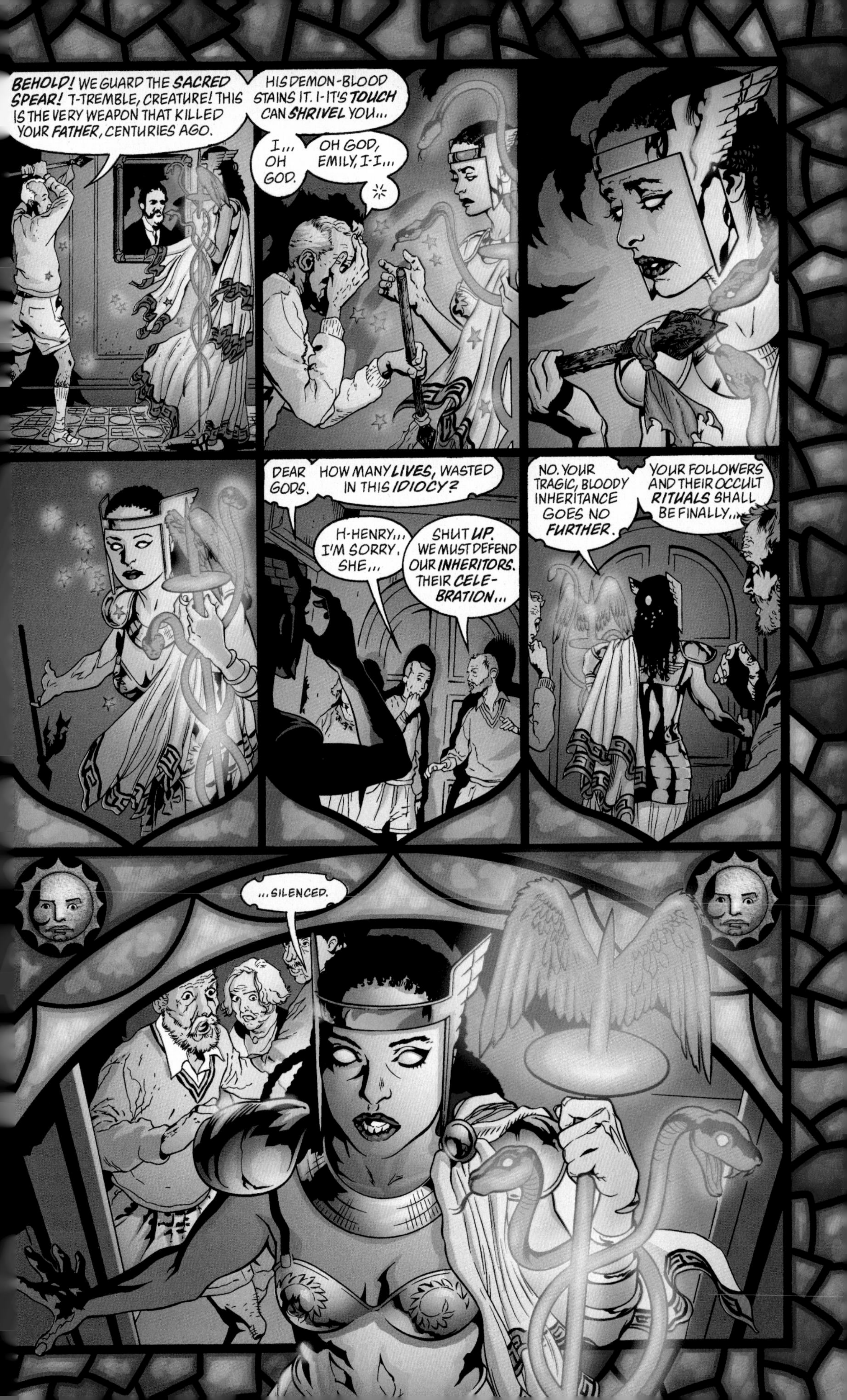

BEHOLD! WE GUARD THE SACRED SPEAR! T-TREMBLE, CREATURE! THIS IS THE VERY WEAPON THAT KILLED YOUR FATHER, CENTURIES AGO.
HIS DEMON-BLOOD STAINS IT. I-IT'S TOUCH CAN SHRIVEL YOU...
I,,, OH GOD.
OH GOD, EMILY, I-I,,,
DEAR GODS.
HOW MANY LIVES, WASTED IN THIS IDIOCY?
H-HENRY,,, I'M SORRY, SHE,,,
SHUT UP. WE MUST DEFEND OUR INHERITORS. THEIR CELE-BRATION...
NO. YOUR TRAGIC, BLOODY INHERITANCE GOES NO FURTHER.
YOUR FOLLOWERS AND THEIR OCCULT RITUALS SHALL BE FINALLY...
...SILENCED.

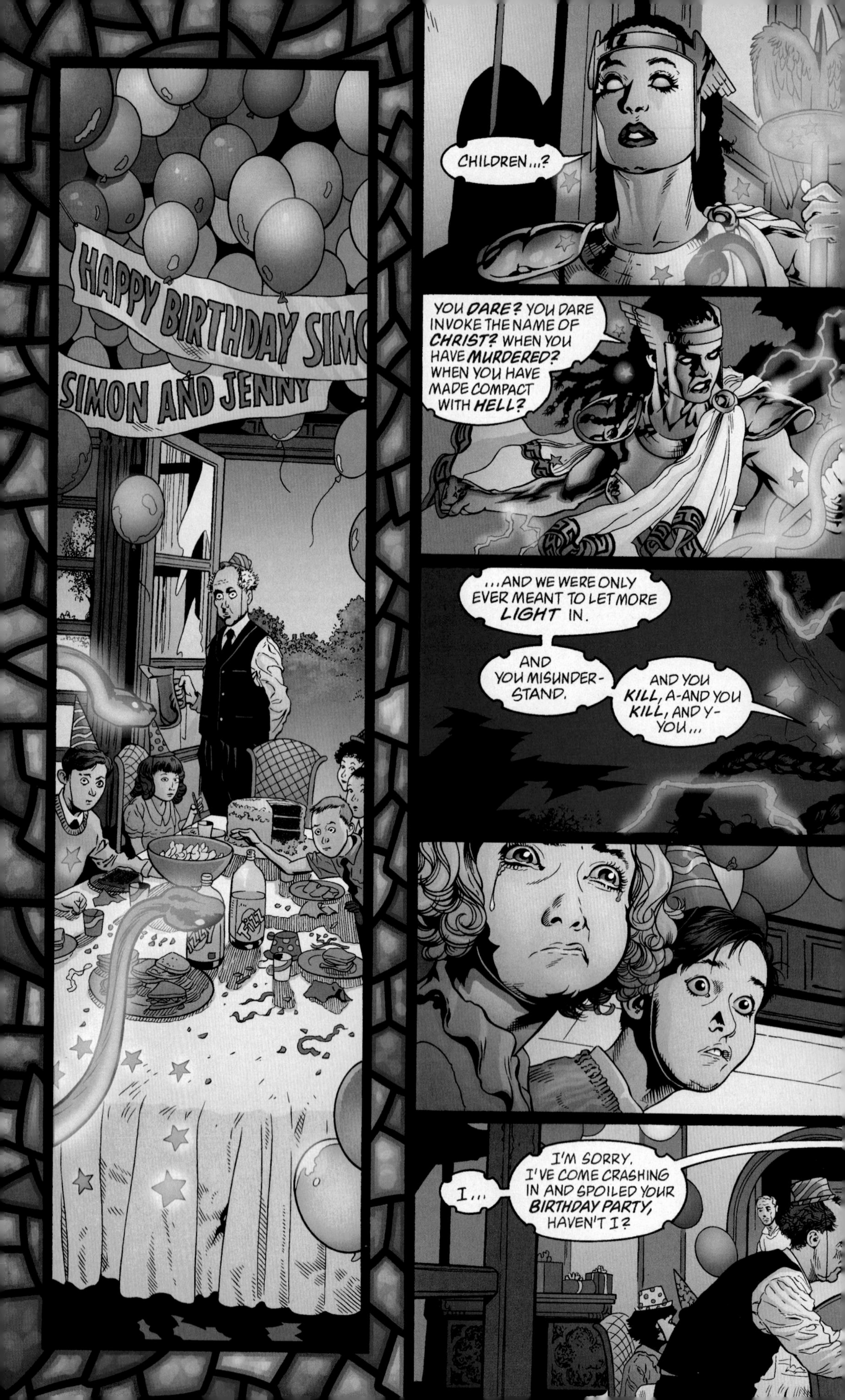
HAPPY BIRTHDAY SIMO
SIMON AND JENNY
FIZZ
CHILDREN...?
YOU DARE? YOU DARE INVOKE THE NAME OF CHRIST? WHEN YOU HAVE MURDERED? WHEN YOU HAVE MADE COMPACT WITH HELL?
...AND WE WERE ONLY EVER MEANT TO LET MORE LIGHT IN.
AND YOU MISUNDER-STAND.
AND YOU KILL, A-AND YOU KILL, AND Y-YOU...
I...
I'M SORRY. I'VE COME CRASHING IN AND SPOILED YOUR BIRTHDAY PARTY, HAVEN'T I?

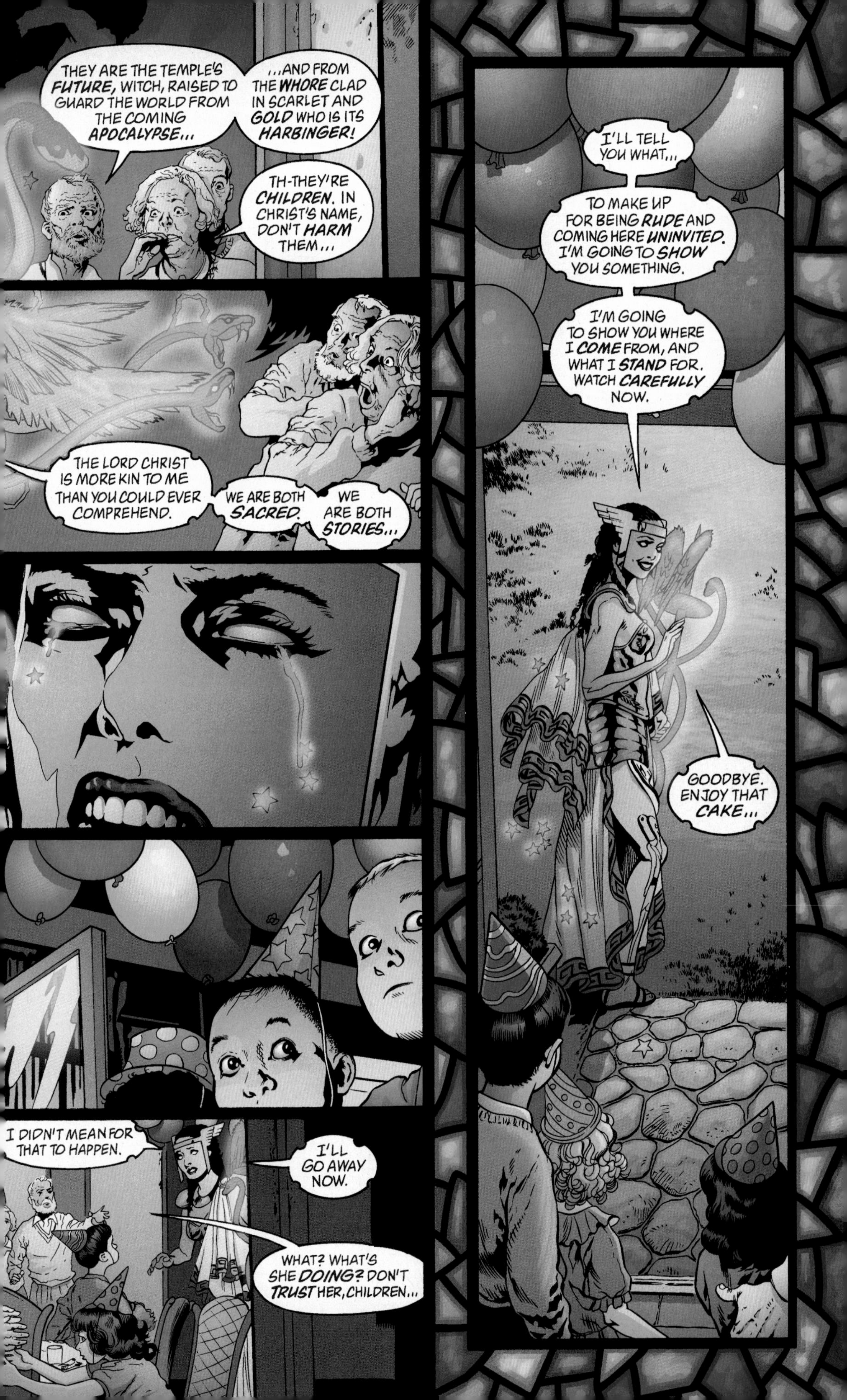
THEY ARE THE TEMPLE'S FUTURE, WITCH, RAISED TO GUARD THE WORLD FROM THE COMING APOCALYPSE...
...AND FROM THE WHORE CLAD IN SCARLET AND GOLD WHO IS ITS HARBINGER!
TH-THEY'RE CHILDREN. IN CHRIST'S NAME, DON'T HARM THEM...
THE LORD CHRIST IS MORE KIN TO ME THAN YOU COULD EVER COMPREHEND.
WE ARE BOTH SACRED.
WE ARE BOTH STORIES...
I DIDN'T MEAN FOR THAT TO HAPPEN.
I'LL GO AWAY NOW.
WHAT? WHAT'S SHE DOING? DON'T TRUST HER, CHILDREN...
I'LL TELL YOU WHAT...
TO MAKE UP FOR BEING RUDE AND COMING HERE UNINVITED, I'M GOING TO SHOW YOU SOMETHING.
I'M GOING TO SHOW YOU WHERE I COME FROM, AND WHAT I STAND FOR. WATCH CAREFULLY NOW.
GOODBYE. ENJOY THAT CAKE...

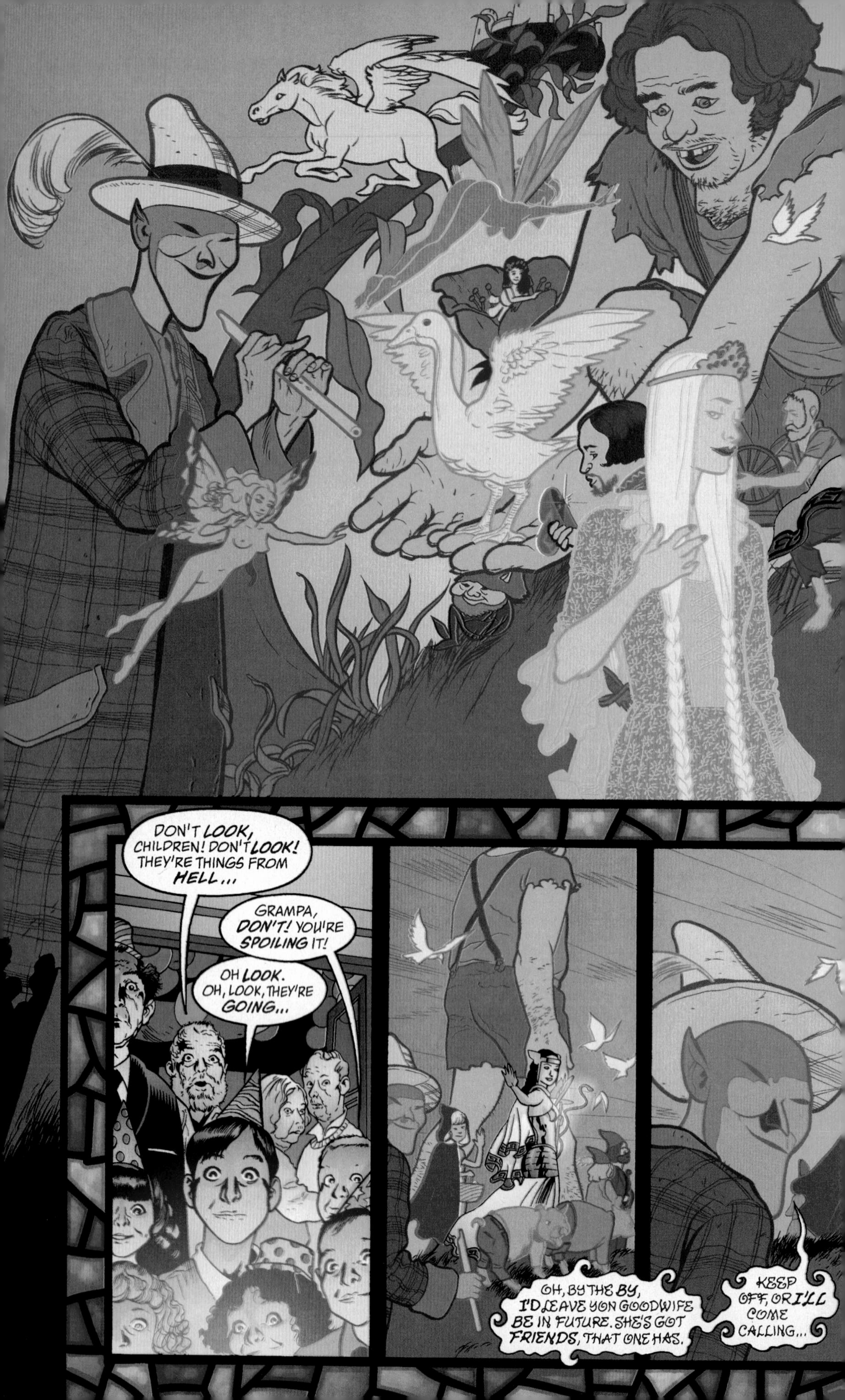

DON'T LOOK, CHILDREN! DON'T LOOK! THEY'RE THINGS FROM HELL...
GRAMPA, DON'T! YOU'RE SPOILING IT!
OH LOOK. OH, LOOK, THEY'RE GOING...
OH, BY THE BY, I'D LEAVE YON GOODWIFE BE IN FUTURE. SHE'S GOT FRIENDS, THAT ONE HAS.
KEEP OFF, OR I'LL COME CALLING...

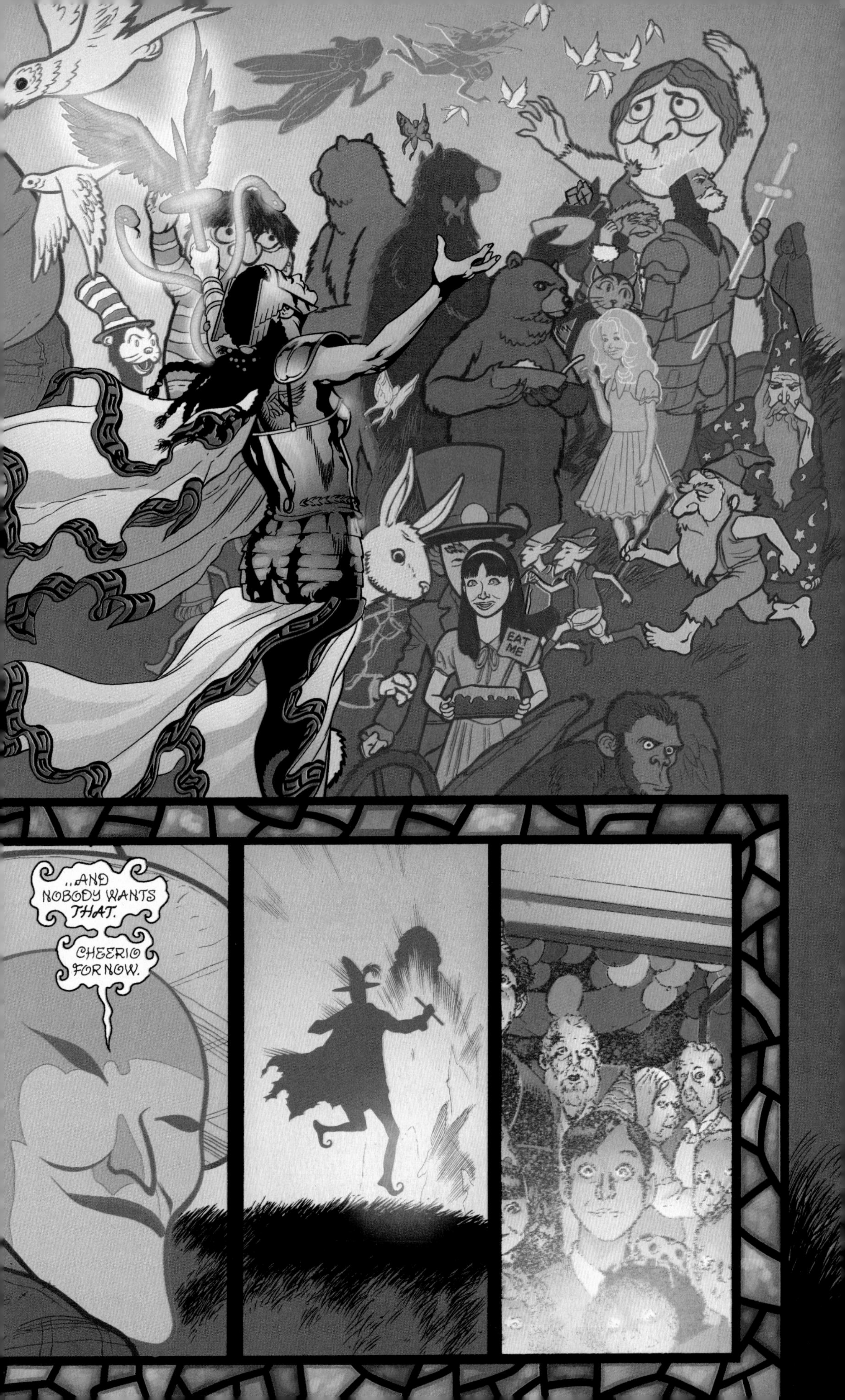
EAT ME
...AND NOBODY WANTS THAT.
CHEERIO FOR NOW.

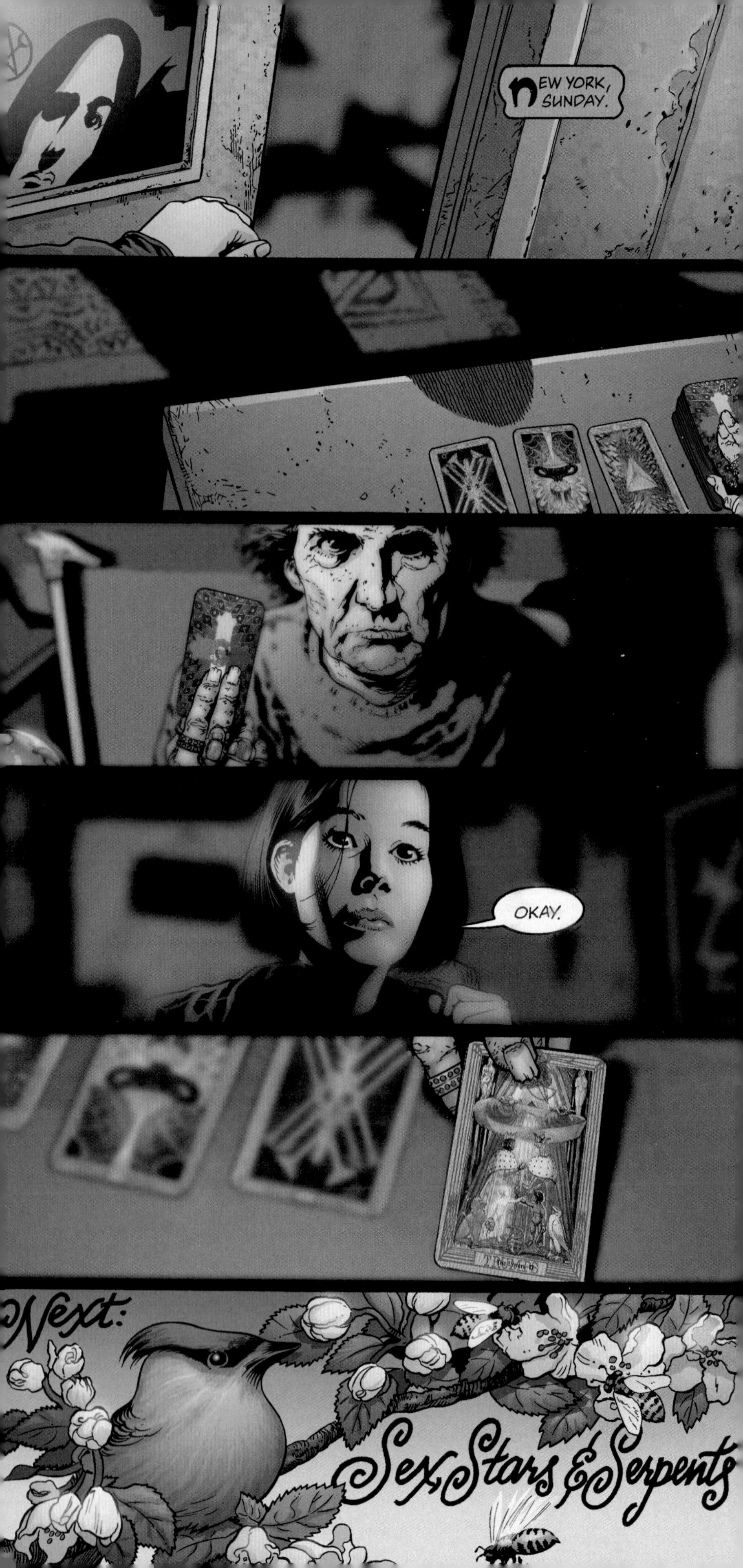
NEW YORK, SUNDAY.
OKAY.
Next: Sex, Stars & Serpents

CHAPTER FOUR

With naught to hide, Promethea's learning moves inside.

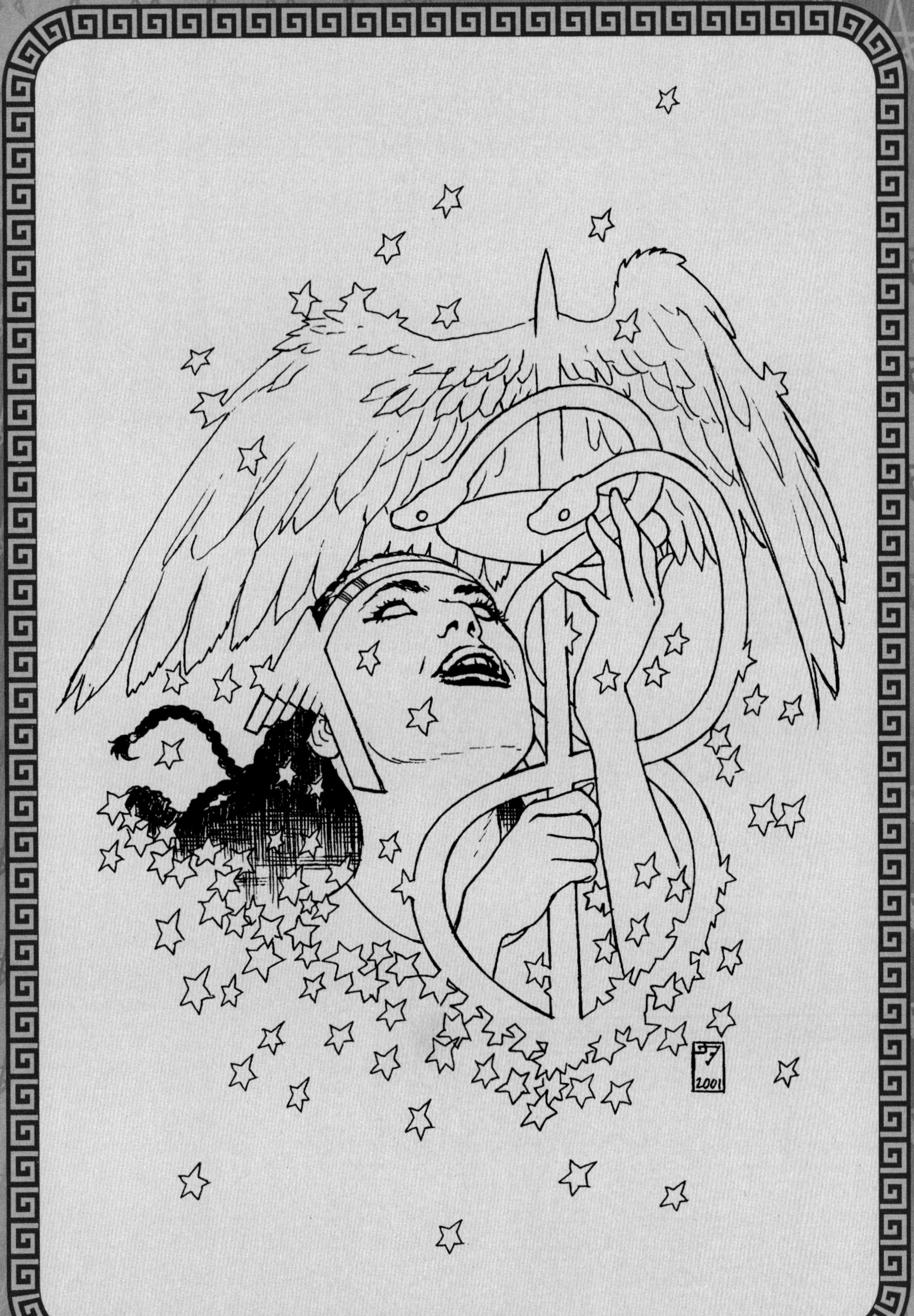

Cover art: J.H. Williams III, Mick Gray & Jeromy Cox

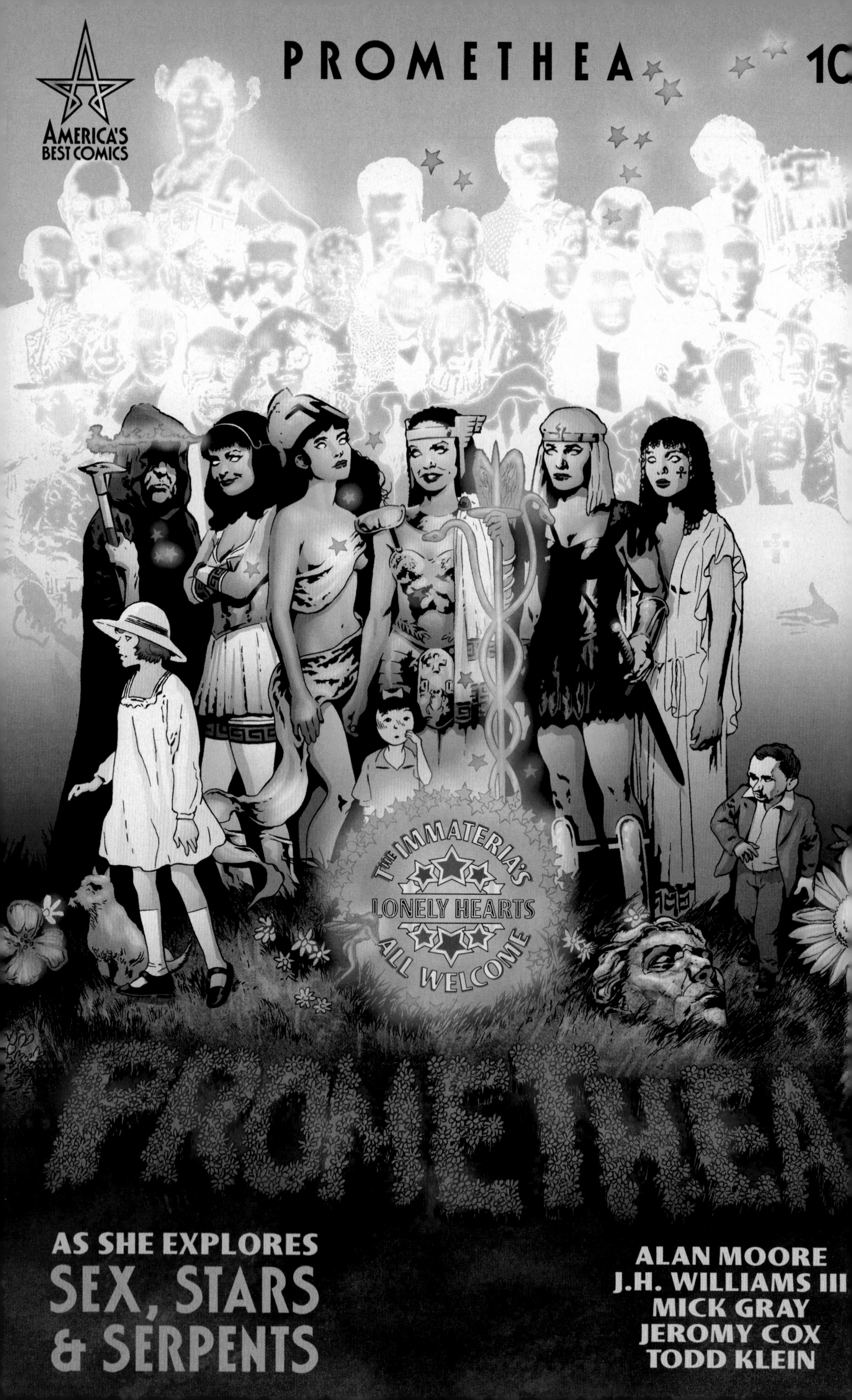
AMERICA'S BEST COMICS
PROMETHEA
10
THE IMMATERIA'S
LONELY HEARTS
ALL WELCOME
PROMETHEA
AS SHE EXPLORES
SEX, STARS
& SERPENTS
ALAN MOORE
J.H. WILLIAMS III
MICK GRAY
JEROMY COX
TODD KLEIN

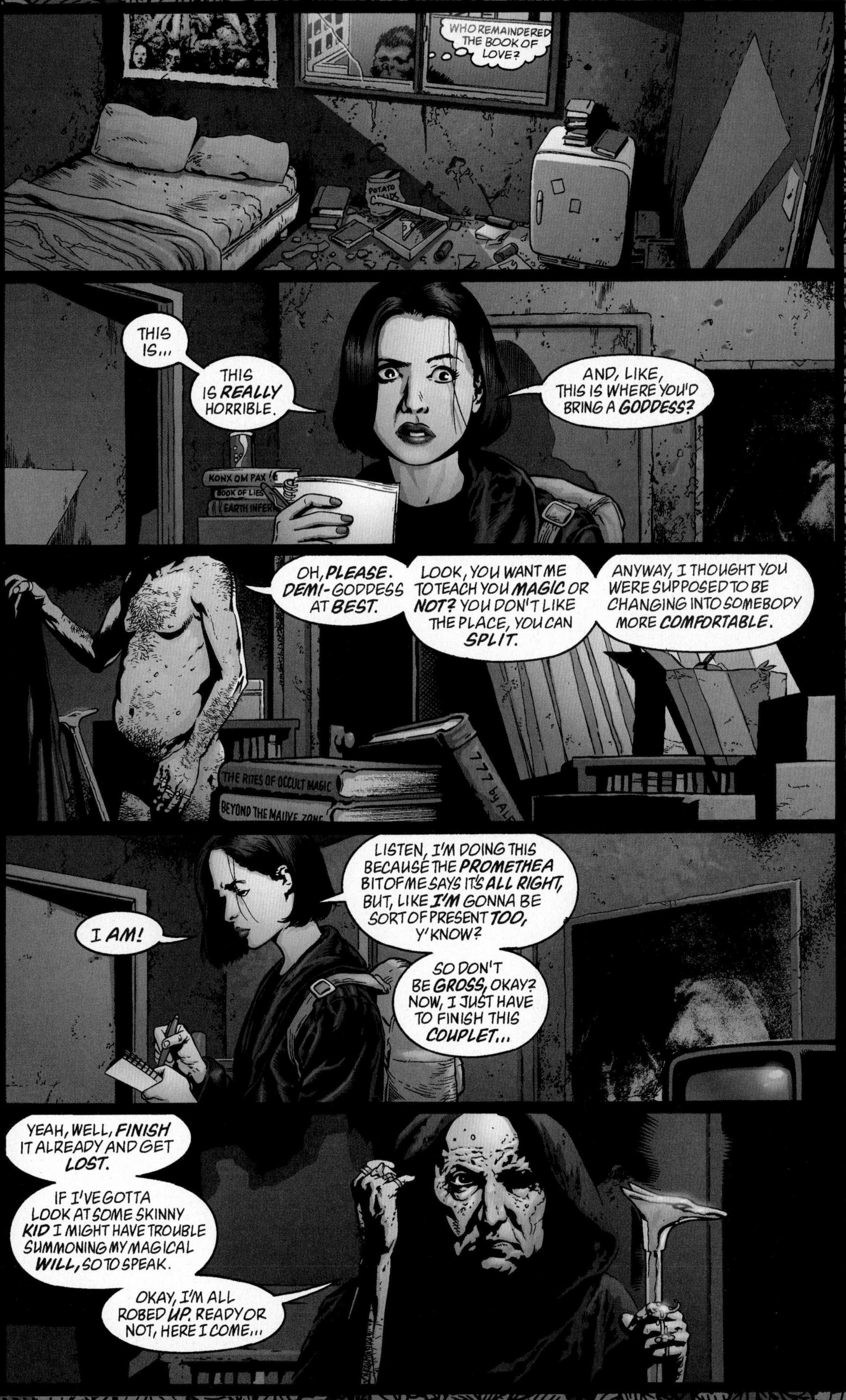
WHO REMAINDERED THE BOOK OF LOVE?
POTATO CHIPS
THIS IS...
THIS IS REALLY HORRIBLE.
AND, LIKE, THIS IS WHERE YOU'D BRING A GODDESS?
KONX OM PAX
BOOK OF LIES
EARTH INFER
OH, PLEASE. DEMI-GODDESS AT BEST.
LOOK, YOU WANT ME TO TEACH YOU MAGIC OR NOT? YOU DON'T LIKE THE PLACE, YOU CAN SPLIT.
ANYWAY, I THOUGHT YOU WERE SUPPOSED TO BE CHANGING INTO SOMEBODY MORE COMFORTABLE.
THE RITES OF OCCULT MAGIC
BEYOND THE MAUVE ZONE
777 by AL
I AM!
LISTEN, I'M DOING THIS BECAUSE THE PROMETHEA BIT OF ME SAYS IT'S ALL RIGHT, BUT, LIKE I'M GONNA BE SORT OF PRESENT TOO, Y'KNOW?
SO DON'T BE GROSS, OKAY? NOW, I JUST HAVE TO FINISH THIS COUPLET...
YEAH, WELL, FINISH IT ALREADY AND GET LOST.
IF I'VE GOTTA LOOK AT SOME SKINNY KID I MIGHT HAVE TROUBLE SUMMONING MY MAGICAL WILL, SO TO SPEAK.
OKAY, I'M ALL ROBED UP. READY OR NOT, HERE I COME...

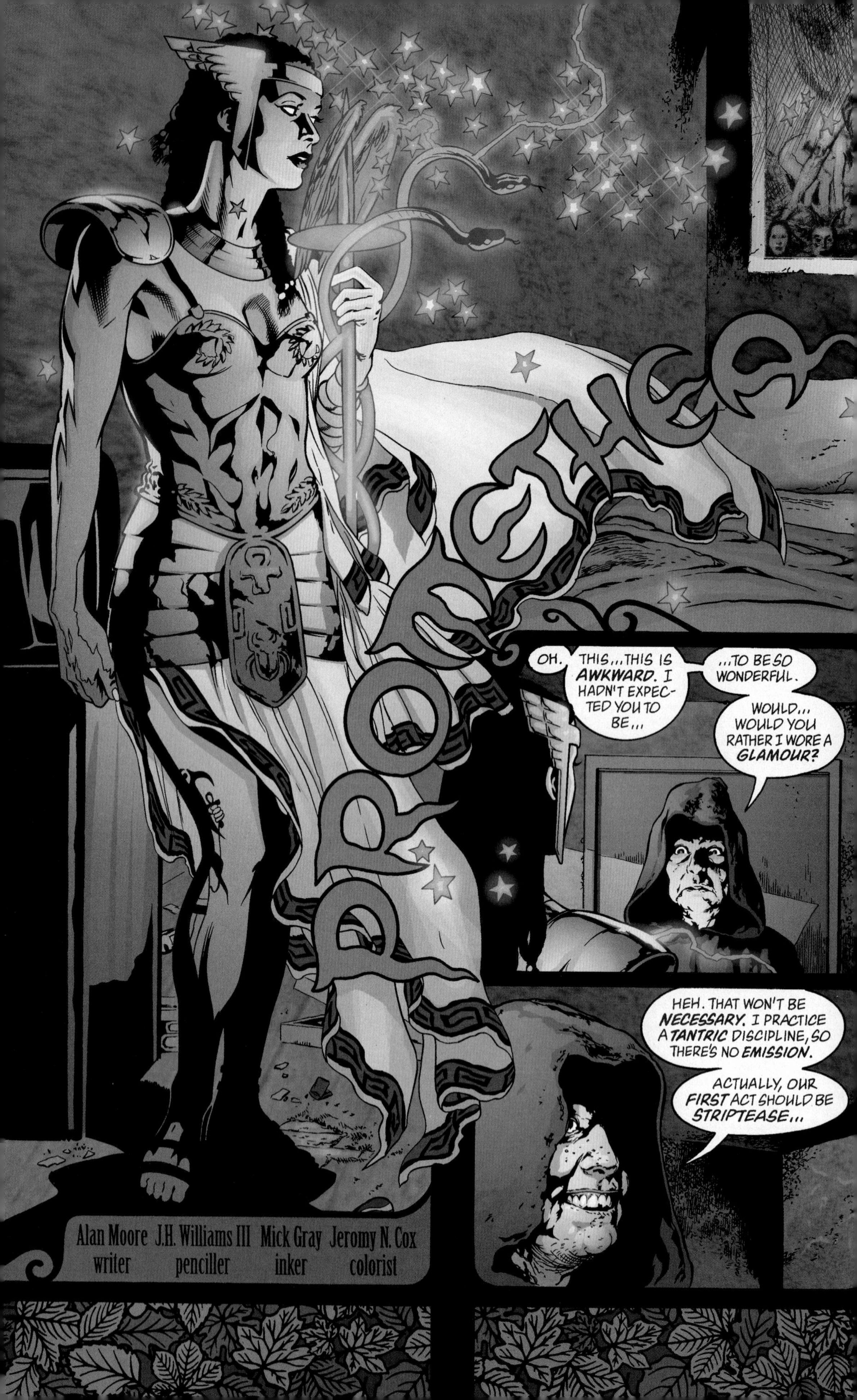
PROMETHEA
OH.
THIS... THIS IS AWKWARD. I HADN'T EXPECTED YOU TO BE...
...TO BE SO WONDERFUL.
WOULD... WOULD YOU RATHER I WORE A GLAMOUR?
HEH. THAT WON'T BE NECESSARY. I PRACTICE A TANTRIC DISCIPLINE, SO THERE'S NO EMISSION.
ACTUALLY, OUR FIRST ACT SHOULD BE STRIPTEASE...
Alan Moore writer
J.H. Williams III penciller
Mick Gray inker
Jeromy N. Cox colorist

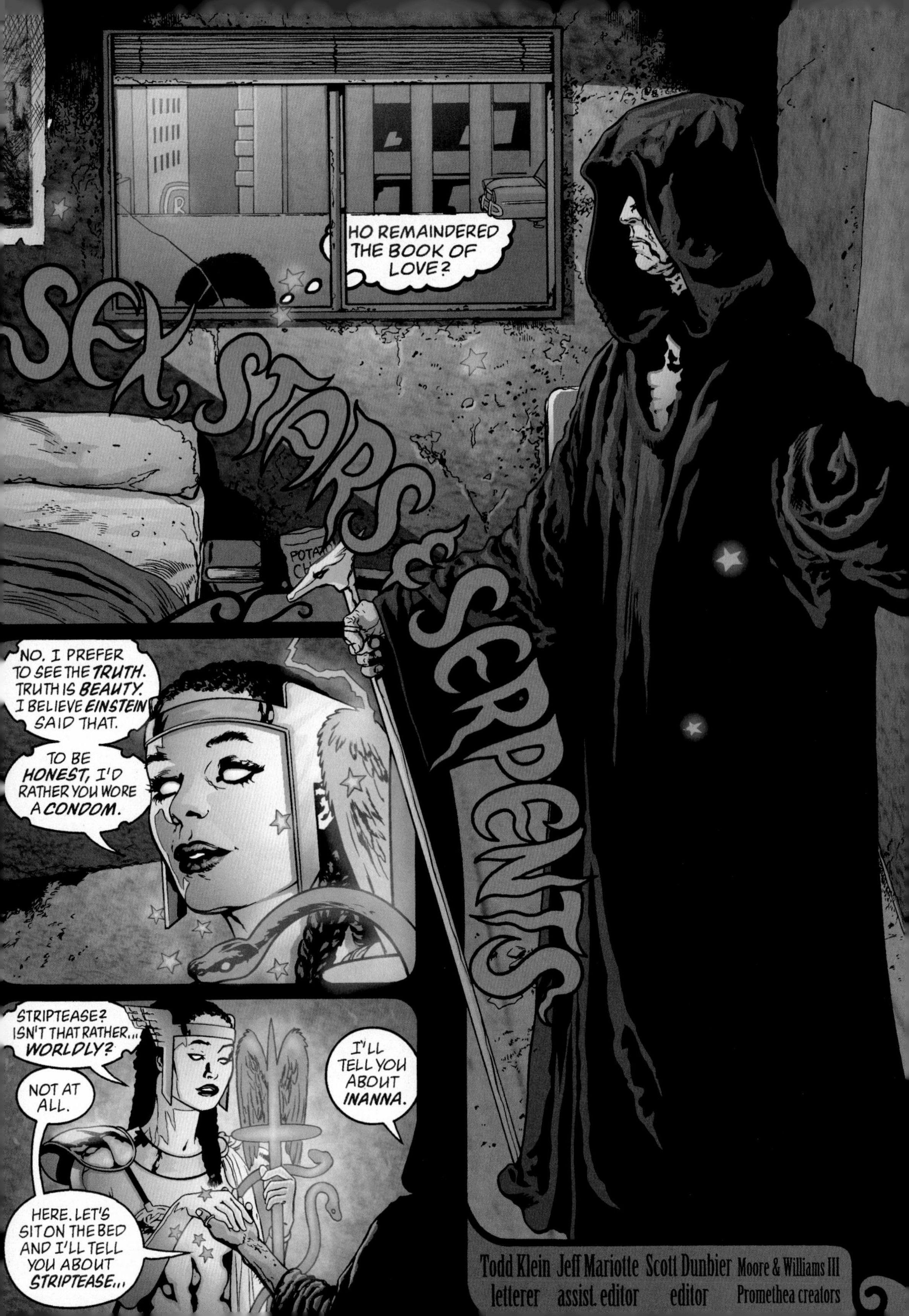

HO REMAINDERED THE BOOK OF LOVE?
SEX, STARS & SERPENTS
NO. I PREFER TO SEE THE TRUTH. TRUTH IS BEAUTY. I BELIEVE EINSTEIN SAID THAT.
TO BE HONEST, I'D RATHER YOU WORE A CONDOM.
STRIPTEASE? ISN'T THAT RATHER... WORLDLY?
NOT AT ALL.
I'LL TELL YOU ABOUT INANNA.
HERE. LET'S SIT ON THE BED AND I'LL TELL YOU ABOUT STRIPTEASE...
Todd Klein letterer
Jeff Mariotte assist. editor
Scott Dunbier editor
Moore & Williams III Promethea creators

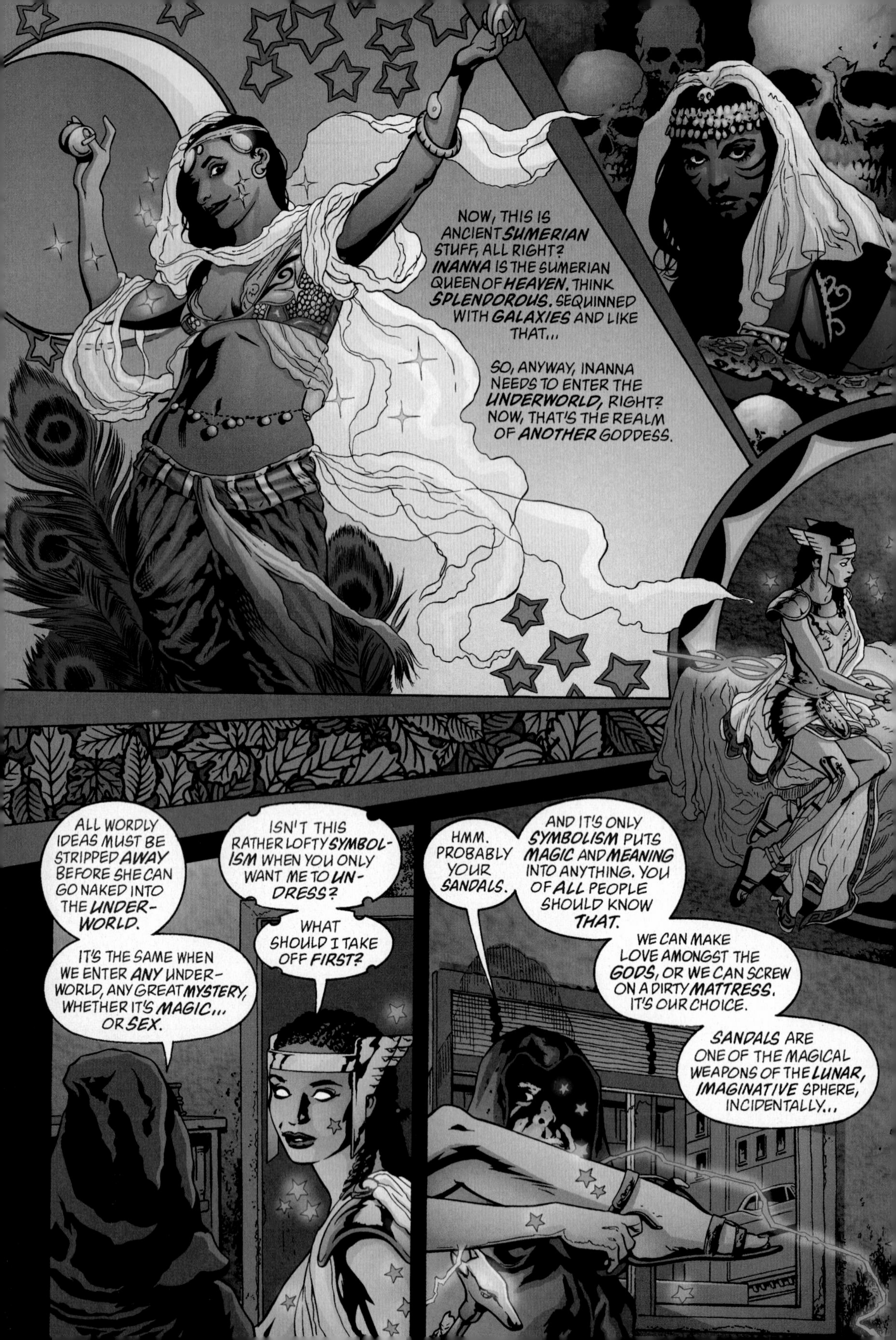
NOW, THIS IS ANCIENT SUMERIAN STUFF, ALL RIGHT? INANNA IS THE SUMERIAN QUEEN OF HEAVEN. THINK SPLENDOROUS. SEQUINNED WITH GALAXIES AND LIKE THAT...
SO, ANYWAY, INANNA NEEDS TO ENTER THE UNDERWORLD, RIGHT? NOW, THAT'S THE REALM OF ANOTHER GODDESS.
ALL WORDLY IDEAS MUST BE STRIPPED AWAY BEFORE SHE CAN GO NAKED INTO THE UNDER-WORLD.
IT'S THE SAME WHEN WE ENTER ANY UNDER-WORLD, ANY GREAT MYSTERY, WHETHER IT'S MAGIC... OR SEX.
ISN'T THIS RATHER LOFTY SYMBOL-ISM WHEN YOU ONLY WANT ME TO UN-DRESS?
WHAT SHOULD I TAKE OFF FIRST?
HMM. PROBABLY YOUR SANDALS.
AND IT'S ONLY SYMBOLISM PUTS MAGIC AND MEANING INTO ANYTHING. YOU OF ALL PEOPLE SHOULD KNOW THAT.
WE CAN MAKE LOVE AMONGST THE GODS, OR WE CAN SCREW ON A DIRTY MATTRESS. IT'S OUR CHOICE.
SANDALS ARE ONE OF THE MAGICAL WEAPONS OF THE LUNAR, IMAGINATIVE SPHERE, INCIDENTALLY...

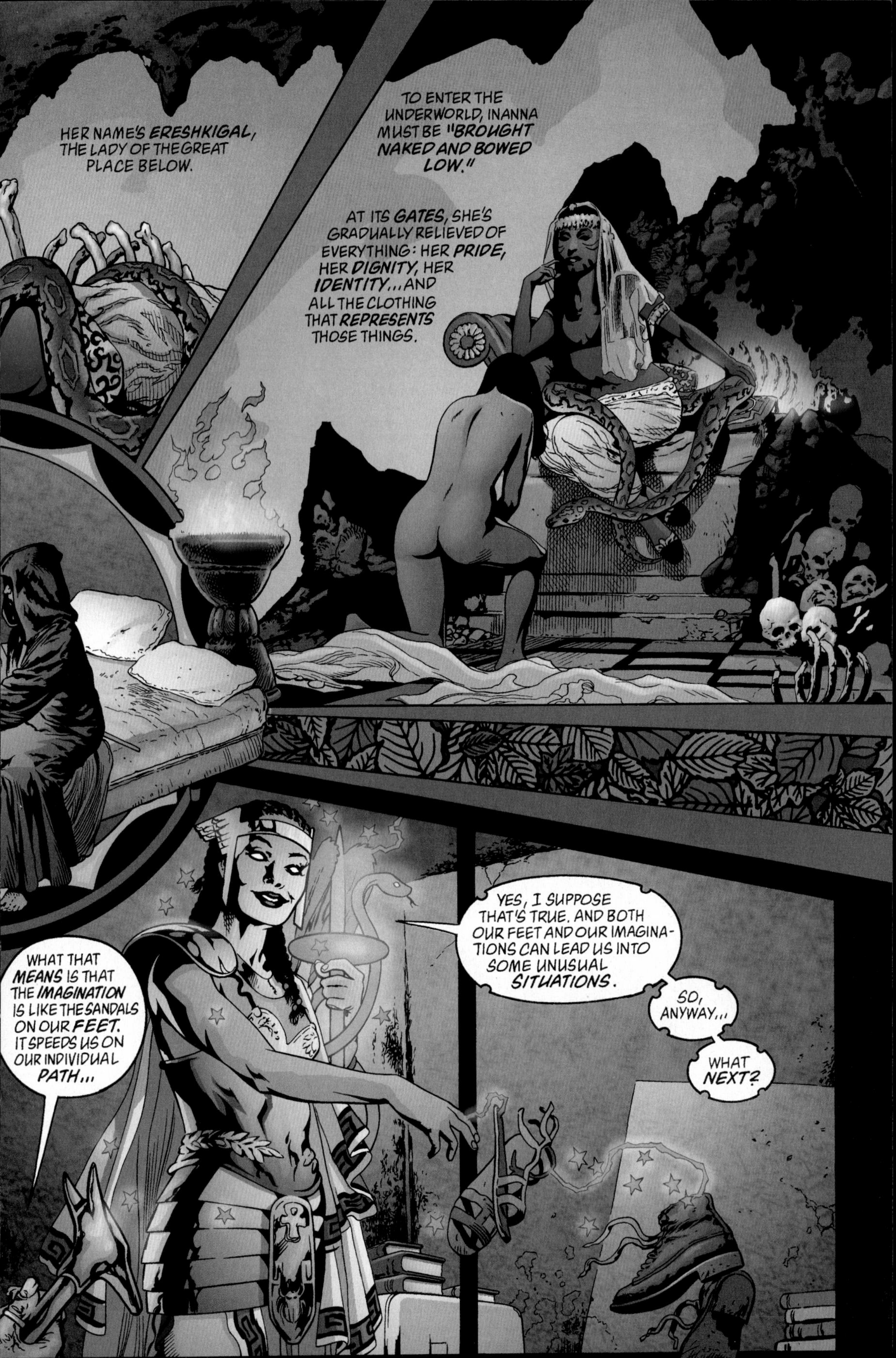

HER NAME'S ERESHKIGAL, THE LADY OF THE GREAT PLACE BELOW.
TO ENTER THE UNDERWORLD, INANNA MUST BE "BROUGHT NAKED AND BOWED LOW."
AT ITS GATES, SHE'S GRADUALLY RELIEVED OF EVERYTHING: HER PRIDE, HER DIGNITY, HER IDENTITY... AND ALL THE CLOTHING THAT REPRESENTS THOSE THINGS.
WHAT THAT MEANS IS THAT THE IMAGINATION IS LIKE THE SANDALS ON OUR FEET. IT SPEEDS US ON OUR INDIVIDUAL PATH...
YES, I SUPPOSE THAT'S TRUE. AND BOTH OUR FEET AND OUR IMAGINATIONS CAN LEAD US INTO SOME UNUSUAL SITUATIONS.
SO, ANYWAY...
WHAT NEXT?

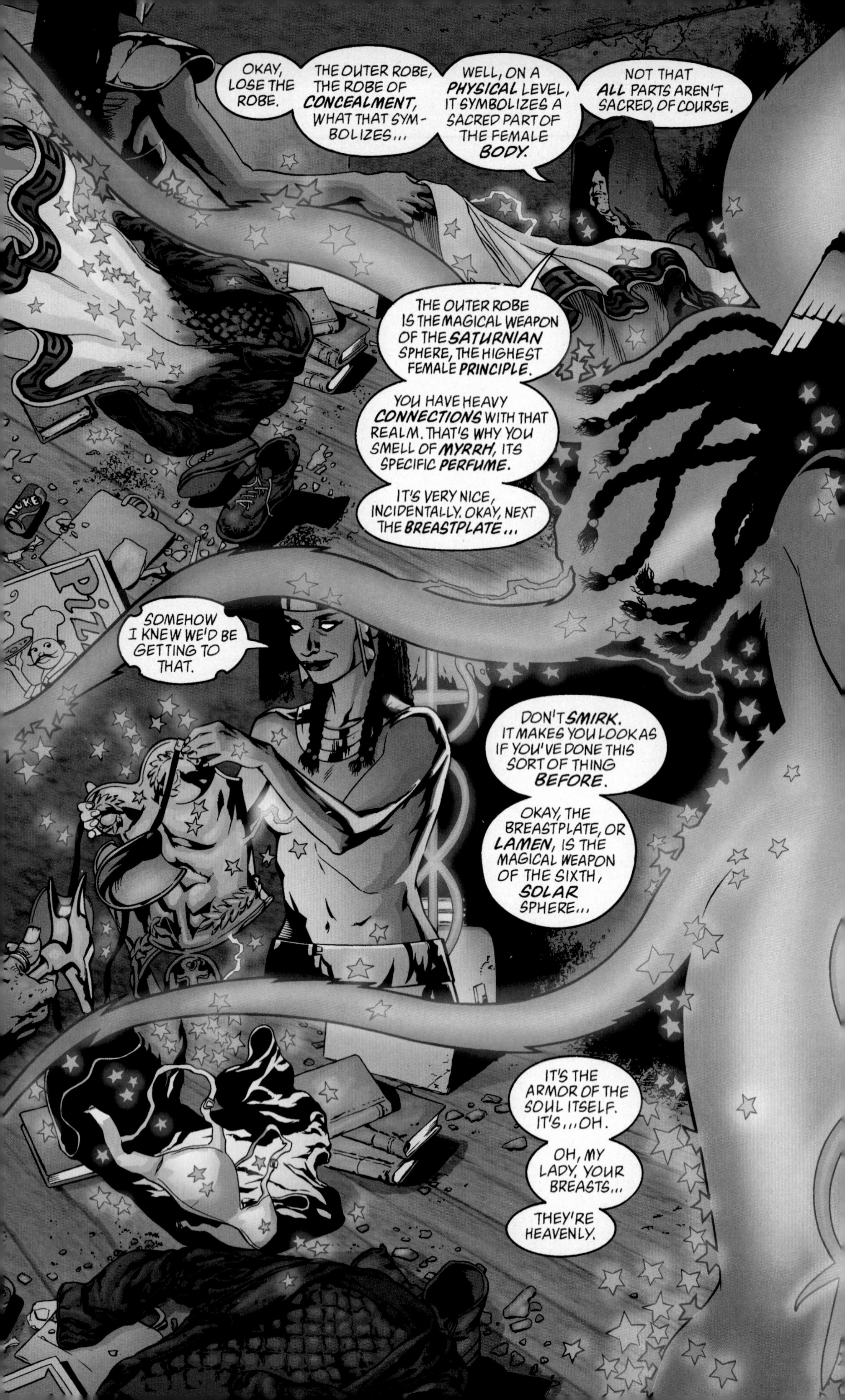
OKAY, LOSE THE ROBE.
THE OUTER ROBE, THE ROBE OF CONCEALMENT, WHAT THAT SYMBOLIZES...
WELL, ON A PHYSICAL LEVEL, IT SYMBOLIZES A SACRED PART OF THE FEMALE BODY.
NOT THAT ALL PARTS AREN'T SACRED, OF COURSE.
THE OUTER ROBE IS THE MAGICAL WEAPON OF THE SATURNIAN SPHERE, THE HIGHEST FEMALE PRINCIPLE.
YOU HAVE HEAVY CONNECTIONS WITH THAT REALM. THAT'S WHY YOU SMELL OF MYRRH, ITS SPECIFIC PERFUME.
IT'S VERY NICE, INCIDENTALLY. OKAY, NEXT THE BREASTPLATE...
SOMEHOW I KNEW WE'D BE GETTING TO THAT.
DON'T SMIRK. IT MAKES YOU LOOK AS IF YOU'VE DONE THIS SORT OF THING BEFORE.
OKAY, THE BREASTPLATE, OR LAMEN, IS THE MAGICAL WEAPON OF THE SIXTH, SOLAR SPHERE...
IT'S THE ARMOR OF THE SOUL ITSELF. IT'S...OH.
OH, MY LADY, YOUR BREASTS...
THEY'RE HEAVENLY.

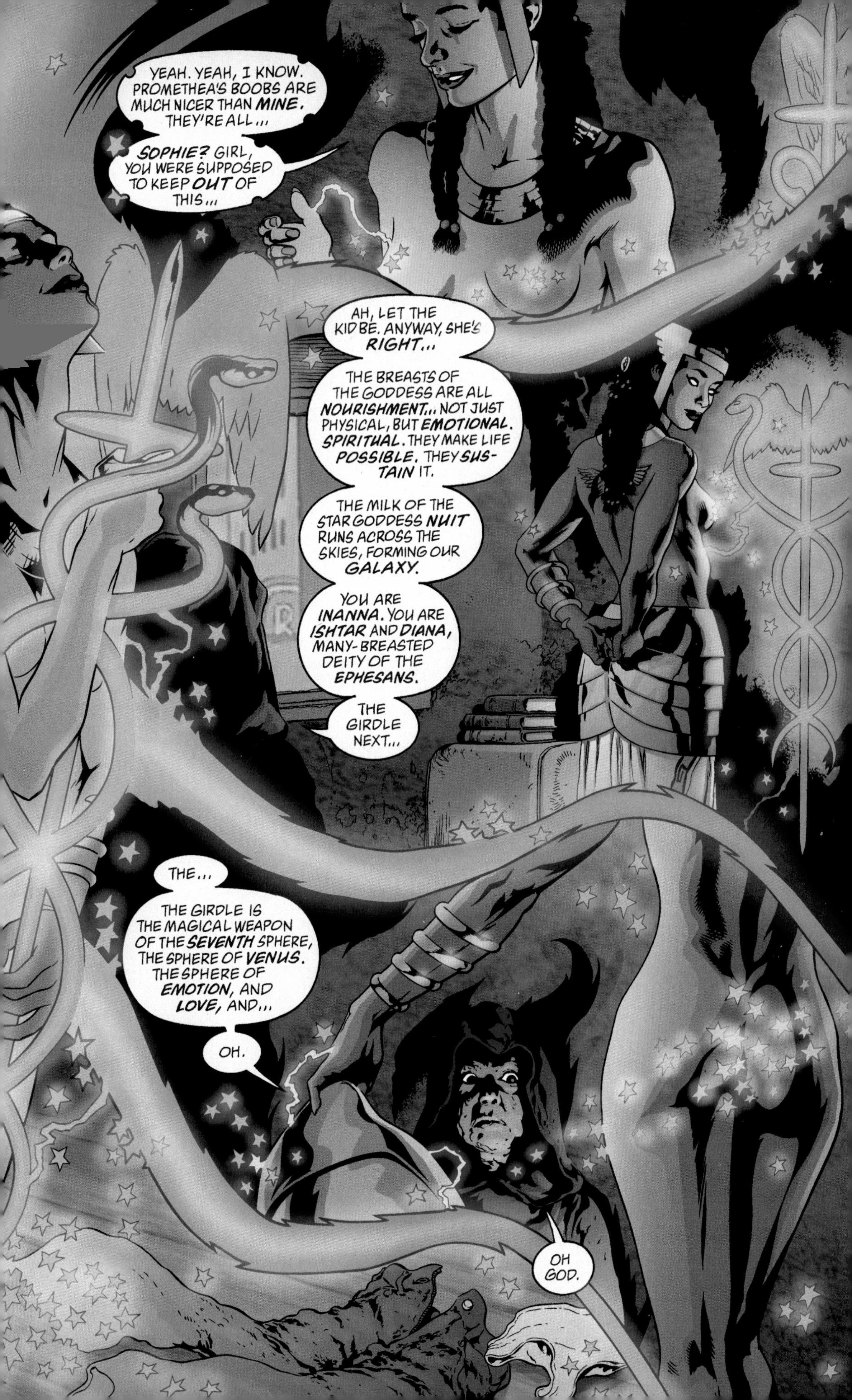
YEAH. YEAH, I KNOW. PROMETHEA'S BOOBS ARE MUCH NICER THAN MINE. THEY'RE ALL...
SOPHIE? GIRL, YOU WERE SUPPOSED TO KEEP OUT OF THIS...
AH, LET THE KID BE. ANYWAY, SHE'S RIGHT...
THE BREASTS OF THE GODDESS ARE ALL NOURISHMENT... NOT JUST PHYSICAL, BUT EMOTIONAL. SPIRITUAL. THEY MAKE LIFE POSSIBLE. THEY SUS-TAIN IT.
THE MILK OF THE STAR GODDESS NUIT RUNS ACROSS THE SKIES, FORMING OUR GALAXY.
YOU ARE INANNA. YOU ARE ISHTAR AND DIANA, MANY-BREASTED DEITY OF THE EPHESANS.
THE GIRDLE NEXT...
THE...
THE GIRDLE IS THE MAGICAL WEAPON OF THE SEVENTH SPHERE, THE SPHERE OF VENUS. THE SPHERE OF EMOTION, AND LOVE, AND...
OH.
OH GOD.

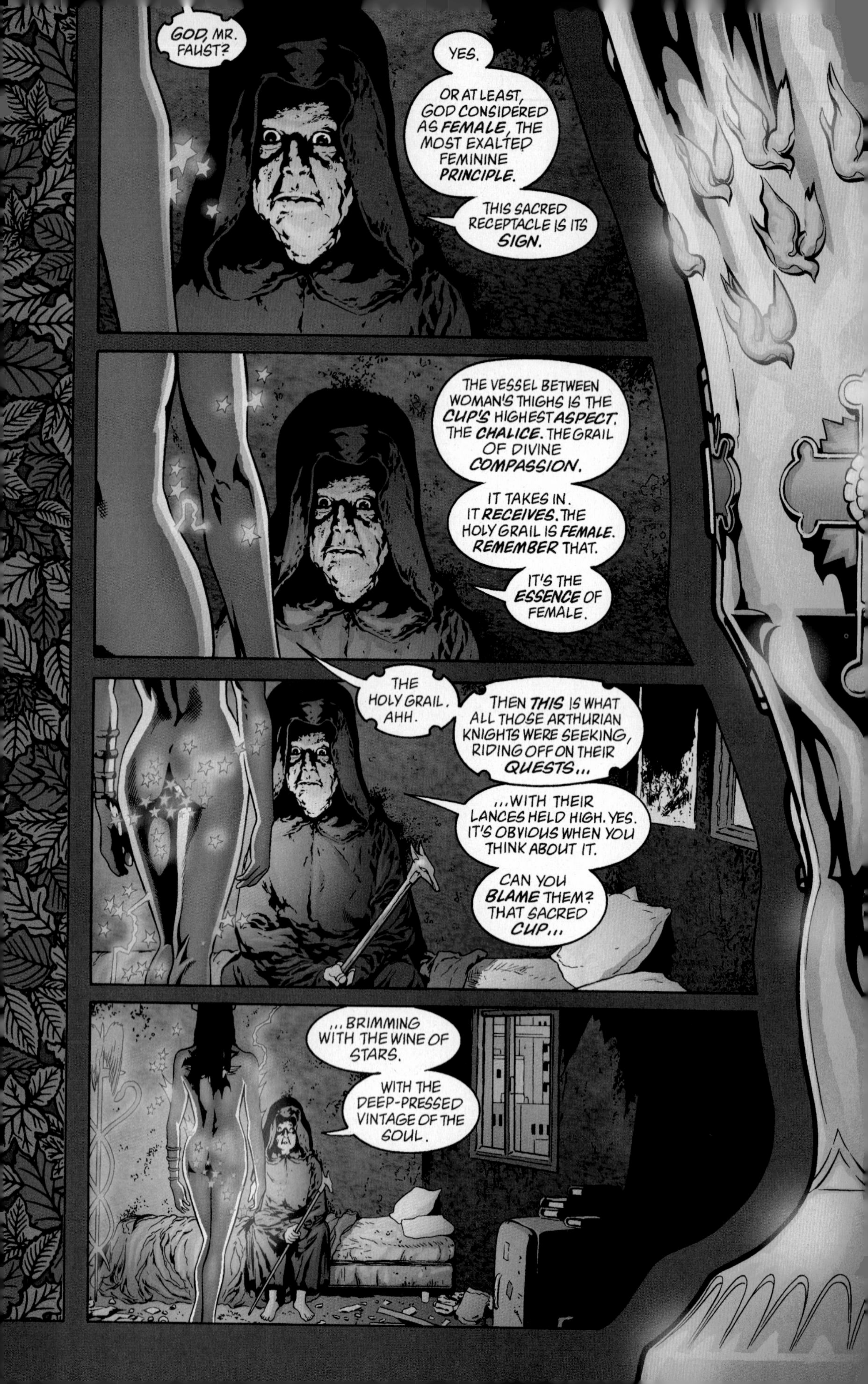
GOD, MR. FAUST?
YES.
OR AT LEAST, GOD CONSIDERED AS FEMALE, THE MOST EXALTED FEMININE PRINCIPLE.
THIS SACRED RECEPTACLE IS ITS SIGN.
THE VESSEL BETWEEN WOMAN'S THIGHS IS THE CUP'S HIGHEST ASPECT. THE CHALICE. THE GRAIL OF DIVINE COMPASSION.
IT TAKES IN. IT RECEIVES. THE HOLY GRAIL IS FEMALE. REMEMBER THAT.
IT'S THE ESSENCE OF FEMALE.
THE HOLY GRAIL. AHH.
THEN THIS IS WHAT ALL THOSE ARTHURIAN KNIGHTS WERE SEEKING, RIDING OFF ON THEIR QUESTS...
...WITH THEIR LANCES HELD HIGH. YES. IT'S OBVIOUS WHEN YOU THINK ABOUT IT.
CAN YOU BLAME THEM? THAT SACRED CUP...
...BRIMMING WITH THE WINE OF STARS.
WITH THE DEEP-PRESSED VINTAGE OF THE SOUL.

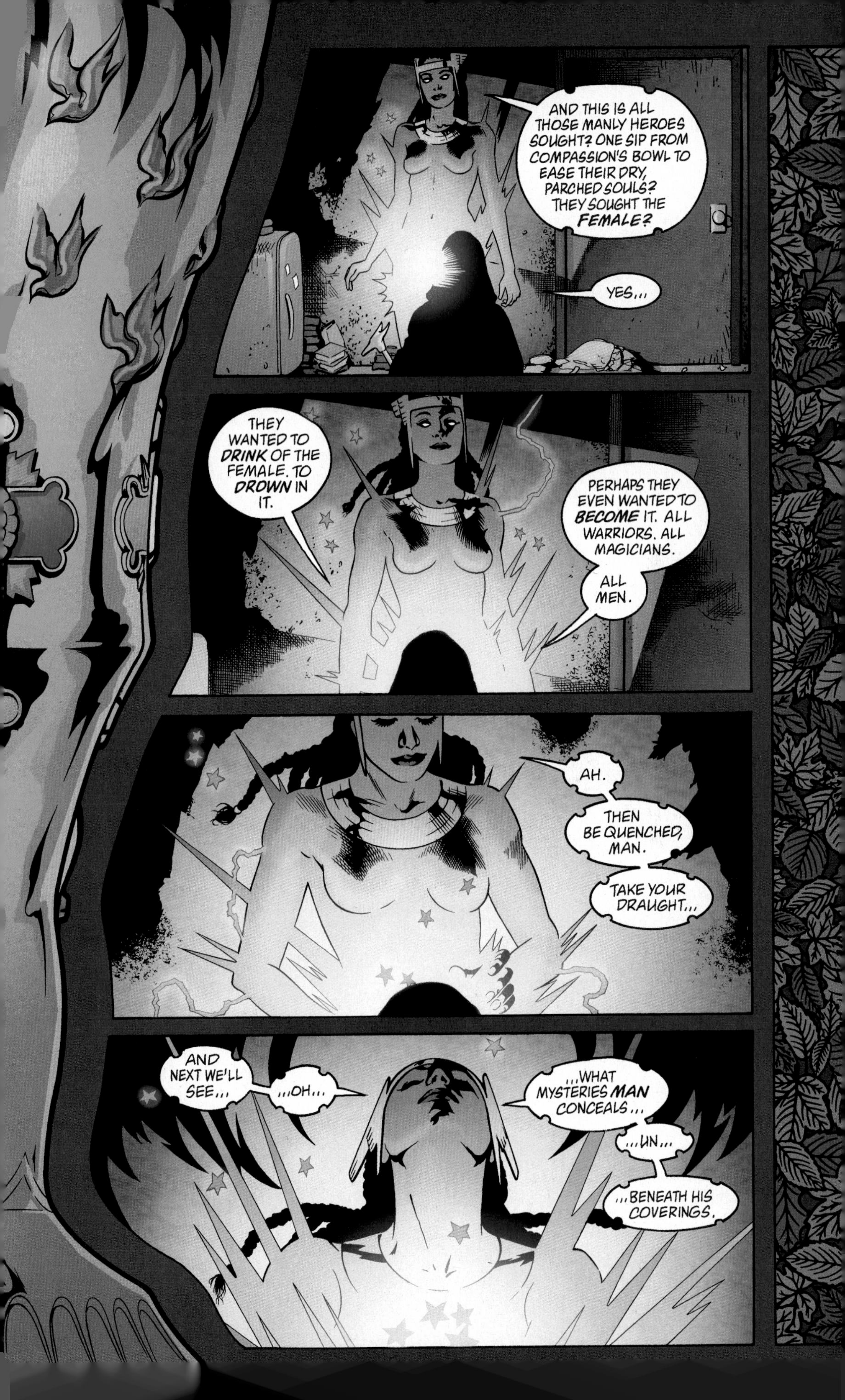

AND THIS IS ALL THOSE MANLY HEROES SOUGHT? ONE SIP FROM COMPASSION'S BOWL TO EASE THEIR DRY, PARCHED SOULS? THEY SOUGHT THE FEMALE?
YES...
THEY WANTED TO DRINK OF THE FEMALE. TO DROWN IN IT.
PERHAPS THEY EVEN WANTED TO BECOME IT. ALL WARRIORS. ALL MAGICIANS.
ALL MEN.
AH.
THEN BE QUENCHED, MAN.
TAKE YOUR DRAUGHT...
AND NEXT WE'LL SEE...
...OH...
...WHAT MYSTERIES MAN CONCEALS...
...UN...
...BENEATH HIS COVERINGS.

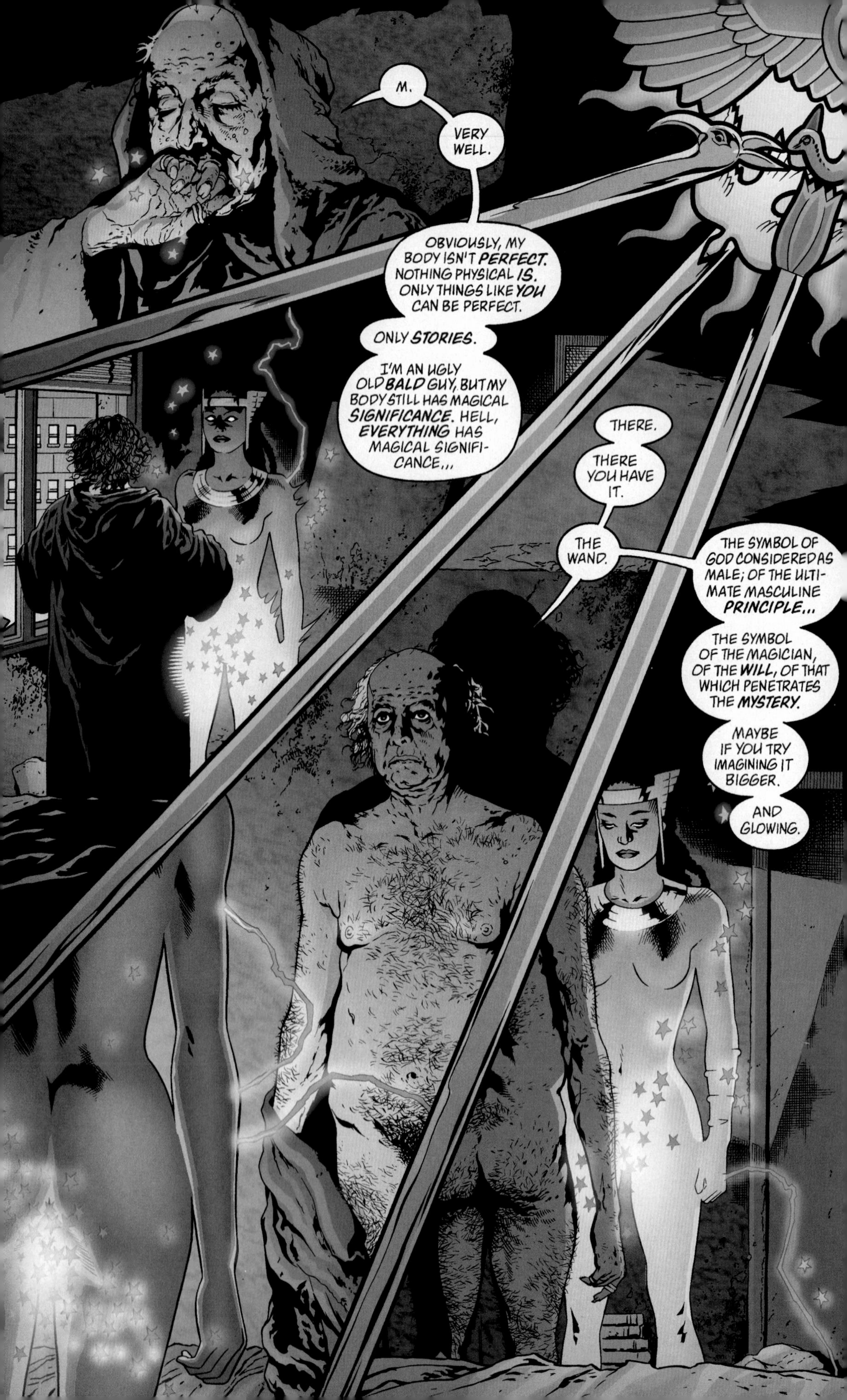
M.
VERY WELL.
OBVIOUSLY, MY BODY ISN'T PERFECT. NOTHING PHYSICAL IS. ONLY THINGS LIKE YOU CAN BE PERFECT.
ONLY STORIES.
I'M AN UGLY OLD BALD GUY, BUT MY BODY STILL HAS MAGICAL SIGNIFICANCE. HELL, EVERYTHING HAS MAGICAL SIGNIFI-CANCE...
THERE.
THERE YOU HAVE IT.
THE WAND.
THE SYMBOL OF GOD CONSIDERED AS MALE; OF THE ULTI-MATE MASCULINE PRINCIPLE...
THE SYMBOL OF THE MAGICIAN, OF THE WILL, OF THAT WHICH PENETRATES THE MYSTERY.
MAYBE IF YOU TRY IMAGINING IT BIGGER.
AND GLOWING.

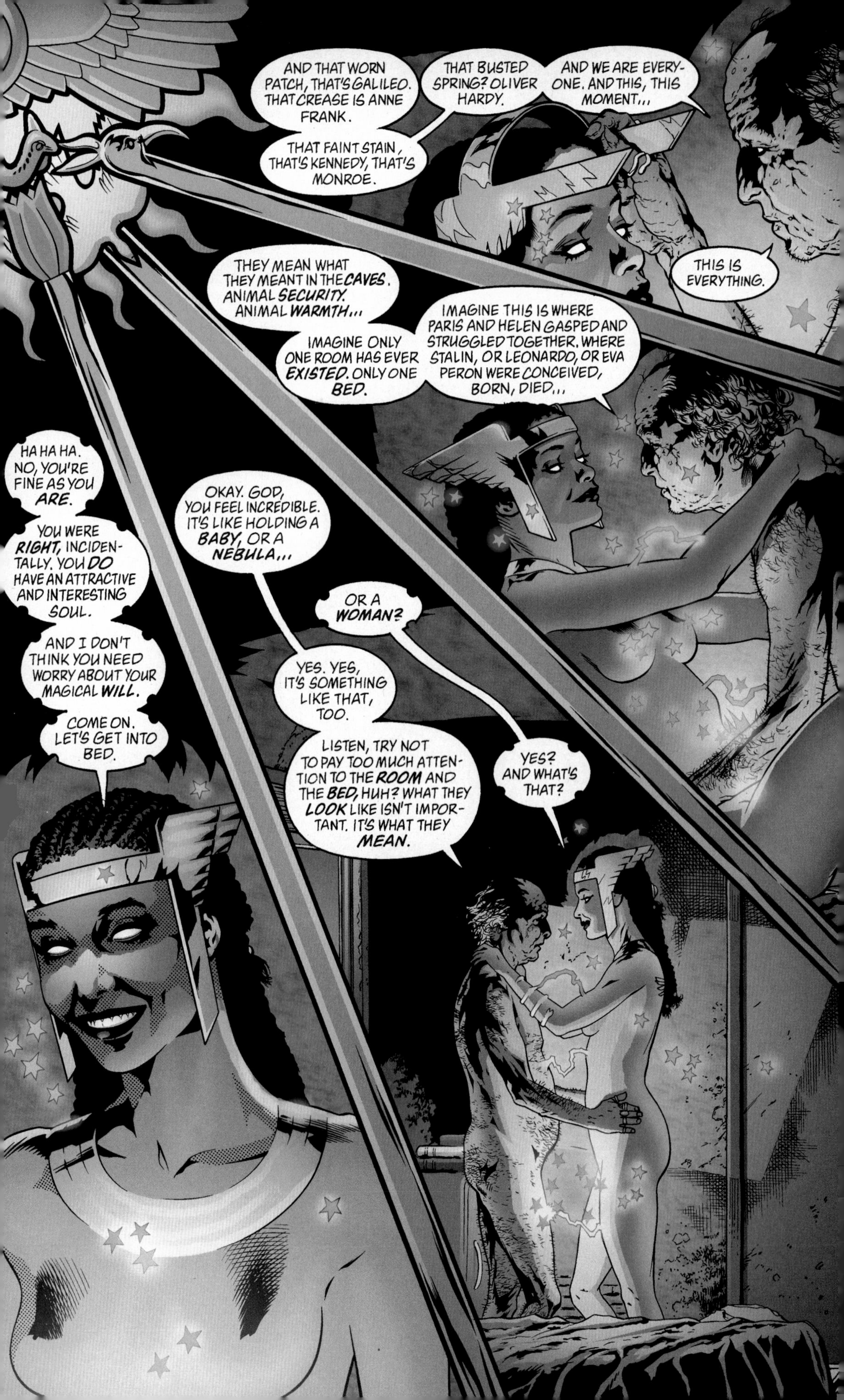
AND THAT WORN PATCH, THAT'S GALILEO. THAT CREASE IS ANNE FRANK.
THAT FAINT STAIN, THAT'S KENNEDY, THAT'S MONROE.
THAT BUSTED SPRING? OLIVER HARDY.
AND WE ARE EVERYONE. AND THIS, THIS MOMENT...
THIS IS EVERYTHING.
THEY MEAN WHAT THEY MEANT IN THE CAVES. ANIMAL SECURITY. ANIMAL WARMTH...
IMAGINE ONLY ONE ROOM HAS EVER EXISTED. ONLY ONE BED.
IMAGINE THIS IS WHERE PARIS AND HELEN GASPED AND STRUGGLED TOGETHER. WHERE STALIN, OR LEONARDO, OR EVA PERON WERE CONCEIVED, BORN, DIED...
HA HA HA. NO, YOU'RE FINE AS YOU ARE.
YOU WERE RIGHT, INCIDENTALLY. YOU DO HAVE AN ATTRACTIVE AND INTERESTING SOUL.
AND I DON'T THINK YOU NEED WORRY ABOUT YOUR MAGICAL WILL.
COME ON. LET'S GET INTO BED.
OKAY. GOD, YOU FEEL INCREDIBLE. IT'S LIKE HOLDING A BABY, OR A NEBULA...
OR A WOMAN?
YES. YES, IT'S SOMETHING LIKE THAT, TOO.
LISTEN, TRY NOT TO PAY TOO MUCH ATTENTION TO THE ROOM AND THE BED, HUH? WHAT THEY LOOK LIKE ISN'T IMPORTANT. IT'S WHAT THEY MEAN.
YES? AND WHAT'S THAT?

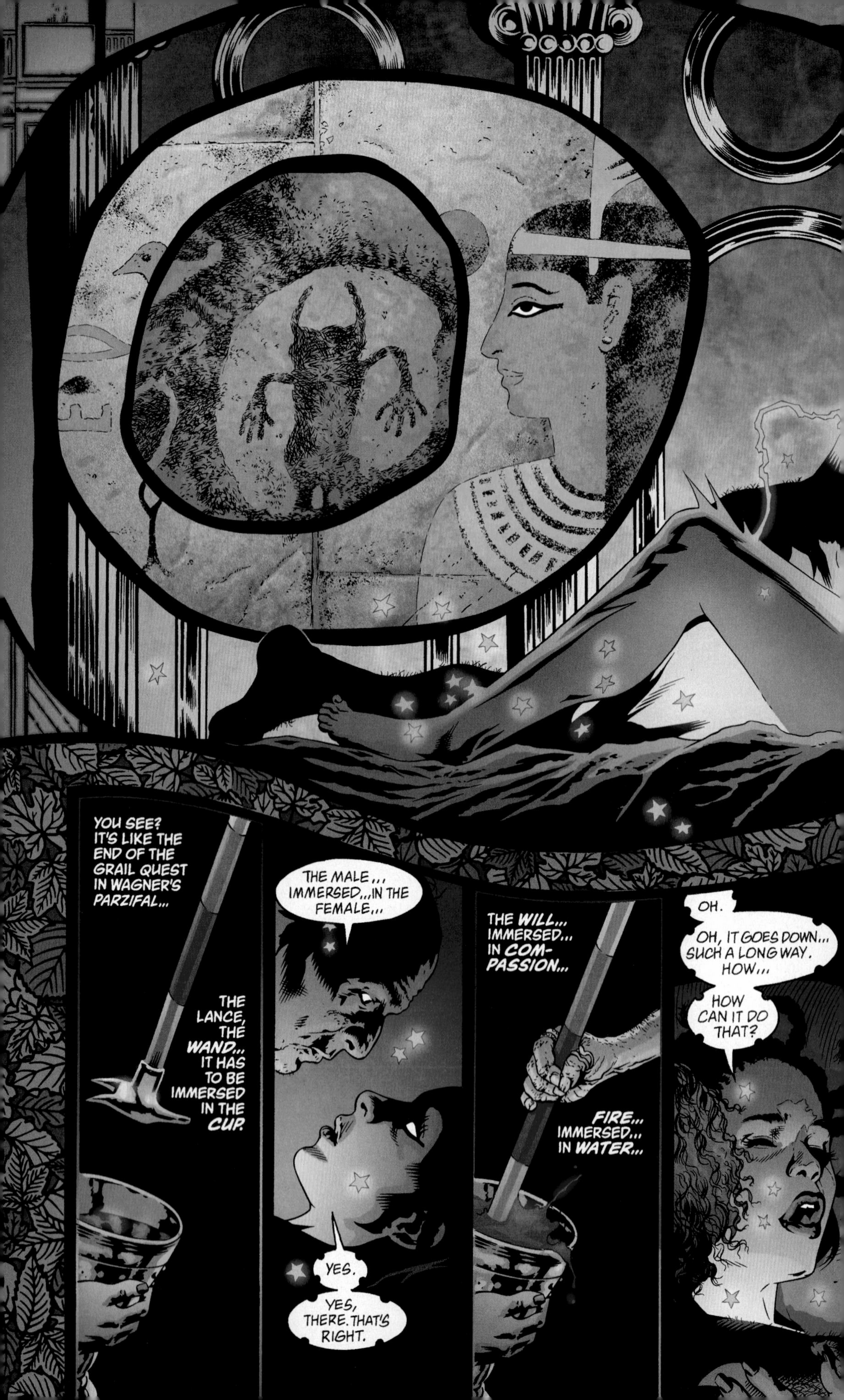
YOU SEE? IT'S LIKE THE END OF THE GRAIL QUEST IN WAGNER'S PARZIFAL...
THE LANCE, THE WAND... IT HAS TO BE IMMERSED IN THE CUP.
THE MALE... IMMERSED... IN THE FEMALE...
YES.
YES, THERE. THAT'S RIGHT.
THE WILL... IMMERSED... IN COMPASSION...
FIRE... IMMERSED... IN WATER...
OH.
OH, IT GOES DOWN... SUCH A LONG WAY. HOW...
HOW CAN IT DO THAT?

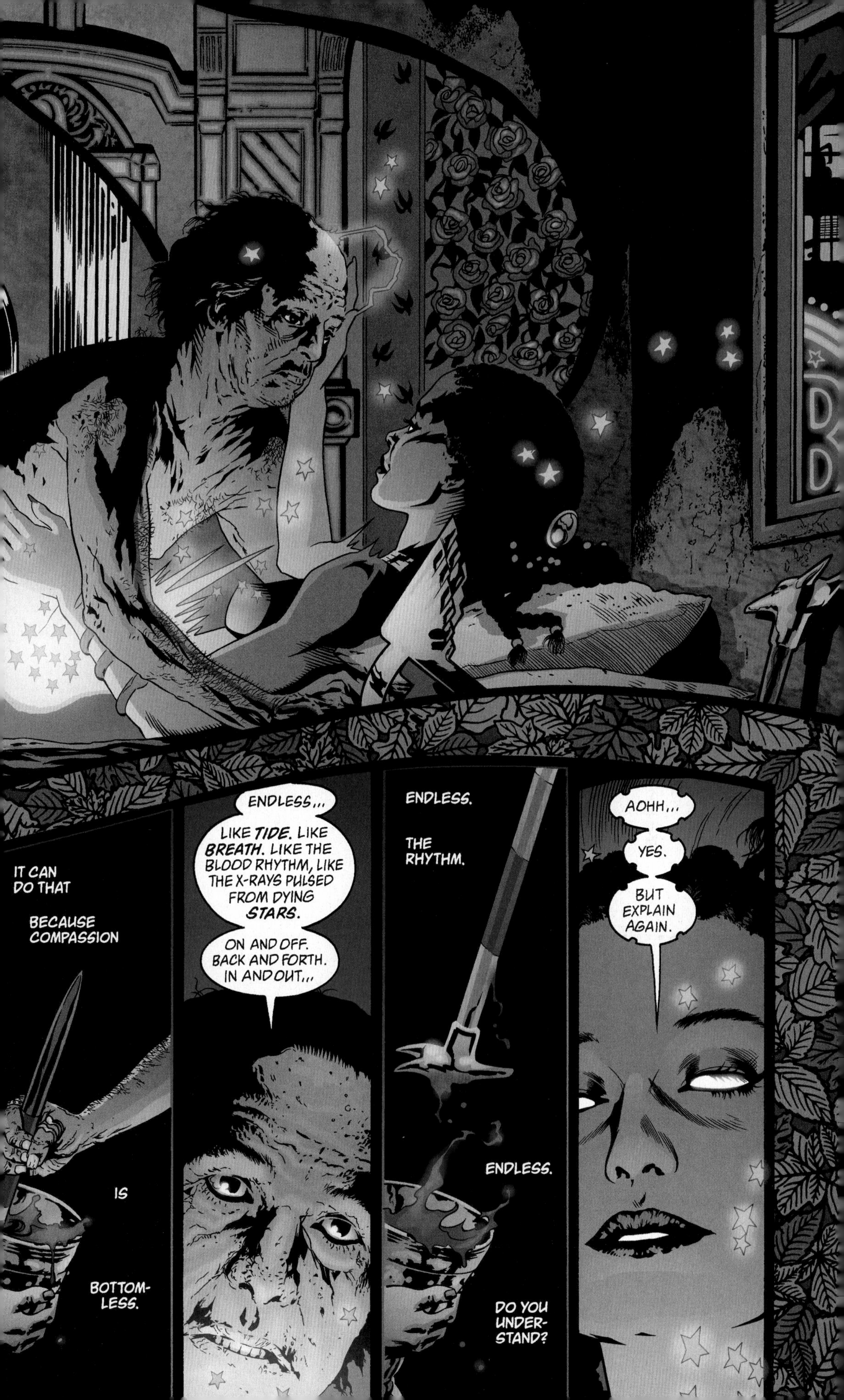

IT CAN DO THAT
BECAUSE COMPASSION
IS
BOTTOM-LESS.
ENDLESS...
LIKE TIDE. LIKE BREATH. LIKE THE BLOOD RHYTHM, LIKE THE X-RAYS PULSED FROM DYING STARS.
ON AND OFF. BACK AND FORTH. IN AND OUT...
ENDLESS.
THE RHYTHM.
ENDLESS.
DO YOU UNDER-STAND?
AOHH...
YES.
BUT EXPLAIN AGAIN.

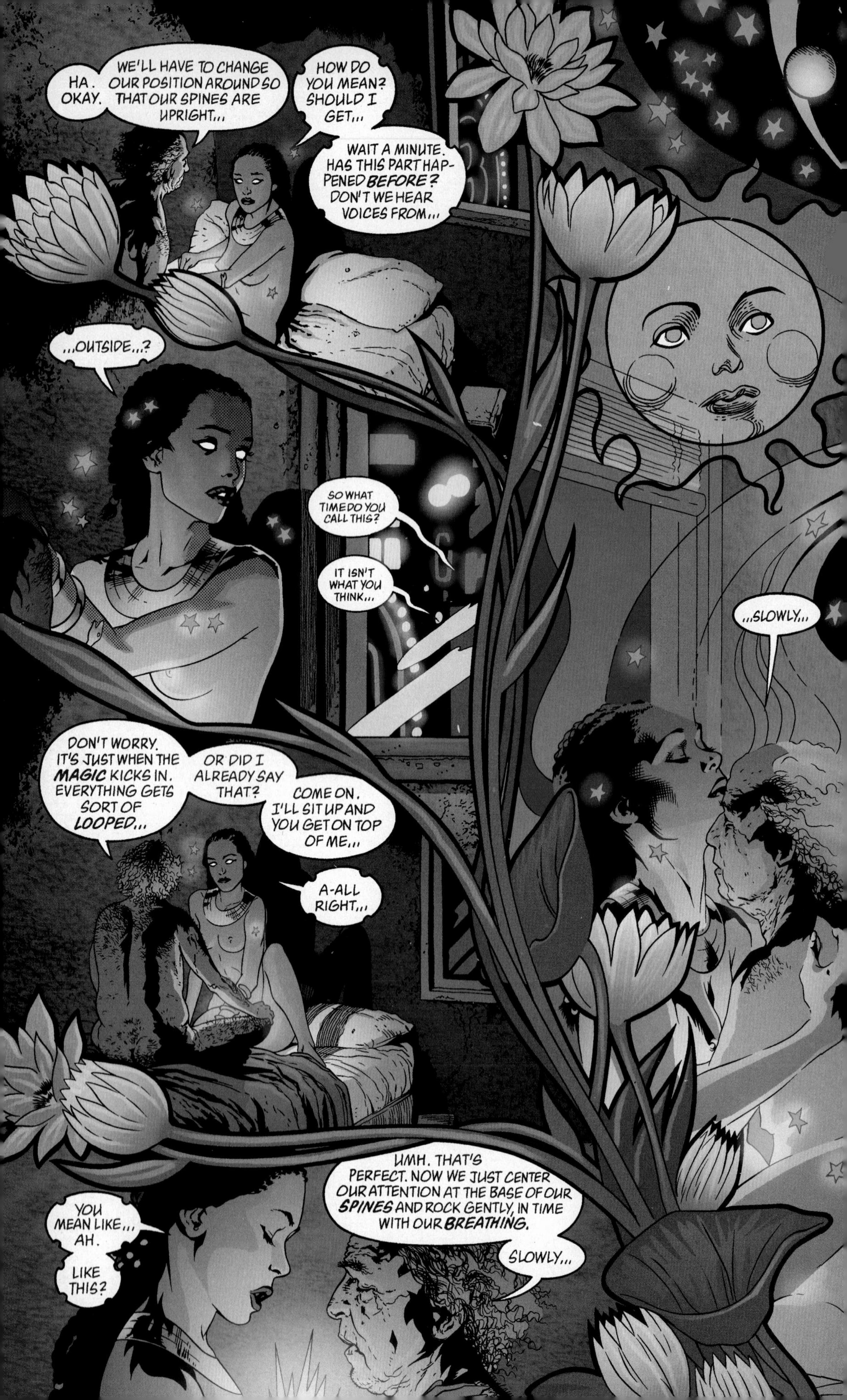
HA. OKAY.
WE'LL HAVE TO CHANGE OUR POSITION AROUND SO THAT OUR SPINES ARE UPRIGHT...
HOW DO YOU MEAN? SHOULD I GET...
WAIT A MINUTE. HAS THIS PART HAPPENED **BEFORE**? DON'T WE HEAR VOICES FROM...
...OUTSIDE...?
SO WHAT TIME DO YOU CALL THIS?
IT ISN'T WHAT YOU THINK...
...SLOWLY...
DON'T WORRY. IT'S JUST WHEN THE **MAGIC** KICKS IN. EVERYTHING GETS SORT OF **LOOPED**...
OR DID I ALREADY SAY THAT?
COME ON. I'LL SIT UP AND YOU GET ON TOP OF ME...
A-ALL RIGHT...
UMH. THAT'S PERFECT. NOW WE JUST CENTER OUR ATTENTION AT THE BASE OF OUR **SPINES** AND ROCK GENTLY, IN TIME WITH OUR **BREATHING**.
SLOWLY...
YOU MEAN LIKE... AH.
LIKE THIS?

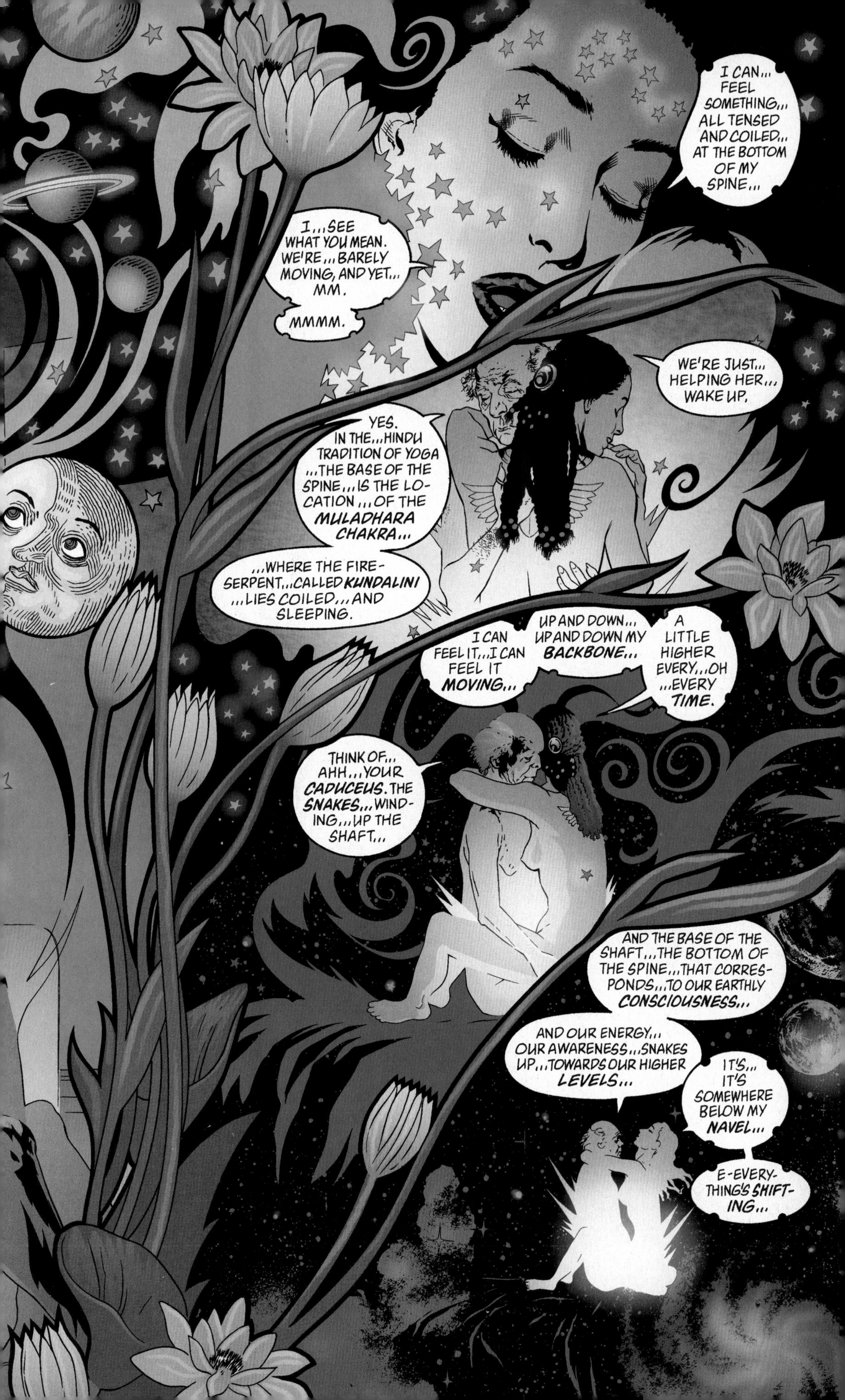
I CAN... FEEL SOMETHING... ALL TENSED AND COILED... AT THE BOTTOM OF MY SPINE...
I... SEE WHAT YOU MEAN. WE'RE... BARELY MOVING, AND YET... MM.
MMMM.
WE'RE JUST... HELPING HER... WAKE UP.
YES. IN THE... HINDU TRADITION OF YOGA ...THE BASE OF THE SPINE... IS THE LOCATION ... OF THE MULADHARA CHAKRA...
...WHERE THE FIRE-SERPENT... CALLED KUNDALINI ...LIES COILED... AND SLEEPING.
I CAN FEEL IT... I CAN FEEL IT MOVING...
UP AND DOWN... UP AND DOWN MY BACKBONE...
A LITTLE HIGHER EVERY... OH ...EVERY TIME.
THINK OF... AHH... YOUR CADUCEUS. THE SNAKES... WINDING... UP THE SHAFT...
AND THE BASE OF THE SHAFT... THE BOTTOM OF THE SPINE... THAT CORRESPONDS... TO OUR EARTHLY CONSCIOUSNESS...
AND OUR ENERGY... OUR AWARENESS... SNAKES UP... TOWARDS OUR HIGHER LEVELS...
IT'S... IT'S SOMEWHERE BELOW MY NAVEL...
E-EVERYTHING'S SHIFTING...

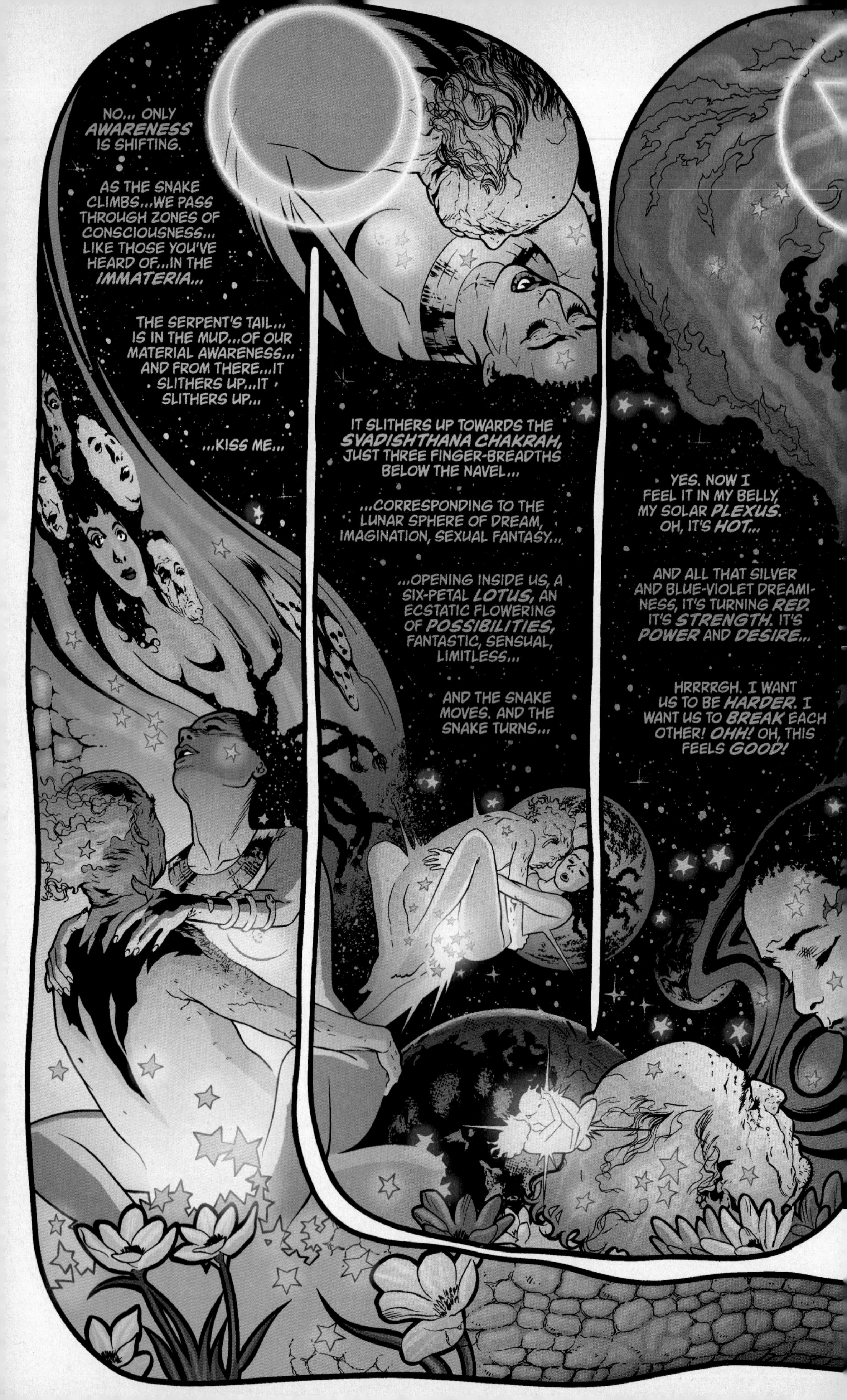

NO... ONLY AWARENESS IS SHIFTING.
AS THE SNAKE CLIMBS...WE PASS THROUGH ZONES OF CONSCIOUSNESS... LIKE THOSE YOU'VE HEARD OF...IN THE IMMATERIA...
THE SERPENT'S TAIL... IS IN THE MUD...OF OUR MATERIAL AWARENESS... AND FROM THERE...IT SLITHERS UP...IT SLITHERS UP...
...KISS ME...
IT SLITHERS UP TOWARDS THE SVADISHTHANA CHAKRAH, JUST THREE FINGER-BREADTHS BELOW THE NAVEL...
...CORRESPONDING TO THE LUNAR SPHERE OF DREAM, IMAGINATION, SEXUAL FANTASY...
...OPENING INSIDE US, A SIX-PETAL LOTUS, AN ECSTATIC FLOWERING OF POSSIBILITIES, FANTASTIC, SENSUAL, LIMITLESS...
AND THE SNAKE MOVES. AND THE SNAKE TURNS...
YES. NOW I FEEL IT IN MY BELLY, MY SOLAR PLEXUS. OH, IT'S HOT...
AND ALL THAT SILVER AND BLUE-VIOLET DREAMINESS, IT'S TURNING RED. IT'S STRENGTH. IT'S POWER AND DESIRE...
HRRRRGH. I WANT US TO BE HARDER. I WANT US TO BREAK EACH OTHER! OHH! OH, THIS FEELS GOOD!

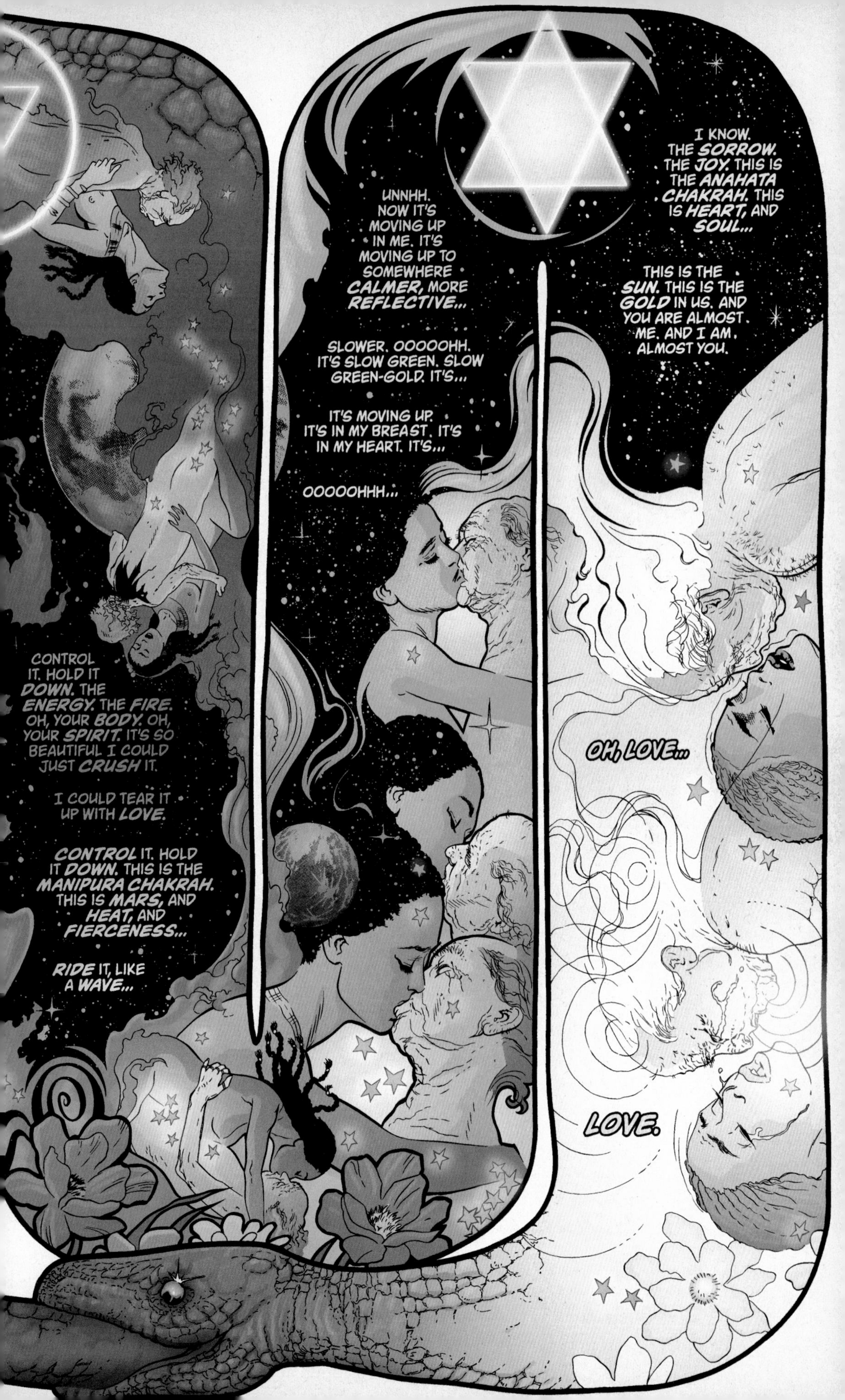
CONTROL IT. HOLD IT DOWN. THE ENERGY. THE FIRE. OH, YOUR BODY. OH, YOUR SPIRIT. IT'S SO BEAUTIFUL I COULD JUST CRUSH IT.
I COULD TEAR IT UP WITH LOVE.
CONTROL IT. HOLD IT DOWN. THIS IS THE MANIPURA CHAKRAH. THIS IS MARS, AND HEAT, AND FIERCENESS...
RIDE IT, LIKE A WAVE...
UNNHH. NOW IT'S MOVING UP IN ME. IT'S MOVING UP TO SOMEWHERE CALMER, MORE REFLECTIVE...
SLOWER. OOOOOHH. IT'S SLOW GREEN. SLOW GREEN-GOLD. IT'S...
IT'S MOVING UP. IT'S IN MY BREAST. IT'S IN MY HEART. IT'S...
OOOOOHHH...
I KNOW. THE SORROW. THE JOY. THIS IS THE ANAHATA CHAKRAH. THIS IS HEART, AND SOUL...
THIS IS THE SUN. THIS IS THE GOLD IN US. AND YOU ARE ALMOST ME. AND I AM ALMOST YOU.
OH, LOVE...
LOVE.

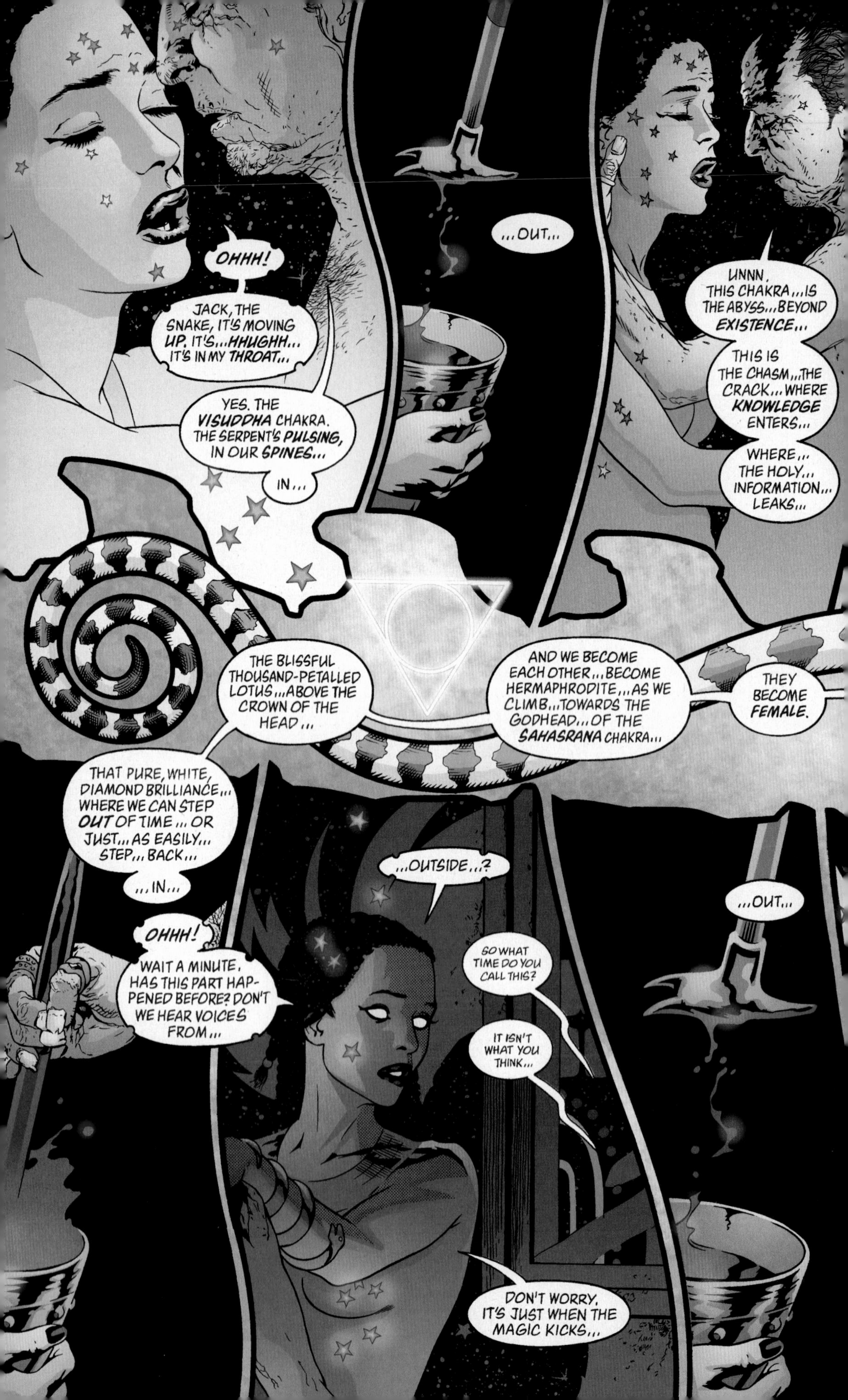
OHHH!
JACK, THE SNAKE, IT'S MOVING UP. IT'S...HHUGHH... IT'S IN MY THROAT...
YES. THE VISUDDHA CHAKRA. THE SERPENT'S PULSING, IN OUR SPINES...
IN...
...OUT...
UNNN. THIS CHAKRA...IS THE ABYSS...BEYOND EXISTENCE...
THIS IS THE CHASM...THE CRACK...WHERE KNOWLEDGE ENTERS...
WHERE... THE HOLY... INFORMATION... LEAKS...
THE BLISSFUL THOUSAND-PETALLED LOTUS...ABOVE THE CROWN OF THE HEAD...
AND WE BECOME EACH OTHER...BECOME HERMAPHRODITE...AS WE CLIMB...TOWARDS THE GODHEAD...OF THE SAHASRANA CHAKRA...
THEY BECOME FEMALE.
THAT PURE, WHITE, DIAMOND BRILLIANCE... WHERE WE CAN STEP OUT OF TIME... OR JUST... AS EASILY... STEP... BACK...
...IN...
...OUTSIDE...?
...OUT...
OHHH!
WAIT A MINUTE, HAS THIS PART HAP-PENED BEFORE? DON'T WE HEAR VOICES FROM...
SO WHAT TIME DO YOU CALL THIS?
IT ISN'T WHAT YOU THINK...
DON'T WORRY, IT'S JUST WHEN THE MAGIC KICKS...

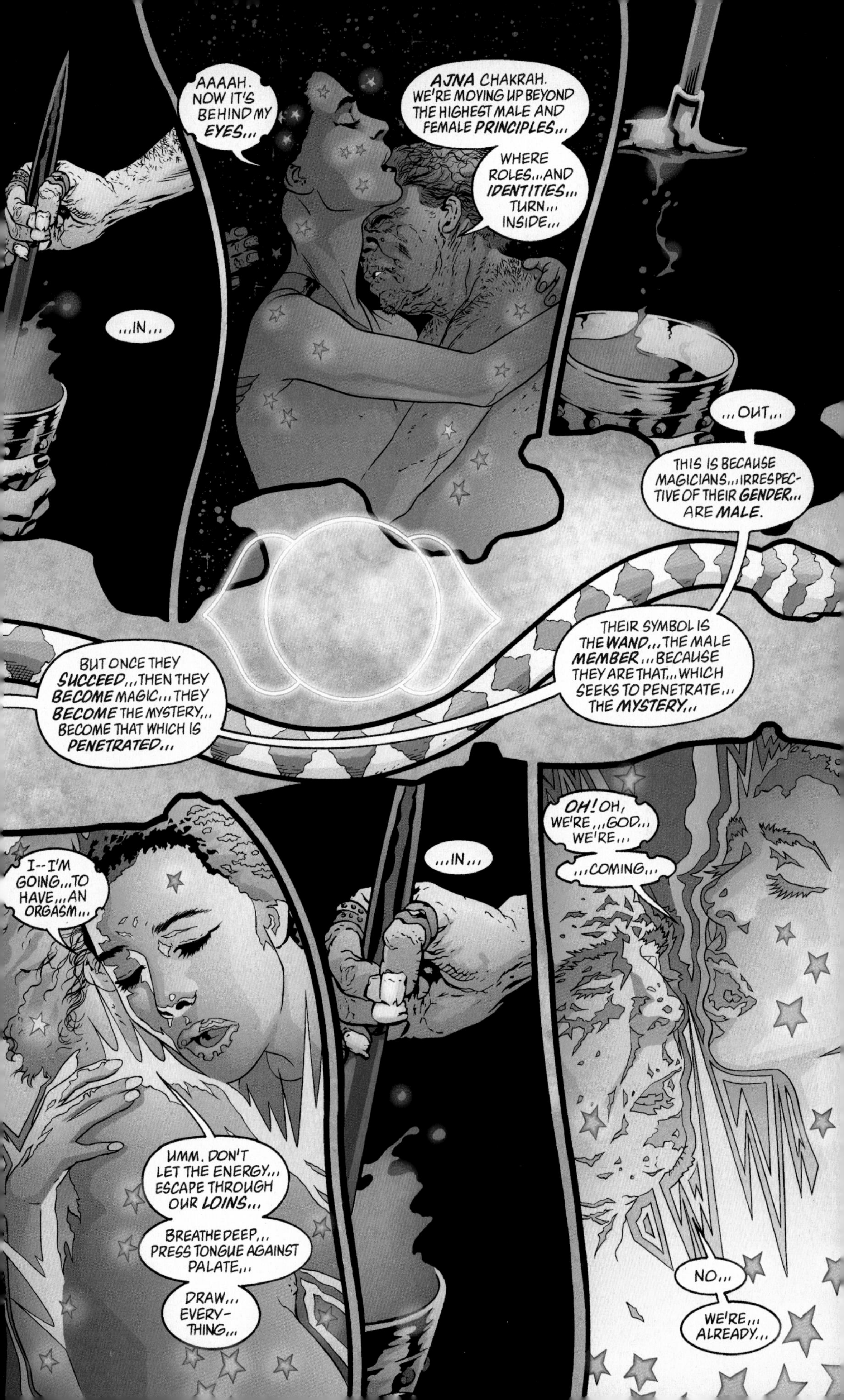
AAAAH. NOW IT'S BEHIND MY EYES...
AJNA CHAKRAH. WE'RE MOVING UP BEYOND THE HIGHEST MALE AND FEMALE PRINCIPLES...
WHERE ROLES...AND IDENTITIES... TURN... INSIDE...
...IN...
...OUT...
THIS IS BECAUSE MAGICIANS...IRRESPECTIVE OF THEIR GENDER... ARE MALE.
THEIR SYMBOL IS THE WAND...THE MALE MEMBER...BECAUSE THEY ARE THAT...WHICH SEEKS TO PENETRATE... THE MYSTERY...
BUT ONCE THEY SUCCEED...THEN THEY BECOME MAGIC...THEY BECOME THE MYSTERY... BECOME THAT WHICH IS PENETRATED...
I--I'M GOING...TO HAVE...AN ORGASM...
...IN...
OH! OH, WE'RE...GOD... WE'RE...
...COMING...
UMM. DON'T LET THE ENERGY... ESCAPE THROUGH OUR LOINS...
BREATHE DEEP... PRESS TONGUE AGAINST PALATE...
DRAW... EVERY-THING...
NO...
WE'RE... ALREADY...

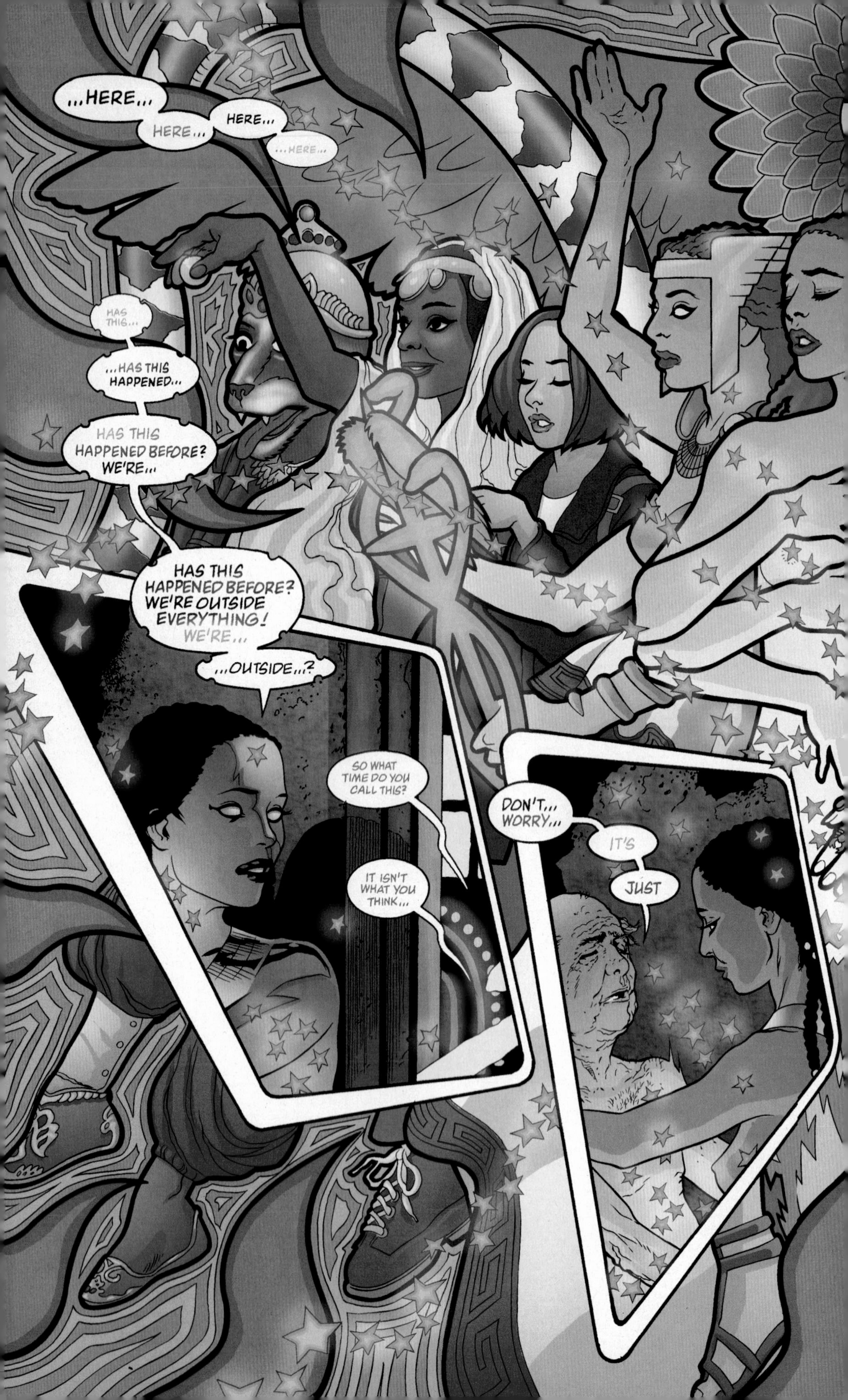
...HERE...
HERE...
HERE...
...HERE...
HAS THIS...
...HAS THIS HAPPENED...
HAS THIS HAPPENED BEFORE? WE'RE...
HAS THIS HAPPENED BEFORE? WE'RE OUTSIDE EVERYTHING! WE'RE...
...OUTSIDE...?
SO WHAT TIME DO YOU CALL THIS?
IT ISN'T WHAT YOU THINK...
DON'T... WORRY...
IT'S
JUST

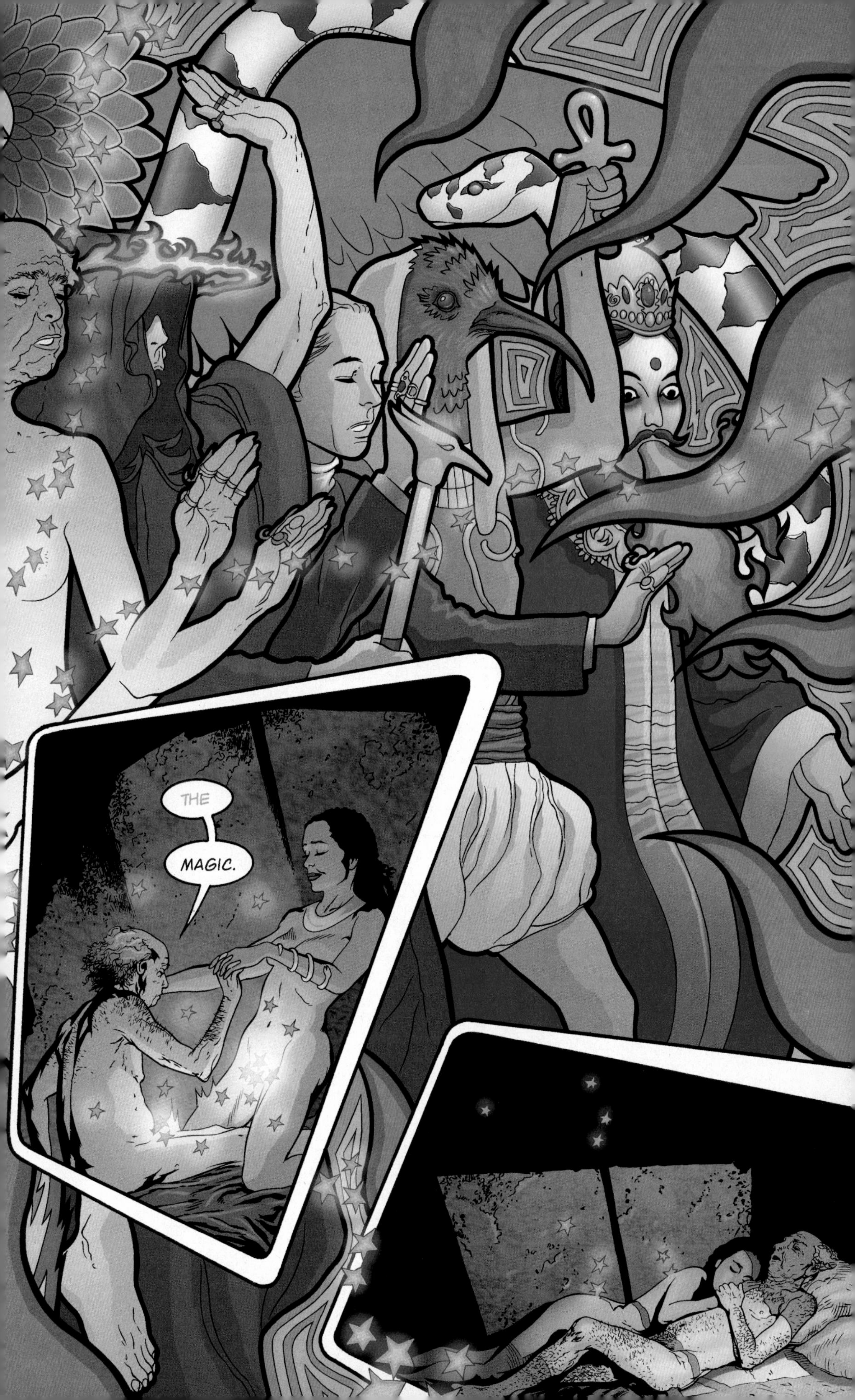
THE
MAGIC.

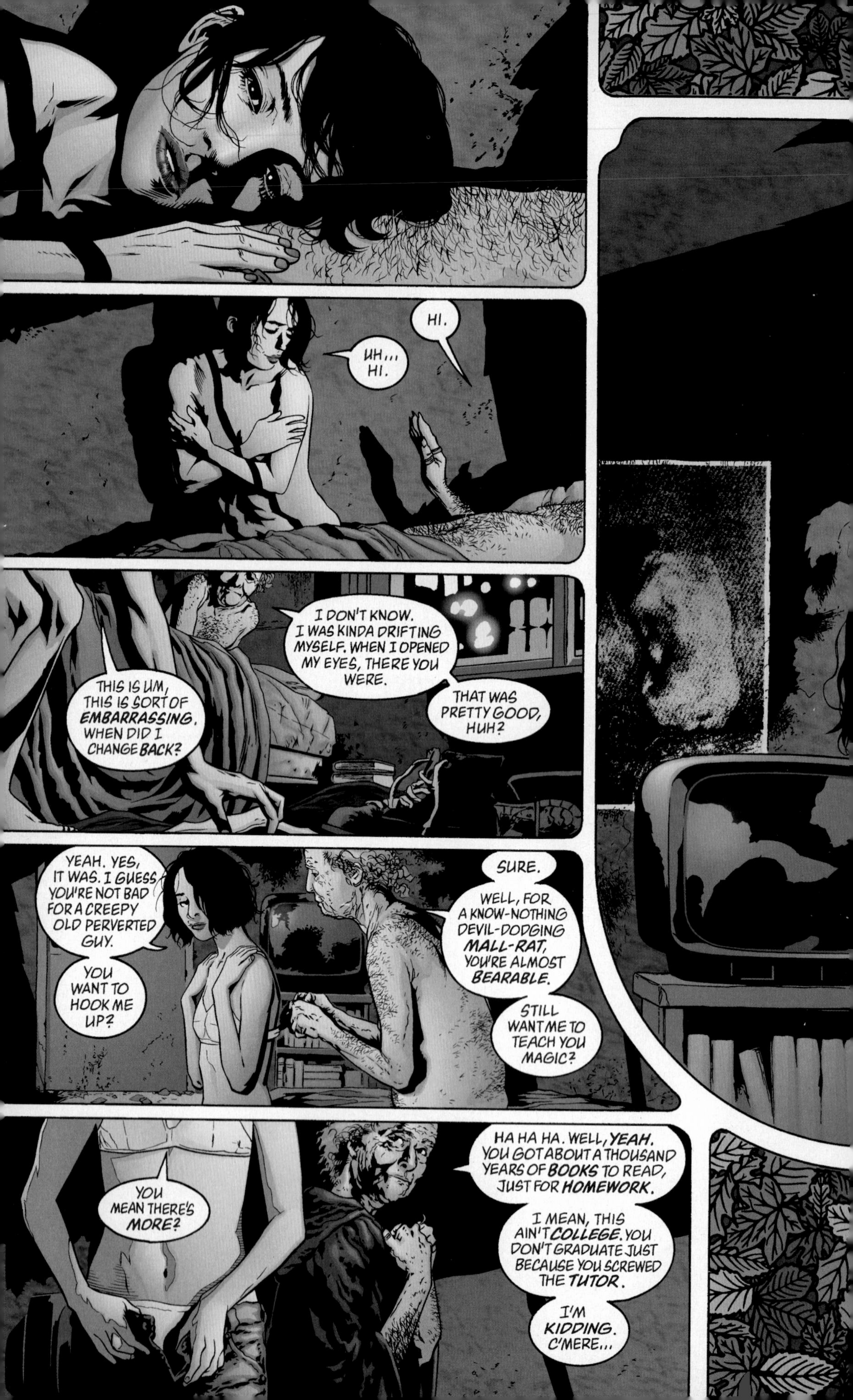
HI.
UH,,, HI.
THIS IS UM, THIS IS SORT OF EMBARRASSING. WHEN DID I CHANGE BACK?
I DON'T KNOW. I WAS KINDA DRIFTING MYSELF. WHEN I OPENED MY EYES, THERE YOU WERE.
THAT WAS PRETTY GOOD, HUH?
YEAH. YES, IT WAS. I GUESS YOU'RE NOT BAD FOR A CREEPY OLD PERVERTED GUY.
SURE.
WELL, FOR A KNOW-NOTHING DEVIL-DODGING MALL-RAT, YOU'RE ALMOST BEARABLE.
YOU WANT TO HOOK ME UP?
STILL WANT ME TO TEACH YOU MAGIC?
YOU MEAN THERE'S MORE?
HA HA HA. WELL, YEAH. YOU GOT ABOUT A THOUSAND YEARS OF BOOKS TO READ, JUST FOR HOMEWORK.
I MEAN, THIS AIN'T COLLEGE. YOU DON'T GRADUATE JUST BECAUSE YOU SCREWED THE TUTOR.
I'M KIDDING. C'MERE...

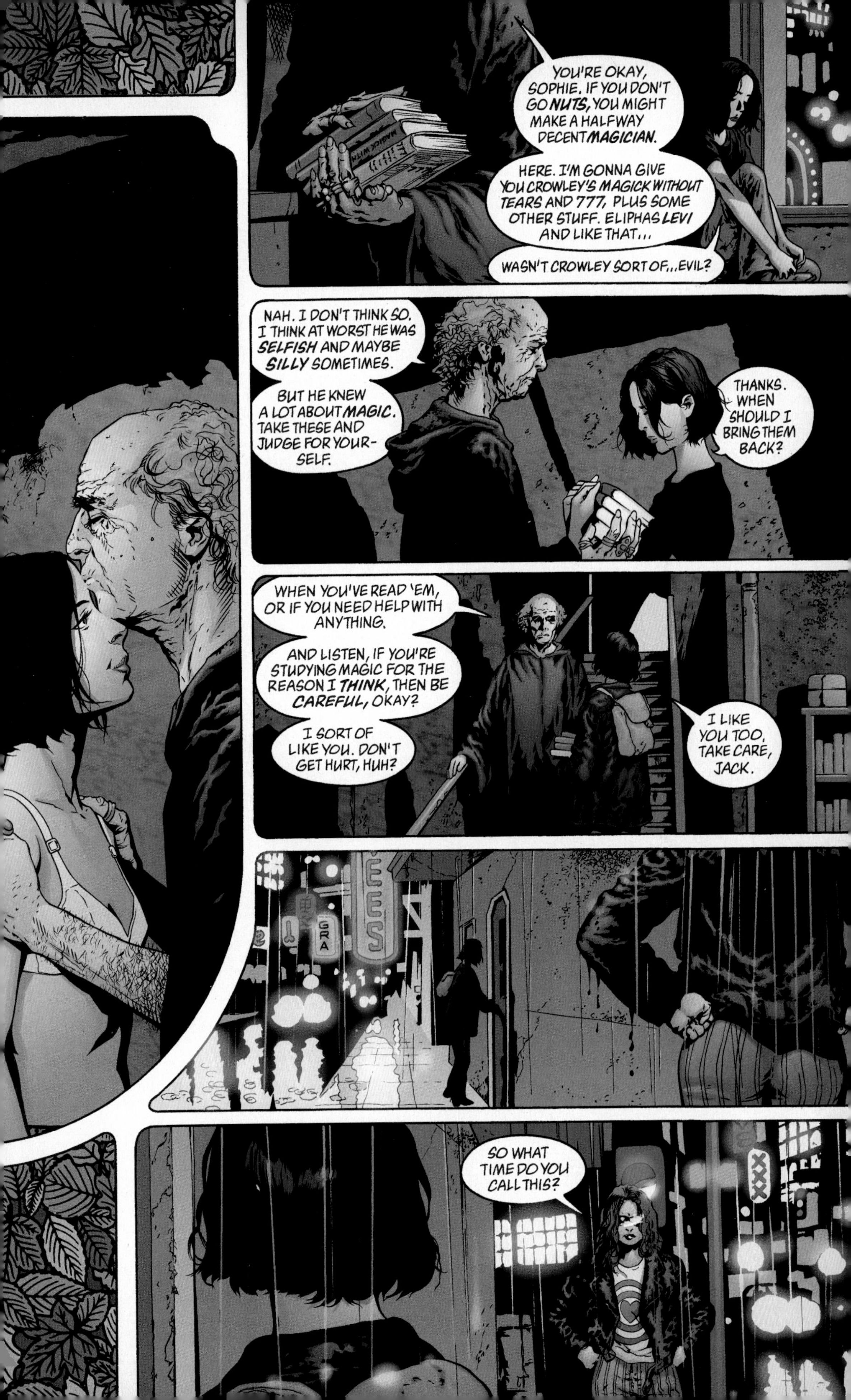

YOU'RE OKAY, SOPHIE. IF YOU DON'T GO NUTS, YOU MIGHT MAKE A HALFWAY DECENT MAGICIAN.
HERE. I'M GONNA GIVE YOU CROWLEY'S MAGICK WITHOUT TEARS AND 777, PLUS SOME OTHER STUFF. ELIPHAS LEVI AND LIKE THAT...
WASN'T CROWLEY SORT OF...EVIL?
NAH. I DON'T THINK SO. I THINK AT WORST HE WAS SELFISH AND MAYBE SILLY SOMETIMES.
BUT HE KNEW A LOT ABOUT MAGIC. TAKE THESE AND JUDGE FOR YOUR-SELF.
THANKS. WHEN SHOULD I BRING THEM BACK?
WHEN YOU'VE READ 'EM, OR IF YOU NEED HELP WITH ANYTHING.
AND LISTEN, IF YOU'RE STUDYING MAGIC FOR THE REASON I THINK, THEN BE CAREFUL, OKAY?
I SORT OF LIKE YOU. DON'T GET HURT, HUH?
I LIKE YOU TOO, TAKE CARE, JACK.
SO WHAT TIME DO YOU CALL THIS?

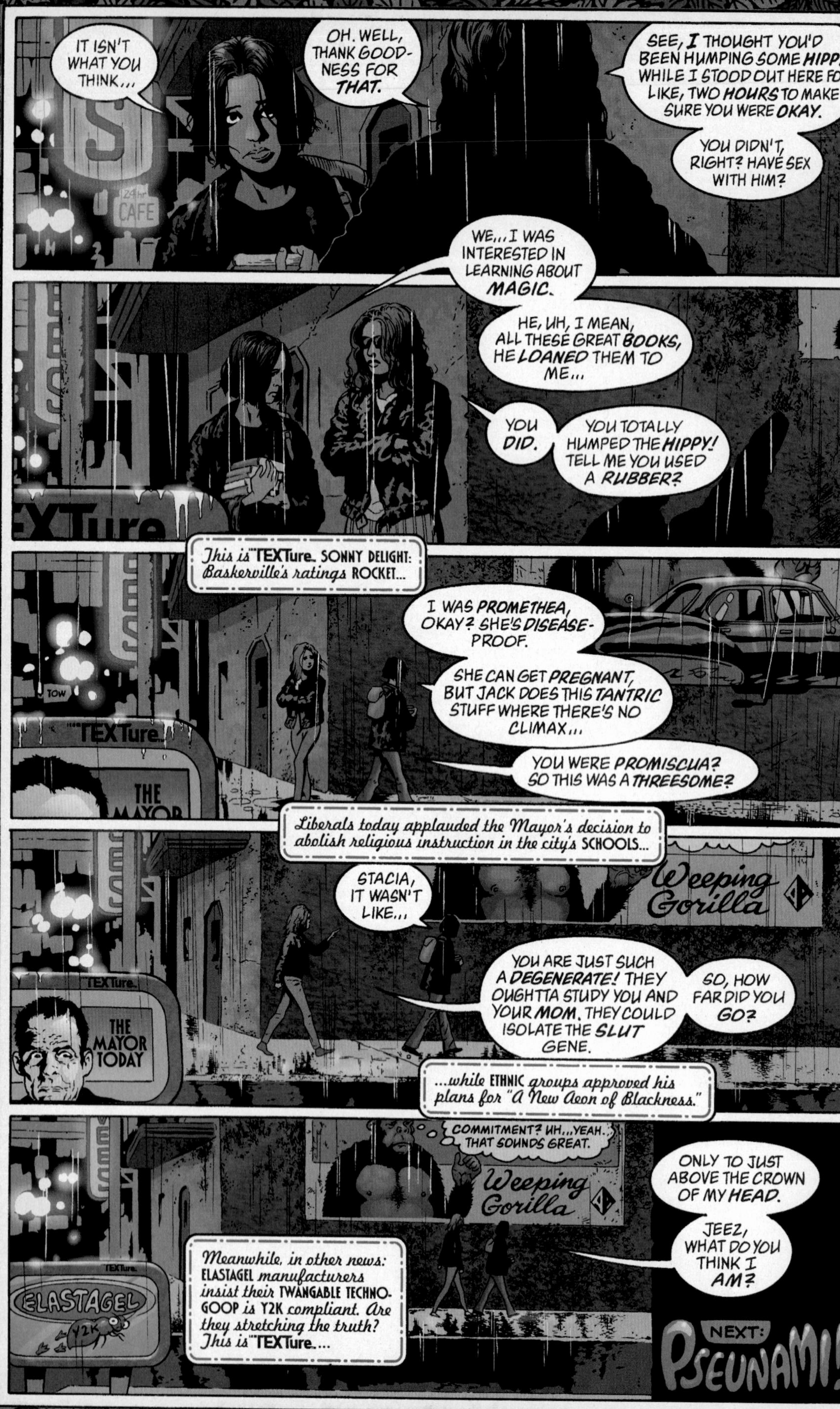

IT ISN'T WHAT YOU THINK...
OH. WELL, THANK GOODNESS FOR THAT.
SEE, I THOUGHT YOU'D BEEN HUMPING SOME HIPPY WHILE I STOOD OUT HERE FOR, LIKE, TWO HOURS TO MAKE SURE YOU WERE OKAY.
YOU DIDN'T, RIGHT? HAVE SEX WITH HIM?
24hr CAFE
WE... I WAS INTERESTED IN LEARNING ABOUT MAGIC.
HE, UH, I MEAN, ALL THESE GREAT BOOKS, HE LOANED THEM TO ME...
YOU DID.
YOU TOTALLY HUMPED THE HIPPY! TELL ME YOU USED A RUBBER?
This is "TEXTure. SONNY DELIGHT: Baskerville's ratings ROCKET...
I WAS PROMETHEA, OKAY? SHE'S DISEASE-PROOF.
SHE CAN GET PREGNANT, BUT JACK DOES THIS TANTRIC STUFF WHERE THERE'S NO CLIMAX...
YOU WERE PROMISCUA? SO THIS WAS A THREESOME?
TEXTure
Liberals today applauded the Mayor's decision to abolish religious instruction in the city's SCHOOLS...
STACIA, IT WASN'T LIKE...
YOU ARE JUST SUCH A DEGENERATE! THEY OUGHTTA STUDY YOU AND YOUR MOM. THEY COULD ISOLATE THE SLUT GENE.
SO, HOW FAR DID YOU GO?
Weeping Gorilla
THE MAYOR TODAY
...while ETHNIC groups approved his plans for "A New Aeon of Blackness."
COMMITMENT? UH...YEAH. THAT SOUNDS GREAT.
Weeping Gorilla
ONLY TO JUST ABOVE THE CROWN OF MY HEAD.
JEEZ, WHAT DO YOU THINK I AM?
Meanwhile, in other news: ELASTAGEL manufacturers insist their TWANGABLE TECHNO-GOOP is Y2K compliant. Are they stretching the truth? This is "TEXTure....
ELASTAGEL
Y2K
NEXT: PSEUNAMI!

CHAPTER FIVE

Can magic's might quell temporal threats this night?

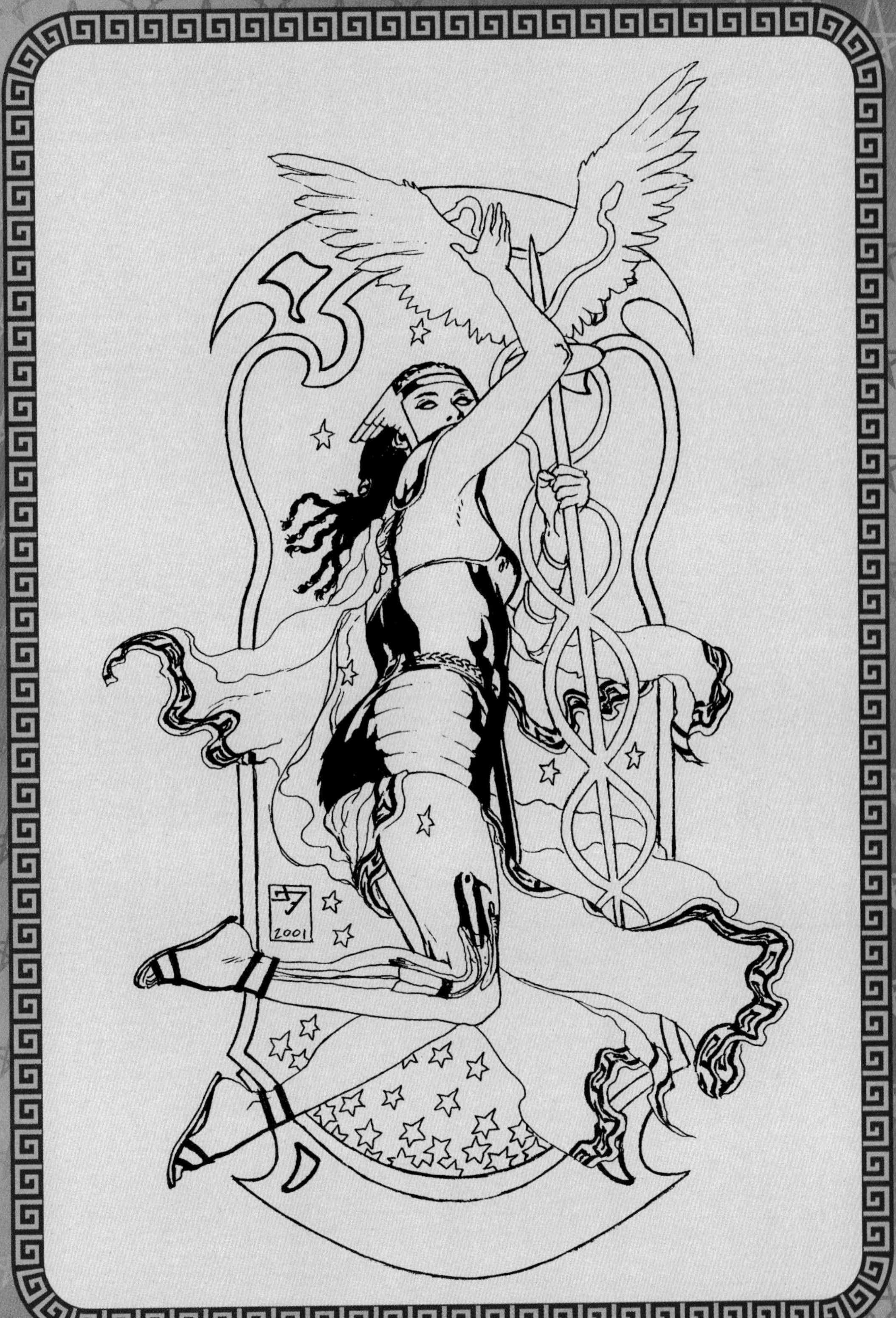
2001

Cover art: J.H. Williams III, Mick Gray & Jeromy Cox

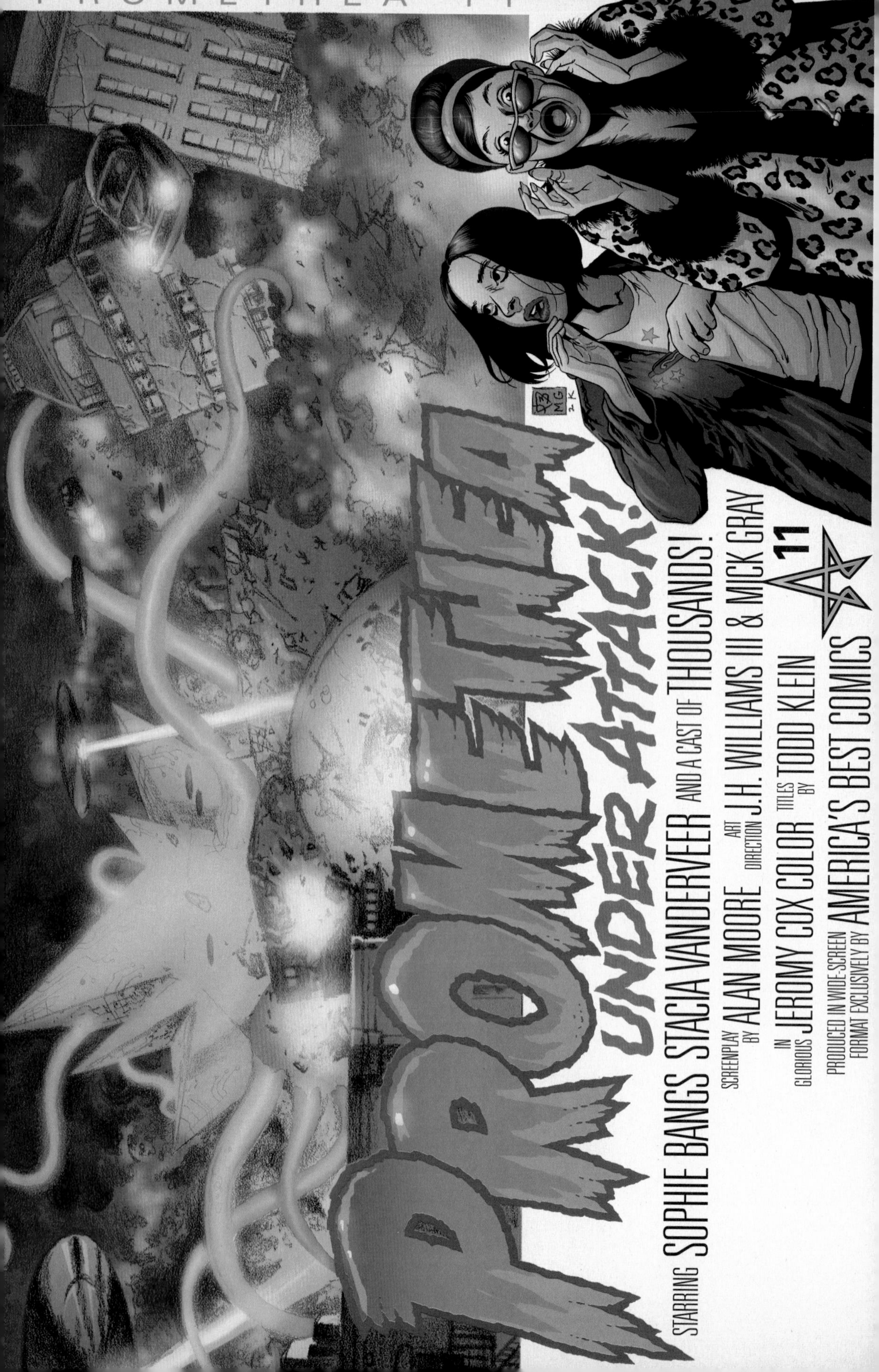
PROMETHEA
UNDER ATTACK!
STARRING SOPHIE BANGS STACIA VANDERVEER AND A CAST OF THOUSANDS!
SCREENPLAY BY ALAN MOORE ART DIRECTION J.H. WILLIAMS III & MICK GRAY
IN GLORIOUS JEROMY COX COLOR TITLES BY TODD KLEIN
PRODUCED IN WIDE-SCREEN FORMAT EXCLUSIVELY BY AMERICA'S BEST COMICS
11

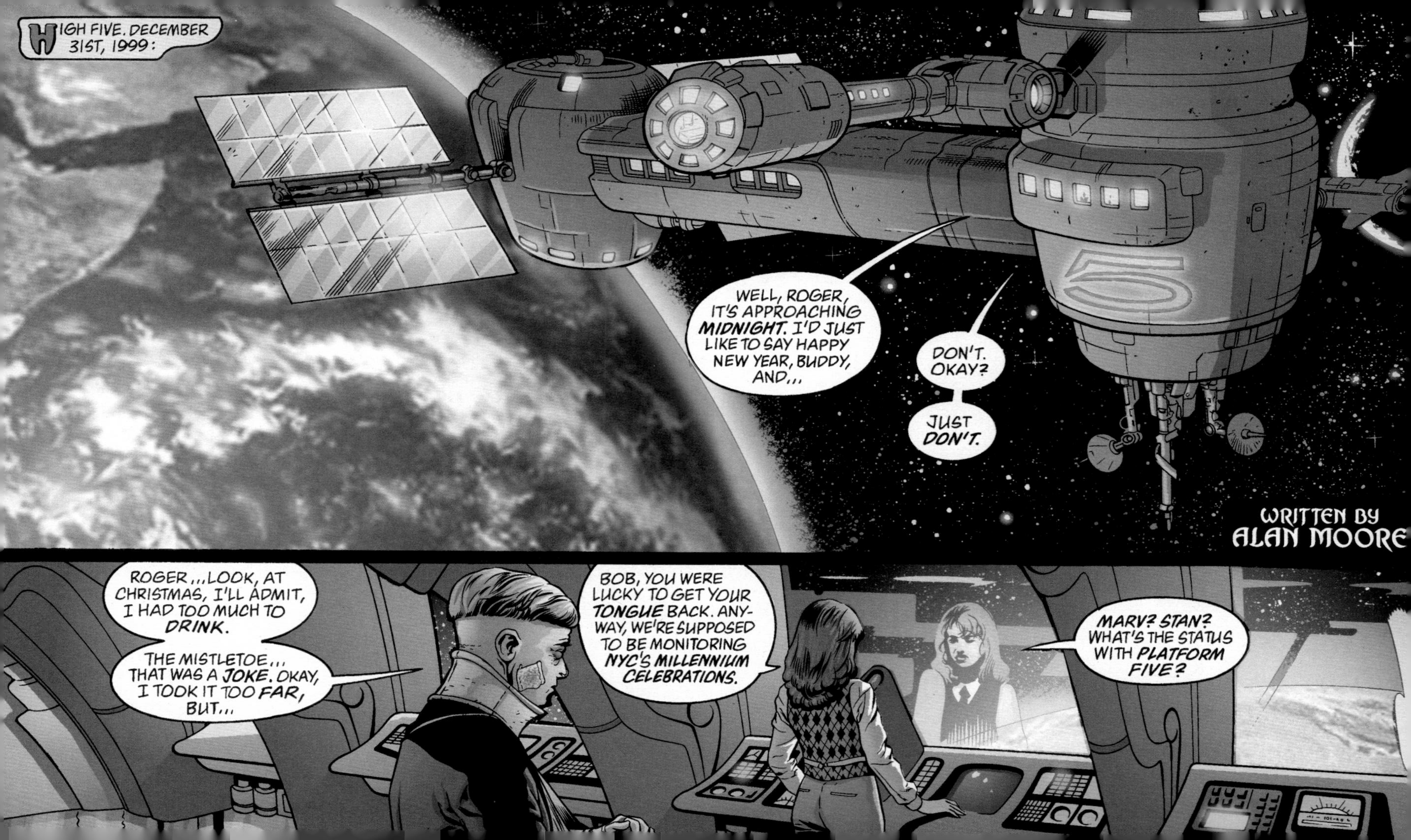
HIGH FIVE. DECEMBER 31ST, 1999:
WELL, ROGER, IT'S APPROACHING MIDNIGHT. I'D JUST LIKE TO SAY HAPPY NEW YEAR, BUDDY, AND...
DON'T. OKAY?
JUST DON'T.
WRITTEN BY ALAN MOORE
ROGER... LOOK, AT CHRISTMAS, I'LL ADMIT, I HAD TOO MUCH TO DRINK.
THE MISTLETOE... THAT WAS A JOKE. OKAY, I TOOK IT TOO FAR, BUT...
BOB, YOU WERE LUCKY TO GET YOUR TONGUE BACK. ANY-WAY, WE'RE SUPPOSED TO BE MONITORING NYC'S MILLENNIUM CELEBRATIONS.
MARV? STAN? WHAT'S THE STATUS WITH PLATFORM FIVE?

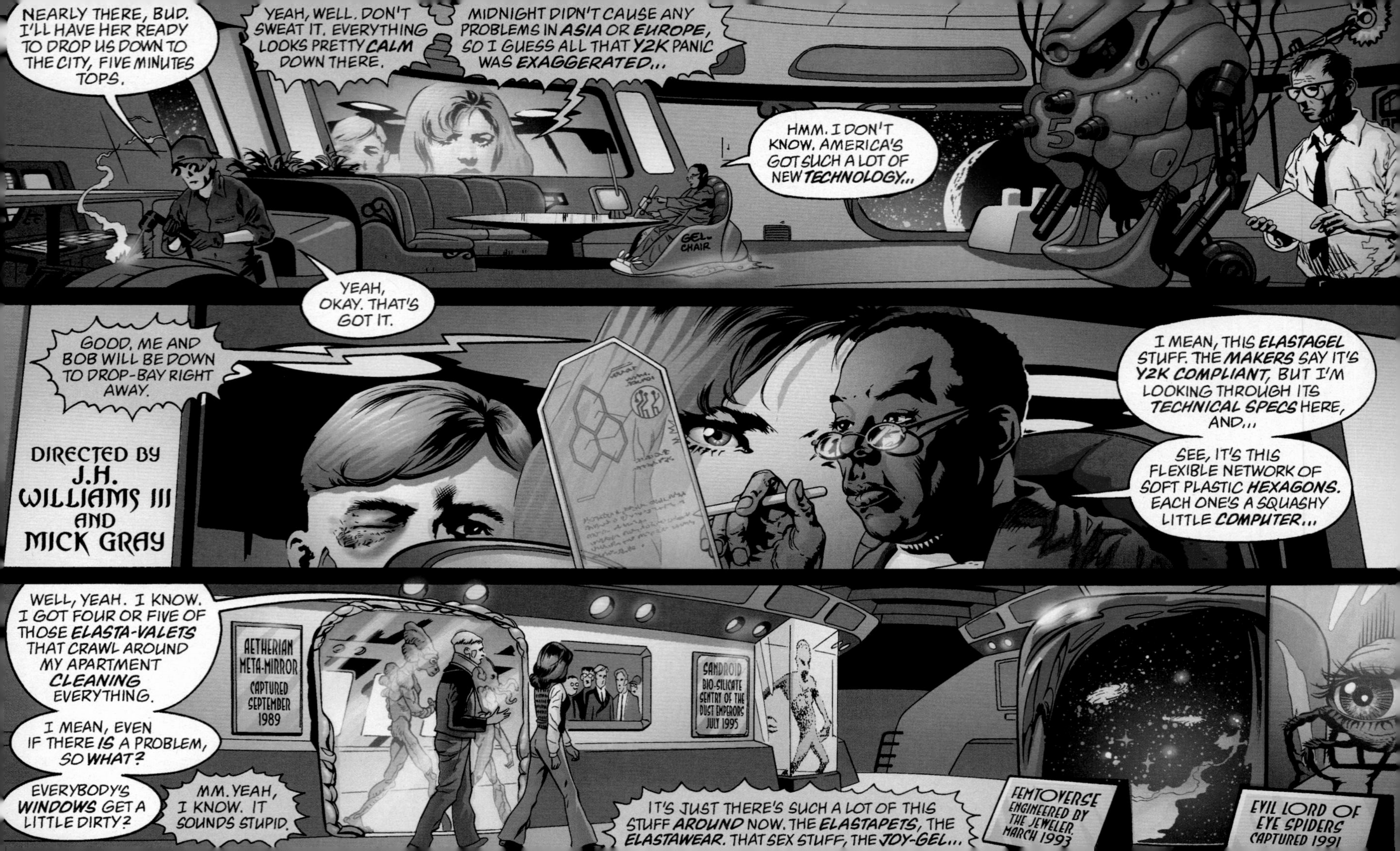
NEARLY THERE, BUD. I'LL HAVE HER READY TO DROP US DOWN TO THE CITY, FIVE MINUTES TOPS.
YEAH, WELL. DON'T SWEAT IT. EVERYTHING LOOKS PRETTY CALM DOWN THERE.
MIDNIGHT DIDN'T CAUSE ANY PROBLEMS IN ASIA OR EUROPE, SO I GUESS ALL THAT Y2K PANIC WAS EXAGGERATED...
HMM. I DON'T KNOW. AMERICA'S GOT SUCH A LOT OF NEW TECHNOLOGY...
GEL-CHAIR
YEAH, OKAY. THAT'S GOT IT.
GOOD, ME AND BOB WILL BE DOWN TO DROP-BAY RIGHT AWAY.
I MEAN, THIS ELASTAGEL STUFF. THE MAKERS SAY IT'S Y2K COMPLIANT, BUT I'M LOOKING THROUGH ITS TECHNICAL SPECS HERE, AND...
SEE, IT'S THIS FLEXIBLE NETWORK OF SOFT PLASTIC HEXAGONS. EACH ONE'S A SQUASHY LITTLE COMPUTER...
DIRECTED BY J.H. WILLIAMS III AND MICK GRAY
WELL, YEAH. I KNOW. I GOT FOUR OR FIVE OF THOSE ELASTA-VALETS THAT CRAWL AROUND MY APARTMENT CLEANING EVERYTHING.
I MEAN, EVEN IF THERE IS A PROBLEM, SO WHAT?
EVERYBODY'S WINDOWS GET A LITTLE DIRTY?
MM. YEAH, I KNOW. IT SOUNDS STUPID.
AETHERIAN META-MIRROR CAPTURED SEPTEMBER 1989
SANDROID BIO-SILICATE SENTRY OF THE DUST EMPERORS JULY 1995
IT'S JUST THERE'S SUCH A LOT OF THIS STUFF AROUND NOW. THE ELASTAPETS, THE ELASTAWEAR. THAT SEX STUFF, THE JOY-GEL...
FEMTOVERSE ENGINEERED BY THE JEWELER MARCH 1993
EVIL LORD OF EYE SPIDERS CAPTURED 1991

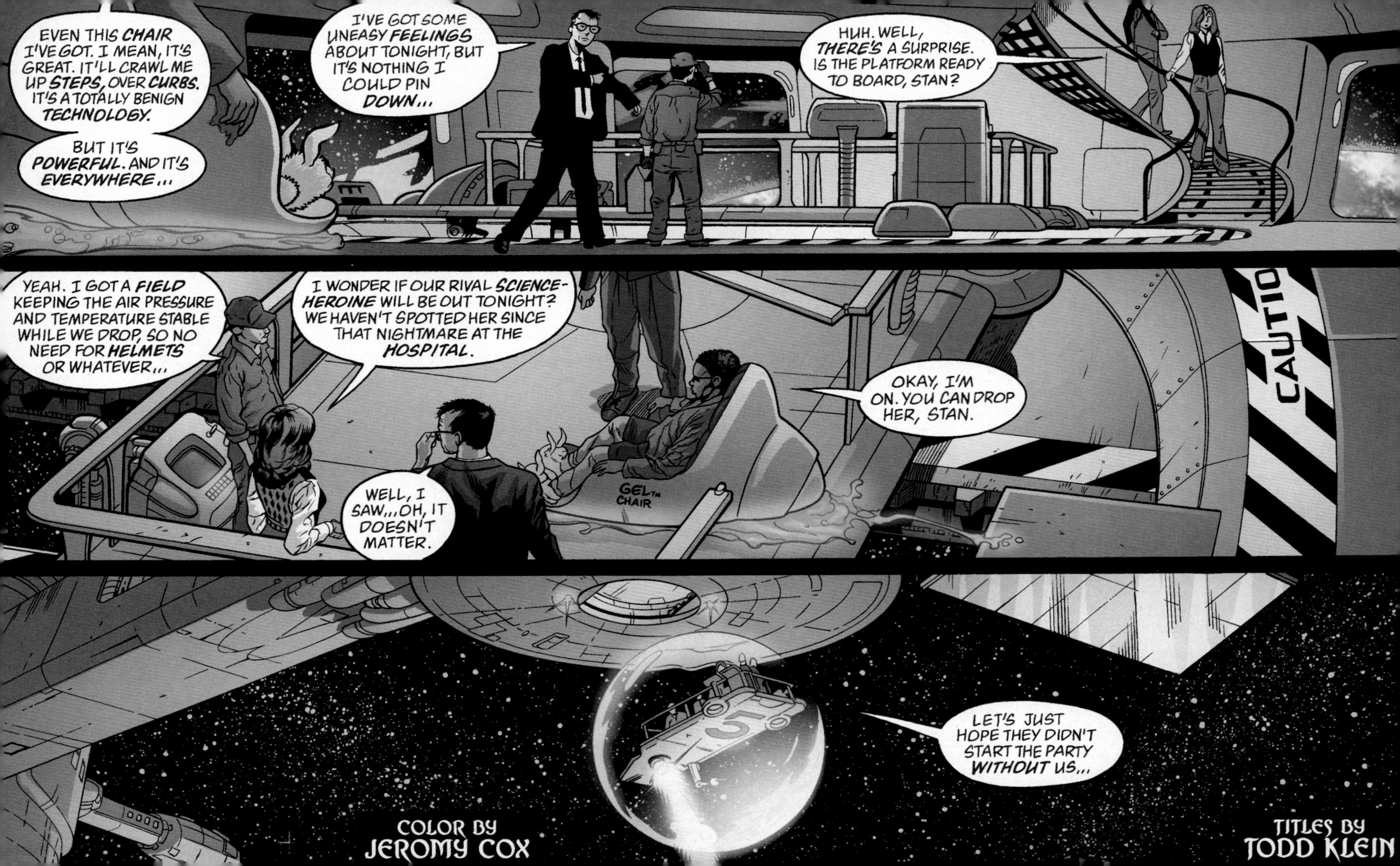
EVEN THIS **CHAIR** I'VE GOT. I MEAN, IT'S GREAT. IT'LL CRAWL ME UP **STEPS**, OVER **CURBS**. IT'S A TOTALLY BENIGN **TECHNOLOGY**.
BUT IT'S **POWERFUL**. AND IT'S **EVERYWHERE**...
I'VE GOT SOME UNEASY **FEELINGS** ABOUT TONIGHT, BUT IT'S NOTHING I COULD PIN **DOWN**...
HUH. WELL, **THERE'S** A SURPRISE. IS THE PLATFORM READY TO BOARD, STAN?
YEAH. I GOT A **FIELD** KEEPING THE AIR PRESSURE AND TEMPERATURE STABLE WHILE WE DROP, SO NO NEED FOR **HELMETS** OR WHATEVER...
I WONDER IF OUR RIVAL **SCIENCE-HEROINE** WILL BE OUT TONIGHT? WE HAVEN'T SPOTTED HER SINCE THAT NIGHTMARE AT THE **HOSPITAL**.
WELL, I SAW... OH, IT DOESN'T MATTER.
GEL™ CHAIR
OKAY, I'M ON. YOU CAN DROP HER, STAN.
CAUTIO
LET'S JUST HOPE THEY DIDN'T START THE PARTY **WITHOUT** US...
COLOR BY JEROMY COX
TITLES BY TODD KLEIN

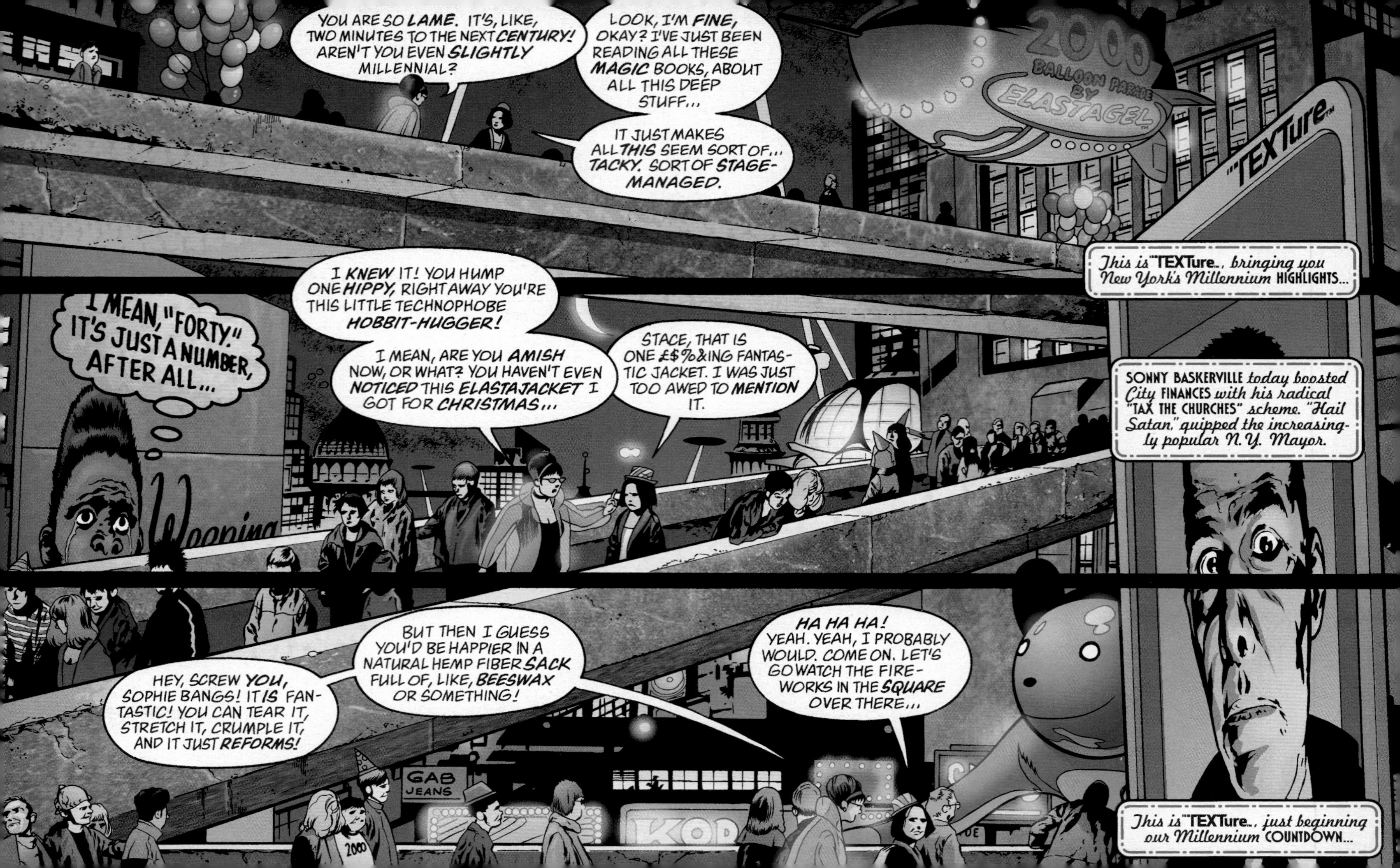

YOU ARE SO LAME. IT'S, LIKE, TWO MINUTES TO THE NEXT CENTURY! AREN'T YOU EVEN SLIGHTLY MILLENNIAL?
LOOK, I'M FINE, OKAY? I'VE JUST BEEN READING ALL THESE MAGIC BOOKS, ABOUT ALL THIS DEEP STUFF...
IT JUST MAKES ALL THIS SEEM SORT OF... TACKY. SORT OF STAGE-MANAGED.
2000 BALLOON PARADE BY ELASTAGEL
"TEXTure"
This is "TEXTure", bringing you New York's Millennium HIGHLIGHTS...
I KNEW IT! YOU HUMP ONE HIPPY, RIGHT AWAY YOU'RE THIS LITTLE TECHNOPHOBE HOBBIT-HUGGER!
I MEAN, ARE YOU AMISH NOW, OR WHAT? YOU HAVEN'T EVEN NOTICED THIS ELASTAJACKET I GOT FOR CHRISTMAS...
STACE, THAT IS ONE £$%&ING FANTASTIC JACKET. I WAS JUST TOO AWED TO MENTION IT.
I MEAN, "FORTY." IT'S JUST A NUMBER, AFTER ALL...
SONNY BASKERVILLE today boosted City FINANCES with his radical "TAX THE CHURCHES" scheme. "Hail Satan," quipped the increasingly popular N.Y. Mayor.
HEY, SCREW YOU, SOPHIE BANGS! IT IS FANTASTIC! YOU CAN TEAR IT, STRETCH IT, CRUMPLE IT, AND IT JUST REFORMS!
BUT THEN I GUESS YOU'D BE HAPPIER IN A NATURAL HEMP FIBER SACK FULL OF, LIKE, BEESWAX OR SOMETHING!
HA HA HA! YEAH. YEAH, I PROBABLY WOULD. COME ON. LET'S GO WATCH THE FIREWORKS IN THE SQUARE OVER THERE...
GAB JEANS
This is "TEXTure", just beginning our Millennium COUNTDOWN...

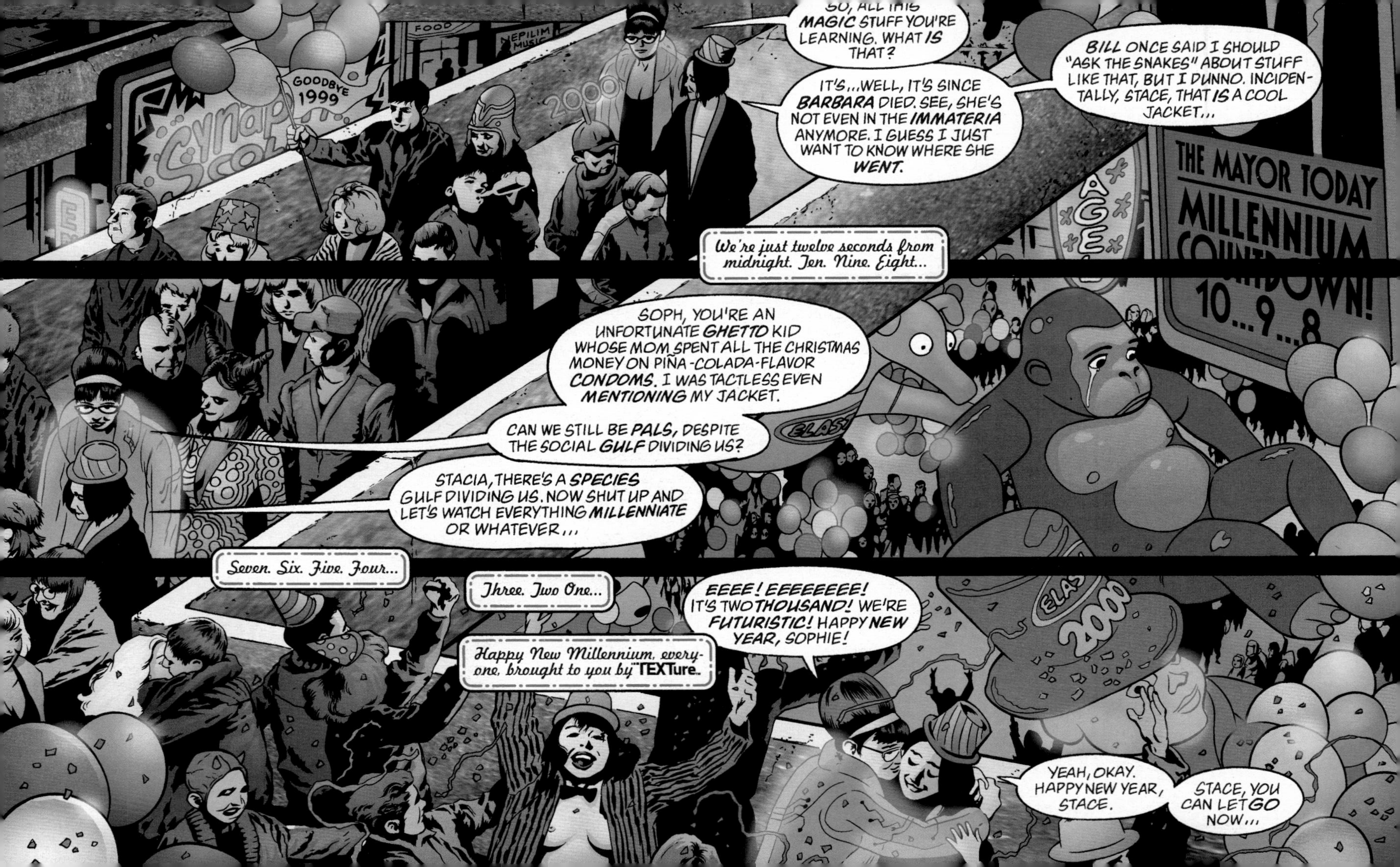
SO, ALL THIS MAGIC STUFF YOU'RE LEARNING. WHAT IS THAT?
IT'S...WELL, IT'S SINCE BARBARA DIED. SEE, SHE'S NOT EVEN IN THE IMMATERIA ANYMORE. I GUESS I JUST WANT TO KNOW WHERE SHE WENT.
BILL ONCE SAID I SHOULD "ASK THE SNAKES" ABOUT STUFF LIKE THAT, BUT I DUNNO. INCIDENTALLY, STACE, THAT IS A COOL JACKET...
GOODBYE 1999
FOOD
NEPILIM MUSIC
2000
THE MAYOR TODAY MILLENNIUM COUNTDOWN! 10...9...8
We're just twelve seconds from midnight. Ten. Nine. Eight...
SOPH, YOU'RE AN UNFORTUNATE GHETTO KID WHOSE MOM SPENT ALL THE CHRISTMAS MONEY ON PIÑA-COLADA-FLAVOR CONDOMS. I WAS TACTLESS EVEN MENTIONING MY JACKET.
CAN WE STILL BE PALS, DESPITE THE SOCIAL GULF DIVIDING US?
STACIA, THERE'S A SPECIES GULF DIVIDING US. NOW SHUT UP AND LET'S WATCH EVERYTHING MILLENNIATE OR WHATEVER...
Seven. Six. Five. Four...
Three. Two One...
EEEE! EEEEEEEE! IT'S TWO THOUSAND! WE'RE FUTURISTIC! HAPPY NEW YEAR, SOPHIE!
Happy New Millennium, everyone, brought to you by TEXTure.
2000
YEAH, OKAY. HAPPY NEW YEAR, STACE.
STACE, YOU CAN LET GO NOW...

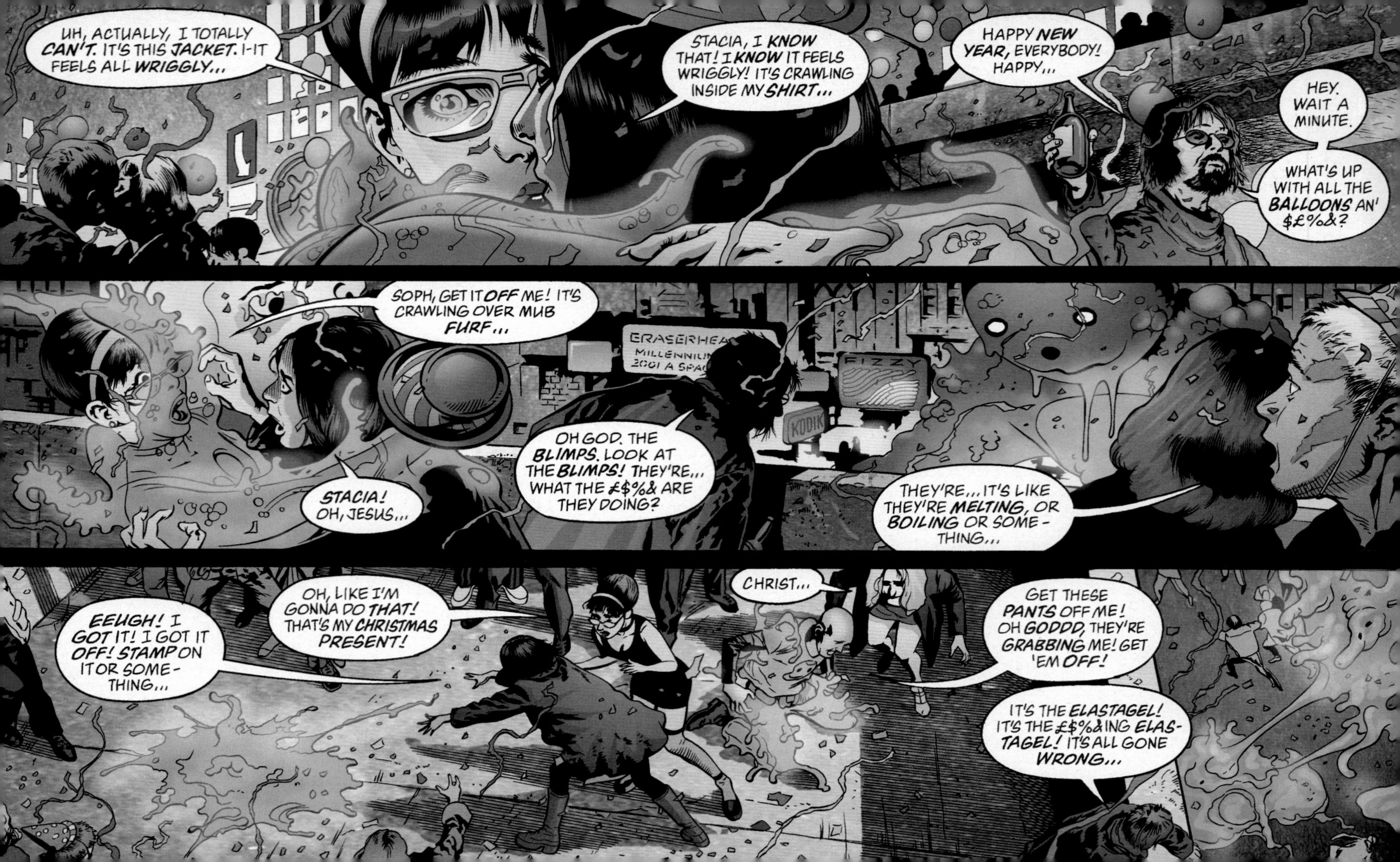
UH, ACTUALLY, I TOTALLY CAN'T. IT'S THIS JACKET. I-IT FEELS ALL WRIGGLY...
STACIA, I KNOW THAT! I KNOW IT FEELS WRIGGLY! IT'S CRAWLING INSIDE MY SHIRT...
HAPPY NEW YEAR, EVERYBODY! HAPPY...
HEY. WAIT A MINUTE.
WHAT'S UP WITH ALL THE BALLOONS AN' $£%&?
SOPH, GET IT OFF ME! IT'S CRAWLING OVER MUB FURF...
STACIA! OH, JESUS...
OH GOD. THE BLIMPS. LOOK AT THE BLIMPS! THEY'RE... WHAT THE £$%& ARE THEY DOING?
ERASERHEA
MILLENNIUM
2001 A SPAC
FIZZY
KODIK
THEY'RE... IT'S LIKE THEY'RE MELTING, OR BOILING OR SOME-THING...
EEUGH! I GOT IT! I GOT IT OFF! STAMP ON IT OR SOME-THING...
OH, LIKE I'M GONNA DO THAT! THAT'S MY CHRISTMAS PRESENT!
CHRIST...
GET THESE PANTS OFF ME! OH GODDD, THEY'RE GRABBING ME! GET 'EM OFF!
IT'S THE ELASTAGEL! IT'S THE £$%&ING ELAS-TAGEL! IT'S ALL GONE WRONG...

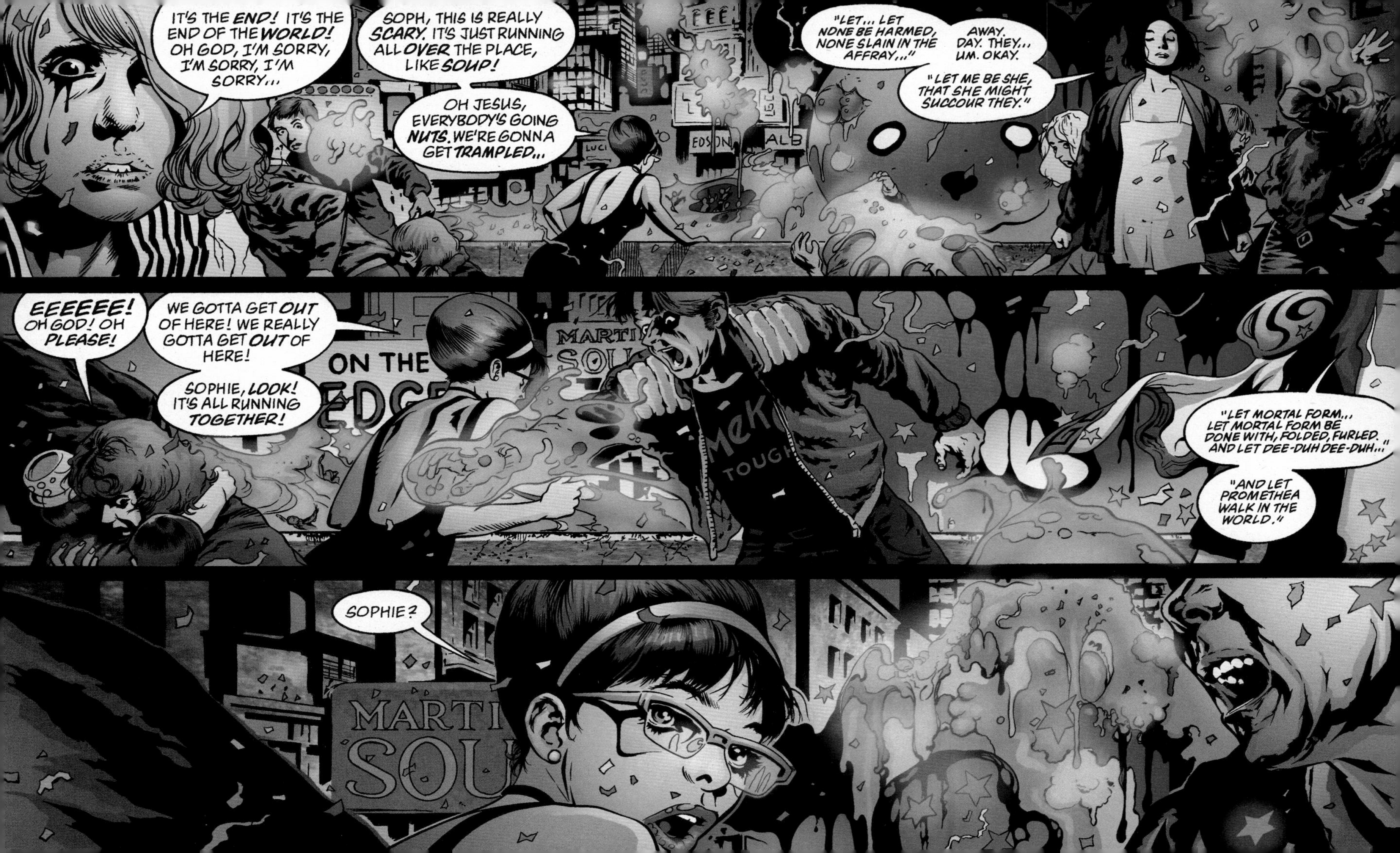
IT'S THE END! IT'S THE END OF THE WORLD! OH GOD, I'M SORRY, I'M SORRY, I'M SORRY...
SOPH, THIS IS REALLY SCARY. IT'S JUST RUNNING ALL OVER THE PLACE, LIKE SOUP!
OH JESUS, EVERYBODY'S GOING NUTS. WE'RE GONNA GET TRAMPLED...
"LET... LET NONE BE HARMED, NONE SLAIN IN THE AFFRAY..."
AWAY. DAY. THEY... UM. OKAY.
"LET ME BE SHE, THAT SHE MIGHT SUCCOUR THEY."
EEEEEE! OH GOD! OH PLEASE!
WE GOTTA GET OUT OF HERE! WE REALLY GOTTA GET OUT OF HERE!
SOPHIE, LOOK! IT'S ALL RUNNING TOGETHER!
ON THE EDG
MARTI SOU
"LET MORTAL FORM... LET MORTAL FORM BE DONE WITH, FOLDED, FURLED. AND LET DEE-DUH DEE-DUH..."
"AND LET PROMETHEA WALK IN THE WORLD."
SOPHIE?
MARTI SOU

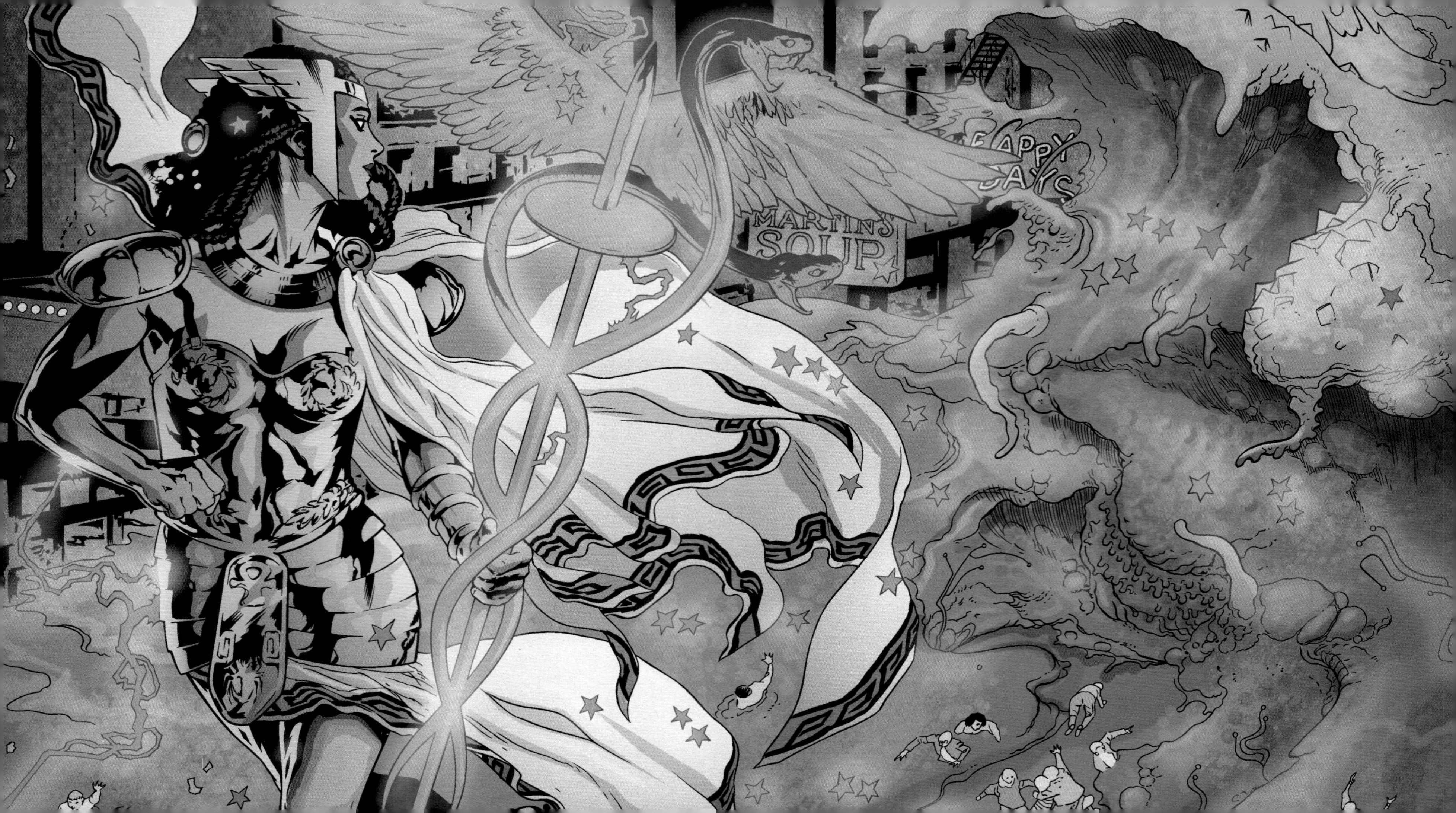
MARTIN'S SOUP

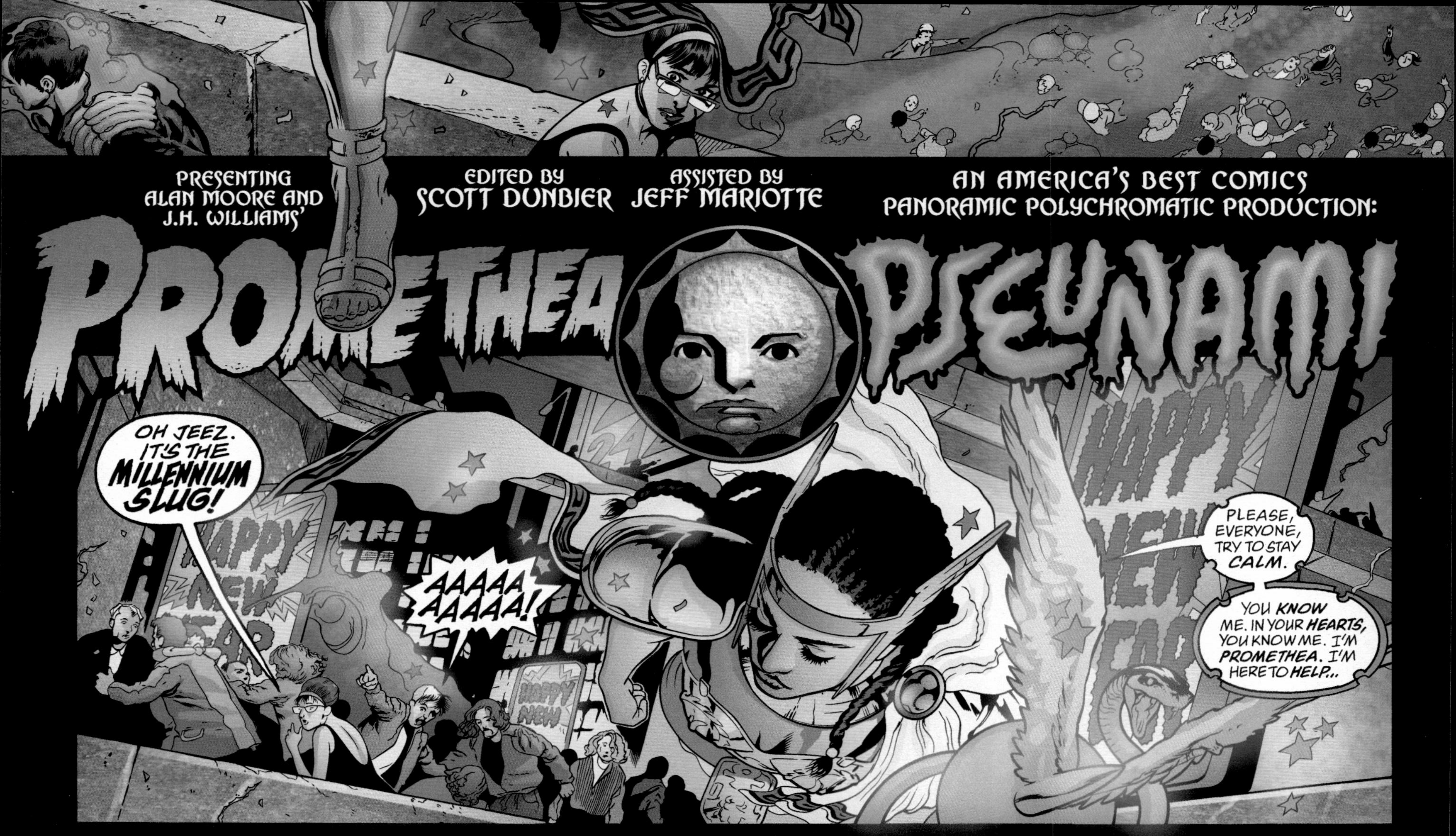

PRESENTING ALAN MOORE AND J.H. WILLIAMS'
EDITED BY SCOTT DUNBIER
ASSISTED BY JEFF MARIOTTE
AN AMERICA'S BEST COMICS PANORAMIC POLYCHROMATIC PRODUCTION:
PROMETHEA
PSEUNAMI
OH JEEZ. IT'S THE MILLENNIUM SLUG!
AAAAA AAAAA!
PLEASE, EVERYONE, TRY TO STAY CALM.
YOU KNOW ME. IN YOUR HEARTS, YOU KNOW ME. I'M PROMETHEA. I'M HERE TO HELP...

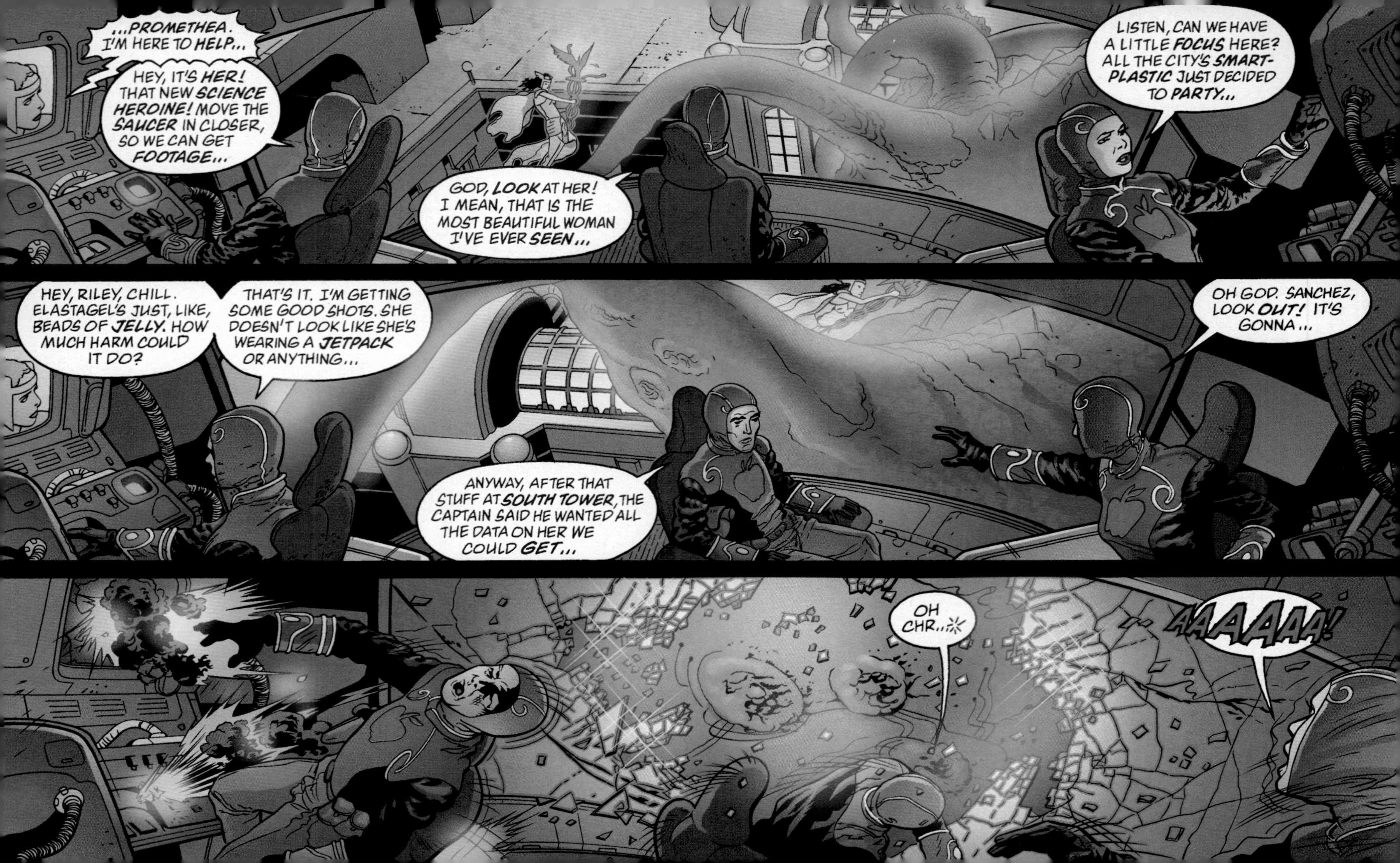
...PROMETHEA. I'M HERE TO HELP...
HEY, IT'S HER! THAT NEW SCIENCE HEROINE! MOVE THE SAUCER IN CLOSER, SO WE CAN GET FOOTAGE...
GOD, LOOK AT HER! I MEAN, THAT IS THE MOST BEAUTIFUL WOMAN I'VE EVER SEEN...
LISTEN, CAN WE HAVE A LITTLE FOCUS HERE? ALL THE CITY'S SMART-PLASTIC JUST DECIDED TO PARTY...
HEY, RILEY, CHILL. ELASTAGEL'S JUST, LIKE, BEADS OF JELLY. HOW MUCH HARM COULD IT DO?
THAT'S IT. I'M GETTING SOME GOOD SHOTS. SHE DOESN'T LOOK LIKE SHE'S WEARING A JETPACK OR ANYTHING...
ANYWAY, AFTER THAT STUFF AT SOUTH TOWER, THE CAPTAIN SAID HE WANTED ALL THE DATA ON HER WE COULD GET...
OH GOD. SANCHEZ, LOOK OUT! IT'S GONNA...
OH CHR...
AAAAAA!

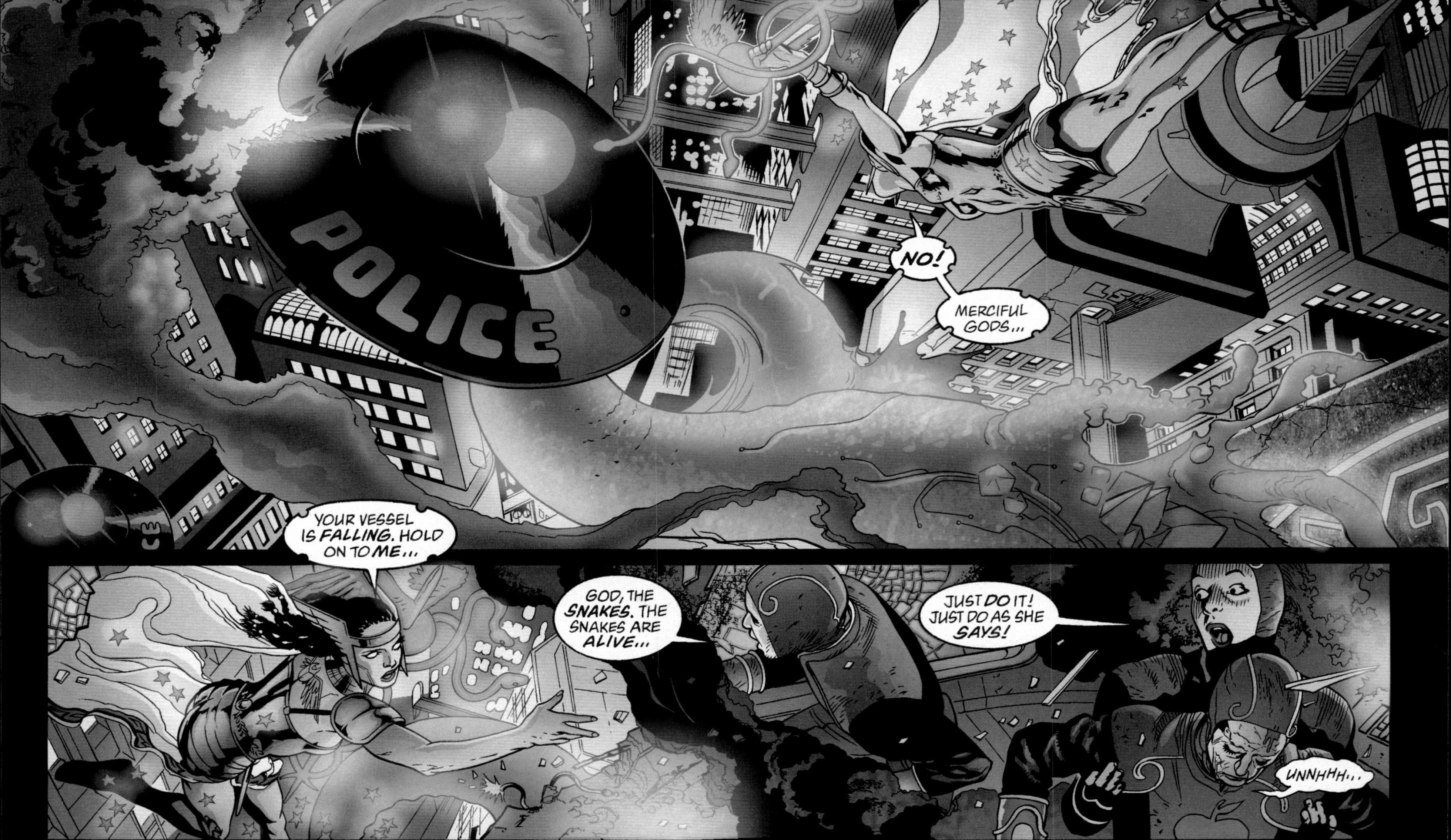
POLICE
NO!
MERCIFUL GODS...
YOUR VESSEL IS FALLING. HOLD ON TO ME...
GOD, THE SNAKES. THE SNAKES ARE ALIVE...
JUST DO IT! JUST DO AS SHE SAYS!
UNNHHH...

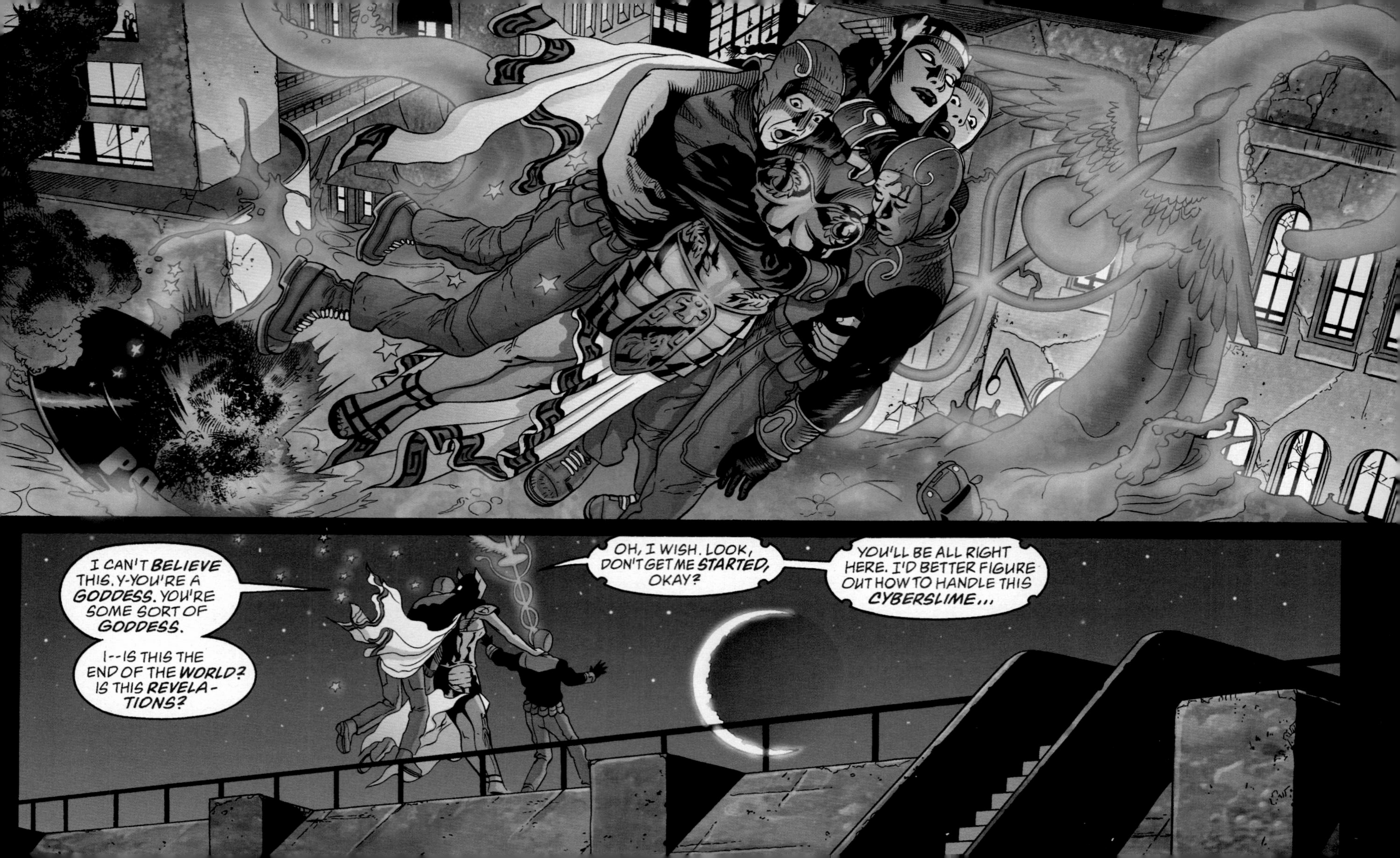
I CAN'T BELIEVE THIS. Y-YOU'RE A GODDESS. YOU'RE SOME SORT OF GODDESS.
I--IS THIS THE END OF THE WORLD? IS THIS REVELATIONS?
OH, I WISH. LOOK, DON'T GET ME STARTED, OKAY?
YOU'LL BE ALL RIGHT HERE. I'D BETTER FIGURE OUT HOW TO HANDLE THIS CYBERSLIME...

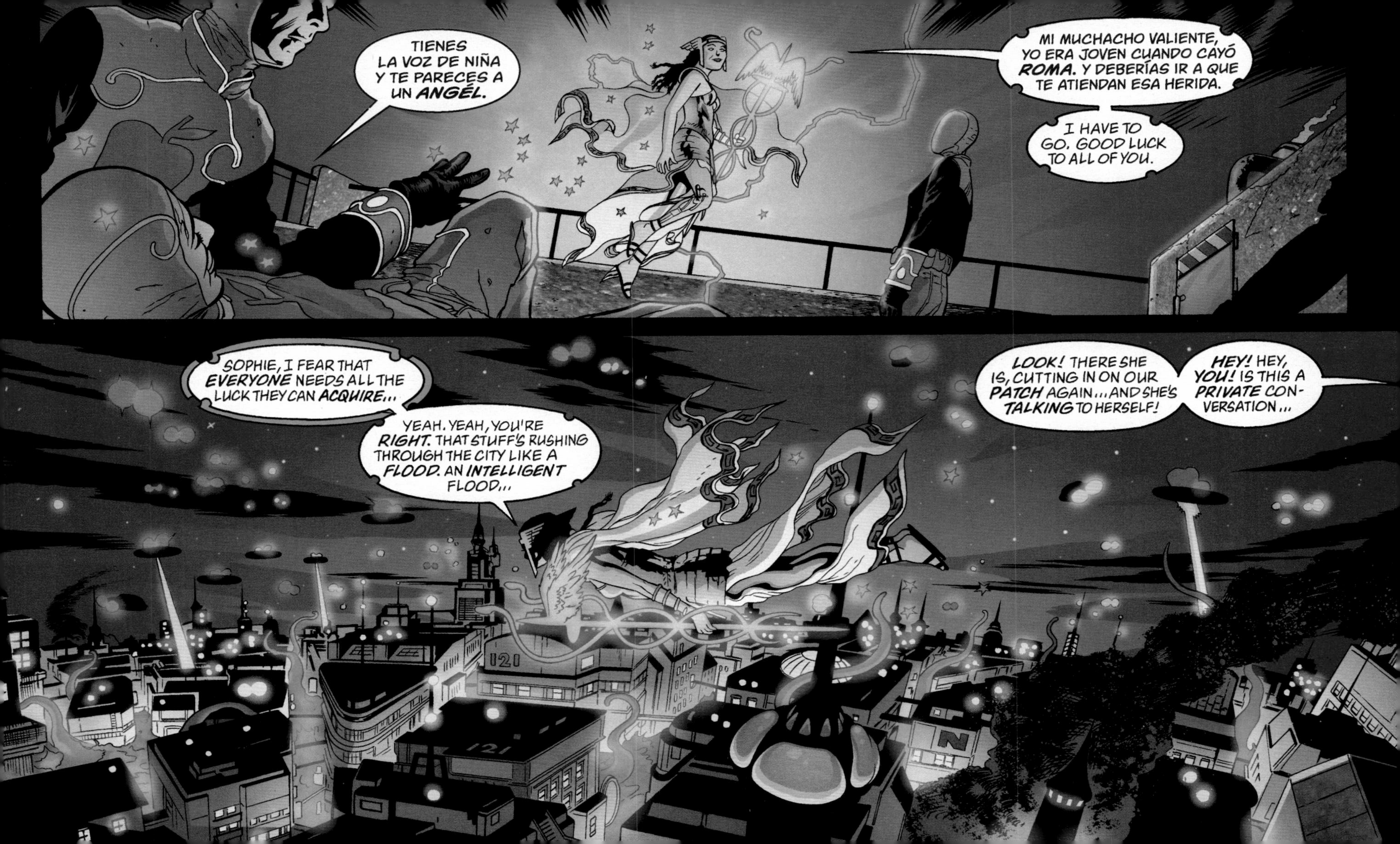
TIENES LA VOZ DE NIÑA Y TE PARECES A UN ANGÉL.
MI MUCHACHO VALIENTE, YO ERA JOVEN CUANDO CAYÓ ROMA. Y DEBERÍAS IR A QUE TE ATIENDAN ESA HERIDA.
I HAVE TO GO. GOOD LUCK TO ALL OF YOU.
SOPHIE, I FEAR THAT EVERYONE NEEDS ALL THE LUCK THEY CAN ACQUIRE...
YEAH. YEAH, YOU'RE RIGHT. THAT STUFF'S RUSHING THROUGH THE CITY LIKE A FLOOD. AN INTELLIGENT FLOOD...
LOOK! THERE SHE IS, CUTTING IN ON OUR PATCH AGAIN... AND SHE'S TALKING TO HERSELF!
HEY! HEY, YOU! IS THIS A PRIVATE CONVERSATION...

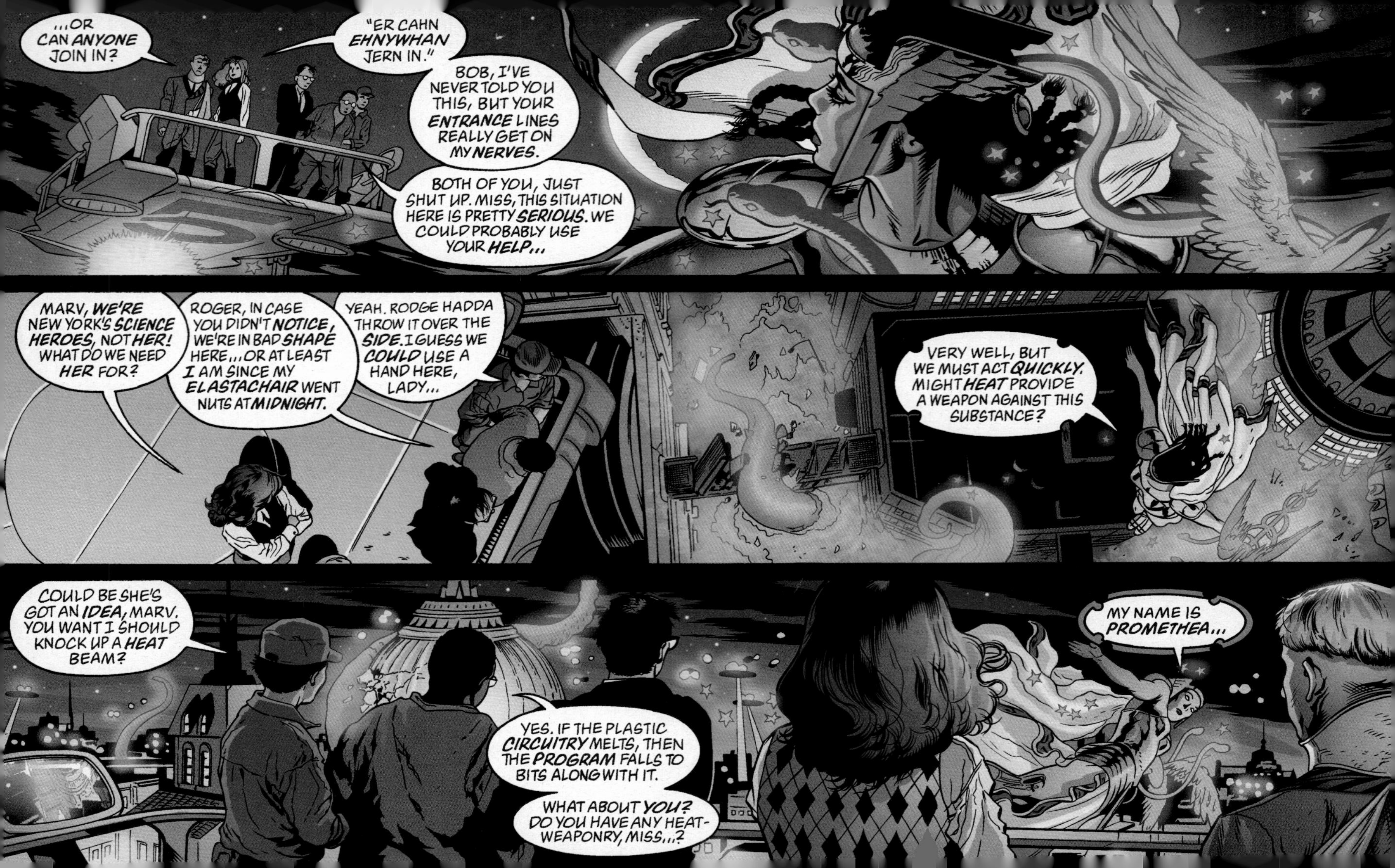
...OR CAN ANYONE JOIN IN?
"ER CAHN EHNYWHAN JERN IN."
BOB, I'VE NEVER TOLD YOU THIS, BUT YOUR ENTRANCE LINES REALLY GET ON MY NERVES.
BOTH OF YOU, JUST SHUT UP. MISS, THIS SITUATION HERE IS PRETTY SERIOUS. WE COULD PROBABLY USE YOUR HELP...
MARV, WE'RE NEW YORK'S SCIENCE HEROES, NOT HER! WHAT DO WE NEED HER FOR?
ROGER, IN CASE YOU DIDN'T NOTICE, WE'RE IN BAD SHAPE HERE... OR AT LEAST I AM SINCE MY ELASTACHAIR WENT NUTS AT MIDNIGHT.
YEAH. RODGE HADDA THROW IT OVER THE SIDE. I GUESS WE COULD USE A HAND HERE, LADY...
VERY WELL, BUT WE MUST ACT QUICKLY. MIGHT HEAT PROVIDE A WEAPON AGAINST THIS SUBSTANCE?
COULD BE SHE'S GOT AN IDEA, MARV. YOU WANT I SHOULD KNOCK UP A HEAT BEAM?
YES. IF THE PLASTIC CIRCUITRY MELTS, THEN THE PROGRAM FALLS TO BITS ALONG WITH IT.
WHAT ABOUT YOU? DO YOU HAVE ANY HEAT-WEAPONRY, MISS...?
MY NAME IS PROMETHEA...

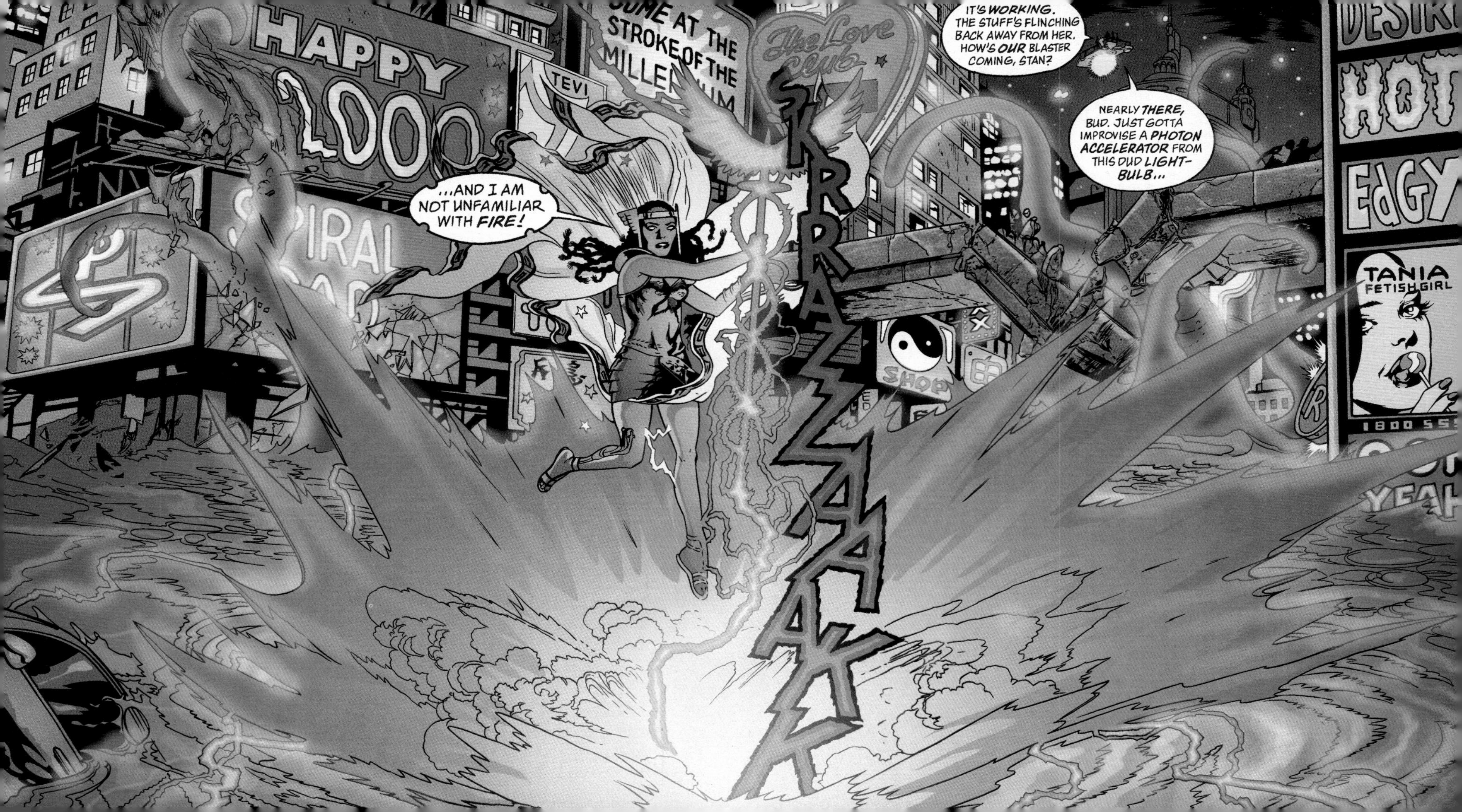
HAPPY 2000
STROKE OF THE
...AND I AM NOT UNFAMILIAR WITH FIRE!
SKRAZZAAKAAK
IT'S WORKING. THE STUFF'S FLINCHING BACK AWAY FROM HER. HOW'S OUR BLASTER COMING, STAN?
NEARLY THERE, BUD. JUST GOTTA IMPROVISE A PHOTON ACCELERATOR FROM THIS DUD LIGHT-BULB...
HOT
EDGY
TANIA
FETISHGIRL

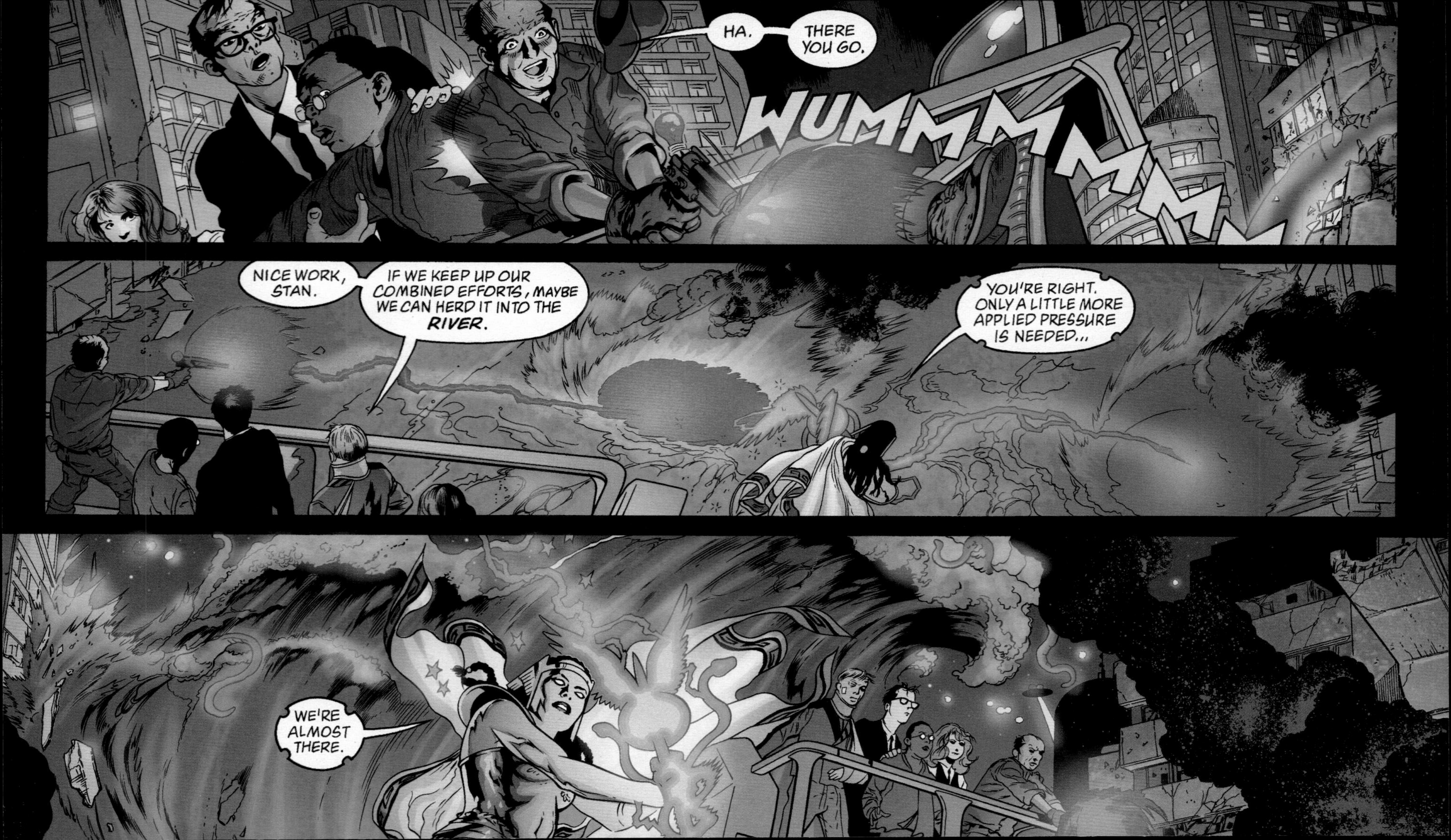
HA.
THERE YOU GO.
WUMMMMMM
NICE WORK, STAN.
IF WE KEEP UP OUR COMBINED EFFORTS, MAYBE WE CAN HERD IT INTO THE RIVER.
YOU'RE RIGHT. ONLY A LITTLE MORE APPLIED PRESSURE IS NEEDED...
WE'RE ALMOST THERE.

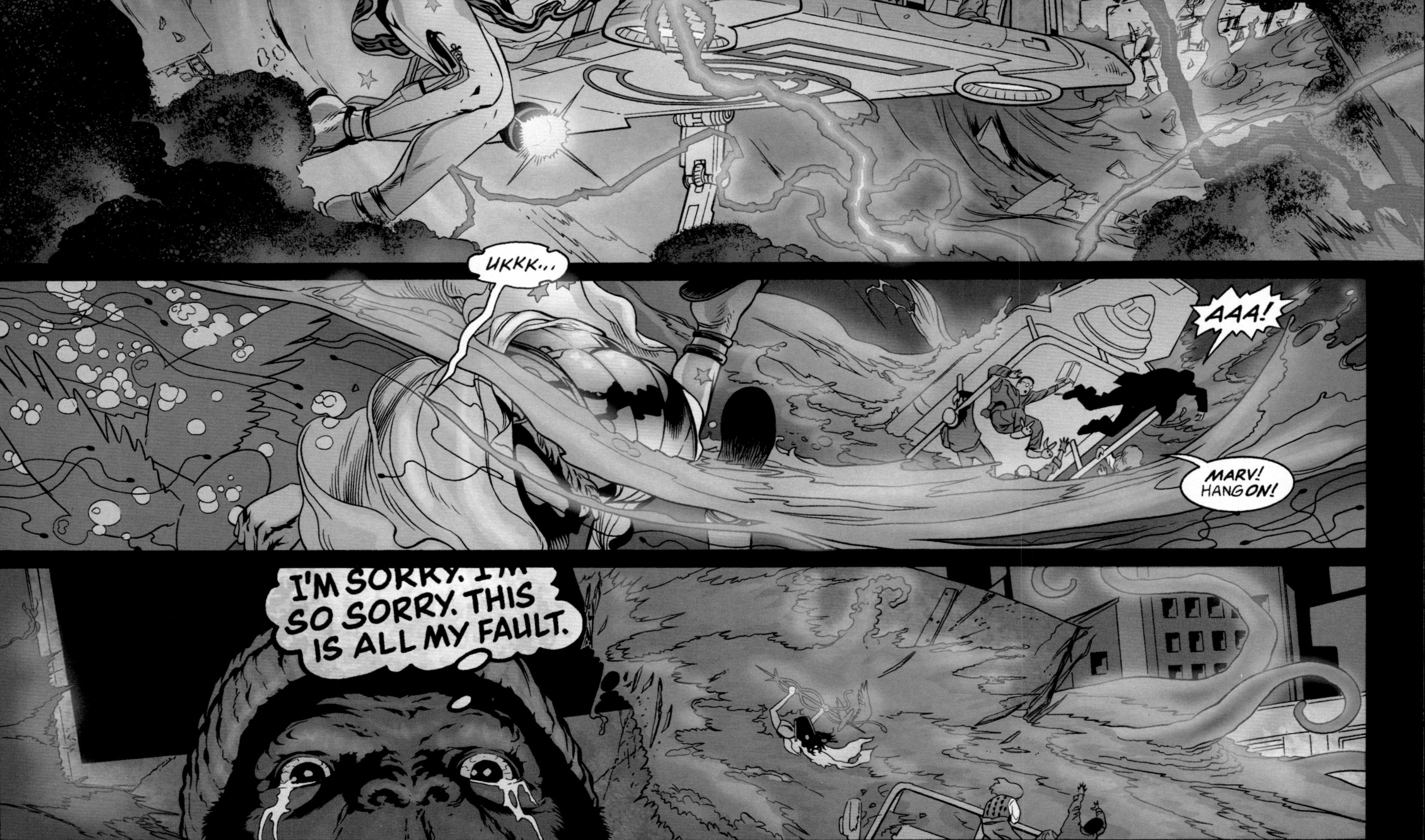
UKKK...
AAA!
MARV! HANG ON!
I'M SORRY. I'M SO SORRY. THIS IS ALL MY FAULT.

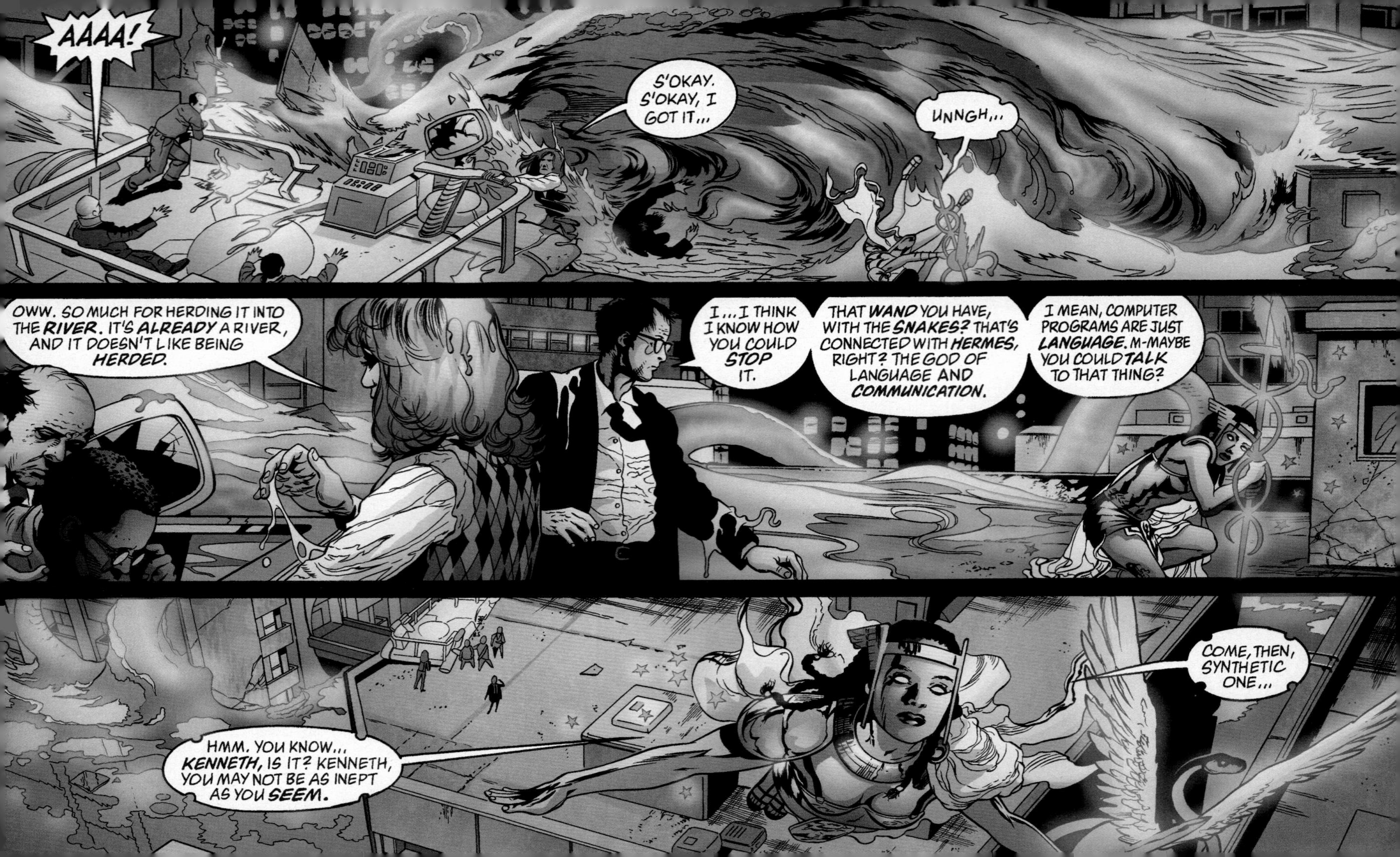
AAAA!
S'OKAY. S'OKAY, I GOT IT...
UNNGH...
OWW. SO MUCH FOR HERDING IT INTO THE RIVER. IT'S ALREADY A RIVER, AND IT DOESN'T LIKE BEING HERDED.
I... I THINK I KNOW HOW YOU COULD STOP IT.
THAT WAND YOU HAVE, WITH THE SNAKES? THAT'S CONNECTED WITH HERMES, RIGHT? THE GOD OF LANGUAGE AND COMMUNICATION.
I MEAN, COMPUTER PROGRAMS ARE JUST LANGUAGE. M-MAYBE YOU COULD TALK TO THAT THING?
HMM. YOU KNOW... KENNETH, IS IT? KENNETH, YOU MAY NOT BE AS INEPT AS YOU SEEM.
COME, THEN, SYNTHETIC ONE...

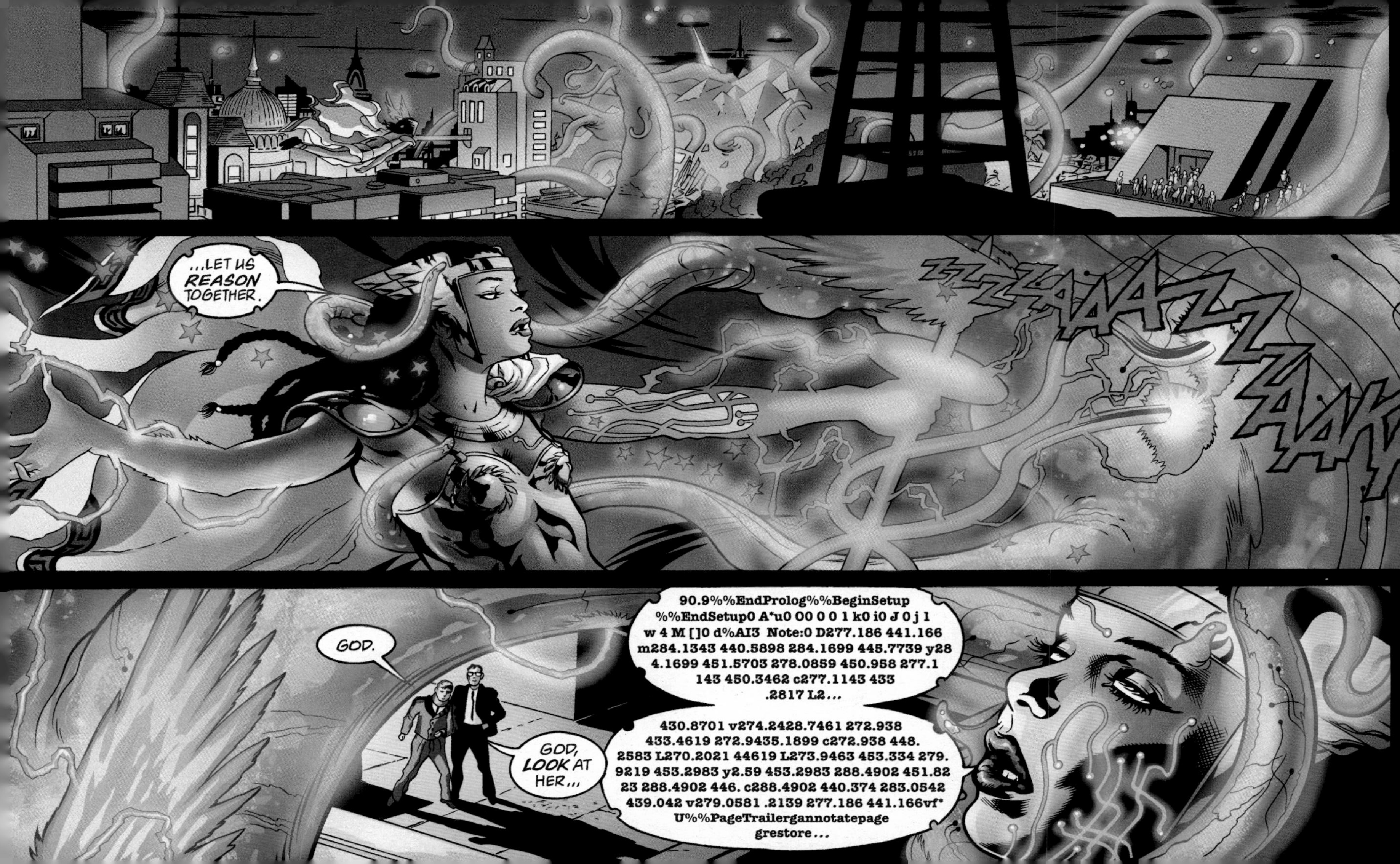
...LET US REASON TOGETHER.
90.9%%EndProlog%%BeginSetup %%EndSetup0 A*u0 O0 0 0 1 k0 i0 J 0 j 1 w 4 M []0 d%AI3 Note:0 D277.186 441.166 m284.1343 440.5898 284.1699 445.7739 y28 4.1699 451.5703 278.0859 450.958 277.1 143 450.3462 c277.1143 433 .2817 L2...
430.8701 v274.2428.7461 272.938 433.4619 272.9435.1899 c272.938 448. 2583 L270.2021 44619 L273.9463 453.334 279. 9219 453.2983 y2.59 453.2983 288.4902 451.82 23 288.4902 446. c288.4902 440.374 283.0542 439.042 v279.0581 .2139 277.186 441.166vf* U%%PageTrailergannotatepage grestore...
GOD, LOOK AT HER...
GOD.

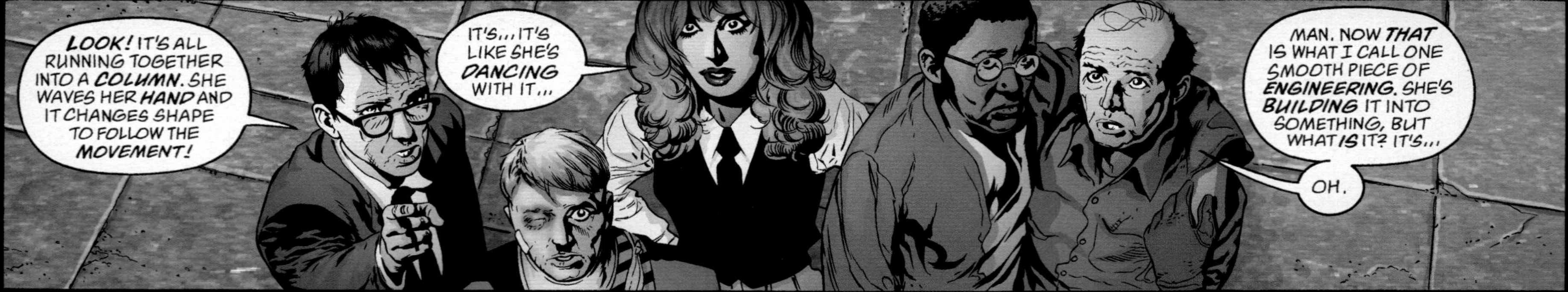
LOOK! IT'S ALL RUNNING TOGETHER INTO A COLUMN. SHE WAVES HER HAND AND IT CHANGES SHAPE TO FOLLOW THE MOVEMENT!
IT'S... IT'S LIKE SHE'S DANCING WITH IT...
MAN. NOW THAT IS WHAT I CALL ONE SMOOTH PIECE OF ENGINEERING. SHE'S BUILDING IT INTO SOMETHING, BUT WHAT IS IT? IT'S...
OH.
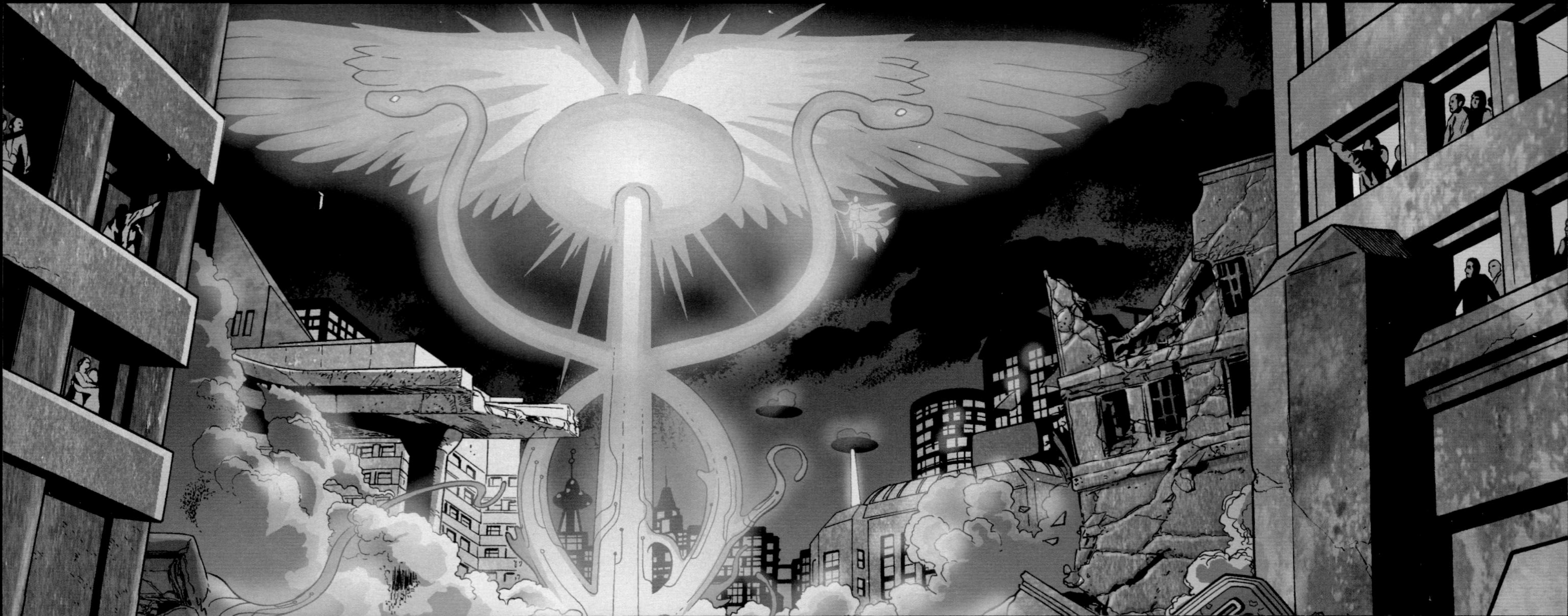

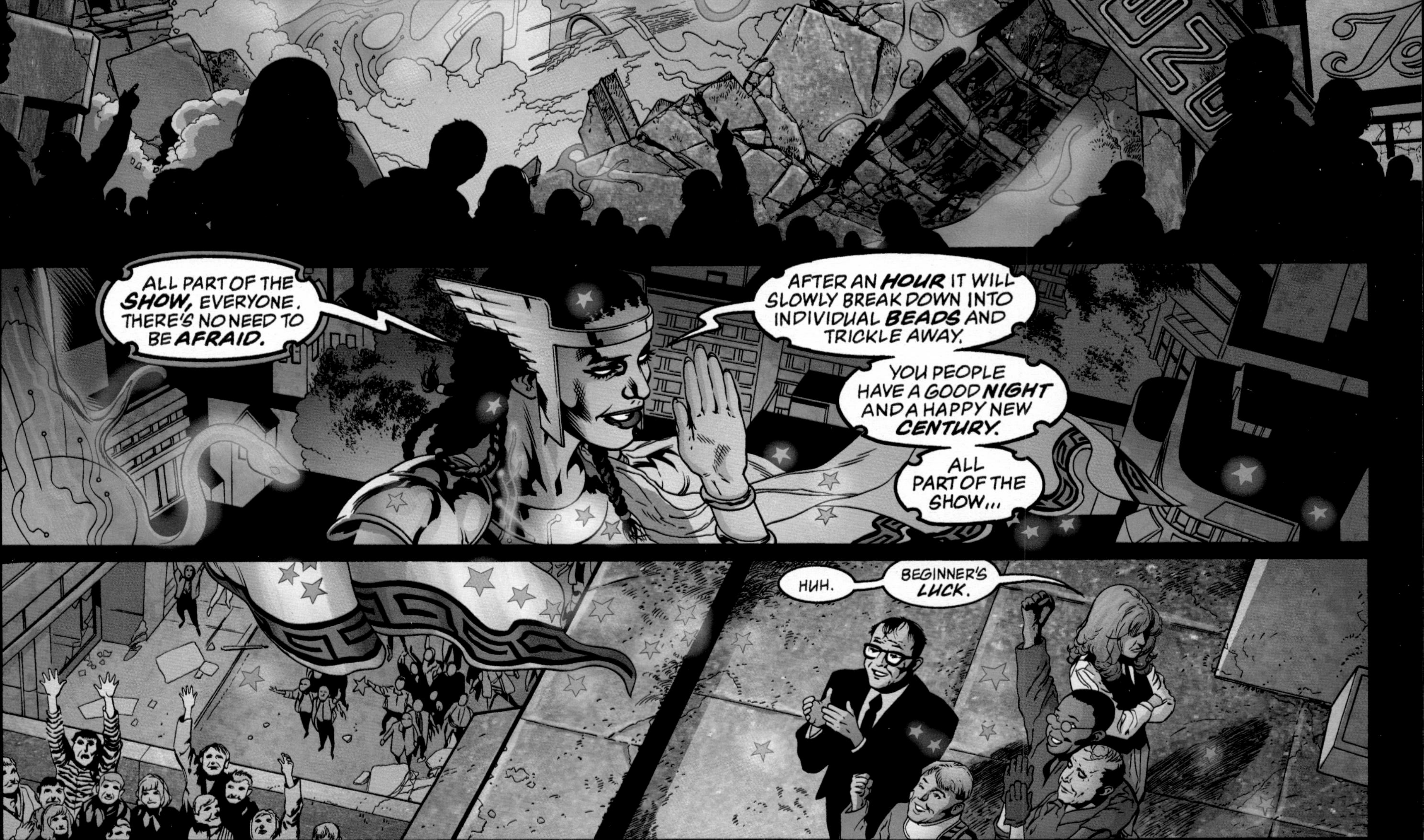
ALL PART OF THE SHOW, EVERYONE. THERE'S NO NEED TO BE AFRAID.
AFTER AN HOUR IT WILL SLOWLY BREAK DOWN INTO INDIVIDUAL BEADS AND TRICKLE AWAY.
YOU PEOPLE HAVE A GOOD NIGHT AND A HAPPY NEW CENTURY.
ALL PART OF THE SHOW...
BEGINNER'S LUCK.
HUH.

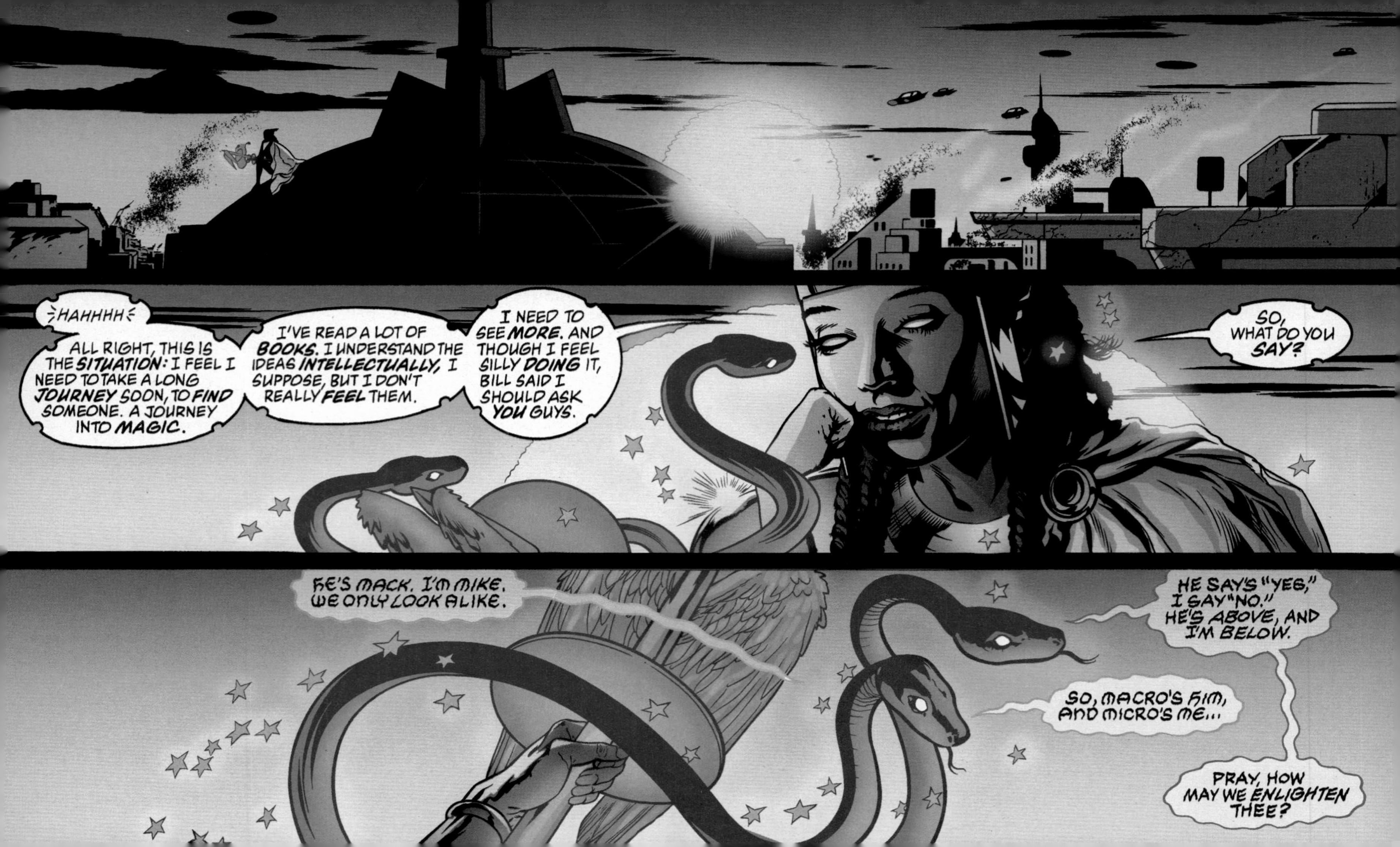

≷HAHHHH≶
ALL RIGHT, THIS IS THE SITUATION: I FEEL I NEED TO TAKE A LONG JOURNEY SOON, TO FIND SOMEONE. A JOURNEY INTO MAGIC.
I'VE READ A LOT OF BOOKS. I UNDERSTAND THE IDEAS INTELLECTUALLY, I SUPPOSE, BUT I DON'T REALLY FEEL THEM.
I NEED TO SEE MORE. AND THOUGH I FEEL SILLY DOING IT, BILL SAID I SHOULD ASK YOU GUYS.
SO, WHAT DO YOU SAY?
HE'S MACK. I'M MIKE. WE ONLY LOOK ALIKE.
HE SAY'S "YES," I SAY "NO." HE'S ABOVE, AND I'M BELOW.
SO, MACRO'S HIM, AND MICRO'S ME...
PRAY, HOW MAY WE ENLIGHTEN THEE?

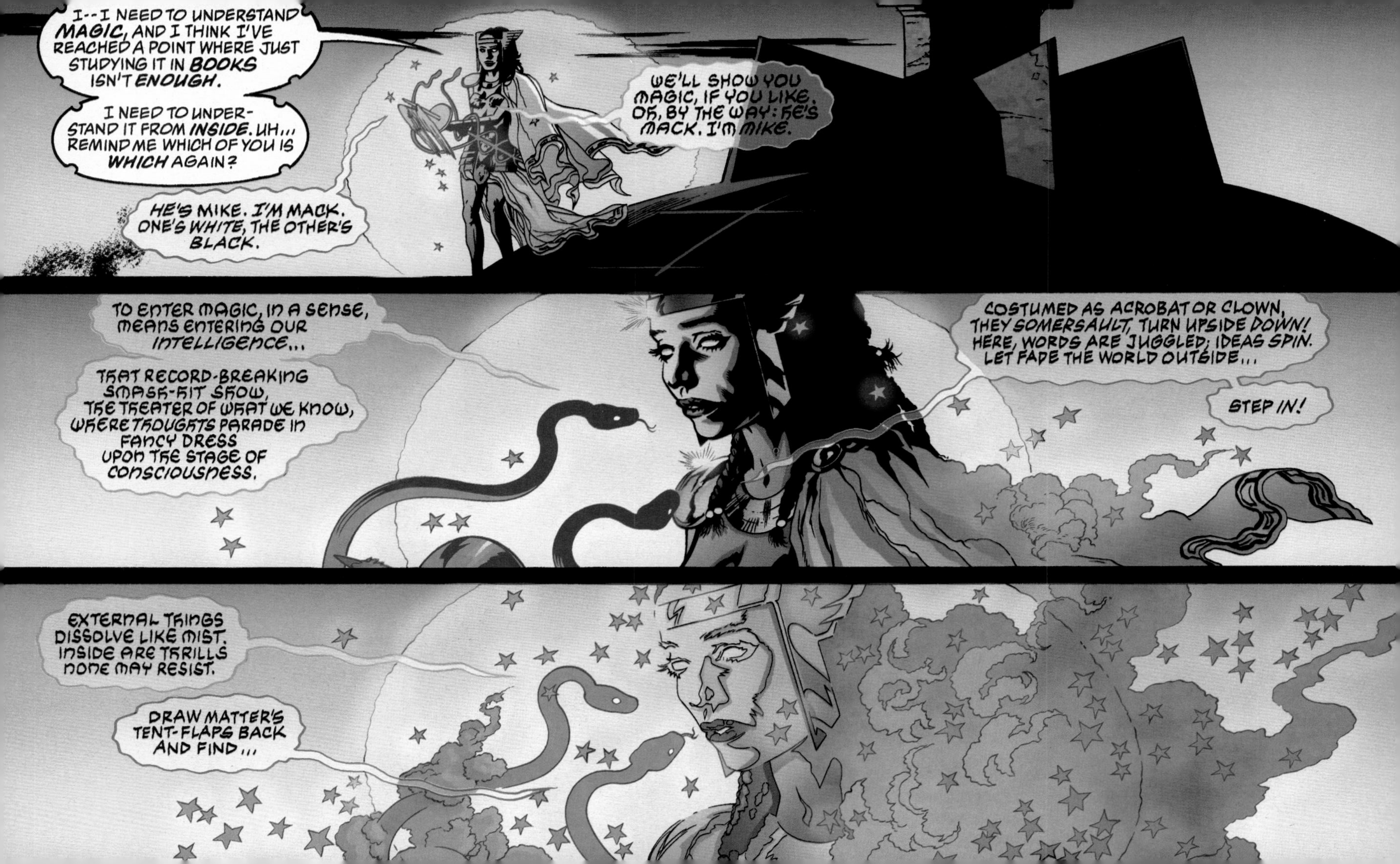
I--I NEED TO UNDERSTAND MAGIC, AND I THINK I'VE REACHED A POINT WHERE JUST STUDYING IT IN BOOKS ISN'T ENOUGH.
I NEED TO UNDER-STAND IT FROM INSIDE. UH... REMIND ME WHICH OF YOU IS WHICH AGAIN?
WE'LL SHOW YOU MAGIC, IF YOU LIKE. OH, BY THE WAY: HE'S MACK. I'M MIKE.
HE'S MIKE. I'M MACK. ONE'S WHITE, THE OTHER'S BLACK.
TO ENTER MAGIC, IN A SENSE, MEANS ENTERING OUR INTELLIGENCE...
THAT RECORD-BREAKING SMASH-HIT SHOW, THE THEATER OF WHAT WE KNOW, WHERE THOUGHTS PARADE IN FANCY DRESS UPON THE STAGE OF CONSCIOUSNESS.
COSTUMED AS ACROBAT OR CLOWN, THEY SOMERSAULT, TURN UPSIDE DOWN! HERE, WORDS ARE JUGGLED; IDEAS SPIN. LET FADE THE WORLD OUTSIDE...
STEP IN!
EXTERNAL THINGS DISSOLVE LIKE MIST. INSIDE ARE THRILLS NONE MAY RESIST.
DRAW MATTER'S TENT-FLAPS BACK AND FIND...

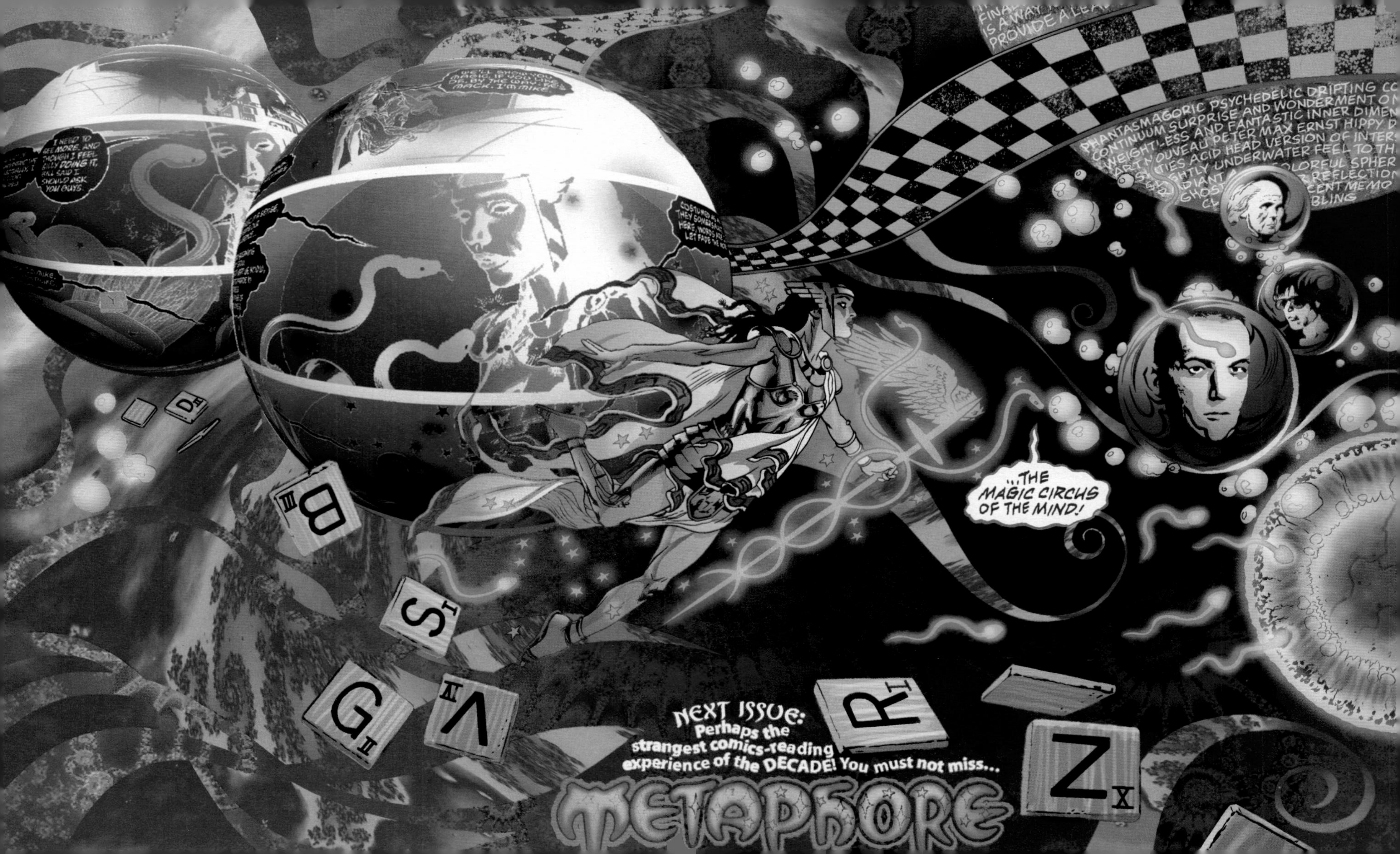

...THE MAGIC CIRCUS OF THE MIND!
NEXT ISSUE: Perhaps the strangest comics-reading experience of the DECADE! You must not miss...
METAPHORE

CHAPTER SIX

Deeper questions have divined a mystic theatre of the mind.

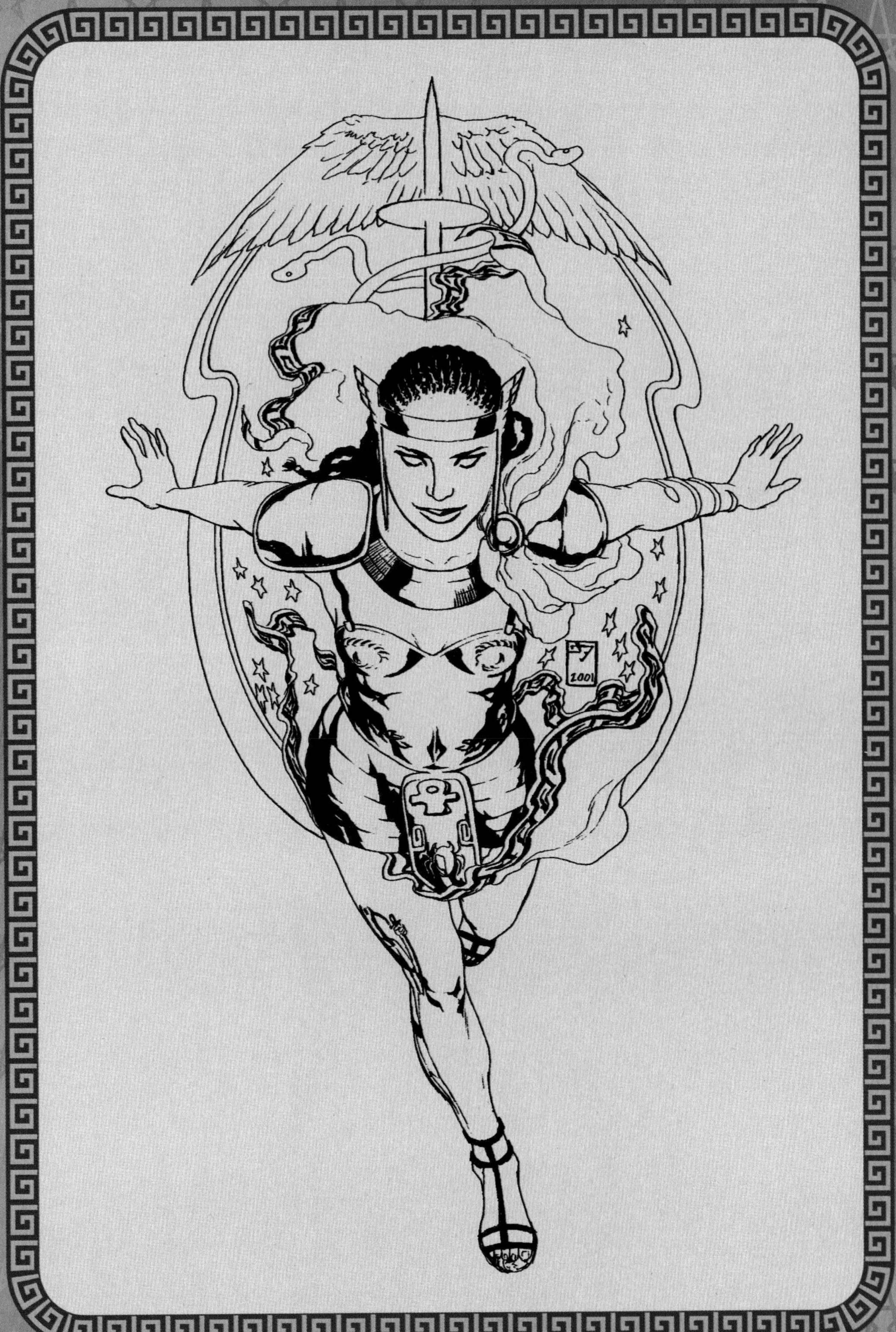

Cover art: J.H. Williams III, Mick Gray & Todd Klein

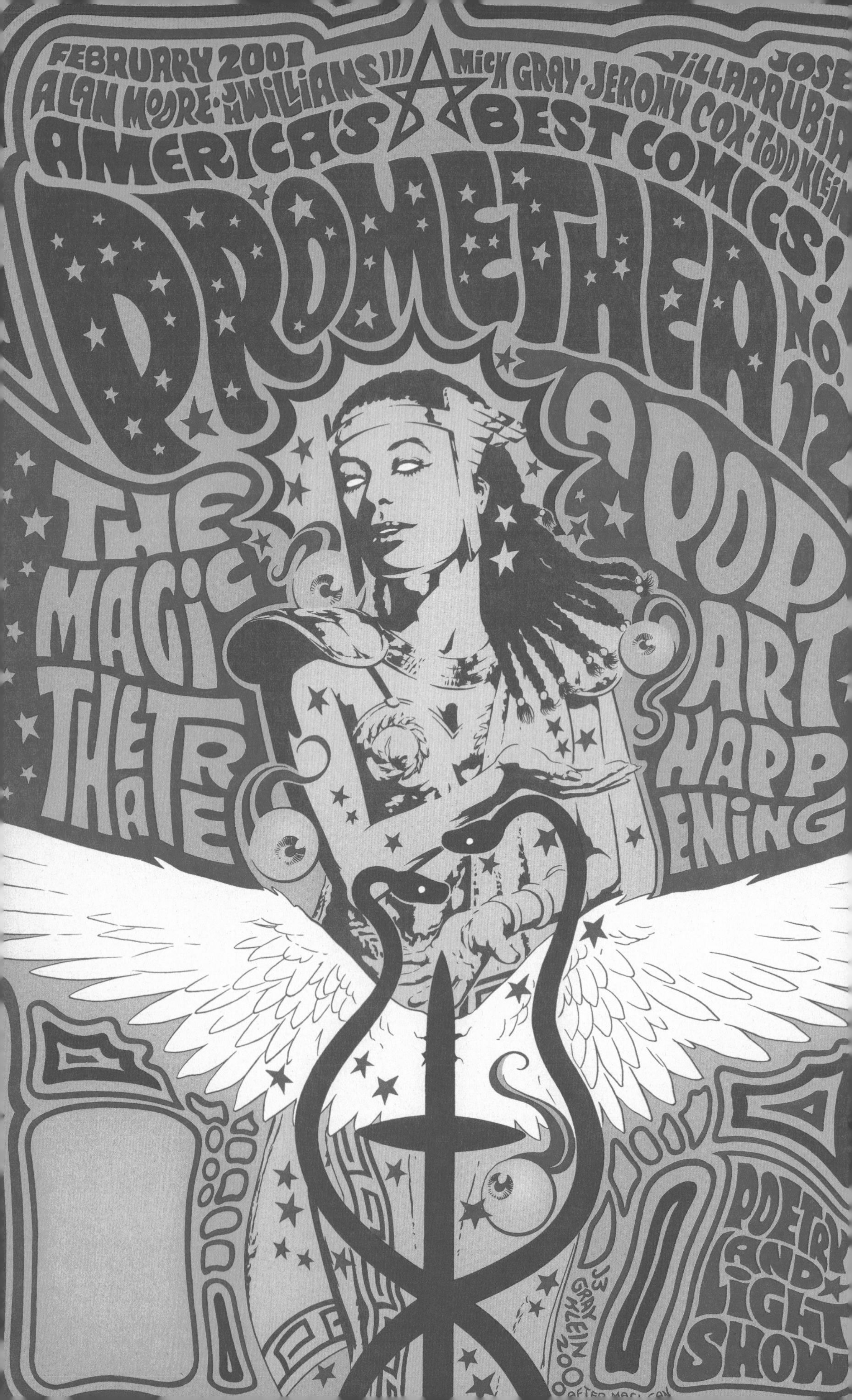
FEBRUARY 2001
ALAN MOORE · J.H. WILLIAMS III
MICK GRAY · JEROMY COX · TODD KLEIN
JOSE VILLARRUBIA
AMERICA'S BEST COMICS!
PROMETHEA NO. 12
THE MAGIC THEATRE
A POP ART HAPPENING
POETRY AND LIGHT SHOW
J3 GRAY KLEIN 2000

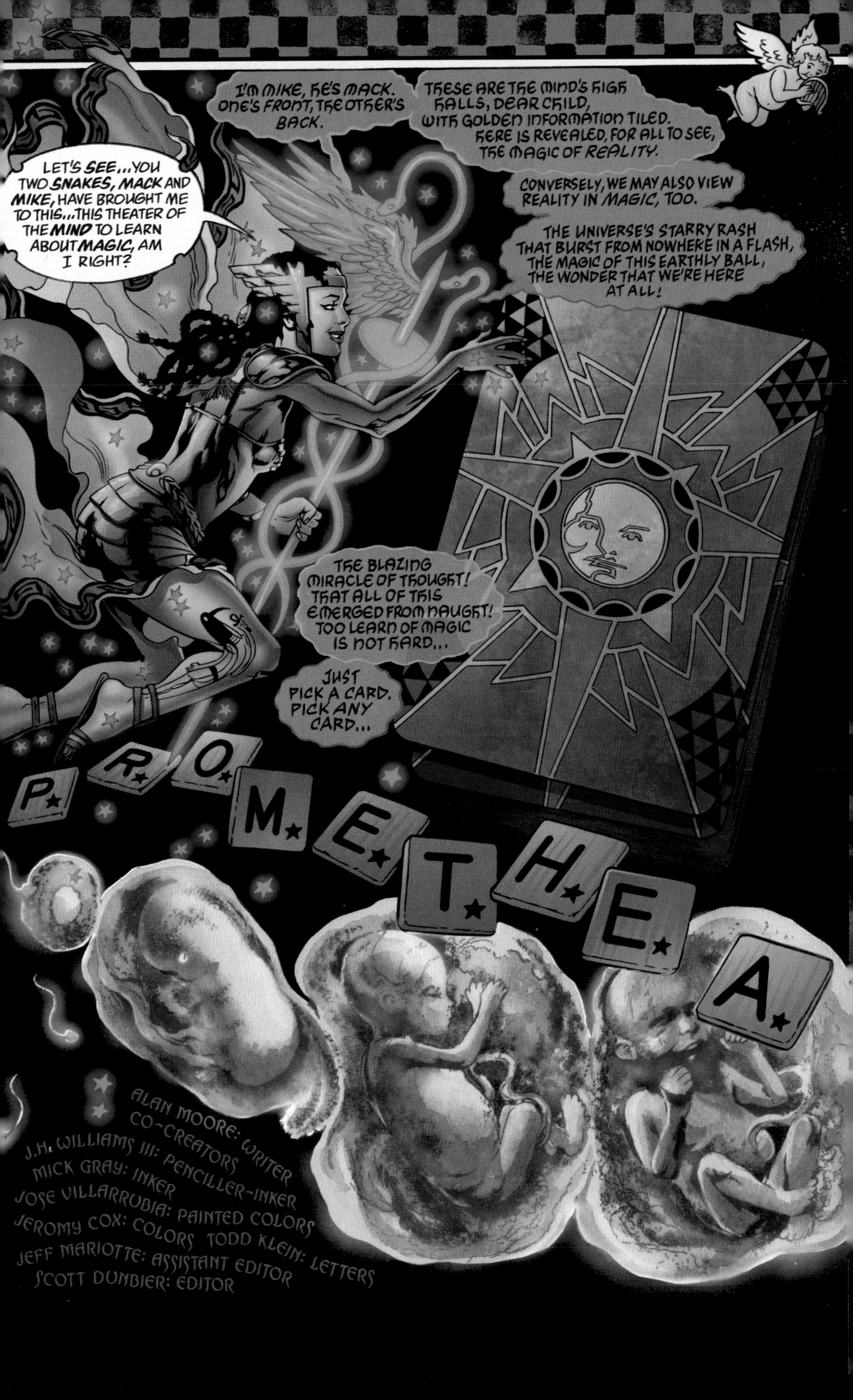
LET'S SEE...YOU TWO SNAKES, MACK AND MIKE, HAVE BROUGHT ME TO THIS...THIS THEATER OF THE MIND TO LEARN ABOUT MAGIC, AM I RIGHT?
I'M MIKE, HE'S MACK. ONE'S FRONT, THE OTHER'S BACK.
THESE ARE THE MIND'S HIGH HALLS, DEAR CHILD, WITH GOLDEN INFORMATION TILED. HERE IS REVEALED, FOR ALL TO SEE, THE MAGIC OF REALITY.
CONVERSELY, WE MAY ALSO VIEW REALITY IN MAGIC, TOO.
THE UNIVERSE'S STARRY RASH THAT BURST FROM NOWHERE IN A FLASH, THE MAGIC OF THIS EARTHLY BALL, THE WONDER THAT WE'RE HERE AT ALL!
THE BLAZING MIRACLE OF THOUGHT! THAT ALL OF THIS EMERGED FROM NAUGHT! TOO LEARN OF MAGIC IS NOT HARD...
JUST PICK A CARD. PICK ANY CARD...
P. R. O. M. E. T. H. E. A.
ALAN MOORE: WRITER
CO-CREATORS
J.H. WILLIAMS III: PENCILLER-INKER
MICK GRAY: INKER
JOSE VILLARRUBIA: PAINTED COLORS
JEROMY COX: COLORS TODD KLEIN: LETTERS
JEFF MARIOTTE: ASSISTANT EDITOR
SCOTT DUNBIER: EDITOR

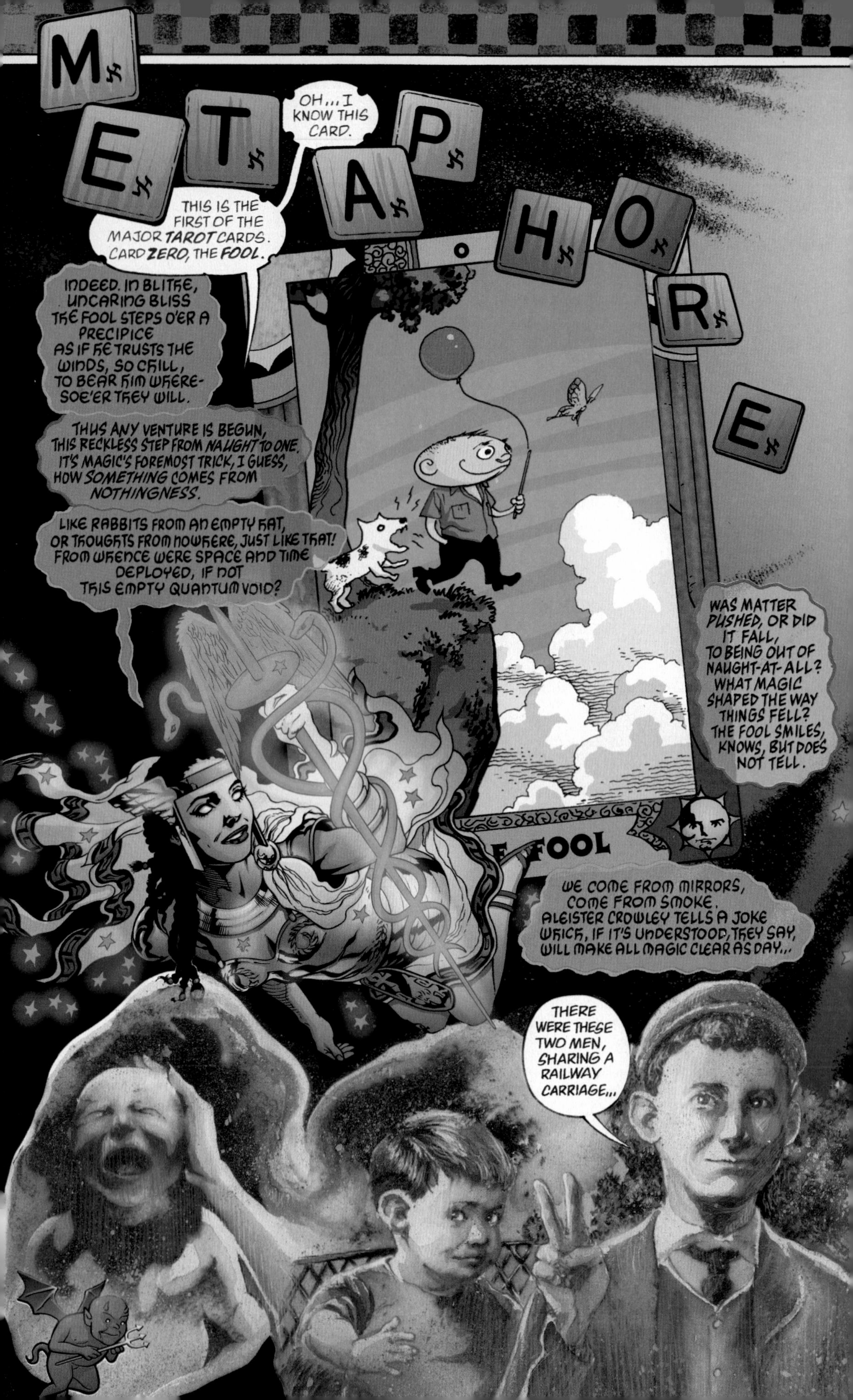

M E T A P H O R E
OH... I KNOW THIS CARD.
THIS IS THE FIRST OF THE MAJOR TAROT CARDS. CARD ZERO, THE FOOL.
INDEED. IN BLITHE, UNCARING BLISS THE FOOL STEPS O'ER A PRECIPICE AS IF HE TRUSTS THE WINDS, SO CHILL, TO BEAR HIM WHERE-SOE'ER THEY WILL.
THUS ANY VENTURE IS BEGUN, THIS RECKLESS STEP FROM NAUGHT TO ONE. IT'S MAGIC'S FOREMOST TRICK, I GUESS, HOW SOMETHING COMES FROM NOTHINGNESS.
LIKE RABBITS FROM AN EMPTY HAT, OR THOUGHTS FROM NOWHERE, JUST LIKE THAT! FROM WHENCE WERE SPACE AND TIME DEPLOYED, IF NOT THIS EMPTY QUANTUM VOID?
WAS MATTER PUSHED, OR DID IT FALL, TO BEING OUT OF NAUGHT-AT-ALL? WHAT MAGIC SHAPED THE WAY THINGS FELL? THE FOOL SMILES, KNOWS, BUT DOES NOT TELL.
FOOL
WE COME FROM MIRRORS, COME FROM SMOKE. ALEISTER CROWLEY TELLS A JOKE WHICH, IF IT'S UNDERSTOOD, THEY SAY, WILL MAKE ALL MAGIC CLEAR AS DAY...
THERE WERE THESE TWO MEN, SHARING A RAILWAY CARRIAGE...

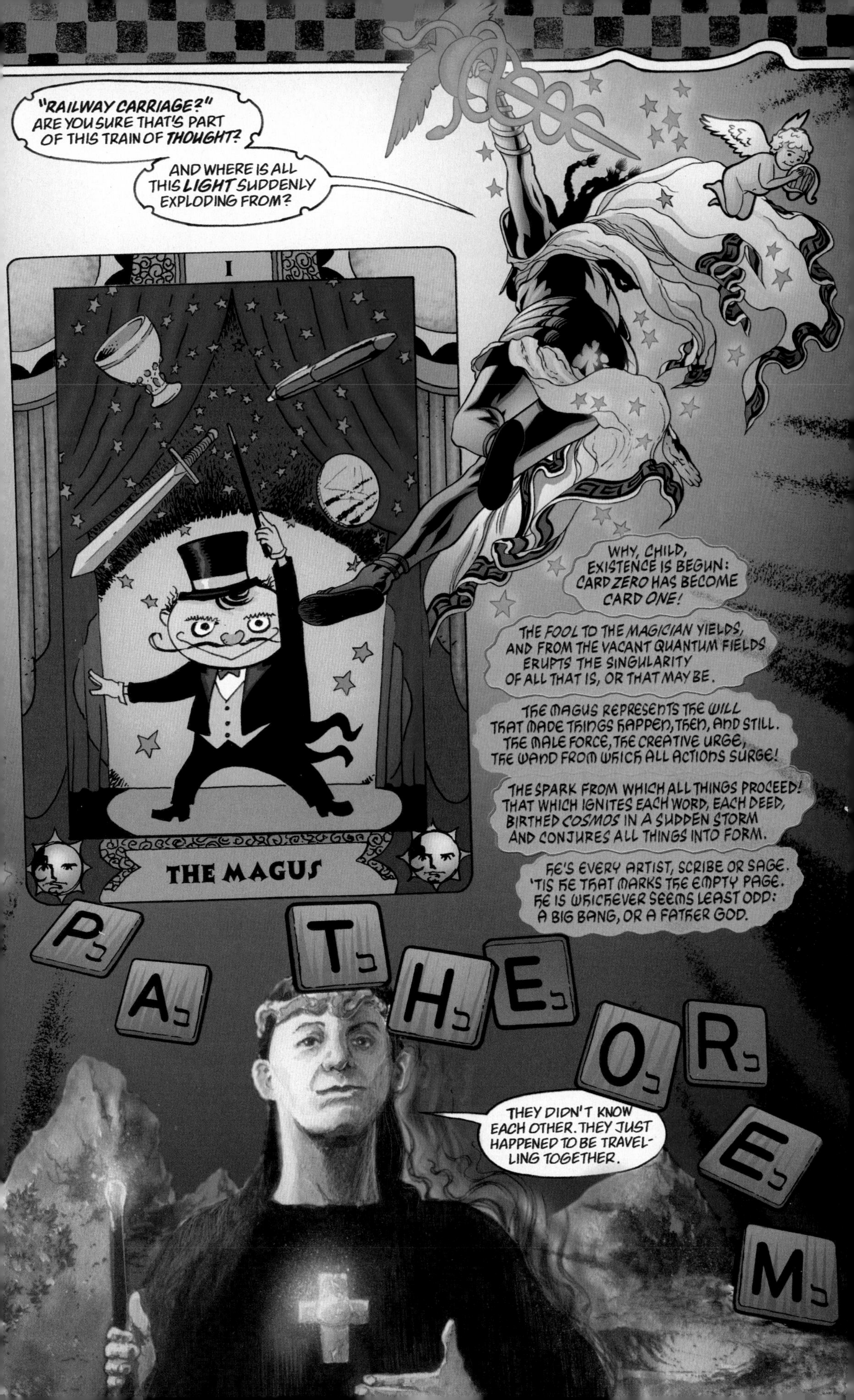
"RAILWAY CARRIAGE?" ARE YOU SURE THAT'S PART OF THIS TRAIN OF THOUGHT?
AND WHERE IS ALL THIS LIGHT SUDDENLY EXPLODING FROM?
I
THE MAGUS
WHY, CHILD, EXISTENCE IS BEGUN: CARD ZERO HAS BECOME CARD ONE!
THE FOOL TO THE MAGICIAN YIELDS, AND FROM THE VACANT QUANTUM FIELDS ERUPTS THE SINGULARITY OF ALL THAT IS, OR THAT MAY BE.
THE MAGUS REPRESENTS THE WILL THAT MADE THINGS HAPPEN, THEN, AND STILL. THE MALE FORCE, THE CREATIVE URGE, THE WAND FROM WHICH ALL ACTIONS SURGE!
THE SPARK FROM WHICH ALL THINGS PROCEED! THAT WHICH IGNITES EACH WORD, EACH DEED, BIRTHED COSMOS IN A SUDDEN STORM AND CONJURES ALL THINGS INTO FORM.
HE'S EVERY ARTIST, SCRIBE OR SAGE. 'TIS HE THAT MARKS THE EMPTY PAGE. HE IS WHICHEVER SEEMS LEAST ODD: A BIG BANG, OR A FATHER GOD.
P A T H E O R E M
THEY DIDN'T KNOW EACH OTHER. THEY JUST HAPPENED TO BE TRAVELLING TOGETHER.

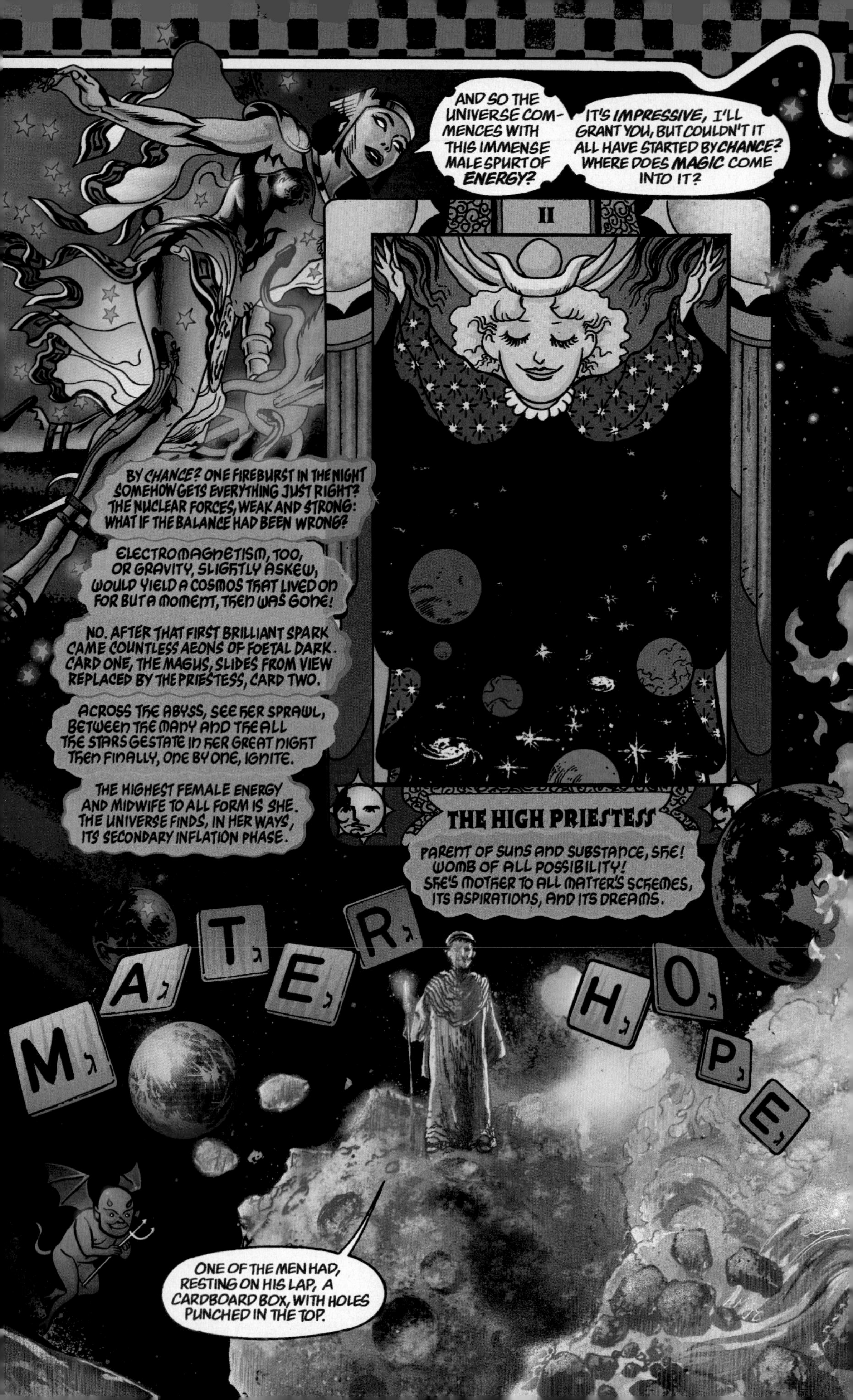

AND SO THE UNIVERSE COMMENCES WITH THIS IMMENSE MALE SPURT OF ENERGY?
IT'S IMPRESSIVE, I'LL GRANT YOU, BUT COULDN'T IT ALL HAVE STARTED BY CHANCE? WHERE DOES MAGIC COME INTO IT?
II
BY CHANCE? ONE FIREBURST IN THE NIGHT SOMEHOW GETS EVERYTHING JUST RIGHT? THE NUCLEAR FORCES, WEAK AND STRONG: WHAT IF THE BALANCE HAD BEEN WRONG?
ELECTROMAGNETISM, TOO, OR GRAVITY, SLIGHTLY ASKEW, WOULD YIELD A COSMOS THAT LIVED ON FOR BUT A MOMENT, THEN WAS GONE!
NO. AFTER THAT FIRST BRILLIANT SPARK CAME COUNTLESS AEONS OF FOETAL DARK. CARD ONE, THE MAGUS, SLIDES FROM VIEW REPLACED BY THE PRIESTESS, CARD TWO.
ACROSS THE ABYSS, SEE HER SPRAWL, BETWEEN THE MANY AND THE ALL THE STARS GESTATE IN HER GREAT NIGHT THEN FINALLY, ONE BY ONE, IGNITE.
THE HIGHEST FEMALE ENERGY AND MIDWIFE TO ALL FORM IS SHE. THE UNIVERSE FINDS, IN HER WAYS, ITS SECONDARY INFLATION PHASE.
THE HIGH PRIESTESS
PARENT OF SUNS AND SUBSTANCE, SHE! WOMB OF ALL POSSIBILITY! SHE'S MOTHER TO ALL MATTER'S SCHEMES, ITS ASPIRATIONS, AND ITS DREAMS.
M A T E R
H O P E
ONE OF THE MEN HAD, RESTING ON HIS LAP, A CARDBOARD BOX, WITH HOLES PUNCHED IN THE TOP.

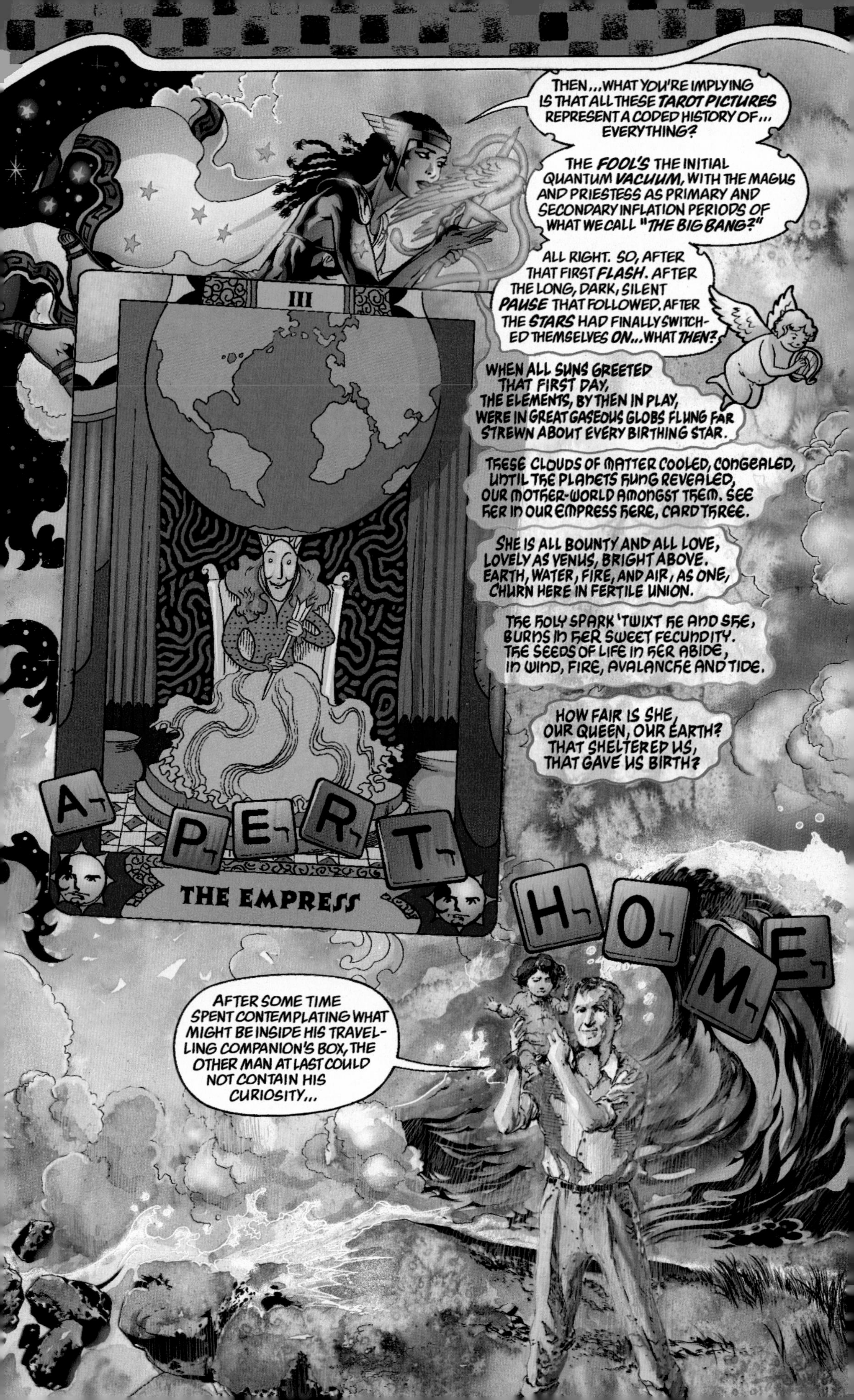
THEN...WHAT YOU'RE IMPLYING IS THAT ALL THESE TAROT PICTURES REPRESENT A CODED HISTORY OF... EVERYTHING?
THE FOOL'S THE INITIAL QUANTUM VACUUM, WITH THE MAGUS AND PRIESTESS AS PRIMARY AND SECONDARY INFLATION PERIODS OF WHAT WE CALL "THE BIG BANG?"
ALL RIGHT. SO, AFTER THAT FIRST FLASH. AFTER THE LONG, DARK, SILENT PAUSE THAT FOLLOWED. AFTER THE STARS HAD FINALLY SWITCHED THEMSELVES ON...WHAT THEN?
WHEN ALL SUNS GREETED THAT FIRST DAY, THE ELEMENTS, BY THEN IN PLAY, WERE IN GREAT GASEOUS GLOBS FLUNG FAR STREWN ABOUT EVERY BIRTHING STAR.
THESE CLOUDS OF MATTER COOLED, CONGEALED, UNTIL THE PLANETS HUNG REVEALED, OUR MOTHER-WORLD AMONGST THEM. SEE HER IN OUR EMPRESS HERE, CARD THREE.
SHE IS ALL BOUNTY AND ALL LOVE, LOVELY AS VENUS, BRIGHT ABOVE. EARTH, WATER, FIRE, AND AIR, AS ONE, CHURN HERE IN FERTILE UNION.
THE HOLY SPARK 'TWIXT HE AND SHE, BURNS IN HER SWEET FECUNDITY. THE SEEDS OF LIFE IN HER ABIDE, IN WIND, FIRE, AVALANCHE AND TIDE.
HOW FAIR IS SHE, OUR QUEEN, OUR EARTH? THAT SHELTERED US, THAT GAVE US BIRTH?
III
THE EMPRESS
A P E R T
H O M E
AFTER SOME TIME SPENT CONTEMPLATING WHAT MIGHT BE INSIDE HIS TRAVELLING COMPANION'S BOX, THE OTHER MAN AT LAST COULD NOT CONTAIN HIS CURIOSITY...

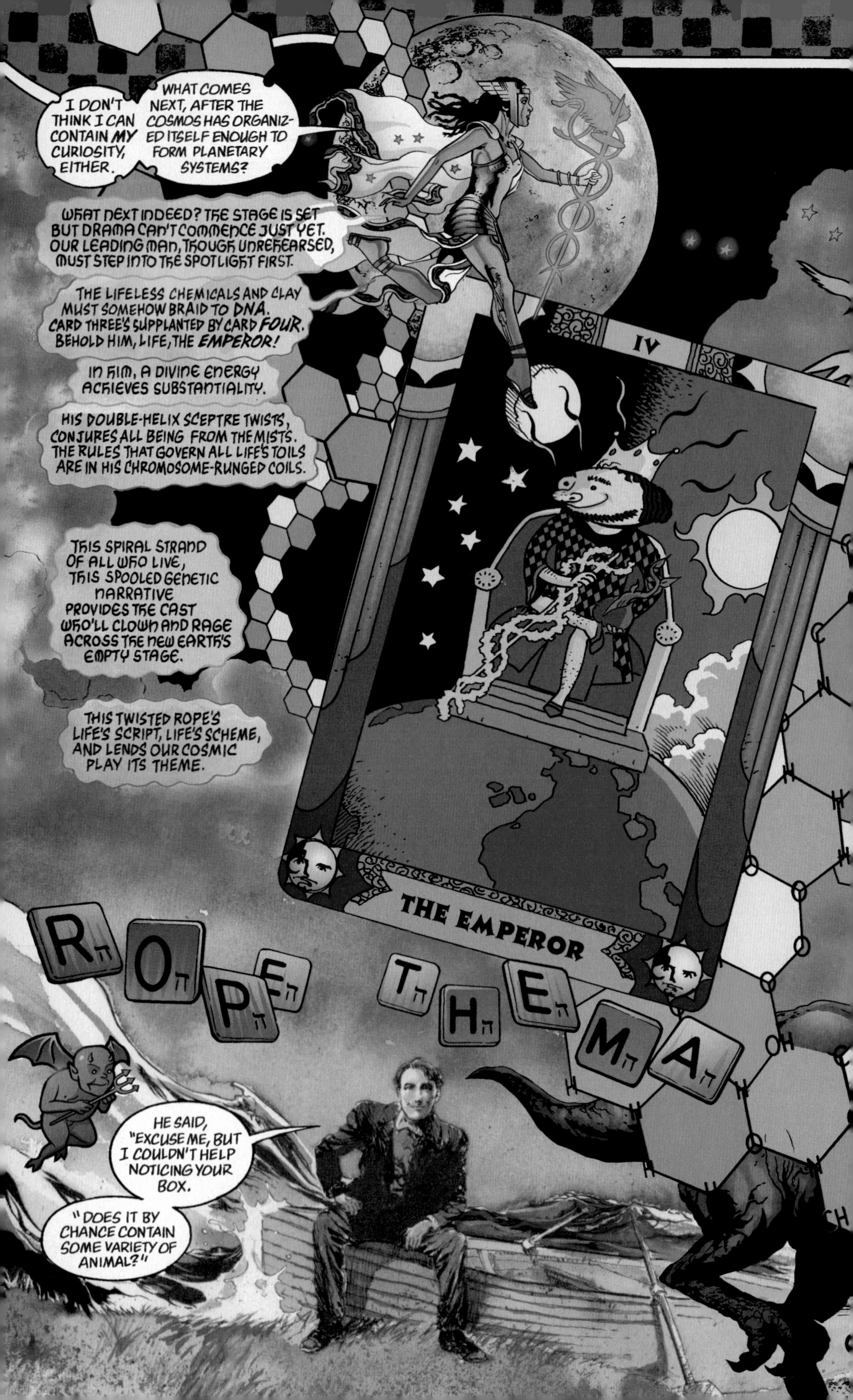

I DON'T THINK I CAN CONTAIN MY CURIOSITY, EITHER.
WHAT COMES NEXT, AFTER THE COSMOS HAS ORGANIZED ITSELF ENOUGH TO FORM PLANETARY SYSTEMS?
WHAT NEXT INDEED? THE STAGE IS SET BUT DRAMA CAN'T COMMENCE JUST YET. OUR LEADING MAN, THOUGH UNREHEARSED, MUST STEP INTO THE SPOTLIGHT FIRST.
THE LIFELESS CHEMICALS AND CLAY MUST SOMEHOW BRAID TO DNA. CARD THREE'S SUPPLANTED BY CARD FOUR. BEHOLD HIM, LIFE, THE EMPEROR!
IN HIM, A DIVINE ENERGY ACHIEVES SUBSTANTIALITY.
HIS DOUBLE-HELIX SCEPTRE TWISTS, CONJURES ALL BEING FROM THE MISTS. THE RULES THAT GOVERN ALL LIFE'S TOILS ARE IN HIS CHROMOSOME-RUNGED COILS.
IV
THE EMPEROR
THIS SPIRAL STRAND OF ALL WHO LIVE, THIS SPOOLED GENETIC NARRATIVE PROVIDES THE CAST WHO'LL CLOWN AND RAGE ACROSS THE NEW EARTH'S EMPTY STAGE.
THIS TWISTED ROPE'S LIFE'S SCRIPT, LIFE'S SCHEME, AND LENDS OUR COSMIC PLAY ITS THEME.
ROPE THEMA
HE SAID, "EXCUSE ME, BUT I COULDN'T HELP NOTICING YOUR BOX.
"DOES IT BY CHANCE CONTAIN SOME VARIETY OF ANIMAL?"

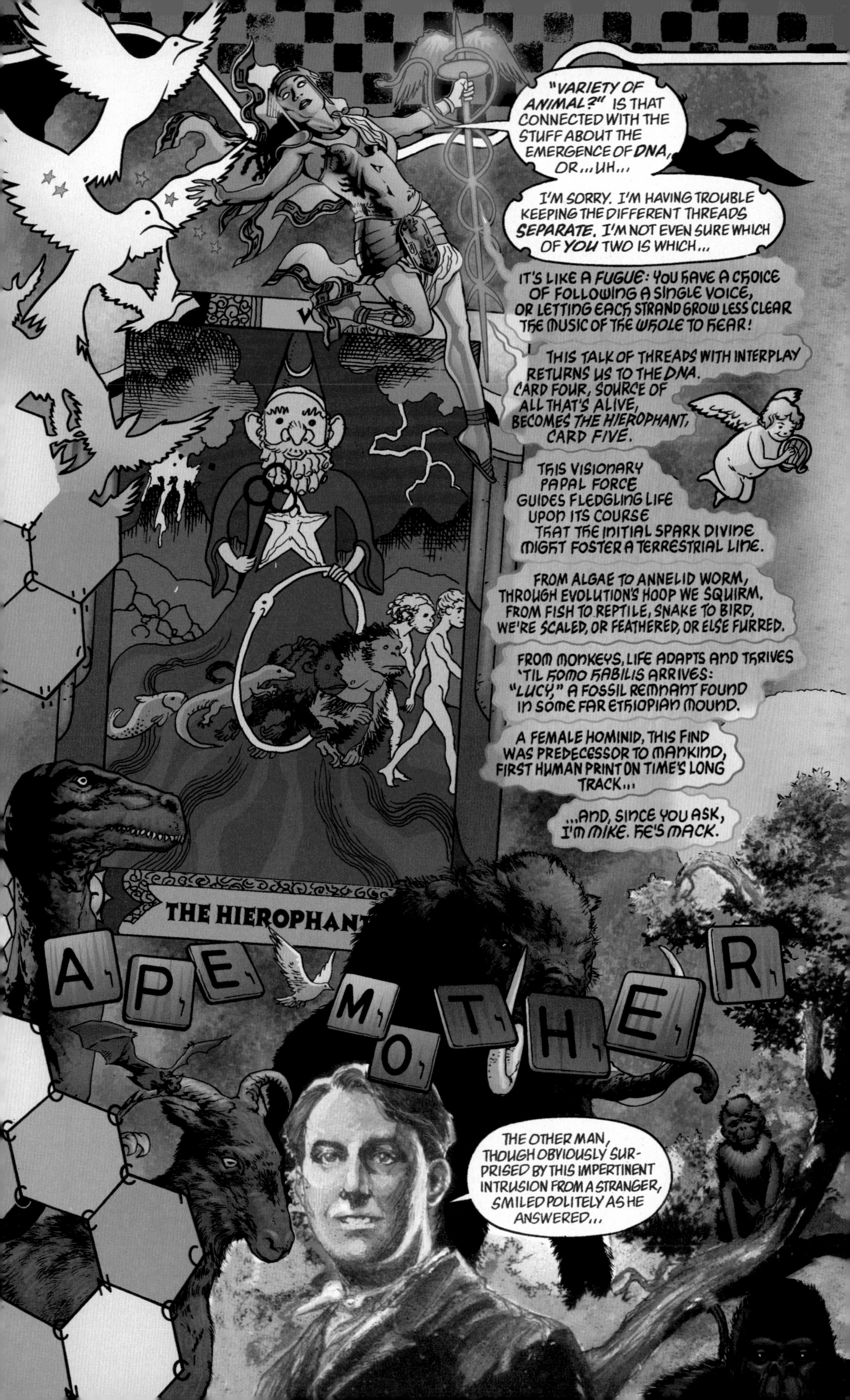
"VARIETY OF ANIMAL?" IS THAT CONNECTED WITH THE STUFF ABOUT THE EMERGENCE OF DNA, OR... UH...
I'M SORRY. I'M HAVING TROUBLE KEEPING THE DIFFERENT THREADS SEPARATE. I'M NOT EVEN SURE WHICH OF YOU TWO IS WHICH...
IT'S LIKE A FUGUE: YOU HAVE A CHOICE OF FOLLOWING A SINGLE VOICE, OR LETTING EACH STRAND GROW LESS CLEAR THE MUSIC OF THE WHOLE TO HEAR!
THIS TALK OF THREADS WITH INTERPLAY RETURNS US TO THE DNA. CARD FOUR, SOURCE OF ALL THAT'S ALIVE, BECOMES THE HIEROPHANT, CARD FIVE.
THIS VISIONARY PAPAL FORCE GUIDES FLEDGLING LIFE UPON ITS COURSE THAT THE INITIAL SPARK DIVINE MIGHT FOSTER A TERRESTRIAL LINE.
FROM ALGAE TO ANNELID WORM, THROUGH EVOLUTION'S HOOP WE SQUIRM, FROM FISH TO REPTILE, SNAKE TO BIRD, WE'RE SCALED, OR FEATHERED, OR ELSE FURRED.
FROM MONKEYS, LIFE ADAPTS AND THRIVES 'TIL HOMO HABILIS ARRIVES: "LUCY," A FOSSIL REMNANT FOUND IN SOME FAR ETHIOPIAN MOUND.
A FEMALE HOMINID, THIS FIND WAS PREDECESSOR TO MANKIND, FIRST HUMAN PRINT ON TIME'S LONG TRACK...
...AND, SINCE YOU ASK, I'M MIKE. HE'S MACK.
THE HIEROPHANT
A P E M O T H E R
THE OTHER MAN, THOUGH OBVIOUSLY SURPRISED BY THIS IMPERTINENT INTRUSION FROM A STRANGER, SMILED POLITELY AS HE ANSWERED...

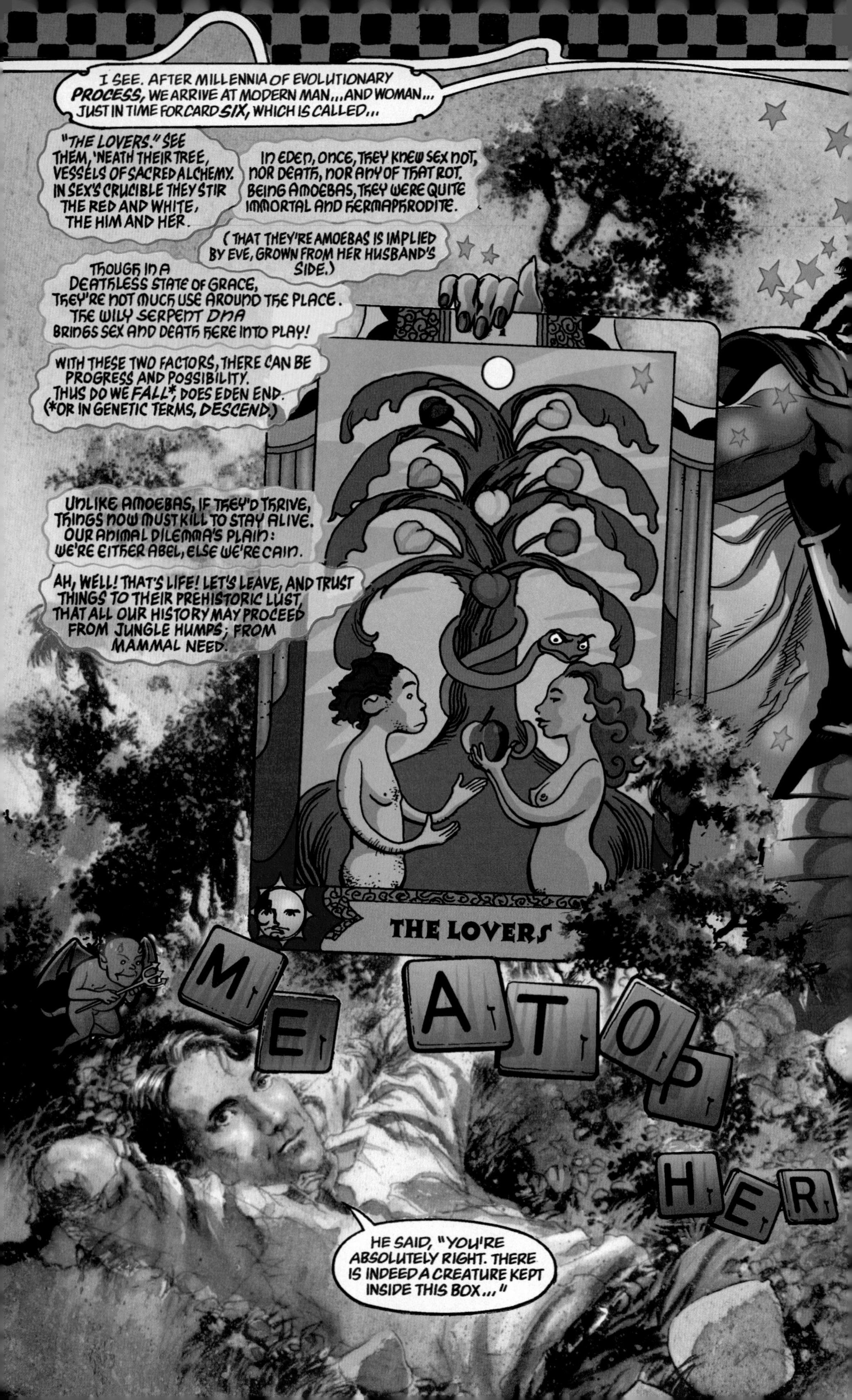
I SEE. AFTER MILLENNIA OF EVOLUTIONARY PROCESS, WE ARRIVE AT MODERN MAN... AND WOMAN... JUST IN TIME FOR CARD SIX, WHICH IS CALLED...
"THE LOVERS." SEE THEM, 'NEATH THEIR TREE, VESSELS OF SACRED ALCHEMY. IN SEX'S CRUCIBLE THEY STIR THE RED AND WHITE, THE HIM AND HER.
IN EDEN, ONCE, THEY KNEW SEX NOT, NOR DEATH, NOR ANY OF THAT ROT. BEING AMOEBAS, THEY WERE QUITE IMMORTAL AND HERMAPHRODITE.
(THAT THEY'RE AMOEBAS IS IMPLIED BY EVE, GROWN FROM HER HUSBAND'S SIDE.)
THOUGH IN A DEATHLESS STATE OF GRACE, THEY'RE NOT MUCH USE AROUND THE PLACE. THE WILY SERPENT DNA BRINGS SEX AND DEATH HERE INTO PLAY!
WITH THESE TWO FACTORS, THERE CAN BE PROGRESS AND POSSIBILITY. THUS DO WE FALL*, DOES EDEN END. (*OR IN GENETIC TERMS, DESCEND.)
UNLIKE AMOEBAS, IF THEY'D THRIVE, THINGS NOW MUST KILL TO STAY ALIVE. OUR ANIMAL DILEMMA'S PLAIN: WE'RE EITHER ABEL, ELSE WE'RE CAIN.
AH, WELL! THAT'S LIFE! LET'S LEAVE, AND TRUST THINGS TO THEIR PREHISTORIC LUST, THAT ALL OUR HISTORY MAY PROCEED FROM JUNGLE HUMPS; FROM MAMMAL NEED.
THE LOVERS
M E A T O P H E R
HE SAID, "YOU'RE ABSOLUTELY RIGHT. THERE IS INDEED A CREATURE KEPT INSIDE THIS BOX..."

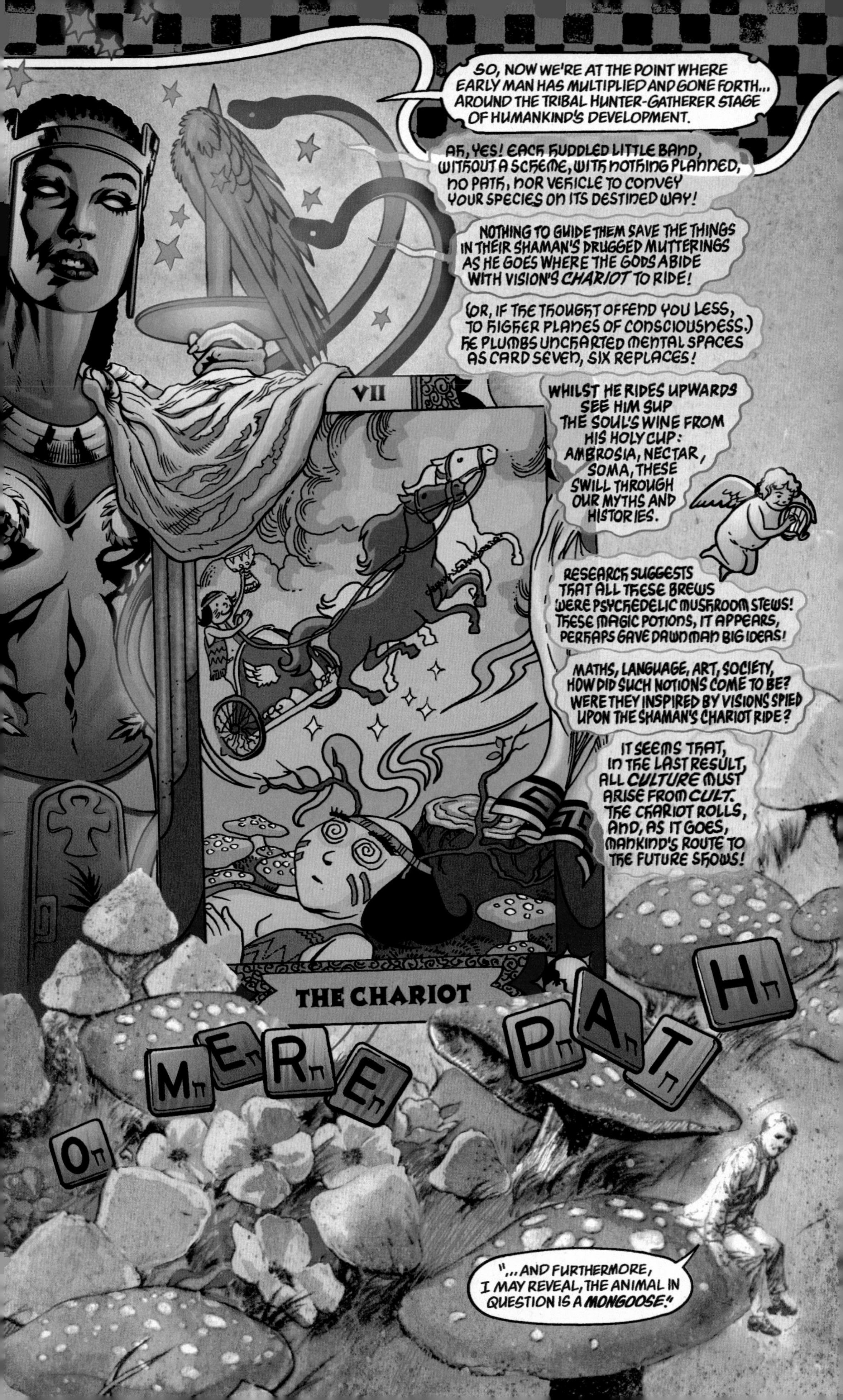
SO, NOW WE'RE AT THE POINT WHERE EARLY MAN HAS MULTIPLIED AND GONE FORTH... AROUND THE TRIBAL HUNTER-GATHERER STAGE OF HUMANKIND'S DEVELOPMENT.
AH, YES! EACH HUDDLED LITTLE BAND, WITHOUT A SCHEME, WITH NOTHING PLANNED, NO PATH, NOR VEHICLE TO CONVEY YOUR SPECIES ON ITS DESTINED WAY!
NOTHING TO GUIDE THEM SAVE THE THINGS IN THEIR SHAMAN'S DRUGGED MUTTERINGS AS HE GOES WHERE THE GODS ABIDE WITH VISION'S CHARIOT TO RIDE!
(OR, IF THE THOUGHT OFFEND YOU LESS, TO HIGHER PLANES OF CONSCIOUSNESS.) HE PLUMBS UNCHARTED MENTAL SPACES AS CARD SEVEN, SIX REPLACES!
VII
WHILST HE RIDES UPWARDS SEE HIM SUP THE SOUL'S WINE FROM HIS HOLY CUP: AMBROSIA, NECTAR, SOMA, THESE SWILL THROUGH OUR MYTHS AND HISTORIES.
RESEARCH SUGGESTS THAT ALL THESE BREWS WERE PSYCHEDELIC MUSHROOM STEWS! THESE MAGIC POTIONS, IT APPEARS, PERHAPS GAVE DAWNMAN BIG IDEAS!
MATHS, LANGUAGE, ART, SOCIETY, HOW DID SUCH NOTIONS COME TO BE? WERE THEY INSPIRED BY VISIONS SPIED UPON THE SHAMAN'S CHARIOT RIDE?
IT SEEMS THAT, IN THE LAST RESULT, ALL CULTURE MUST ARISE FROM CULT. THE CHARIOT ROLLS, AND, AS IT GOES, MANKIND'S ROUTE TO THE FUTURE SHOWS!
THE CHARIOT
O MERE PATH
"...AND FURTHERMORE, I MAY REVEAL, THE ANIMAL IN QUESTION IS A MONGOOSE."

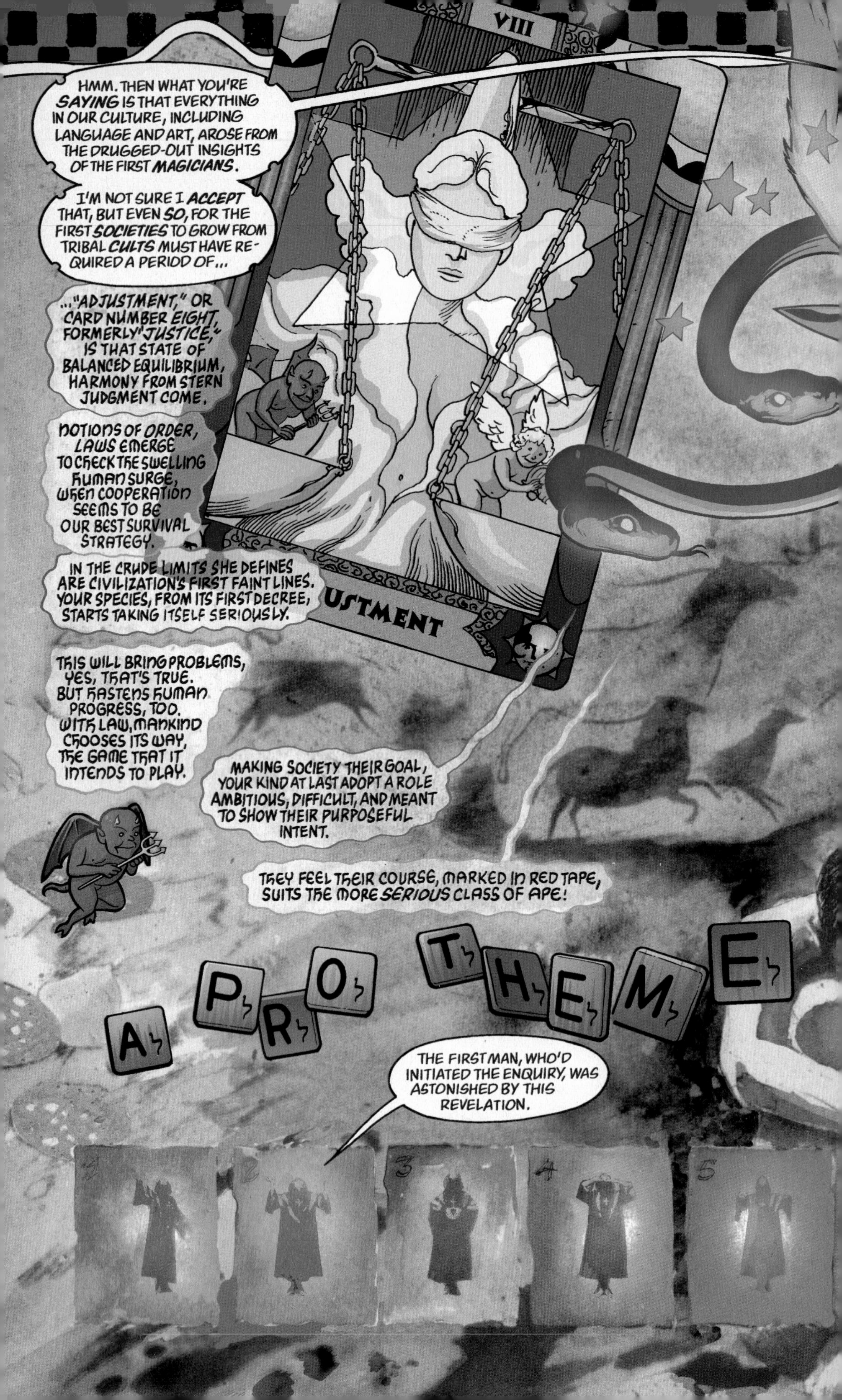
VIII
HMM. THEN WHAT YOU'RE SAYING IS THAT EVERYTHING IN OUR CULTURE, INCLUDING LANGUAGE AND ART, AROSE FROM THE DRUGGED-OUT INSIGHTS OF THE FIRST MAGICIANS.
I'M NOT SURE I ACCEPT THAT, BUT EVEN SO, FOR THE FIRST SOCIETIES TO GROW FROM TRIBAL CULTS MUST HAVE REQUIRED A PERIOD OF...
..."ADJUSTMENT," OR CARD NUMBER EIGHT, FORMERLY "JUSTICE," IS THAT STATE OF BALANCED EQUILIBRIUM, HARMONY FROM STERN JUDGMENT COME.
NOTIONS OF ORDER, LAWS EMERGE TO CHECK THE SWELLING HUMAN SURGE, WHEN COOPERATION SEEMS TO BE OUR BEST SURVIVAL STRATEGY.
IN THE CRUDE LIMITS SHE DEFINES ARE CIVILIZATION'S FIRST FAINT LINES. YOUR SPECIES, FROM ITS FIRST DECREE, STARTS TAKING ITSELF SERIOUSLY.
USTMENT
THIS WILL BRING PROBLEMS, YES, THAT'S TRUE. BUT HASTENS HUMAN PROGRESS, TOO. WITH LAW, MANKIND CHOOSES ITS WAY, THE GAME THAT IT INTENDS TO PLAY.
MAKING SOCIETY THEIR GOAL, YOUR KIND AT LAST ADOPT A ROLE AMBITIOUS, DIFFICULT, AND MEANT TO SHOW THEIR PURPOSEFUL INTENT.
THEY FEEL THEIR COURSE, MARKED IN RED TAPE, SUITS THE MORE SERIOUS CLASS OF APE!
A PRO THEME
THE FIRST MAN, WHO'D INITIATED THE ENQUIRY, WAS ASTONISHED BY THIS REVELATION.
1
2
3
4
5

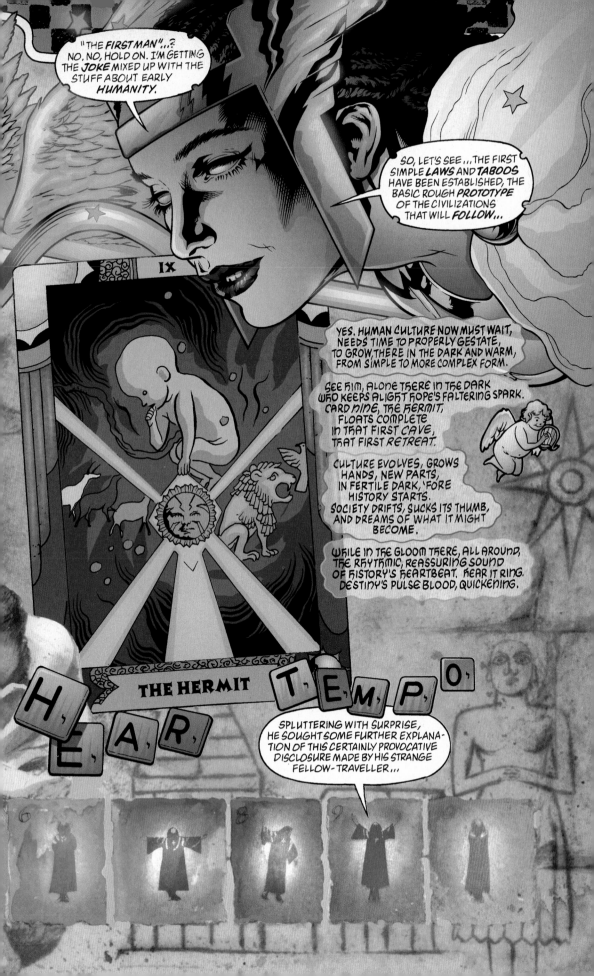

"THE *FIRST MAN*"..? NO, NO, HOLD ON. I'M GETTING THE *JOKE* MIXED UP WITH THE STUFF ABOUT EARLY *HUMANITY*.

SO, LET'S SEE ...THE FIRST SIMPLE *LAWS* AND *TABOOS* HAVE BEEN ESTABLISHED, THE BASIC ROUGH *PROTOTYPE* OF THE CIVILIZATIONS THAT WILL *FOLLOW*...

IX

YES. HUMAN CULTURE NOW MUST WAIT, NEEDS TIME TO PROPERLY GESTATE, TO GROW, THERE IN THE DARK AND WARM, FROM SIMPLE TO MORE COMPLEX FORM.

SEE HIM, ALONE THERE IN THE DARK WHO KEEPS ALIGHT HOPE'S FALTERING SPARK. CARD *NINE*, THE HERMIT, FLOATS COMPLETE IN THAT FIRST *CAVE*, THAT FIRST *RETREAT*.

CULTURE EVOLVES, GROWS HANDS, NEW PARTS, IN FERTILE DARK, 'FORE HISTORY STARTS. SOCIETY DRIFTS, SUCKS ITS THUMB, AND DREAMS OF WHAT IT MIGHT BECOME.

WHILE IN THE GLOOM THERE, ALL AROUND, THE RHYTHMIC, REASSURING SOUND OF HISTORY'S HEARTBEAT. HEAR IT RING. DESTINY'S PULSE BLOOD, QUICKENING.

THE HERMIT

H E A R   T E M P O,

SPLUTTERING WITH SURPRISE, HE SOUGHT SOME FURTHER EXPLANATION OF THIS CERTAINLY PROVOCATIVE DISCLOSURE MADE BY HIS STRANGE FELLOW-TRAVELLER...

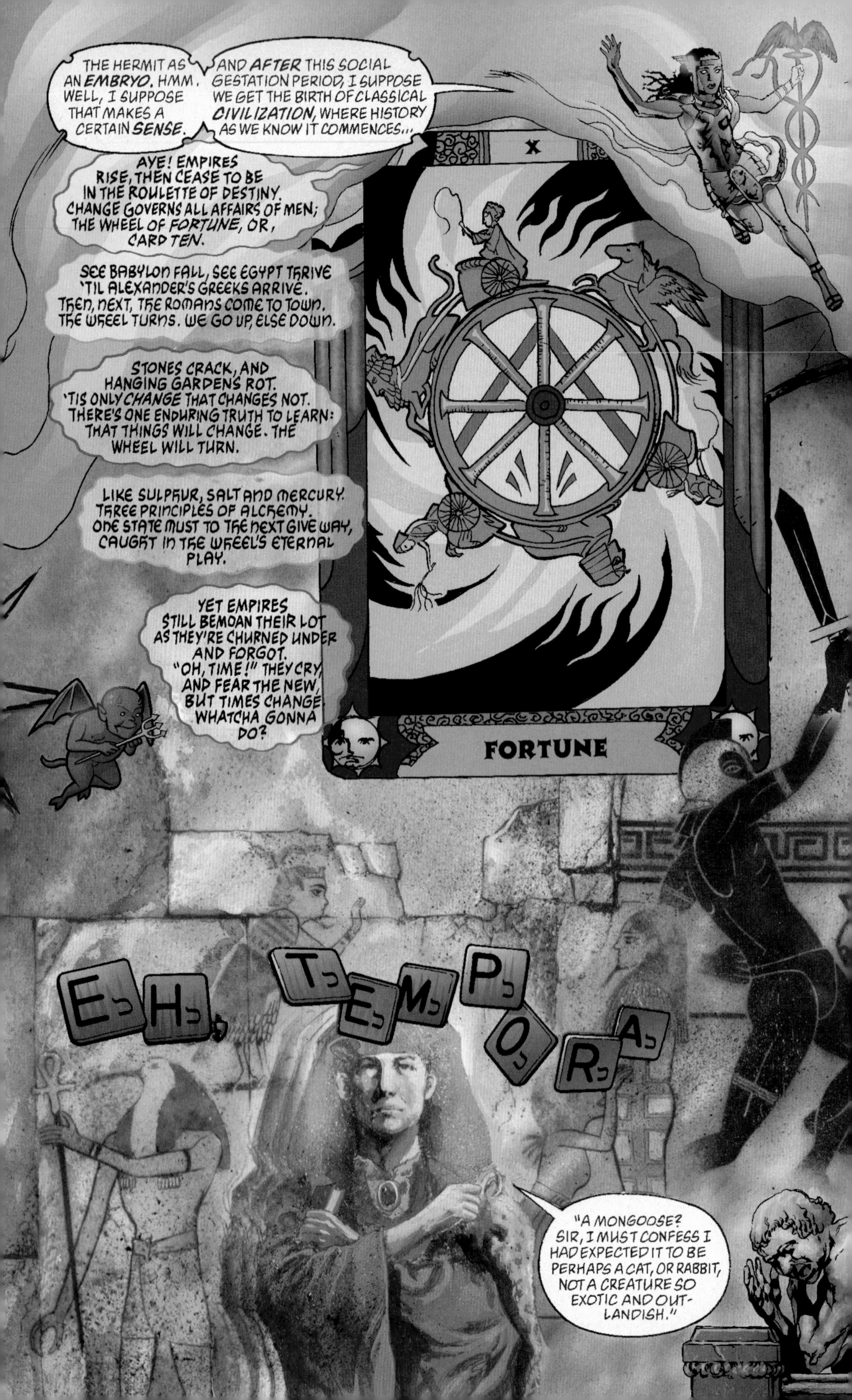
THE HERMIT AS AN EMBRYO. HMM. WELL, I SUPPOSE THAT MAKES A CERTAIN SENSE.
AND AFTER THIS SOCIAL GESTATION PERIOD, I SUPPOSE WE GET THE BIRTH OF CLASSICAL CIVILIZATION, WHERE HISTORY AS WE KNOW IT COMMENCES...
AYE! EMPIRES RISE, THEN CEASE TO BE IN THE ROULETTE OF DESTINY. CHANGE GOVERNS ALL AFFAIRS OF MEN; THE WHEEL OF FORTUNE, OR, CARD TEN.
SEE BABYLON FALL, SEE EGYPT THRIVE 'TIL ALEXANDER'S GREEKS ARRIVE. THEN, NEXT, THE ROMANS COME TO TOWN. THE WHEEL TURNS. WE GO UP, ELSE DOWN.
STONES CRACK, AND HANGING GARDENS ROT. 'TIS ONLY CHANGE THAT CHANGES NOT. THERE'S ONE ENDURING TRUTH TO LEARN: THAT THINGS WILL CHANGE. THE WHEEL WILL TURN.
LIKE SULPHUR, SALT AND MERCURY. THREE PRINCIPLES OF ALCHEMY. ONE STATE MUST TO THE NEXT GIVE WAY, CAUGHT IN THE WHEEL'S ETERNAL PLAY.
YET EMPIRES STILL BEMOAN THEIR LOT AS THEY'RE CHURNED UNDER AND FORGOT. "OH, TIME!" THEY CRY, AND FEAR THE NEW, BUT TIMES CHANGE. WHATCHA GONNA DO?
X
FORTUNE
EH, TEMPORA
"A MONGOOSE? SIR, I MUST CONFESS I HAD EXPECTED IT TO BE PERHAPS A CAT, OR RABBIT, NOT A CREATURE SO EXOTIC AND OUT-LANDISH."

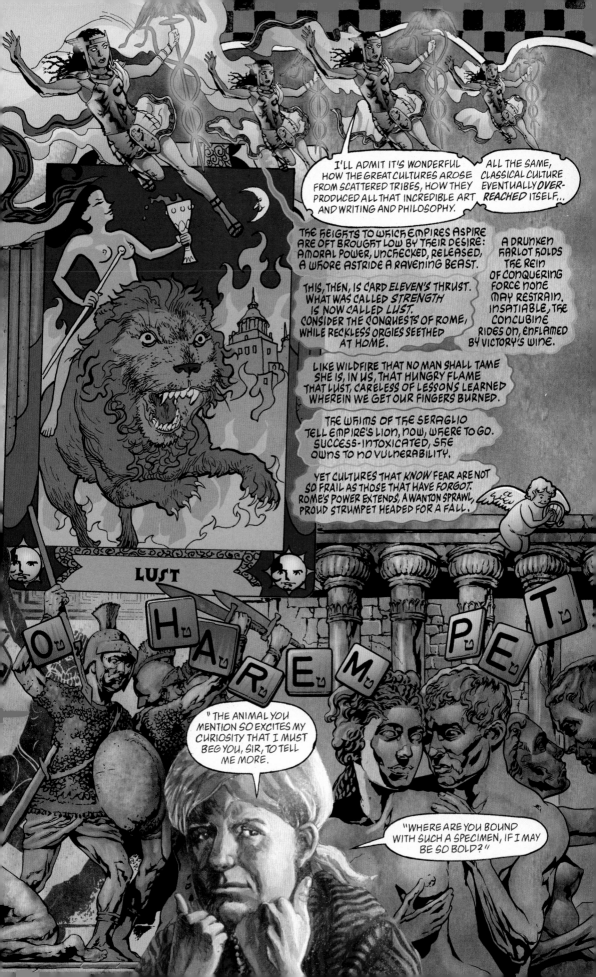

I'LL ADMIT IT'S WONDERFUL HOW THE GREAT CULTURES AROSE FROM SCATTERED TRIBES, HOW THEY PRODUCED ALL THAT INCREDIBLE ART AND WRITING AND PHILOSOPHY.

ALL THE SAME, CLASSICAL CULTURE EVENTUALLY *OVER-REACHED* ITSELF...

THE HEIGHTS TO WHICH EMPIRES ASPIRE
ARE OFT BROUGHT LOW BY THEIR DESIRE:
AMORAL POWER, UNCHECKED, RELEASED,
A WHORE ASTRIDE A RAVENING BEAST.

A DRUNKEN HARLOT HOLDS THE REIN OF CONQUERING FORCE NONE MAY RESTRAIN. INSATIABLE, THE CONCUBINE RIDES ON, ENFLAMED BY VICTORY'S WINE.

THIS, THEN, IS CARD ELEVEN'S THRUST.
WHAT WAS CALLED *STRENGTH*
IS NOW CALLED *LUST.*
CONSIDER THE CONQUESTS OF ROME,
WHILE RECKLESS ORGIES SEETHED
AT HOME.

LIKE WILDFIRE THAT NO MAN SHALL TAME
SHE IS, IN US, THAT HUNGRY FLAME
THAT LUST, CARELESS OF LESSONS LEARNED
WHEREIN WE GET OUR FINGERS BURNED.

THE WHIMS OF THE SERAGLIO
TELL EMPIRE'S LION, NOW, WHERE TO GO.
SUCCESS-INTOXICATED, SHE
OWNS TO NO VULNERABILITY.

YET CULTURES THAT *KNOW* FEAR ARE NOT
SO FRAIL AS THOSE THAT HAVE FORGOT.
ROME'S POWER EXTENDS, A WANTON SPRAWL,
PROUD STRUMPET HEADED FOR A FALL.

LUST

" THE ANIMAL YOU MENTION SO EXCITES MY CURIOSITY THAT I MUST BEG YOU, SIR, TO TELL ME MORE.

"WHERE ARE YOU BOUND WITH SUCH A SPECIMEN, IF I MAY BE SO BOLD?"

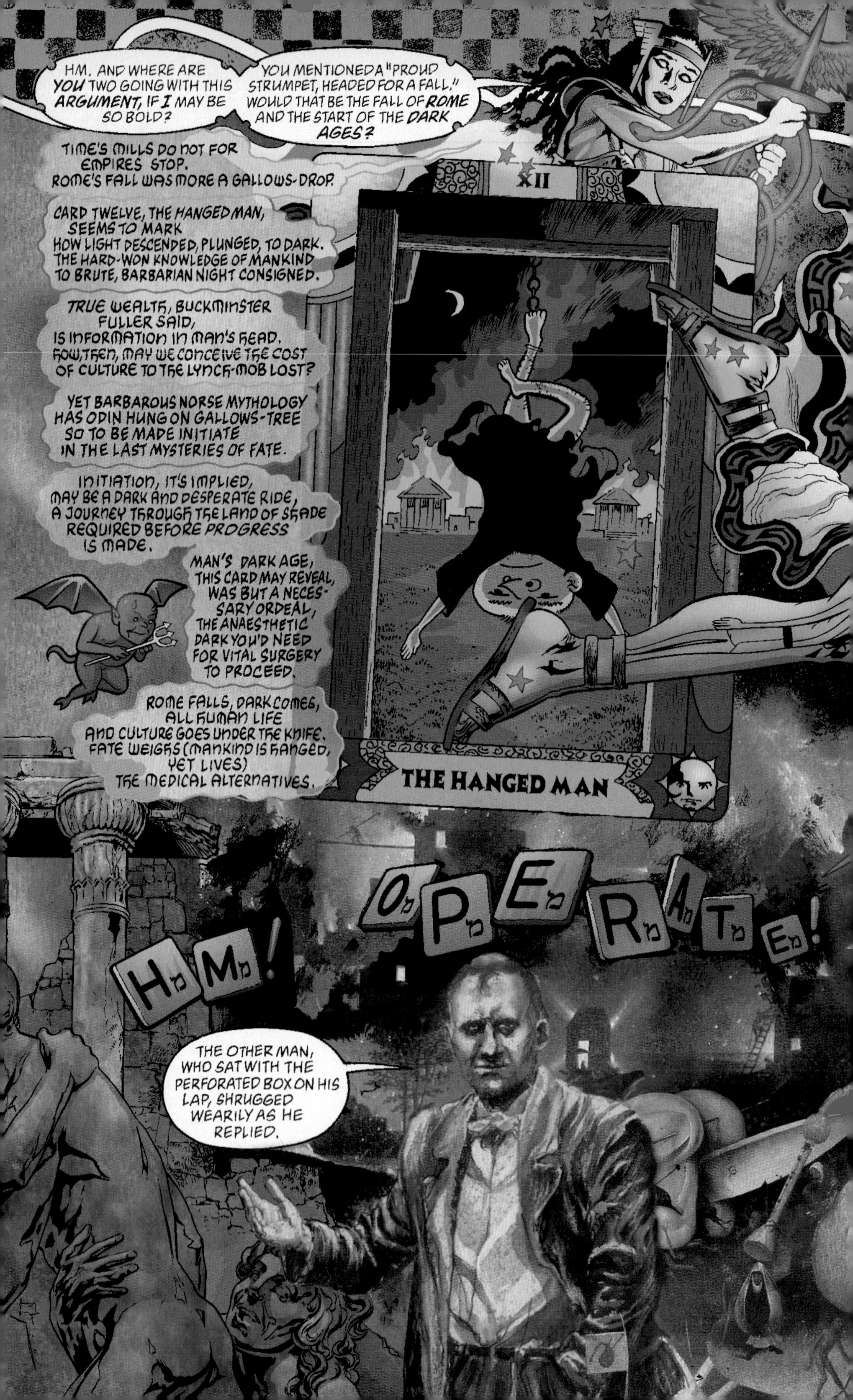

HM. AND WHERE ARE YOU TWO GOING WITH THIS ARGUMENT, IF I MAY BE SO BOLD?
YOU MENTIONED A "PROUD STRUMPET, HEADED FOR A FALL." WOULD THAT BE THE FALL OF ROME AND THE START OF THE DARK AGES?
TIME'S MILLS DO NOT FOR EMPIRES STOP. ROME'S FALL WAS MORE A GALLOWS-DROP.
CARD TWELVE, THE HANGED MAN, SEEMS TO MARK HOW LIGHT DESCENDED, PLUNGED, TO DARK. THE HARD-WON KNOWLEDGE OF MANKIND TO BRUTE, BARBARIAN NIGHT CONSIGNED.
TRUE WEALTH, BUCKMINSTER FULLER SAID, IS INFORMATION IN MAN'S HEAD. HOW, THEN, MAY WE CONCEIVE THE COST OF CULTURE TO THE LYNCH-MOB LOST?
YET BARBAROUS NORSE MYTHOLOGY HAS ODIN HUNG ON GALLOWS-TREE SO TO BE MADE INITIATE IN THE LAST MYSTERIES OF FATE.
INITIATION, IT'S IMPLIED, MAY BE A DARK AND DESPERATE RIDE, A JOURNEY THROUGH THE LAND OF SHADE REQUIRED BEFORE PROGRESS IS MADE.
MAN'S DARK AGE, THIS CARD MAY REVEAL, WAS BUT A NECES-SARY ORDEAL, THE ANAESTHETIC DARK YOU'D NEED FOR VITAL SURGERY TO PROCEED.
ROME FALLS, DARK COMES, ALL HUMAN LIFE AND CULTURE GOES UNDER THE KNIFE. FATE WEIGHS (MANKIND IS HANGED, YET LIVES) THE MEDICAL ALTERNATIVES.
XII
THE HANGED MAN
HM!
OPERATE!
THE OTHER MAN, WHO SAT WITH THE PERFORATED BOX ON HIS LAP, SHRUGGED WEARILY AS HE REPLIED.

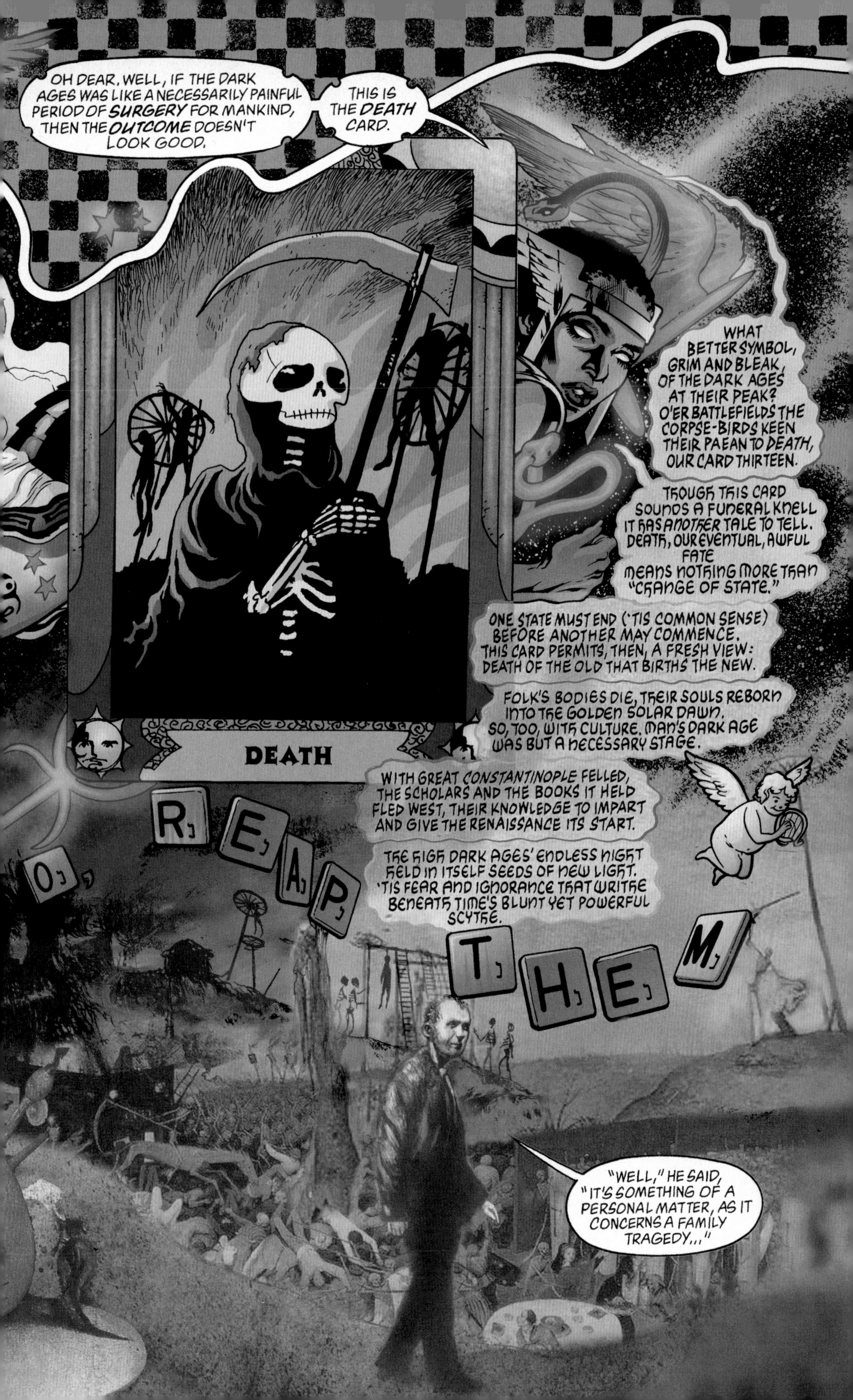

OH DEAR. WELL, IF THE DARK AGES WAS LIKE A NECESSARILY PAINFUL PERIOD OF SURGERY FOR MANKIND, THEN THE OUTCOME DOESN'T LOOK GOOD.
THIS IS THE DEATH CARD.
DEATH
WHAT BETTER SYMBOL, GRIM AND BLEAK, OF THE DARK AGES AT THEIR PEAK? O'ER BATTLEFIELDS THE CORPSE-BIRDS KEEN THEIR PAEAN TO DEATH, OUR CARD THIRTEEN.
THOUGH THIS CARD SOUNDS A FUNERAL KNELL IT HAS ANOTHER TALE TO TELL. DEATH, OUR EVENTUAL, AWFUL FATE MEANS NOTHING MORE THAN "CHANGE OF STATE."
ONE STATE MUST END ('TIS COMMON SENSE) BEFORE ANOTHER MAY COMMENCE. THIS CARD PERMITS, THEN, A FRESH VIEW: DEATH OF THE OLD THAT BIRTHS THE NEW.
FOLK'S BODIES DIE, THEIR SOULS REBORN INTO THE GOLDEN SOLAR DAWN. SO, TOO, WITH CULTURE. MAN'S DARK AGE WAS BUT A NECESSARY STAGE.
WITH GREAT CONSTANTINOPLE FELLED, THE SCHOLARS AND THE BOOKS IT HELD FLED WEST, THEIR KNOWLEDGE TO IMPART AND GIVE THE RENAISSANCE ITS START.
THE HIGH DARK AGES' ENDLESS NIGHT HELD IN ITSELF SEEDS OF NEW LIGHT. 'TIS FEAR AND IGNORANCE THAT WRITHE BENEATH TIME'S BLUNT YET POWERFUL SCYTHE.
O, REAP THEM
"WELL," HE SAID, "IT'S SOMETHING OF A PERSONAL MATTER, AS IT CONCERNS A FAMILY TRAGEDY..."

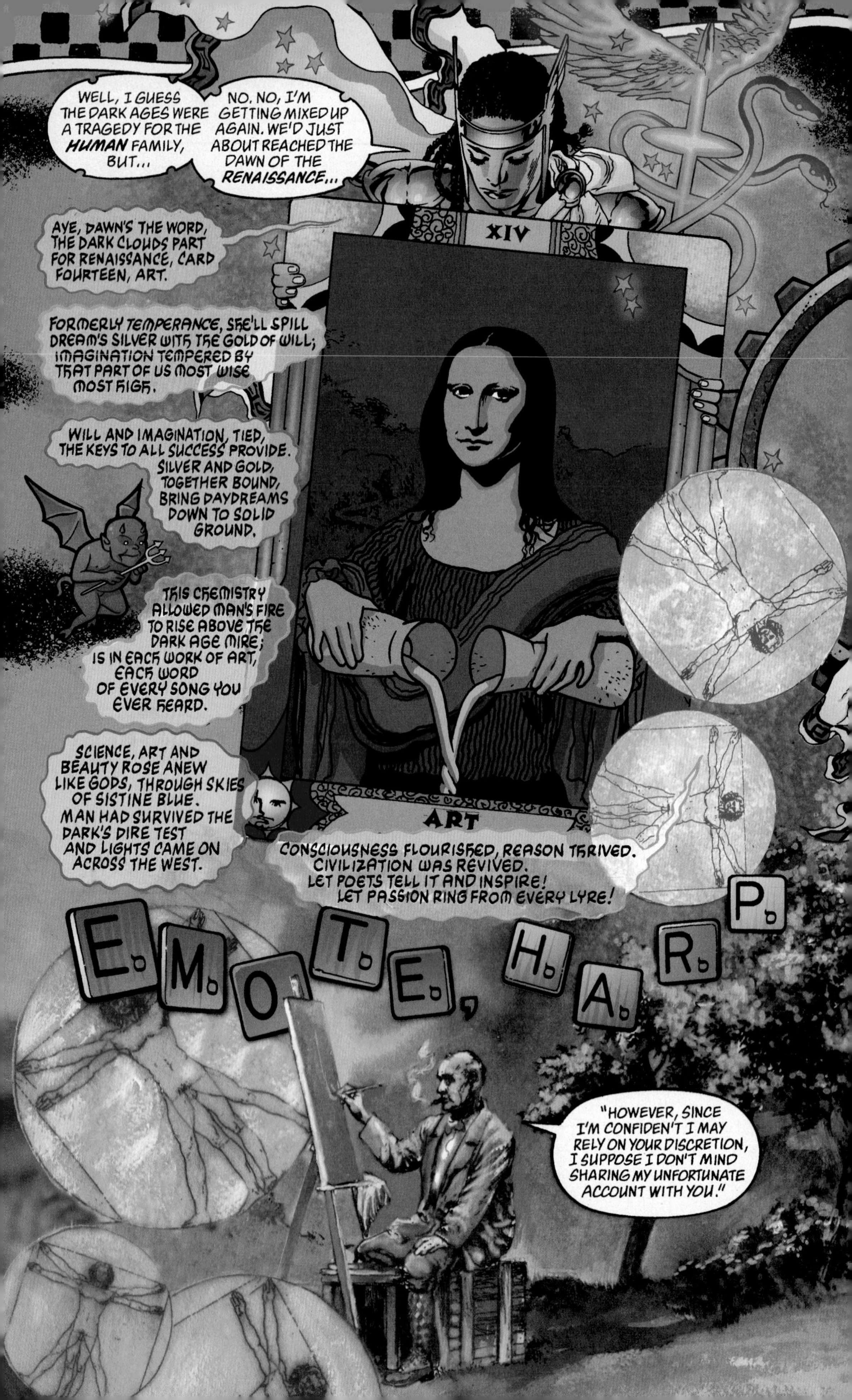

WELL, I GUESS THE DARK AGES WERE A TRAGEDY FOR THE *HUMAN* FAMILY, BUT...
NO. NO, I'M GETTING MIXED UP AGAIN. WE'D JUST ABOUT REACHED THE DAWN OF THE *RENAISSANCE*...
AYE, DAWN'S THE WORD, THE DARK CLOUDS PART FOR RENAISSANCE, CARD FOURTEEN, ART.
XIV
FORMERLY *TEMPERANCE*, SHE'LL SPILL DREAM'S SILVER WITH THE GOLD OF WILL; IMAGINATION TEMPERED BY THAT PART OF US MOST WISE MOST HIGH.
WILL AND IMAGINATION, TIED, THE KEYS TO ALL SUCCESS PROVIDE. SILVER AND GOLD, TOGETHER BOUND, BRING DAYDREAMS DOWN TO SOLID GROUND.
THIS CHEMISTRY ALLOWED MAN'S FIRE TO RISE ABOVE THE DARK AGE MIRE; IS IN EACH WORK OF ART, EACH WORD OF EVERY SONG YOU EVER HEARD.
SCIENCE, ART AND BEAUTY ROSE ANEW LIKE GODS, THROUGH SKIES OF SISTINE BLUE. MAN HAD SURVIVED THE DARK'S DIRE TEST AND LIGHTS CAME ON ACROSS THE WEST.
ART
CONSCIOUSNESS FLOURISHED, REASON THRIVED. CIVILIZATION WAS REVIVED. LET POETS TELL IT AND INSPIRE! LET PASSION RING FROM EVERY LYRE!
EMOTE, HARP
"HOWEVER, SINCE I'M CONFIDENT I MAY RELY ON YOUR DISCRETION, I SUPPOSE I DON'T MIND SHARING MY UNFORTUNATE ACCOUNT WITH YOU."

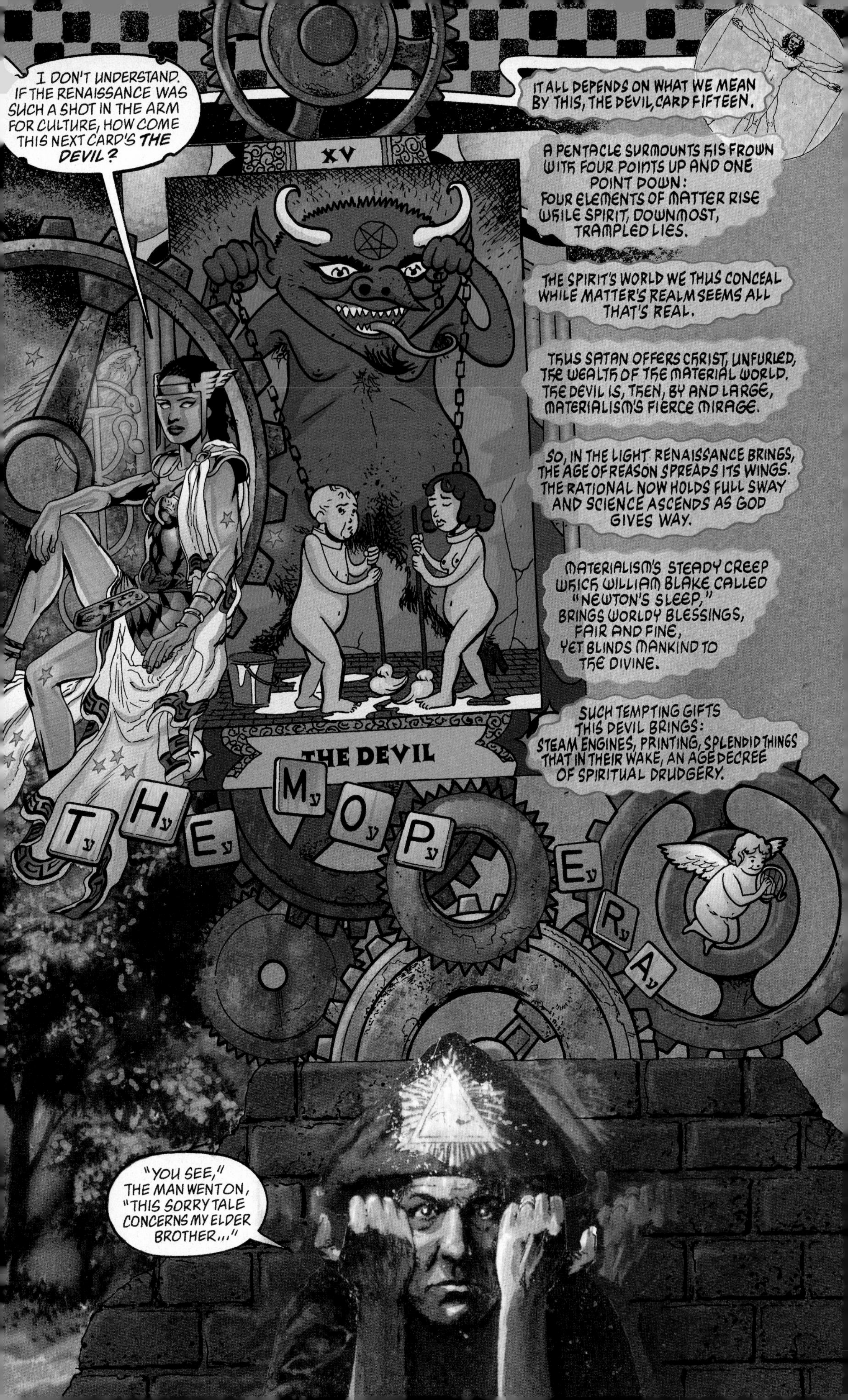
I DON'T UNDERSTAND. IF THE RENAISSANCE WAS SUCH A SHOT IN THE ARM FOR CULTURE, HOW COME THIS NEXT CARD'S **THE DEVIL?**
IT ALL DEPENDS ON WHAT WE MEAN BY THIS, THE DEVIL, CARD FIFTEEN.
XV
A PENTACLE SURMOUNTS HIS FROWN WITH FOUR POINTS UP AND ONE POINT DOWN: FOUR ELEMENTS OF MATTER RISE WHILE SPIRIT, DOWNMOST, TRAMPLED LIES.
THE SPIRIT'S WORLD WE THUS CONCEAL WHILE MATTER'S REALM SEEMS ALL THAT'S REAL.
THUS SATAN OFFERS CHRIST, UNFURLED, THE WEALTH OF THE MATERIAL WORLD. THE DEVIL IS, THEN, BY AND LARGE, MATERIALISM'S FIERCE MIRAGE.
SO, IN THE LIGHT RENAISSANCE BRINGS, THE AGE OF REASON SPREADS ITS WINGS. THE RATIONAL NOW HOLDS FULL SWAY AND SCIENCE ASCENDS AS GOD GIVES WAY.
MATERIALISM'S STEADY CREEP WHICH WILLIAM BLAKE CALLED "NEWTON'S SLEEP," BRINGS WORLDY BLESSINGS, FAIR AND FINE, YET BLINDS MANKIND TO THE DIVINE.
SUCH TEMPTING GIFTS THIS DEVIL BRINGS: STEAM ENGINES, PRINTING, SPLENDID THINGS THAT IN THEIR WAKE, AN AGE DECREE OF SPIRITUAL DRUDGERY.
THE DEVIL
THE MOPERA
"YOU SEE," THE MAN WENT ON, "THIS SORRY TALE CONCERNS MY ELDER BROTHER..."

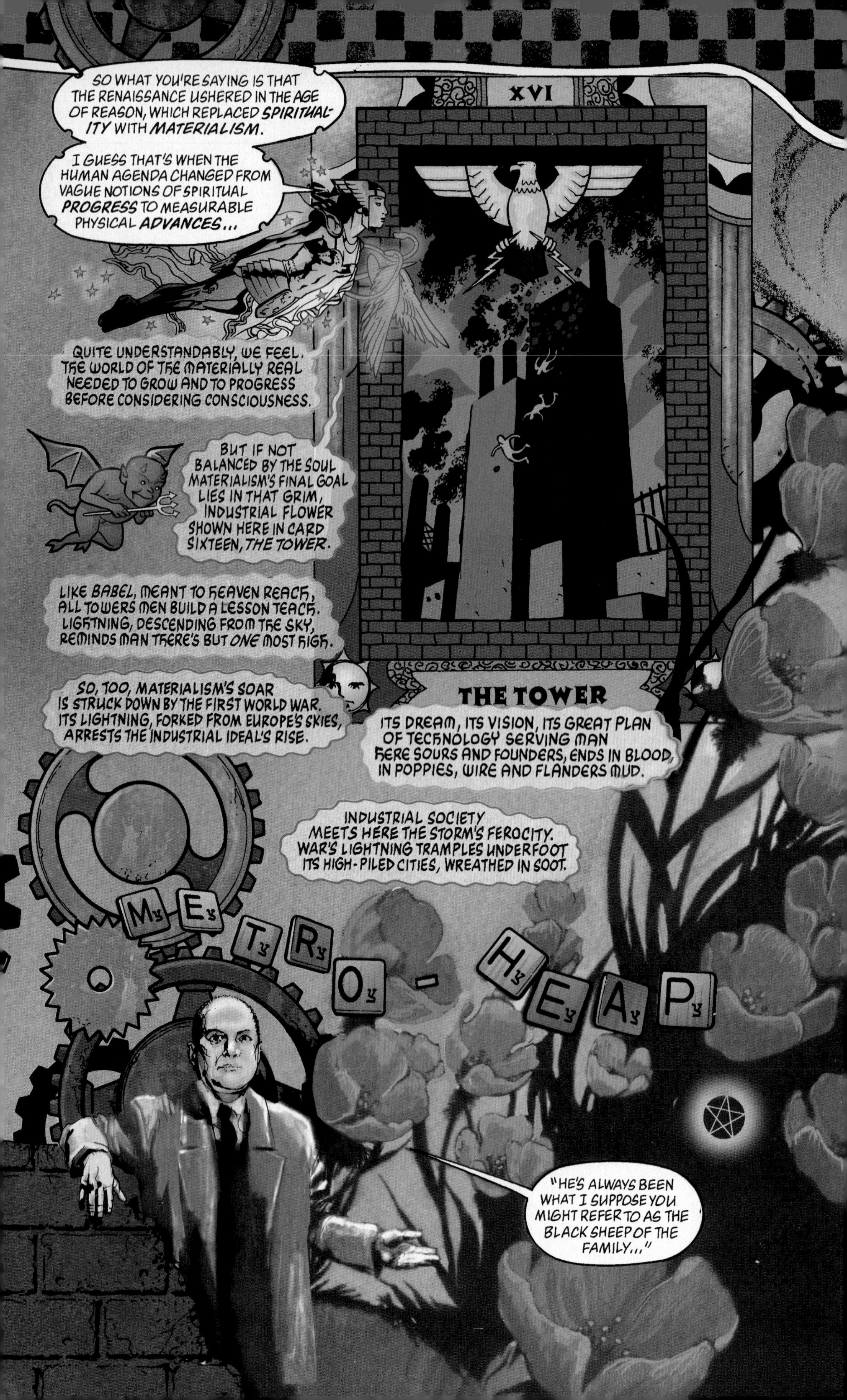
XVI
SO WHAT YOU'RE SAYING IS THAT THE RENAISSANCE USHERED IN THE AGE OF REASON, WHICH REPLACED SPIRITUALITY WITH MATERIALISM.
I GUESS THAT'S WHEN THE HUMAN AGENDA CHANGED FROM VAGUE NOTIONS OF SPIRITUAL PROGRESS TO MEASURABLE PHYSICAL ADVANCES...
QUITE UNDERSTANDABLY, WE FEEL, THE WORLD OF THE MATERIALLY REAL NEEDED TO GROW AND TO PROGRESS BEFORE CONSIDERING CONSCIOUSNESS.
BUT IF NOT BALANCED BY THE SOUL MATERIALISM'S FINAL GOAL LIES IN THAT GRIM, INDUSTRIAL FLOWER SHOWN HERE IN CARD SIXTEEN, THE TOWER.
LIKE BABEL, MEANT TO HEAVEN REACH, ALL TOWERS MEN BUILD A LESSON TEACH. LIGHTNING, DESCENDING FROM THE SKY, REMINDS MAN THERE'S BUT ONE MOST HIGH.
THE TOWER
SO, TOO, MATERIALISM'S SOAR IS STRUCK DOWN BY THE FIRST WORLD WAR. ITS LIGHTNING, FORKED FROM EUROPE'S SKIES, ARRESTS THE INDUSTRIAL IDEAL'S RISE.
ITS DREAM, ITS VISION, ITS GREAT PLAN OF TECHNOLOGY SERVING MAN HERE SOURS AND FOUNDERS, ENDS IN BLOOD, IN POPPIES, WIRE AND FLANDERS MUD.
INDUSTRIAL SOCIETY MEETS HERE THE STORM'S FEROCITY. WAR'S LIGHTNING TRAMPLES UNDERFOOT ITS HIGH-PILED CITIES, WREATHED IN SOOT.
METRO-HEAP
"HE'S ALWAYS BEEN WHAT I SUPPOSE YOU MIGHT REFER TO AS THE BLACK SHEEP OF THE FAMILY..."

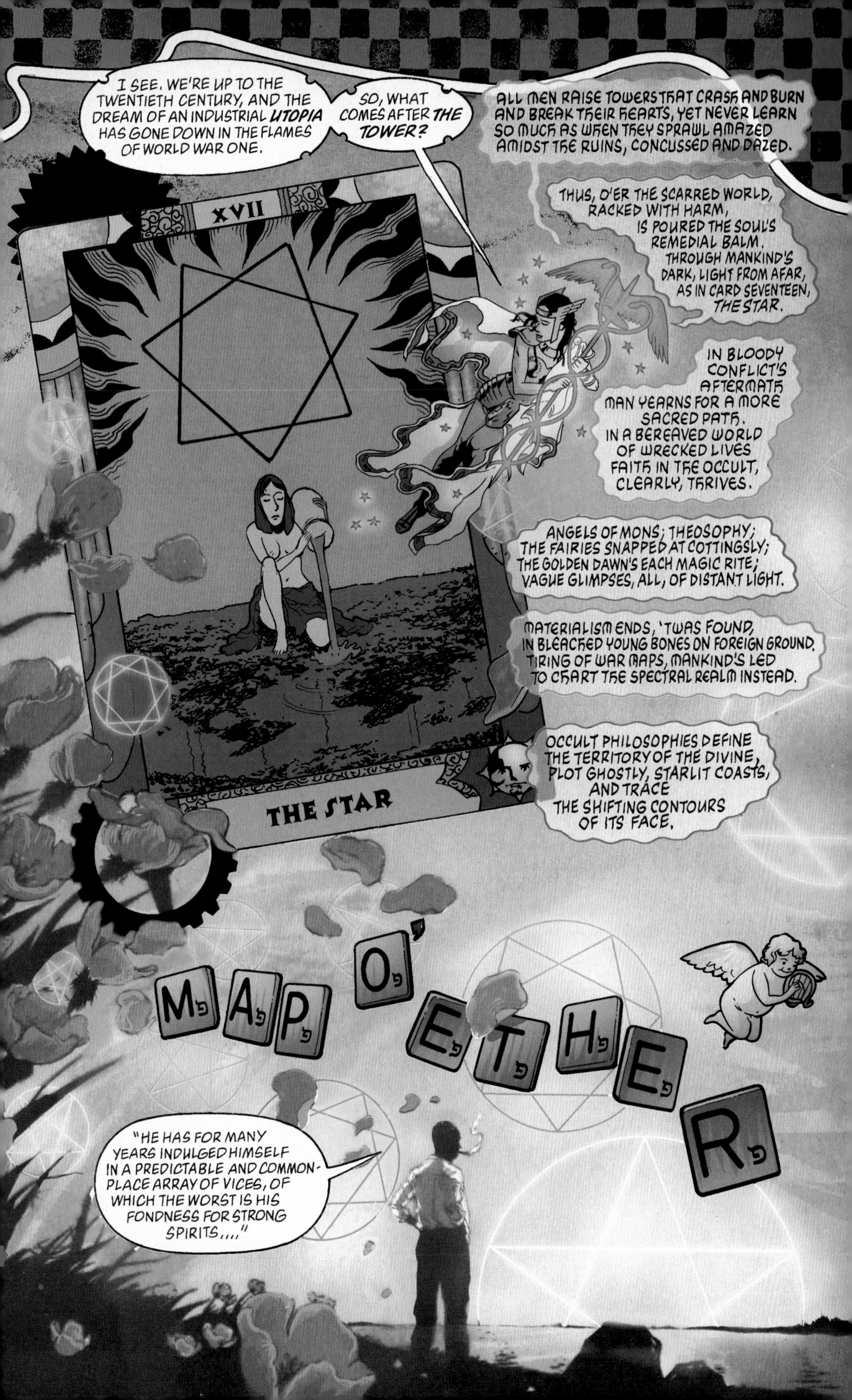
I SEE. WE'RE UP TO THE TWENTIETH CENTURY, AND THE DREAM OF AN INDUSTRIAL *UTOPIA* HAS GONE DOWN IN THE FLAMES OF WORLD WAR ONE.
SO, WHAT COMES AFTER *THE TOWER?*
ALL MEN RAISE TOWERS THAT CRASH AND BURN AND BREAK THEIR HEARTS, YET NEVER LEARN SO MUCH AS WHEN THEY SPRAWL AMAZED AMIDST THE RUINS, CONCUSSED AND DAZED.
THUS, O'ER THE SCARRED WORLD, RACKED WITH HARM, IS POURED THE SOUL'S REMEDIAL BALM. THROUGH MANKIND'S DARK, LIGHT FROM AFAR, AS IN CARD SEVENTEEN, *THE STAR.*
XVII
THE STAR
IN BLOODY CONFLICT'S AFTERMATH MAN YEARNS FOR A MORE SACRED PATH. IN A BEREAVED WORLD OF WRECKED LIVES FAITH IN THE OCCULT, CLEARLY, THRIVES.
ANGELS OF MONS; THEOSOPHY; THE FAIRIES SNAPPED AT COTTINGSLY; THE GOLDEN DAWN'S EACH MAGIC RITE; VAGUE GLIMPSES, ALL, OF DISTANT LIGHT.
MATERIALISM ENDS, 'TWAS FOUND, IN BLEACHED YOUNG BONES ON FOREIGN GROUND. TIRING OF WAR MAPS, MANKIND'S LED TO CHART THE SPECTRAL REALM INSTEAD.
OCCULT PHILOSOPHIES DEFINE THE TERRITORY OF THE DIVINE, PLOT GHOSTLY, STARLIT COASTS, AND TRACE THE SHIFTING CONTOURS OF ITS FACE.
MAP O' ETHER
"HE HAS FOR MANY YEARS INDULGED HIMSELF IN A PREDICTABLE AND COMMON-PLACE ARRAY OF VICES, OF WHICH THE WORST IS HIS FONDNESS FOR STRONG SPIRITS,..."

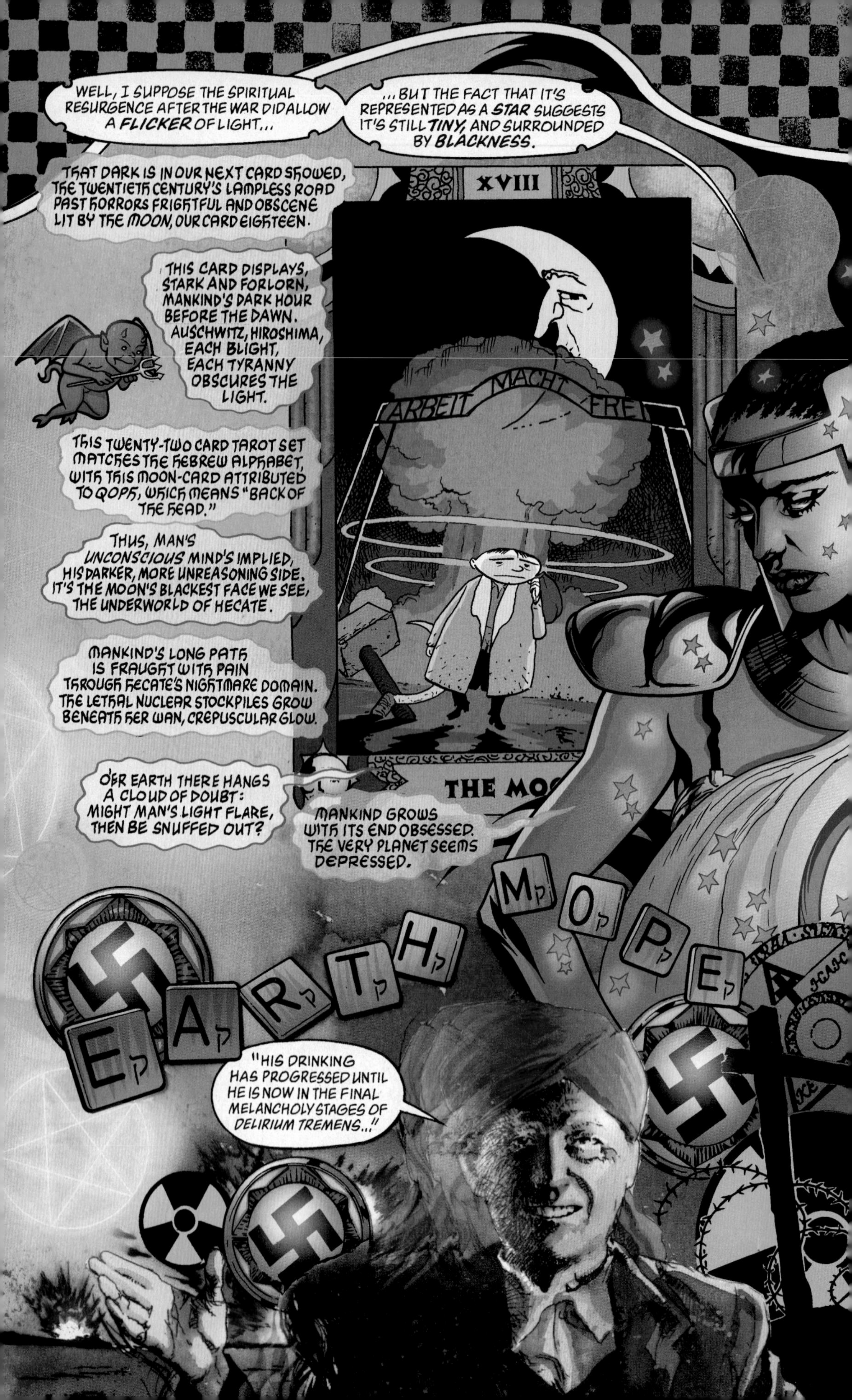
WELL, I SUPPOSE THE SPIRITUAL RESURGENCE AFTER THE WAR DID ALLOW A FLICKER OF LIGHT...
...BUT THE FACT THAT IT'S REPRESENTED AS A STAR SUGGESTS IT'S STILL TINY, AND SURROUNDED BY BLACKNESS.
THAT DARK IS IN OUR NEXT CARD SHOWED, THE TWENTIETH CENTURY'S LAMPLESS ROAD PAST HORRORS FRIGHTFUL AND OBSCENE LIT BY THE MOON, OUR CARD EIGHTEEN.
XVIII
THIS CARD DISPLAYS, STARK AND FORLORN, MANKIND'S DARK HOUR BEFORE THE DAWN. AUSCHWITZ, HIROSHIMA, EACH BLIGHT, EACH TYRANNY OBSCURES THE LIGHT.
ARBEIT MACHT FREI
THIS TWENTY-TWO CARD TAROT SET MATCHES THE HEBREW ALPHABET, WITH THIS MOON-CARD ATTRIBUTED TO QOPH, WHICH MEANS "BACK OF THE HEAD."
THUS, MAN'S UNCONSCIOUS MIND'S IMPLIED, HIS DARKER, MORE UNREASONING SIDE. IT'S THE MOON'S BLACKEST FACE WE SEE, THE UNDERWORLD OF HECATE.
MANKIND'S LONG PATH IS FRAUGHT WITH PAIN THROUGH HECATE'S NIGHTMARE DOMAIN. THE LETHAL NUCLEAR STOCKPILES GROW BENEATH HER WAN, CREPUSCULAR GLOW.
THE MOO
O'ER EARTH THERE HANGS A CLOUD OF DOUBT: MIGHT MAN'S LIGHT FLARE, THEN BE SNUFFED OUT?
MANKIND GROWS WITH ITS END OBSESSED. THE VERY PLANET SEEMS DEPRESSED.
EARTH MOPE
"HIS DRINKING HAS PROGRESSED UNTIL HE IS NOW IN THE FINAL MELANCHOLY STAGES OF DELIRIUM TREMENS..."

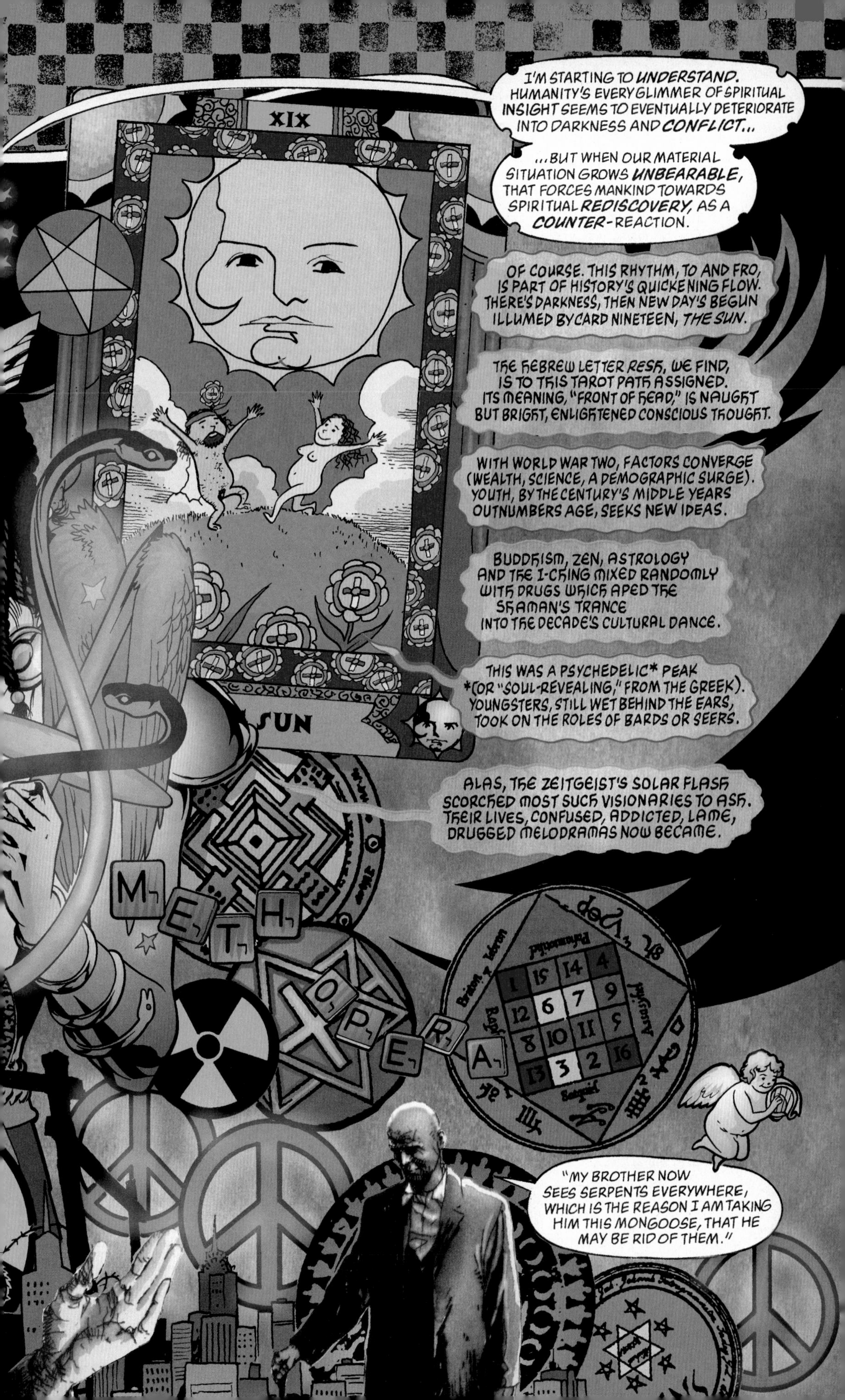

I'M STARTING TO UNDERSTAND. HUMANITY'S EVERY GLIMMER OF SPIRITUAL INSIGHT SEEMS TO EVENTUALLY DETERIORATE INTO DARKNESS AND CONFLICT...
...BUT WHEN OUR MATERIAL SITUATION GROWS UNBEARABLE, THAT FORCES MANKIND TOWARDS SPIRITUAL REDISCOVERY, AS A COUNTER-REACTION.
XIX
OF COURSE. THIS RHYTHM, TO AND FRO, IS PART OF HISTORY'S QUICKENING FLOW. THERE'S DARKNESS, THEN NEW DAY'S BEGUN ILLUMED BY CARD NINETEEN, THE SUN.
THE HEBREW LETTER RESH, WE FIND, IS TO THIS TAROT PATH ASSIGNED. ITS MEANING, "FRONT OF HEAD," IS NAUGHT BUT BRIGHT, ENLIGHTENED CONSCIOUS THOUGHT.
WITH WORLD WAR TWO, FACTORS CONVERGE (WEALTH, SCIENCE, A DEMOGRAPHIC SURGE). YOUTH, BY THE CENTURY'S MIDDLE YEARS OUTNUMBERS AGE, SEEKS NEW IDEAS.
BUDDHISM, ZEN, ASTROLOGY AND THE I-CHING MIXED RANDOMLY WITH DRUGS WHICH APED THE SHAMAN'S TRANCE INTO THE DECADE'S CULTURAL DANCE.
SUN
THIS WAS A PSYCHEDELIC* PEAK *(OR "SOUL-REVEALING," FROM THE GREEK). YOUNGSTERS, STILL WET BEHIND THE EARS, TOOK ON THE ROLES OF BARDS OR SEERS.
ALAS, THE ZEITGEIST'S SOLAR FLASH SCORCHED MOST SUCH VISIONARIES TO ASH. THEIR LIVES, CONFUSED, ADDICTED, LAME, DRUGGED MELODRAMAS NOW BECAME.
M E T H
O P E R A
1 15 14 4
12 6 7 9
8 10 11 5
13 3 2 16
"MY BROTHER NOW SEES SERPENTS EVERYWHERE, WHICH IS THE REASON I AM TAKING HIM THIS MONGOOSE, THAT HE MAY BE RID OF THEM."

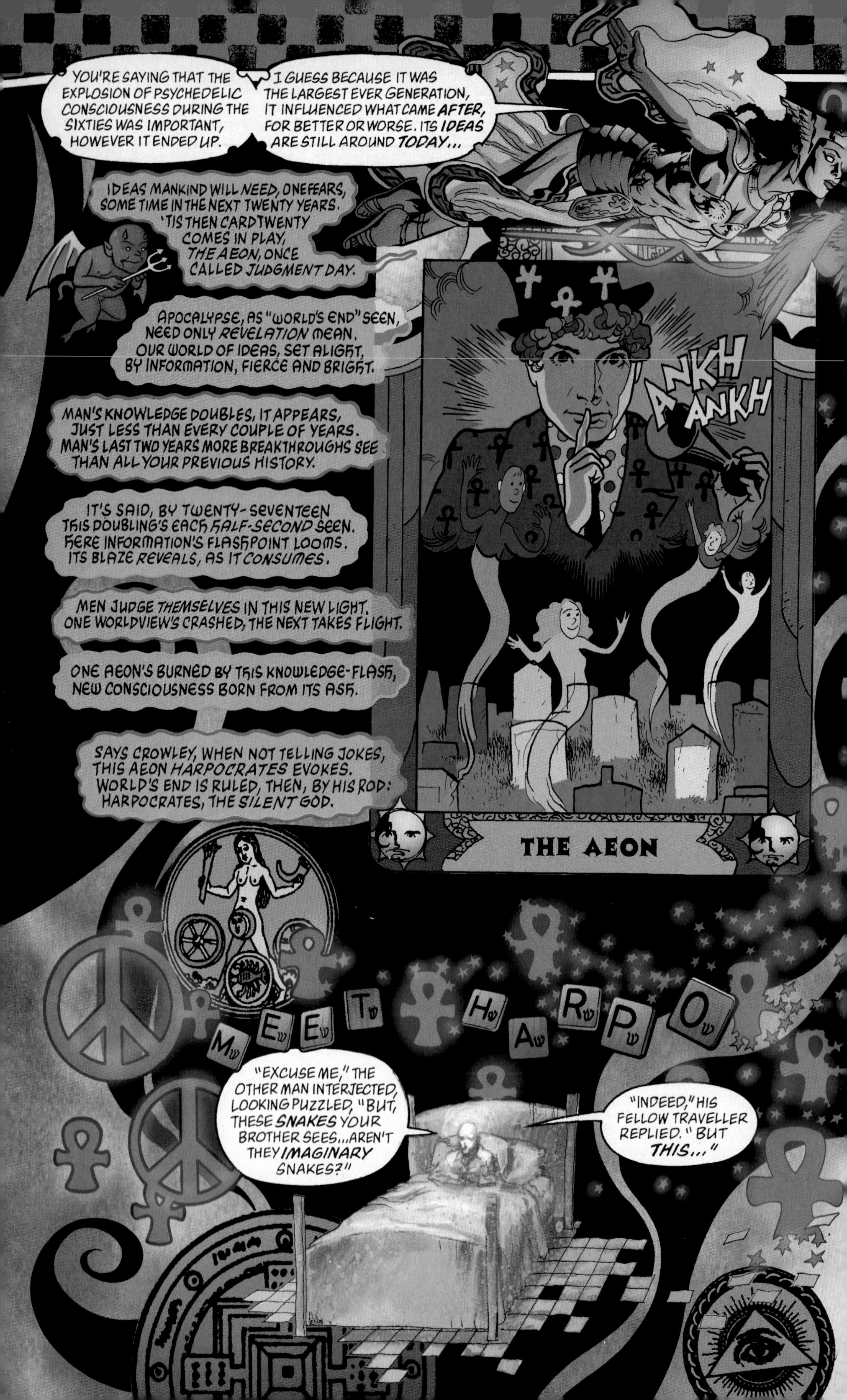
YOU'RE SAYING THAT THE EXPLOSION OF PSYCHEDELIC CONSCIOUSNESS DURING THE SIXTIES WAS IMPORTANT, HOWEVER IT ENDED UP.
I GUESS BECAUSE IT WAS THE LARGEST EVER GENERATION, IT INFLUENCED WHAT CAME AFTER, FOR BETTER OR WORSE. ITS IDEAS ARE STILL AROUND TODAY...
IDEAS MANKIND WILL NEED, ONE FEARS, SOME TIME IN THE NEXT TWENTY YEARS. 'TIS THEN CARD TWENTY COMES IN PLAY, THE AEON, ONCE CALLED JUDGMENT DAY.
APOCALYPSE, AS "WORLD'S END" SEEN, NEED ONLY REVELATION MEAN. OUR WORLD OF IDEAS, SET ALIGHT, BY INFORMATION, FIERCE AND BRIGHT.
MAN'S KNOWLEDGE DOUBLES, IT APPEARS, JUST LESS THAN EVERY COUPLE OF YEARS. MAN'S LAST TWO YEARS MORE BREAKTHROUGHS SEE THAN ALL YOUR PREVIOUS HISTORY.
IT'S SAID, BY TWENTY-SEVENTEEN THIS DOUBLING'S EACH HALF-SECOND SEEN. HERE INFORMATION'S FLASHPOINT LOOMS. ITS BLAZE REVEALS, AS IT CONSUMES.
MEN JUDGE THEMSELVES IN THIS NEW LIGHT. ONE WORLDVIEW'S CRASHED, THE NEXT TAKES FLIGHT.
ONE AEON'S BURNED BY THIS KNOWLEDGE-FLASH, NEW CONSCIOUSNESS BORN FROM ITS ASH.
SAYS CROWLEY, WHEN NOT TELLING JOKES, THIS AEON HARPOCRATES EVOKES. WORLD'S END IS RULED, THEN, BY HIS ROD: HARPOCRATES, THE SILENT GOD.
ANKH ANKH ANKH
THE AEON
MEET HARPO
"EXCUSE ME," THE OTHER MAN INTERJECTED, LOOKING PUZZLED, "BUT, THESE SNAKES YOUR BROTHER SEES... AREN'T THEY IMAGINARY SNAKES?"
"INDEED," HIS FELLOW TRAVELLER REPLIED. "BUT THIS..."

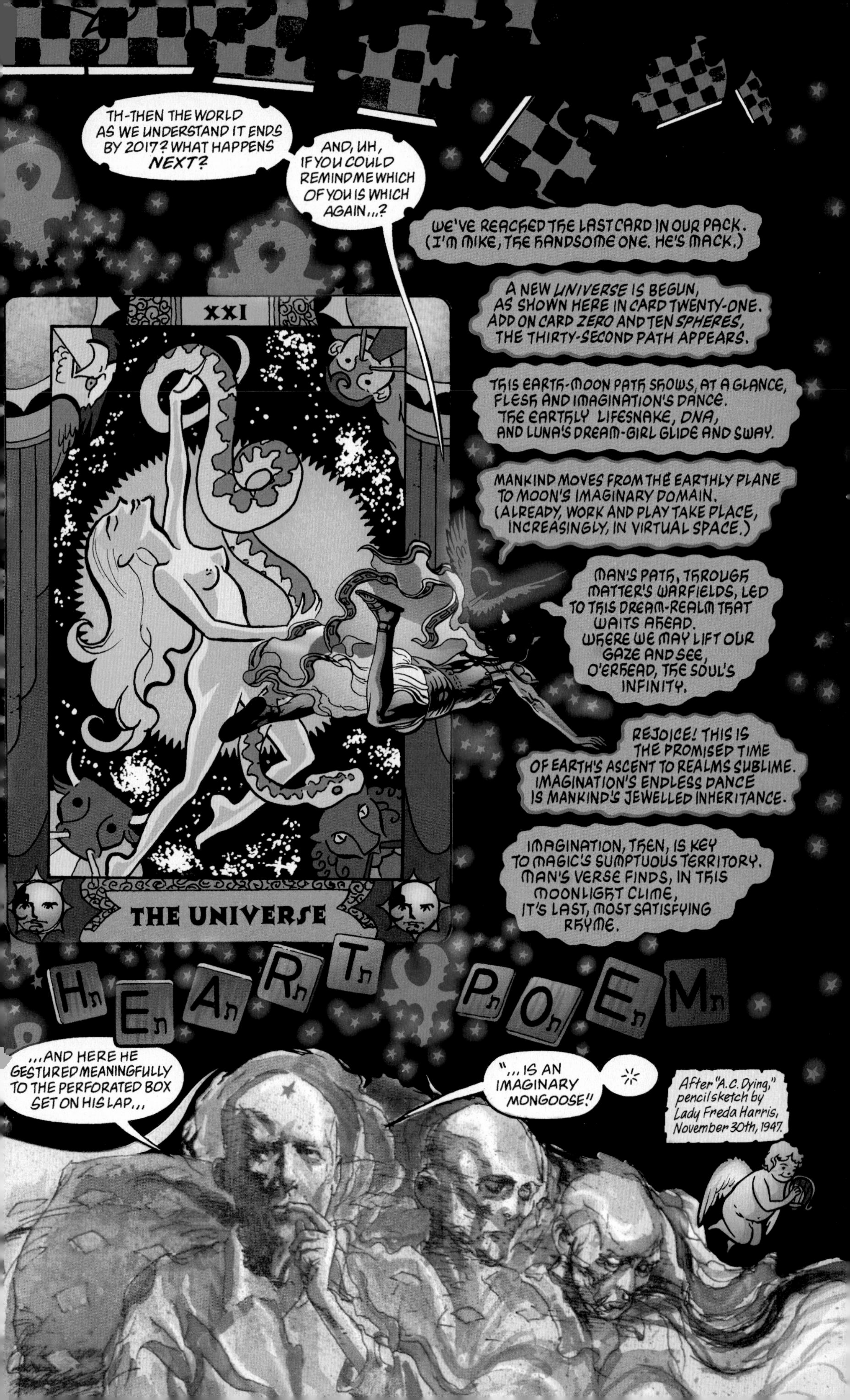

TH-THEN THE WORLD AS WE UNDERSTAND IT ENDS BY 2017? WHAT HAPPENS NEXT?
AND, UH, IF YOU COULD REMIND ME WHICH OF YOU IS WHICH AGAIN...?
WE'VE REACHED THE LAST CARD IN OUR PACK. (I'M MIKE, THE HANDSOME ONE. HE'S MACK.)
A NEW UNIVERSE IS BEGUN, AS SHOWN HERE IN CARD TWENTY-ONE. ADD ON CARD ZERO AND TEN SPHERES, THE THIRTY-SECOND PATH APPEARS.
THIS EARTH-MOON PATH SHOWS, AT A GLANCE, FLESH AND IMAGINATION'S DANCE. THE EARTHLY LIFESNAKE, DNA, AND LUNA'S DREAM-GIRL GLIDE AND SWAY.
MANKIND MOVES FROM THE EARTHLY PLANE TO MOON'S IMAGINARY DOMAIN. (ALREADY, WORK AND PLAY TAKE PLACE, INCREASINGLY, IN VIRTUAL SPACE.)
MAN'S PATH, THROUGH MATTER'S WARFIELDS, LED TO THIS DREAM-REALM THAT WAITS AHEAD. WHERE WE MAY LIFT OUR GAZE AND SEE, O'ERHEAD, THE SOUL'S INFINITY.
REJOICE! THIS IS THE PROMISED TIME OF EARTH'S ASCENT TO REALMS SUBLIME. IMAGINATION'S ENDLESS DANCE IS MANKIND'S JEWELLED INHERITANCE.
IMAGINATION, THEN, IS KEY TO MAGIC'S SUMPTUOUS TERRITORY. MAN'S VERSE FINDS, IN THIS MOONLIGHT CLIME, IT'S LAST, MOST SATISFYING RHYME.
XXI
THE UNIVERSE
HEART POEM
...AND HERE HE GESTURED MEANINGFULLY TO THE PERFORATED BOX SET ON HIS LAP...
"...IS AN IMAGINARY MONGOOSE!"
After "A.C. Dying," pencil sketch by Lady Freda Harris, November 30th, 1947.

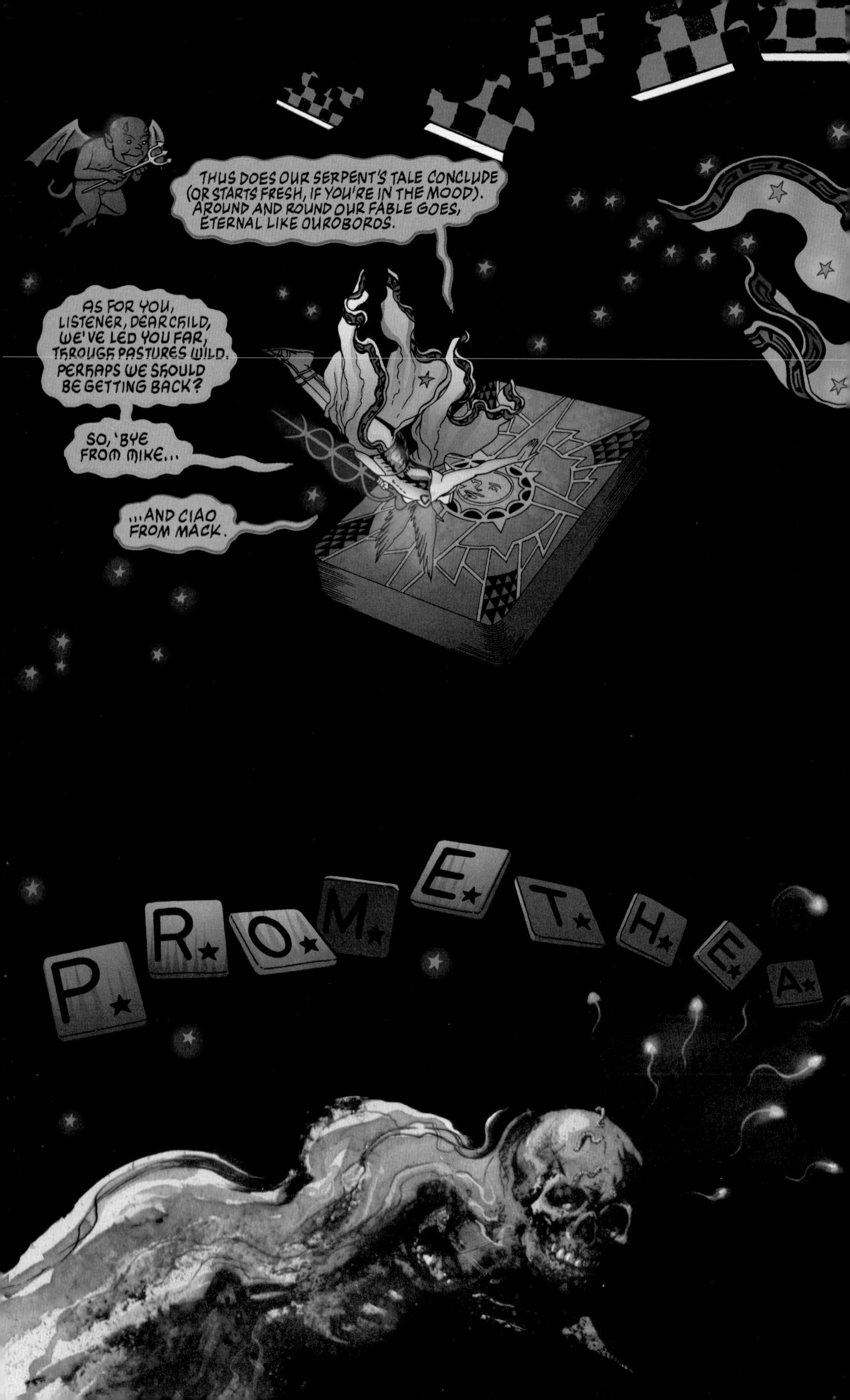
THUS DOES OUR SERPENT'S TALE CONCLUDE (OR STARTS FRESH, IF YOU'RE IN THE MOOD). AROUND AND ROUND OUR FABLE GOES, ETERNAL LIKE OUROBOROS.
AS FOR YOU, LISTENER, DEARCHILD, WE'VE LED YOU FAR, THROUGH PASTURES WILD. PERHAPS WE SHOULD BE GETTING BACK?
SO, 'BYE FROM MIKE...
...AND CIAO FROM MACK.
PROMETHEA

DEDICATIONS

To Leah, Amber, and Melinda;

To all my family, all my friends.

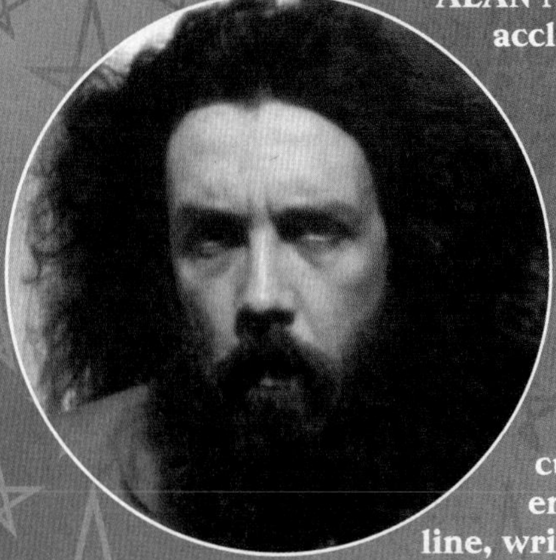

ALAN MOORE is perhaps the most acclaimed writer in the graphic story medium, having garnered many awards for such works as WATCHMEN, V FOR VENDETTA, FROM HELL, MIRACLEMAN, SWAMP THING and SUPREME, among others, along with the many fine artists he has collaborated with on those works. He is currently masterminding the entire America's Best Comics line, writing TOM STRONG, TOP 10 and TOMORROW STORIES in addition to PROMETHEA, with more in the planning stages. He resides in central England.

Foremost to my wife, Wendy, for all her help in the production of Promethea. The work wouldn't be the same without her. To Alan, my friend, for his truly magical mind and talent. I have learned much from him. To Mick (the best inker of all) and Holly, our friendship means a great deal to me. To Todd for his friendship and insightful vision. To Scott for having faith in me. To Jeromy for his fantastic palette and sense of humor. To Jose for his friendship and inspiration. To all my friends and family.

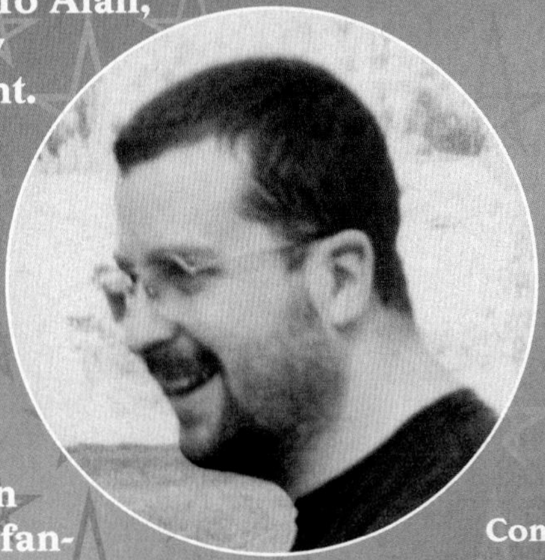

J.H. WILLIAMS III, penciller and co-creator of PROMETHEA, entered the comics field in 1991 and immediately began getting attention for his finely crafted work on such titles as BATMAN and STARMAN. He's been praised for SON OF SUPERMAN and another co-creation, CHASE, has produced numerous covers for DC Comics (with Jeromy Cox) and Marvel Comics (with Jose Villarrubia), and is currently writing D.E.O. stories for DC Comics' secret files and other projects with Chase co-creator D. Curtis Johnson. J.H. and his wife, Wendy, live in California.

To Genevieve for reminding me what life is really about, and to my wonderful wife, Holly, for giving me that reminder. To my mom and dad for all their love and support of whatever I wanted to do. To my great friend Ron Magee, for sending me down to Slave Labor Graphics twelve years ago. And to all the people who read our books...this ink's for you!

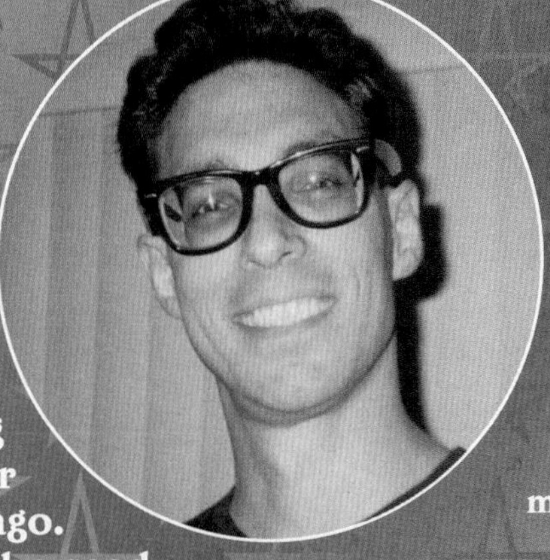

MICK GRAY, a longtime comics inker, began his collaboration with Williams in 1995, and his accurate attention to every detail and nuance on such titles as BATMAN, CHASE and SON OF SUPERMAN, not to mention PROMETHEA, continue to make this an exclusive team. Mick and his wife, Holly, also live in California.

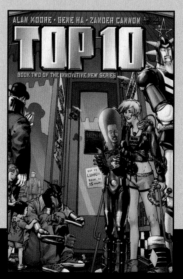